LEGALITY

LEGALITY

Scott J. Shapiro

The Belknap Press of Harvard University Press

Cambridge, Massachusetts,

London, England

2011

Library of Congress Cataloging-in-Publication Data

Shapiro, Scott
Legality / Scott J. Shapiro.
p. cm.
Includes bibliographical references and index.
ISBN 978-0-674-05566-7 (alk. paper)
1. Jurisprudence.   2. Law—Philosophy.   3. Legal positivism.   I. Title.
K230.S525L44 2010   2010018677
340'.1—dc22

For Alison

CONTENTS

LEGALITY

1

WHAT IS LAW
(AND WHY SHOULD WE CARE)?

What Is Jurisprudence?

When I was applying to high school, my mother advised me to enter "medical jurisprudence" in the section of my application reserved for "future career." Of course I had no idea what medical jurisprudence was: I had never even heard the word "jurisprudence" before. But partly in order to placate my mother and partly because I didn't have any other ideas about my future career, I followed her advice. Inexplicably, they let me into the school anyway.

Thirty years later, I now know that "jurisprudence" in that instance was really just a fancy, and slightly archaic, way of saying "law." And so I can infer that someone who practices medical jurisprudence is someone who practices medical law—though, to be honest, I am still murky on what *exactly* medical law is or would be. And, similarly, I know that when lawyers speak in grand terms of, say, "Fourth Amendment jurisprudence," they mean to refer to the Fourth Amendment to the United States Constitution and the legal doctrine that surrounds it.

I also know now that the term "jurisprudence" has a couple of other well-established uses as well. It is, for example, often employed to denote the *academic study* of the law: that is, the branch of learning in which law professors and legal scholars participate. Following this usage, those who practice jurisprudence are concerned with describing the law of particular legal systems. This typically involves developing theories that set out the general principles that structure a given area of legal doctrine and then going on to enumerate the detailed rules that exemplify the aforementioned principles. Employed in this way, then, "medical jurisprudence" would refer not to the legal rules that regulate medical matters, as in my first example, but rather to a scholarly subdiscipline, like

1

solid-state physics or Japanese linguistics. It is worth noting too that this usage comports with etymology, since the Latin word *jurisprudentia* means "knowledge of the law."

Most legal academics in English-speaking countries do not however describe themselves as "jurisprudes."[1] The word "jurisprudence" is generally reserved for the *philosophical* study of the law; and a jurisprude, insofar as the word is used at all, is someone who engages in this particular kind of philosophically oriented study. In keeping with this, it is worth noting that the label "Jurisprudence" is not applied to *every* single course title in American and British law schools but is reserved rather for courses that focus on the philosophical issues that the law raises. Some scholars have in fact even aimed for further nuance by distinguishing between jurisprudence on the one hand and legal philosophy on the other. But since the significance of this proposed distinction frankly escapes me, I am going to set it aside in what follows and use the terms "jurisprudence" and "legal philosophy" interchangeably instead.

Jurisprudence: Normative and Analytical

The philosophical discipline of jurisprudence is typically divided into two subareas: normative and analytical. Normative jurisprudence deals with the *moral* foundations of the law, while analytical jurisprudence examines its *metaphysical* foundations. Let's discuss each in turn.

Normative jurisprudence is the study of the law from a moral perspective and comprises two branches, which I will refer to as *interpretive* and *critical*. *Interpretive* jurisprudes seek to provide an account of the *actual* moral underpinnings or logic of current law. Thus, for example, they might take up the question of why our criminal law punishes criminals. Is it to deter people from committing crimes or to rehabilitate them? Do we punish in order to incapacitate offenders for a certain time or to ensure that they get their just deserts? To take another example, the interpretive theorist is interested in identifying the moral point or function of contract law. Does the law hold contractual parties liable when they make certain contracts because they promised? Or is it because economic efficiency demands that we hold people to their bargains? And so on.

Those who work in the *critical* branch of normative jurisprudence are interested in a different question. Instead of attempting to describe the *actual* moral foundations of current law, they want to know what, from a moral point of view, the law *should* be. So, for example, a critical theorist does not describe why our existing criminal law punishes criminals, as the interpretive theorist would do, but focuses rather on whether criminals should be punished at all. The object is not simply to recover the moral logic of current criminal law but to see if that logic is justified. As their names suggest, critical legal studies, critical race theory, and feminist legal theory are all examples of critical normative jurisprudence. Each of them is concerned with evaluating existing legal systems according to moral criteria, by showing how current law covertly and unfairly privileges certain groups (capitalists, white people, men) at the expense of others (workers, racial minorities, women).

Analytical jurisprudence, by contrast, is not concerned with morality. Rather, it analyzes the nature of law and legal entities, and its objects of study include legal systems, laws, rules, rights, authority, validity, obligation, interpretation, sovereignty, courts, proximate causation, property, crime, tort, negligence, and so on. Analytical jurisprudes want to determine the fundamental nature of these particular objects of study by asking analytical questions such as: What distinguishes legal systems from games, etiquette, and religion? Are all laws rules? Are legal rights a type of moral right? Is legal reasoning a special kind of reasoning? Is legal causation the same as ordinary, everyday causation? Is property best understood as a bundle of rights? What distinguishes torts from crimes? And so on.[2]

What Is "What Is Law?"?

This book is primarily concerned with analytical jurisprudence. My aim throughout the chapters that follow will be roughly threefold: to take up the overarching question of "What is law?"; to examine some historically influential answers to this question; and, finally, to propose a new, and hopefully better, account of my own.

I realize of course that there are many people out there who wonder why anyone would or should read a book about analytical jurisprudence, let alone *write* one. I have learned the hard way that the relevance of this kind of inquiry is far from obvious to a large number of people, including legal scholars, and is generally regarded with much more skepticism than normative jurisprudence. There is of course an obvious and understandable reason for this. The moral questions that normative jurisprudes address bear directly on the burning questions of our day, such as: Why punish criminals? Should women have a legally protected right to terminate their pregnancies? Do competent adults have the right to die? Should same-sex couples have the right to marry? What are the limits of state authority in a time of global terrorism? Pretty much everyone understands that the morality of law constitutes a relevant, if not vital, area of inquiry.

Questions to do with the fundamental nature of the law—traditionally formulated as "What is Law?"—seem, by contrast, to exercise and engage a small minority of people. For one thing, there is a very clear and obvious sense in which people *do* know what law is. Virtually everyone is aware that legal systems are composed of courts, legislatures, and police and would have little trouble identifying them from pictures or descriptions. Indeed, legal institutions are highly prominent entities that trumpet their official status every chance they get. Most people also realize that these institutions regulate large portions of contemporary life. They do so by making and enforcing rules that prohibit physical assault, theft, and other immoral activities and that govern property relations, the voluntary undertaking of obligations, and family structure. There are of course heavy tomes that set out these rules and legions of professionals who exist solely to dispense advice about their meaning and implications. It is in fact possible that lawyers and law students are most skeptical about analytical jurisprudence precisely because they really do know a lot about the law already. What remains to be seen in these cases is how posing the question "What is Law?" at a high level of abstraction, as analytical jurisprudes are wont to do, can increase their knowledge. Should analytical jurisprudence matter to anyone other than philosophers and, if so, why?

It is of course impossible to make any real progress with this question— the question of relevance—without first becoming clear about the kind of issues that analytic jurisprudes seek to answer. When one studies *the nature of law,* what *exactly* is one studying? What does the question "What is law?" mean anyway? Getting a firm grip on this question is essential to understanding why it might be worth asking in the first place.

"Law"

Clearly, the key term in this context is "law," and the first thing to notice about this term is its ambiguity. In many cases, "law" functions as what linguists call a mass term, like "snow" or "meat," and thus refers to an uncountable quantity of legal norms. When we ask, for example, whether a particular legal system has much telecommunications law (a question similar in type to that of whether there is much snow outside) we are employing this particular usage. But, unlike many other mass terms, "law" can also take an indefinite article. You can't play with *a* snow, but you *can* create, apply, study, detest, or obey *a* law. In this first sense, "law" is like "rock" or "lamb": by themselves, they are mass terms but, when they are preceded by an indefinite article or pluralized, they convert into count terms. And so, just as we can ask how many rocks are in the garden, we can also ask if a particular country or legal system has *many* laws governing telecommunications.

The term "law" is also frequently used to refer to a particular social organization. We can say, for example, that the law normally claims the right to use force to ensure compliance with its rules. In this example, "law" does not refer to an indefinite collection of legal norms but rather to an organization that creates, applies, and enforces such norms. And, in cases like this, law *can* receive a definite article—we can talk about "the law"—while to add an indefinite article or pluralize it is to change its meaning.

The term "legal system" is plagued by a similar ambiguity. Following one usage, a legal system is a particular system of rules. For example: the American legal system is constituted by the sum total of all the laws of the United States and their interrelations. In other cases, however, the term "legal system" denotes a particular institution or organization. In these cases, the American legal system is understood as an organization constituted by senators, judges, cabinet secretaries, filing clerks, police officers, and so on. Or, to put it somewhat differently: in the first sense of "legal system," legal systems are constituted by *norms;* in the second sense, they are constituted by *people.*

Since the terms "law" and "legal system" are ambiguous, the questions "What is law?" and "What are legal systems?" are inevitably ambiguous as well. It is hard to know if they refer to an inquiry into the nature of legal norms or an inquiry into the nature of legal organizations. When the first genre of inquiry is assumed, the philosophical analysis will tend to focus on the following sorts of questions: When do legal norms exist? What is their logical structure? Are there different kinds of legal norms? What are the interrelations between different norms in a legal system? When the second genre of inquiry is assumed, the analysis will turn to other kinds of questions, such as: What does the organization do?

What is it supposed to do? What is its general structure? Why do particular legal systems have the specific institutional structures they have? How are the various participants in these systems related to one another?

Analytical jurisprudes have, by and large, taken the first of these two possible routes. They study legal phenomena by analyzing the norms that legal organizations produce rather than the organizations that produce them. In this respect, legal philosophy has resisted the "organizational turn" followed by many other academic disciplines. For the past century, psychologists, anthropologists, sociologists, economists, and political scientists have focused on organizations in order to study individual and group behavior in institutional settings as well as the behavior of institutions themselves. This focus has been extraordinarily fruitful, spawning several new fields, including bureaucracy theory, transaction-cost economics, scientific management, legislative studies, and systems theory. Legal scholars have of course been investigating and analyzing the proper regulation of organizations, such as legislatures, courts, publicly held corporations, employee-owned cooperatives, banks, churches, schools, trade associations, and so on, for a long time. The Legal Process School led by the lawyers Henry Hart and Albert Sacks was an extremely influential approach to the American legal system that analyzed the law through an organizational lens. And in recent years, philosophers of action have begun to analyze the nature of groups in general and collective action in particular.

Legal philosophy has nevertheless remained more or less unaffected by the kind of organizational analysis that has become such a prominent and productive feature of these other disciplines. Given that it is hard to imagine anyone who would deny that legal systems are organizations run by groups from particular cultures, or that they have distinctive institutional structures that are designed to achieve certain political objectives, this apparent lack of interest is surprising. To use an economic analogy, we can think of the law as a kind of firm whose subdivisions include legislatures, administrative agencies, courts, and police departments. This firm does not, of course, produce anything that is sold in the market—it produces laws. But, just as the economist asks why economic actors organize themselves into firms instead of engaging in continuous market-based, arm's-length bargaining, so too philosophers can productively ask why moral agents form legal systems that produce rules rather than deliberate about and negotiate over the terms of social interaction among themselves. As I will try to show, answering such a question not only illuminates the nature of legal organizations—their distinctive mission, modus operandi, and so on; it is also a prerequisite for tackling questions about the nature of legal norms. In other words, we cannot understand what laws are unless we understand how and for what purposes legal systems produce them in the first place.

I will return to these themes in greater detail in subsequent chapters. My point here has been simply to highlight the ambiguous nature of the terms "law" and "legal system" in a preliminary way so as to be able to resolve the ambiguities and thereby identify the core questions of analytical jurisprudence more precisely. As a practical matter, however, the evocations are largely harmless and I will use these terms in an ambiguous fashion when being more exact would be cumbersome.

If one wanted to be fussy, of course, one could avoid the ambiguities we have identified here entirely by speaking about legality, that is, about the property of being law. Legal norms and legal organizations both instantiate the same property—they are both *legal* things. Thus, I will sometimes speak directly about legality, in which case I will be referring to a property that can be instantiated by rules, organizations, officials, texts, concepts, statements, judgments, and so on.[3]

Law, the Law, and "Law"

It is important to distinguish the question "What is law?" from the similar-sounding question "What is *the* law?" The latter is of course a familiar, garden-variety legal question. It reflects a desire to understand what the law is on a *particular* matter and is the kind of question a client would be likely to ask his or her lawyer. The former question, by contrast, does *not* concern the current state of *the* law. It reflects a philosophical effort to understand *the nature of law in general.*

It is also important to distinguish between the question "What is law?" and the question "What is 'law'?" The latter question concerns the meaning of the word "law," not the nature of the word's referent, namely, law. It is nevertheless sometimes thought that the latter, semantic question is the one that preoccupies analytical jurisprudence—that legal philosophers are mainly attempting to define the *word* "law." But this impression is mistaken. Legal philosophy is not lexicography. It is not an elaborate attempt to contribute to the Oxford English Dictionary but rather an effort to understand *the nature of a social institution and its products.*

One obvious reason why legal philosophy is not solely concerned with the definition of "law" is that "law" is an English word and non-English-speakers can and do engage in legal philosophy. Furthermore, it is not even possible for an English-speaker to do legal philosophy simply by considering the proper use of the word "law," for the word is radically over- and underinclusive at once. It is overinclusive insofar as many things that English-speakers refer to as "law" are not law in the relevant sense, for example, divine law, the moral law, Boyle's law, the law of cosines, and so on.[4] Legal philosophers are not concerned with everything to which any one could conceivably apply the term "law" but rather with *legal* laws and *legal* systems. Conversely, the word "law" is underinclusive as well. As Jeremy Bentham pointed out, English-speaking lawyers normally reserve this word for those rules that have been enacted by legislatures. For example, we say that Congress passed a law, but the Environmental Protection Agency enacted a *regulation.* Similarly, the president issues an executive *order,* not an executive law.[5] Thus, if we attended solely to linguistic usage, we might be fooled into thinking that only Congress makes law, when in fact most of the law in the United States is created in the executive, not the legislative, branch.[6]

The Nature of a Thing

As we have seen, then, to ask "What is law?" is to inquire into the fundamental nature of law. In this section I would like to unpack this question further by asking what exactly it is that we want to know when we inquire into the nature of something.

One possibility is that we are asking about the thing's *identity,* that is, what it is to be that thing. For example, philosophers who study epistemology are inquiring into the nature of knowledge. To ask "What is knowledge" is to ask what it is about knowledge that makes it *knowledge.* The classic answer to the question maintains that knowledge is true and justified belief. This is an answer to the question because it claims that what makes an instance of knowledge *knowledge* is that it is a belief that is at once true and justified.

In general, to ask about the identity of X is to ask what it is about X that makes it X and not Y or Z or any other such thing. Call this the "Identity Question." A correct answer to the Identity Question must supply the set of properties that make (possible or actual) instances of X the things that they are. The identity of water, to take another example, is

H_2O because water is just H_2O. Being H_2O is what makes water *water*. With respect to law, accordingly, to answer the question "What is law?" on this interpretation is to discover what makes all and only instances of law instances of *law* and not something else.

It is also possible that an inquiry into the nature of an entity will not be primarily concerned with the Identity Question. In these instances, we are not so much interested in what makes the object the thing that it is but rather in what *necessarily follows from* the fact that it is what it is and not something else. I'm going to refer to this here as the "Implication Question."

Consider the number 3. Arguably, what makes the number 3 the number 3 is that it is the number that comes after 2. The identity of 3, therefore, is being the successor of 2. However, when mathematicians study the number 3, they are clearly interested in more than its identity. Mathematicians want to know all of its mathematical properties. They want to know, in other words, what *follows* from the fact that a certain number is the number 3 and not some other number. To take a trivial finding, mathematicians have discovered that 3 is a prime number. While being a prime number is not part of the number 3's identity (being the successor of 2 is), we might still say that it is part of the nature of 3 because being 3 necessarily entails being prime. Put in another way, being prime is part of the nature of being 3 because if a number is not prime, then it is impossible for it to be 3.

In this second sense of "nature," to discover an entity's nature is in part to discover those properties that it *necessarily* has. An object has a property necessarily just in case it could not fail to have it. Thus, to discover the law's nature, in this second sense, would be in part to discover its necessary properties, that is, those properties that law could not fail to have.

It is important to note that when philosophers ask about the nature of an object, they do not care about *every* property that it possesses necessarily. It is necessarily true, for example, that every piece of knowledge is identical with itself and that the number 3 is not married to the number 7. But their inquiry into the nature of knowledge or numbers does not seek to discover and catalog all these properties because, although necessary, they are also uninteresting. They are uninteresting in part because they are not *distinctive* of the entities in question. Everything is identical to itself and is incapable of marrying the number 7. When asking about the nature of law, for example, we want to know which properties law necessarily possesses in virtue of being an instance of law and not a game, social etiquette, religion, or some other thing.

Another reason why these properties are uninteresting is that knowing that the entities possess these properties does not answer any interesting question. No one wonders about whether knowledge is self-identical or what the marital status of a given number is. Of course, whether philosophers will find a certain necessary property interesting is to some extent context specific: it depends on which issues and phenomena seem most perplexing at a given time. As a result, we should not expect any theory of law to be complete. Each generation identifies new questions, and these newly salient challenges affect which properties legal philosophers will seek to catalog and study.

It should also be pointed out that when philosophers ask the Implication Question about an object, they are interested not just in what necessarily follows from the fact that the object in question has a certain identity but also in what does *not* necessarily follow. They care, in other words, about the object's contingent properties as well. For example, many legal philosophers have been eager to show that whether there is a moral obligation to obey the law is a contingent feature of legal systems. Thus they maintain that part of the answer to the Implication Question is that it does *not* follow from the fact that something is law that its subjects have a moral obligation to obey. Others, of course, believe just the opposite: they claim that it does necessarily follow from the fact that something is law that it is morally obligatory. On this view, moral legitimacy would be part of the nature of legality in the second sense.

As we have seen, then, when one inquires into the nature of an object, one might be asking either of two possible questions.[7] One might be asking about the identity of the object—what makes it the thing that it is? Or one might be asking about the necessary implications of its identity— what necessarily follows (or does not follow) from the fact that it is what it is and not something else?

The Structure of the Social World

Since my discussion thus far has been rather abstract, I'd like now to reformulate these questions about the nature of law in slightly more concrete terms. We all realize of course that we classify the social world in very complex and subtle ways. We don't, for example, just refer to particular individuals or humanity in general; we distinguish extensively and elaborately among many different sorts of social groups. We talk about different families, ethnic groups, religious groups, clubs, nations, classes, tribes, work forces, student bodies, faculty departments, sports teams, political parties, personality types, TV fans, and so on.

We also speak, of course, about legal officials. Judges, legislators, regulators, prosecutors, and police officers are generally grouped together as officers of the law in order to distinguish them from those who lack legal power to act. And, not only do we distinguish between legal and nonlegal groups within a particular community, we also differentiate between legal groups across communities. We consider French judges, ministers, legislators, and law enforcement personnel to be part of the French legal system and not of, say, the British legal system. Likewise, we regard British officials as belonging to the same system, but not to the French system.

And, just as we distinguish between different groups, we also differentiate between systems of rules. We refer, for example, to the rules of Christianity, the Smith family, American middle-class etiquette, the Rotary club, French law, morality, medieval canon law, chess, Cambridge University, the Olympic Committee, and so forth.

The fact that we distinguish between different groups and systems of rules reflects an important fact about our social world: namely, that it is highly pluralistic. For a world in which everyone held the same basic beliefs and values and in which the activity of each group was seen as a contribution to an overarching and shared objective would be one in which there was no need to distinguish between different groups and their rules in such an elaborate fashion. The question "Whose rule is that?" would not be particularly urgent precisely because everyone would regard all rules as equally valid. And despite the fact that there would be many different sources of rules in such a world, its inhabitants would not think it important to classify rules on the basis of their pedigree or point of origin.

The ideological diversity of the modern world, by contrast, compels us to distinguish between various groups and the competing demands that they place on us. If we are told that there is a rule prohibiting some action, say, eating meat, we would want to know *whose* rule it is. If it is a moral rule, then we might heed it if we can be persuaded that eating meat is actually immoral (or at least feel guilty if we don't). But if meat eating is merely against the law, we might choose to disobey it and risk the repercussions. There are other possibilities as well: the rule may be our friend's rule and we might decide to follow it in his presence in order to support our friend's decision to become a vegetarian. Or it might be a rule of the church in which we were raised and whose teachings we no longer follow as adults. Or our interlocutor might simply be reminding us of our new vegetarian diet.

Thus, we might say that one of the prime philosophical motivations for asking the question "What is law?" is to try to make sense of one important part of our elaborate scheme of social classification. When we understand this as a search for the identity of law, the task is a taxonomical one. When we say that a given rule is a legal rule, what makes it a *legal* rule and not a rule of etiquette, chess, Catholicism, Microsoft, morality, or my friend's conception of morality? And when we say that a rule is a rule of French law, what makes it the case that it is a rule of *French* law and not American, Chinese, Jewish, or Iranian law? These questions challenge us to make explicit the principles that underpin our commonsense conception of the social world.

Alternatively, the question "What is law?" may be understood as the search for the necessary and interesting properties of law. In asking the Implication Question, we are not concerned with why something counts as an instance of law but rather with what necessarily follows or does not follow from that fact. In other words, what must be true of a rule because it is a *legal* rule and not a rule of etiquette, chess, Catholicism . . . and so forth? Does it mean that someone will be punished if he doesn't follow it? Does it mean that he now has a moral obligation to obey it? Do we reason with the rule differently from the way that we reason with non-legal rules? These questions attempt to make the logic of our social classifications explicit. They prod us to detail what follows, as a matter of necessity, from the fact that something falls into one box on our social grid and not another.

Legal philosophers have not always been interested in pursuing the Identity and the Implication questions at once.[8] As we will see, some philosophers, such as Austin, have focused on the law's identity, while others, such as Hart and Dworkin, have been far more concerned with its necessary implications. I want here to try to address both problems. That is to say, I will be concerned in what follows not only with the question of what makes law *law* but also with the related question of what necessarily follows from the fact that something is law.

Conceptual Analysis

Analytical philosophers have traditionally approached both identity and implication questions by means of a distinctive methodology. This method goes by several different names: "conceptual analysis," "descriptive metaphysics," "reflective equilibrium," and "rational reconstruction." For simplicity, and out of deference to tradition, I will refer to it here as conceptual analysis.[9]

Before I proceed, I should point out that philosophical methodology is, of course, extremely controversial and that philosophers are not all agreed on this issue. There may in fact be no one who completely agrees with the methodology of conceptual analysis that I'm about to describe. I hope nevertheless that my description will capture, at least in broad outline, a methodology widely employed by philosophers in general, and legal philosophers in particular.[10] It is also the methodology that I intend to employ in this book.

Truisms

Conceptual analysis can easily be thought of as a kind of detective work. Imagine that someone is murdered. The detective will first look for evidence at the crime scene, collecting as many clues as she can. She will study those clues hoping that the evidence, coupled with her knowledge of the world and human psychology, will help eliminate many of the suspects and lead her to the identity of the killer.

In conceptual analysis, the philosopher also collects clues and uses the process of elimination for a specific purpose, namely, to elucidate the identity of the entity that falls under the concept in question. The major difference between the philosopher and the police detective is that the evidence that the latter collects and analyzes concerns *true* states of affairs whereas the former is primarily interested in *truistic* ones. The philosophical clues, in other words, are not merely true, but *self-evidently* so.[11]

The key to conceptual analysis, then, is the gathering of truisms about a given entity. Everyone who has mastered the concept of, say, knowledge accepts or would be disposed to accept a certain number of truisms about knowledge. For example, it is a truism that one cannot know some fact unless one believes that fact. This is an obvious truth about knowledge. It is also a truism that if one knows something, one is not wrong about it. If one does not know that knowledge implies truth, then one does not know what knowledge is. Other truisms about knowledge include: "If you know that p, you are highly confident that p"; "Experts know more about their area of expertise than nonexperts"; "If someone knows that p, it is a good idea to defer to them with respect to p"; "To know a fact about the world, one must have some evidence supporting one's judgment"; "If I believe that p and you believe that not-p, then at most one of us can be in the know"; "It is possible for two people to know the same fact"; "Knowledge is useful for achieving one's ends" and so on.

Again, truisms are the clues that help us determine the identity of the object in question. Although it is not necessary that our answer satisfy every single truism, we must try to come up with a theory that accounts for as many of them as possible. For if our account flouts too many of them, we will have changed the subject and will no longer be giving an account of the intended entity but of something else entirely.

For example, philosophers have thought that knowledge is true, justified belief because such a theory best fits a comprehensive truistic description of the entity in question. The claim that instances of knowledge must be beliefs accounts for the fact that one cannot know something if one does not believe it, and it also explains how it is possible for two people to know the same fact. That knowledge consists of beliefs that are true explains why knowledge is inconsistent with error, why knowing things about the world is useful, why two people who have contradictory beliefs cannot both be in the know, and so forth. That knowledge consists of beliefs that are not only true but also justified accounts for the fact that knowledge warrants deference, that experts know more than nonexperts, that knowledge about the world requires supporting evidence, and so on.

Having determined the answer to the Identity Question in this way, the philosopher may then go on to infer additional necessary truths about the entity in question for the purposes of answering the Implication Question.[12] For example, once we arrive at our characterization of knowledge as true, justified belief, we can see that knowledge is "agglomerable," which is to say that if one knows that p and one knows that q, and one believes that p and q, then it necessarily follows that one knows that p and q. This is so because (1) one possesses the belief that p and q; (2) one will be justified in believing that p and q because one believes that p and believes that q; and (3) both p and q are true given that one knows that p and knows that q. Hence, it follows necessarily from the fact that knowledge is true, justified belief that one will know that p and q just in case one knows that p and knows that q and believes that p and q.

Truisms about Law

To answer the Identity and Implication questions about law, then, the legal philosopher must assemble a preliminary list of truisms about law. Doing this does not however mean identifying what the layperson would recognize as obvious truths about the law. It means identifying those truths that those who have a good understanding of how legal institutions operate (lawyers, judges, legislators, legal scholars, and so on) take to be self-evident, or at least would take to be so on due reflection.

In assembling a list of truisms about law, the legal philosopher must include truisms about *basic legal institutions* ("All legal systems have judges," "Courts interpret the law," "One of the functions of courts is to resolve disputes," "Every legal system has institutions for changing the law"); *legal norms* ("Some laws are rules," "Some laws impose obligations," "Laws can apply to those who created them," "Laws are always members of legal systems"); *legal authority* ("Legal authority is conferred by legal rules," "Legal authorities have the power to obligate even when their judgments are wrong," "In every legal system, some person or institution has supreme authority to make certain laws"); *motivation* ("Simply knowing that the law requires one to act in a certain way does not motivate one to act in that way," "It is possible to obey the law even though one does not think that one is morally obligated to do so," "One can be a legal official even though one is alienated from one's job"); *objectivity* ("There are right answers to some legal questions," "Courts sometimes make mistakes when interpreting the law," "Some people know more about the law than others") and so on.

To establish the identity of law, the legal philosopher aims to determine what the law must be if it is to have the properties specified in the above list. Suppose, for example, that someone proposes the following account of the nature of law: The law is whatever courts say it is. Although this is a popular theory among many politicians and law professors, it is clear that this account fails as an instance of conceptual analysis insofar as it flouts many legal truisms. For if the law is whatever the courts say it is, then courts must be legally infallible—they could never be in the wrong. This conclusion nevertheless violates the objectivity truism, mentioned above, which maintains that courts can make mistakes when interpreting the law. And it also violates other truisms that I have not listed, such as the following: that some courts have better legal judgment than others, that appellate courts exist in part to correct legal errors, and that the reason why it is often possible to predict what courts will do is we think that courts often correctly follow preexisting law. This account flouts so many truisms that it cannot be seen as revealing the identity of the entity referenced by our concept of law. The theory, in other words, can be true only if we change the subject and talk about some other object entirely.

Disagreements in Conceptual Analysis

The fact that our theories about the identity of law must be tested against the set of statements that strike informed individuals as self-evidently true of course raises a vexing question: what happens when we disagree about whether some statement is a truism or not? For example, it seems to me an obvious truth about the nature of legality that regimes that are morally illegitimate may still have law. I say this because it is easy for me to imagine legal systems that are evil.[13] In fact, human history is littered with examples of precisely such wicked regimes; in the last century alone, there have been the Nazis, the Soviet Union, the Taliban, the Iraqi Baathists, and the Burmese junta, to name only a few of the many possible candidates.

Yet not everyone agrees with my intuitions in this regard. Some legal philosophers deny that the Nazis, the Soviets, the Taliban, and others had law, claiming that these regimes merely had "law-like" systems instead. These reactions strike me as idiosyncratic, but the fact that many people whom I respect have these reactions highlights a particularly disturbing aspect of conceptual analysis. Conceptual analysis, as we have seen, depends on our ability to assemble a list of obvious truths. But when we deal with questions about, for example, whether the Nazis had law, we often find that people's responses about what is obviously and self-evidently true differ significantly. Some think it is obvious that the Nazis had law; others think it is equally obvious that they did not. Because each intuition will lead to a very different theory of law, it is imperative that we resolve this conflict. Yet, conceptual analysis seems to provide no way to adjudicate between rival intuitions.

One possibility that should not be discounted is that the conflict is irresolvable. People might actually possess different concepts of law, and their clashing opinions may be manifestations of this fact. It is possible that we may actually be referring to different things when we use the word "law," as when I ask you the location of the nearest bank hoping that you will point me to a financial institution, but you instead tell me that the nearest bank is along the Hudson River. If so, conceptual analysis of law would not be possible because there would be no object to which we are all referring when we use the word "law."

Another, more plausible possibility, however, is that those who deny that the Nazis had law recognize that their view goes somewhat against the grain but affirm it precisely because they feel that rival theories cannot account for certain important truisms about the law as well as their theory can. The claim that the Nazis did not have law, in other words, is not a truistic *input* to conceptual analysis but rather its theoretical *output*. For example, one might feel that the only way to account for the fact that legal authorities have the legal *right* to rule and are capable of imposing legal *obligations* on their subjects compels us to impute moral legitimacy to them and hence to deny to wicked regimes such as the Nazis the status of law. On this interpretation, the conflict regarding the legality of a wicked regime would indeed be resolvable. To adjudicate between intuitions, one would need to examine the theories of which they are a part in order to see which better accommodates the *entire* set of considered judgments about the law. Although we are obviously in no position to do this right now, I hope to be better equipped to do this later on in the book.

What I do want to emphasize at this point is the provisional role that intuitions play in conceptual analysis. While conceptual analysis proceeds on the basis of our intuitions, it is obviously important that we not take any of our reactions as sacrosanct and unrevisable. The fact that an account does not square with some of our intuitions—that it requires us, say, to deny that the Nazis had law—may count against that account but it is by no means fatal to it. We must consider the totality of our reactions and be willing to give up some of our views when they don't cohere with other judgments to which we assign a higher priority and are therefore less willing to abandon. In this respect, conceptual analysis is an exercise in rational reconstruction. Unless our understanding of an entity is perfect, it is possible that we will be mistaken, at least somewhat, about what is self-evidently true of the entity in question. Conceptual analysis aims to identify the sources of confusion and help us to resolve them.

Relatedly, we should not infer from the fact that conceptual analysis is supposed to *start* from truistic judgments that it will necessarily *end* in truistic theories.[14] Indeed, there would be no point in engaging in conceptual analysis if the identity of some entity were obvious to everyone. A proper answer to the Identity Question seeks to account for the truistic judgments and explain why those truisms are true. But such an explanation need not itself be truistic. Many of those who are presented with the answer to an Identity Question may not be able to "see" that it is the best account of the entity in question, let alone that it is self-evidently the best account.[15]

The fact, therefore, that theories about the nature of law are contested should not be taken to impugn conceptual analysis. Just as two detectives can disagree about which suspect committed the crime, two philosophers can disagree about what makes an entity the thing that it is. In both cases, the persons in question are attempting to figure out which account best explains the more or less common body of evidence. And in both cases, people can disagree because at least one side engages in fallacious reasoning, overlooks relevant evidence, lacks imagination, indulges in wishful thinking, or brings to bear a different worldview than their interlocutor.[16]

Strategies for the Imagination

As any philosopher will attest, conceptual analysis is a tricky enterprise. Unlike mathematics and logic, both of which possess algorithms for demonstrably proving theorems, philosophy lacks established procedures for guaranteeing that one has discovered an entity's identity. As a result, philosophers never know whether they have simply overlooked some crucial consideration. There is always the lingering possibility that they have pronounced a property to be part of a thing's nature merely because they were not clever or fortunate enough to construct the right counterexample.

The analysis of knowledge as true, justified belief is a case in point. This account had been accepted by philosophers for over two thousand years until Edmund Gettier came along in 1963 and showed that it was untenable.[17] He did this by devising vignettes in which it was clear that the protagonist had a true, justified belief but did not have knowledge. One such example goes as follows: Suppose you see a very realistic statue of a cow in a field, but you mistakenly think it's a real cow. It turns out, however, that there is a cow in the meadow standing right behind the statue. Now, although you believe that there is a cow in the field, and that belief is true and justified (remember the statue looks just like a real cow), we would not say that you *knew* that there was a cow in the field (after all, you saw a statue of a cow, not an actual cow). This shows that knowledge is not just true, justified belief but something else as well. Philosophers have been on the lookout for that something else ever since.

In what follows, we will see that same dynamic at work in the field of jurisprudence. Accounts of the nature of legality that endured for generations have frequently been felled by a few neat counterexamples. The fact that conceptual analysis is fallible, of course, does not invalidate it as a method of reasoning. After all, scientific reasoning is not foolproof either. But these considerations do underscore the need for caution. They indicate that we should not be overly confident in our assertions that a given property is part of a thing's nature. If anything, the history of philosophy teaches us to be humble in metaphysical matters and to proceed carefully and cautiously.

But conceptual analysis is thorny not only because ingenious counterexamples are hard to conjure up. Perhaps the bigger difficulty is the ever-present danger of overlooking the obvious. As I have noted, when we inspect our concepts, we look for truisms, statements so unobjectionable that they hardly need mentioning. But it is precisely their unremarkable character that makes these truisms so easy to miss. Simply staring at paradigms of law and hoping that connections will pop into our minds is bound to be unproductive, not to mention extremely boring.

In order to elucidate those properties that may be hiding in plain sight, we need to develop compensatory strategies. Let me mention four such strategies. This list is by no means exhaustive—it merely represents a few helpful techniques for doing conceptual analysis, all of which I will go on to use throughout this book.

The first strategy, which I will call the "Comparative Strategy," is an old standard in jurisprudential circles. It aims to stimulate thought through the heavy use of comparisons on the premise that examining institutions and practices that are similar, but not identical, to law, such as games, organized crime, religion, corporations, clubs, etiquette, popular morality, and so forth, will better equip us to appreciate the distinctive aspects of law itself.

Theorists who utilize the Comparative Strategy, especially those who have been influenced by the Ordinary Language School of philosophy that prevailed in Britain during the middle of the last century, typically rely heavily on assessments of linguistic usage. Legal philosophers compare how we speak about various sorts of institutions and practices and try to exploit disparities in use as clues to how these various institutions or practices differ from one another. Hart aptly summarized the point of this exercise: "Many important distinctions, which are not immediately obvious, between types of social situation or relationships may be best brought to light by an examination of the standard uses of the relevant expressions and of the way in which these depend on a social context, itself often left unstated."[18] Hart concluded with a quote from J. L. Austin, perhaps the exemplary practitioner of this form of the Comparative Strategy in modern philosophy. "In this field of study it is particularly true that we may use, as Professor J. L. Austin said, 'a sharpened awareness of words to sharpen our perception of the phenomena.' "[19]

Another traditional method is to analyze puzzles generated by the concept in question and hope that cracking these riddles will yield insight into the character of a thing that falls under the concept. Since the concept of law is a veritable cornucopia of paradoxes, jurisprudes have frequently availed themselves of the "Puzzle-Solving Strategy." I plan to employ it repeatedly in the course of the book, as we examine a number of puzzles involving legal authority, legal obligation, and legal interpretation.

A large portion of the book will be devoted to one paradox in particular. This riddle, which I call the "Possibility Puzzle" and introduce in the next chapter, is an extraordinarily vexing one: it purports to show, by way of seemingly undeniable logic, that legal systems could never have come into existence. Thus, our belief that law is a human invention that currently exists must be an illusion. As we will see, the main disagreements in legal philosophy can profitably be viewed as disputes about the proper solution to the Possibility Puzzle. And, as we will also see, resolving this puzzle and showing how legal institutions are indeed possible will provide invaluable clues for revealing the law's fundamental nature.

A third technique for answering the question "What is law?" involves building a hypothetical legal system. The "Constructivist Strategy," as I will call it, starts with a very simple, easily understandable nonlegal situation. It then uses this scenario to launch a comparison with the law and tries to imagine what would be necessary to transform it into a legal system. Hart's well-known reconstruction of John Austin's theory of law employs precisely this technique. As Hart showed, one way to understand Austin's theory of law is to imagine it as starting with the simple situation of a gunman demanding money from a person under the threat of harm. It then compares how a gunman demanding money from someone differs from a legal authority demanding obedience from someone. Finally, it suggests how to modify the gunman case so that, after the various adjustments are made, the gunman has turned into the legal sovereign and a legal system has been created.

There are, of course, many other ways to try to build a hypothetical legal system. In Chapter 5, for example, I begin not with a gunman but with a simple egalitarian group activity of cooking together. I then consider the conditions under which it would be advisable for one person to have authority over another and the minimal changes that must occur in order for hierarchical relations to be created. The hypothetical continues by considering the various limitations of such a simple governance structure and the various minimal changes that must take place in order to solve such problems. The construction ends when the hierarchical structure that emerges is so complex and sophisticated that it can justifiably be considered a legal system.

The Constructivist Strategy is an invaluable tool for legal philosophers, and its value derives from the way in which it makes it possible for them to determine several crucial pieces of information. First, it enables philosophers to rule out those properties that are merely contingent features of legality. For if it is possible to build a legal system without using certain objects or appealing to certain concepts, then these objects and concepts cannot be necessary ingredients of law. Second, the Constructivist Strategy helps philosophers uncover those properties that are essential for the existence of law. Because the construction of the hypothetical legal system is supposed to be as economical as possible, the process aims to reveal the minimal core of law, those building blocks that are absolutely needed to establish a legal system and nothing more.[20] Third, the Constructivist Strategy enables the development of noncircular analyses of law. By building legal systems from exclusively nonlegal building blocks, legal philosophers can ensure that they do not appeal to the law in order to explain law.

The last technique, which might be called the "Anecdotal Strategy," attempts to stimulate thought about law through the examination of anthropological and historical evidence about the formation and operation of legal systems. The aim is to discover what actual participants in the practice consider to be valuable about legal institutions in general, and about their design in particular.

This strategy is relatively novel. Philosophers seldom look to history or other legal cultures when engaging in conceptual analysis, and for good reason. Since philosophers are usually not trained as historians or anthropologists, there is the risk that they will either misrepresent the facts or oversimplify their interpretation (or both). But while it is important to bear in mind the potential hazards of interdisciplinary research, it seems to me that ignoring legal history and anthropology also deprives philosophers of an extremely important source of inspiration and ideas. In this book, therefore, I hope to experiment with the Anecdotal Strategy. I will refer to historical episodes or anthropological research on several occasions in order to make the theory of law that I am developing more vivid and to suggest the plausibility of my general approach.

These four strategies—the Comparative, Puzzle-Solving, Constructivist, and Anecdotal—are indispensable tools for engaging in conceptual analysis. They exercise the imagination and thereby promote the discovery of truths that are elusive precisely because they are so plainly true. They also suggest new approaches and models for explaining such truisms, thus enabling philosophers to gain purchase on the identity of the law and its necessary implications.

Why Care?

As I noted earlier, one doesn't need especially acute powers of social observation to be aware that analytical jurisprudence is not everyone's cup of tea. In my experience, most legal academics and practitioners find the question "What is law?" distinctly unmoving. Unlike philosophers, they simply don't see the point of worrying or speculating about the nature of law and frequently dismiss such questions as formal and arid, far too scholastic to be of any real interest or value. Richard Posner captured this sentiment well in his Clarendon Lectures: "I have nothing against philosophical speculation. But one would like it to have some pay-off; *something* ought to turn on the answer to the question 'What is law?' if the question is to be worth asking by people who could use their time in other socially valuable ways. Nothing does turn on it."[21]

In some cases, this aversion to analytical jurisprudence is simply one manifestation of a distaste for, or skepticism about, philosophy in general. Many people undoubtedly perceive philosophizing as a bizarre and silly activity, valuable chiefly as fodder for brilliant Monty Python sketches. My hunch, however, is that most people's antipathy to modern jurisprudence does not reflect a hostility to philosophical thinking in general but rather a number of basic misunderstandings about the project of analytical jurisprudence specifically.

We encountered one such confusion earlier when we considered the widespread assumption that the question "What is law?" is just an inquiry into the meaning of a word—or, in other words, a merely semantic exercise.[22] Those who operate on this assumption find it difficult to fathom why philosophers would spend so much time on "mere semantics." But as we have seen, analytical jurisprudence is *not* primarily a linguistic inquiry; it is an attempt to uncover the basic principles that structure a highly significant part of our social world.

Others may have developed an aversion to analytical jurisprudence because they associate it with a particular debate within the discipline. Many people seem to think that the main debate in jurisprudence is about whether there are moral constraints on legal validity or, to put it slightly differently, whether a rule can be so unjust that it cannot be properly characterized as law. The Fugitive Slave Act of 1850, for example, is an example of one such stunningly unjust rule. It obligated federal marshals or other officials to arrest anyone suspected of being a runaway slave, and stipulated that this obligation could be triggered by nothing more than a claimant's sworn testimony. The suspected slave had no right to testify on his or her own behalf or demand a jury trial in order to contest these allegations. Finally, those who failed to comply with the law were subject to a $1,000 fine.

In such cases, a philosopher might easily ask: was the Fugitive Slave Act *really* a law or was it so unjust as to be undeserving of this title? Legal positivists respond to this question by claiming that there are no necessary moral constraints on the criteria of legality. A very unjust rule can still be a law as long as it satisfies the criteria of legal validity applied by the institutions of the legal system in question. Thus, from the positivists' perspective, the Fugitive Slave Act belonged to the body of federal law in antebellum America, its manifestly unjust and immoral character notwithstanding. From the perspective of natural law theorists, however, some of the rules that regimes sanction may simply be too unjust to be counted as law.[23] Thus, even though the fugitive slave laws were considered to be lawful at the time, antebellum lawyers were in fact wrong to respond to them as such, since the Fugitive Slave Act was legally null and void.

The fact that this debate represented the public face of jurisprudence for many generations may be one reason that some legal observers concluded that jurisprudence was less than riveting or at least insufficiently interesting or important to merit an entire field of study. I have some sympathy for those who think to themselves: "Who cares what you call an unjust rule! If you want to call it a law, call it a law; if you want to call it a nonlaw, don't call it a law." Of course, the real question is not what you *call* an unjust rule, but rather what an unjust rule *is*. But I also recognize this genre of response as an expression of frustration at the amount of energy put into answering a question that hardly seems worth the effort.

I have tried to show here, however, that the question "What is law?" encompasses much more than the issue of whether an unjust rule can still be a law. Philosophers of law are for the most part engaged in a much broader inquiry into the identity of law and its implications. To be sure, the latter questions bear on the relation between law and morality and to that extent must take up the issue of whether there are moral constraints on legality. One cannot fully understand the nature of the law without also coming to grips with the question of whether an unjust rule is still a law. But knowing the answer to this latter question would teach us very little about the nature of law in general.

I also suspect that few skeptics will be satisfied by any of the clarifications or arguments I have offered thus far. For the principal objection to analytical jurisprudence almost certainly has to do with its perceived lack of relevance. The objection here seems to boil down to this: questions such as "What is law?" *don't have any practical significance.*

Complaints about the "irrelevance" of jurisprudence are of course neither new nor surprising. In 1879 the great British constitutional scholar A. V. Dicey proclaimed that "[j]urisprudence is a word that stinks in the nostrils of a practicing barrister."[24] Lawyers are pragmatic both by temperament and necessity—their job, after all, is to help their clients, and if they repeatedly fail in this regard, their livelihood is at risk. Why should lawyers care about a discipline that studies their practice without telling them anything that will affect how they engage in it? Those who study, teach, and write about tort law can arguably be said to contribute to the practice of tort law. But those who inquire into *the nature of law* seem to have no discernible effect on the *practice of law* of any kind. What, then, *is* the point of jurisprudence? To many members of the bar, and legions of law students, the answer is by no means obvious.

My aim in what follows is to show that, contrary to these venerable jurists, a great deal *does* turn on the question of "What is Law?" In fact, I will argue that it is not possible to address many of the most pressing practical matters that concern lawyers—including who has the legal authority to regulate which conduct and how to interpret legal texts—without addressing the analytical questions that have traditionally preoccupied philosophers of law as well. One of the main goals of this book will thus be to show that analytical jurisprudence has profound practical implications for the practice of law—or, in other words, that the answer to what the law is *in any particular case* depends crucially on the answer to what law is *in general*.

In a nutshell, my reasoning here is as follows: In order to prove conclusively that the law is thus-and-so in a particular jurisdiction, it is not enough to know who has authority within the jurisdiction, which texts they have approved, and how to interpret them. One must also know a general philosophical truth, namely, how legal authority and proper interpretive methodology are established in general. In other words, one must know which facts *ultimately* determine the existence and content of legal systems. For without this information it is not possible to show definitively that a given person has legal authority in a particular jurisdiction and how their texts ought to be interpreted. In short, if one wants to demonstrate conclusively that the law is thus-and-so in any particular case, one must know certain philosophical truths about the nature of law in general—precisely the information that analytic jurisprudence seeks to provide.

Since this point is extremely important to my argument, I would like to dwell on it a bit longer. In the next section I want to say something more about why our ability to answer the legal question "What is *the* law?" depends on our ability to answer the philosophical question "What *is* law?"

The Ultimate Determinants of Legal Facts

Let me begin by introducing the notion of a *legal fact*.[25] A legal fact is a fact about either the existence or the content of a particular legal system. It is a legal fact, for example, that Bulgaria has a legal system. Similarly, it is a legal fact that the law in California prohibits driving in excess of 65 miles per hour.

Legal facts are never *ultimate* facts. In other words, whenever a law or legal system exists, it always does so in virtue of some other facts. For example, if it is against the law to jaywalk in New York City, then this legal fact obtains in virtue of the fact that, say, the city council voted to approve a bill that set out in writing that jaywalking is prohibited within the city and the fact that the mayor signed this bill. By contrast, the existence of any particular quark does not depend on the existence of any other fact (assuming that quarks are fundamental particles). Its existence is ultimate—there is no other fact in virtue of which the quark exists.

The recognition that legal facts are always determined by other facts shapes the practice of legal argumentation in a fundamental way. Suppose we want to show someone that the law is thus-and-so in a particular jurisdiction. Since legal facts are not ultimate, we can only make our case by pointing to the existence of other facts that determine that the law is thus-and-so in the jurisdiction. In the case of legislative, administrative, or judicial rules, we would be required to argue that those with legal authority within the relevant jurisdiction approved certain legal texts and their proper interpretation supports our claim about the law.

Similarly, suppose that our interlocutor denies that the persons we identified have legal authority within the jurisdiction. Because the authoritative status of the persons in question is a legal fact, it cannot be ultimate either. We will therefore be compelled to respond to our interlocutor by making reference to other facts, such as the existence of relevant valid laws that confer such authority.

This dynamic of contestation and rejoinder can continue still further. Imagine that our interlocutor denies that the laws to which we have just referred are valid within the jurisdiction and accordingly concludes that they are incapable of conferring authority. We might reply by adverting to the existence of still other laws that confer authority on officials to create the authority-conferring laws in question. Indeed, we might trace the existence of the laws conferring authority all the way back to the fundamental rules of the legal system. In the United States, for example, in order to establish claims of legal authority within the federal system, one must show that they eventually derive from the United States Constitution. Facts regarding the existence of federal law, therefore, are always partially determined by facts about constitutional law.

The fact that legal facts are never ultimate raises an obvious query: what happens when we run out of legal facts upon which to rely? Suppose, for example, that our interlocutor is so obstinate that he denies that the fundamental rules of the legal system that we are referencing are legally valid. Or imagine that someone claims that the United States Constitution is not legally binding on federal and state officials in the United States. Perhaps she rejects the idea that state conventions had the authority to ratify the Constitution and claims instead that the Articles of Confederation are still in force.[26] Since the Constitution is fundamental law, we cannot appeal to further legal facts to justify its existence. How might we then respond to these skeptical claims? What facts might we appeal to in order to establish the authoritative status of fundamental laws such as the Constitution?

Legal Positivism and Natural Law

In the philosophy of law, there have been two different answers to this sort of question. The first kind of answer, advanced by legal positivists, is that all legal facts are ultimately determined by social facts alone.[27] For those who endorse this answer, claims about the existence or content of a legal system must ultimately be established by referring to what people think, intend, claim, say, or do. Positivists disagree with one another about the nature of these ultimate social facts, but one plausible version goes as follows: the fact that legal officials treat the state conventions as having had the power to ratify the Constitution makes it the case that the Constitution is legally binding on them. Thus, following the positivist account, the practice of U.S. legal officials is ultimately responsible for the content of all federal law.

The second position, advanced by natural lawyers, holds that legal facts are ultimately determined by moral *and* social facts.[28] For those who hold this position, claims of legal authority and proper interpretation must in the end be justified through morally sound reasoning. Although natural lawyers disagree with one another about the nature of these ultimate moral facts, one plausible version of their position is as follows: the fact that the Constitution was ratified by all of the state conventions invests it with moral authority and hence legal authority. The Constitution is legally binding, on this view, not because it *is* but rather because it *ought* to be followed.

I will have much more to say about these positions in the chapters to come. But there are two initial things to note about this debate. First, the disagreement between legal positivists and natural lawyers concerns the *necessary properties of law* and, therefore, *the nature of law*. The positivist believes that it is a necessary property of the law that its existence and content is ultimately determined by social facts alone. In this respect, the positivist treats the law like custom: it is in the nature of both law and custom that facts about their existence or content are ultimately determined by social facts alone (it is a custom to eat turkey on Thanksgiving just because people take it upon themselves to eat turkey on Thanksgiving). By contrast, natural lawyers claim that it is a necessary property of the law that its existence and content are ultimately determined by social and moral facts, and they believe that the nature of law is similar in this regard to the nature of political morality.

Second, and more importantly, this philosophical debate has important implications for practice. These implications may be obscured by our example of the Constitution insofar as everyone agrees that it is legally authoritative and binding on all federal and state officials in the United States. No one seriously doubts this legal fact, and as a result, philosophical disagreements about which facts determine the authority of state constitutional conventions are merely academic. To take a different example, however, American lawyers do not all agree with one another about the correct way to *interpret* the Constitution. And it is here that philosophical disagreements about the nature of law can make a profound practical difference.

To see this, consider the ongoing debate about the constitutionality of the death penalty in the United States. The Eighth Amendment to the United States Constitution states: "Excessive bail shall not be required, nor excessive fines imposed, nor cruel and unusual punishments inflicted."[29] This constitutional provision has given rise to endless discussions about whether it should be read as prohibiting punishments that are actually cruel or only those that were thought to be cruel by those who drafted and ratified the provision. Following the first interpretation, the death penalty would be unconstitutional only if state-sponsored executions could be shown to be actually cruel. Following the second interpretation, the death penalty is definitely constitutional because it is clear from other provisions in the Constitution that the framers thought that the death penalty *was* constitutional.

Notice that this interpretive disagreement is a dispute about what determines the content of United States constitutional law. The first position states that the plain meaning of the text determines the content of the Eighth Amendment prohibition (because "cruel" means cruel, U.S. law prohibits punishments that are actually cruel). The second position states that the intentions of the framers determine the content of the Eighth Amendment (because "cruel" must be interpreted according to the beliefs of the framers, U.S. law prohibits punishment that the framers thought was cruel).

The crucial question here is: how are we to resolve this disagreement? What determines the content of the Eighth Amendment: plain meaning or original intent (or perhaps something else)? And it is here that the debate between the legal positivists and natural lawyers becomes relevant. For the only way to figure out whether plain meaning or original intent determines United States constitutional law is to know which facts *ultimately* determine the content of *all* law. So, for example, if the positivists are right, the only way to demonstrate that one interpretive methodology or another is correct is to point to the social fact or facts that make it so, perhaps by showing that courts routinely follow one methodology and not the other. On the other hand, if the natural lawyer is right, then the only way to establish one's position is by engaging in moral and political philosophy. Thus, for example, one might argue for one methodology over another by showing that considerations of democratic theory support reading the Constitution in a certain way.

What this line of reasoning implies is that analytical jurisprudence is capable of making a crucial practical difference. For there is often no way to resolve specific disagreements about *the* law without first resolving disagreements about *the nature of law* in general. In order to show conclusively that the law is thus-and-so in a particular case, it is not enough to assert that the law was created by someone with authority and that one is interpreting the legal texts properly. One must also be capable of demonstrating that one is *justified* in ascribing legal authority to that person and in interpreting their texts accordingly.

It is in this sense that the resolution of certain legal disputes depends on the ability to resolve certain philosophical disputes as well. If the positivist is right and the existence and content of legal systems are ultimately determined by social facts alone, then the only way to demonstrate conclusively that a person has legal authority or that one is interpreting legal texts properly is by engaging in sociological inquiry. Only by looking to what people think, intend, claim, say, or do can the lawyer definitively demonstrate that the law is thus-and-so in any particular instance. On the other hand, if the natural law theorist is right and the existence and content of legal systems are ultimately determined by moral facts as well, then it is impossible to demonstrate conclusively what the law is in any particular case without engaging in moral inquiry. Moral philosophy would be indispensable for establishing the truth of legal propositions because it would be essential for establishing the validity of claims about legal authority and proper interpretive methodology.

Labels

What I hope I have shown here is that doubts about the relevance of analytical jurisprudence are unwarranted insofar as questions about the nature of law have direct and important implications for legal practice. When legal disputes are predicated on conflicting claims about who has authority in a particular system or how its texts ought to be interpreted, it will often be necessary to advert to philosophical truths about what ultimately determines legal authority or interpretive methodology in every legal system.

My hunch is that lawyers' failure to recognize the relationship between these two questions derives from their unduly cramped understanding of what legal philosophers are up to when they investigate the nature of law. As we have seen, it is widely assumed that legal philosophers are responding primarily to concerns about a *label*, trying to figure out either what the label "law" means or where to apply it. A jurisprudential theory, on this narrow view, is a labeling theory, which involves providing either a definition of a word or a procedure for deciding whether to affix it to some object or another.

It is undeniably true that legal philosophers have sometimes made it seem as though they were responding to labeling anxieties. As we noted earlier, legal theorists have worried whether rules like the Fugitive Slave Act of 1850 really merit the label "law" or whether the Nazis really had a legal system. Philosophers have also debated whether international law is law or whether "primitive" cultures have legal systems. But it is a mistake to think that concerns about proper labeling practices have by any means occupied the bulk of their time and effort. Most of the time, of course, it is perfectly obvious when something is law. For example, we have no doubt that the United States has a legal system and that the Eighth Amendment to its Constitution is existing law. Yet, as we saw in the first half of the chapter, the mere fact that we know that something has the property of legality does not exhaust our philosophical curiosity. For there are two questions that arise in relation to any bona fide example of law, namely, *what makes it law* and *what necessarily follows from that fact.* Jurisprudential theories, in other words, are less interested in whether something merits the label "law" than in why it merits this label when it does and what the implications are. The label "law" is not the major *output* of the theory—it is the *input.*

As we noted before, when legal positivists and natural lawyers disagree about which facts ultimately determine the existence and content of the law, they are disagreeing about *the necessary features of law.* In other words, they are at odds about the right answer to the Implication Question. The positivist believes that it necessarily follows from the fact that something is law that its existence and content are ultimately determined by social facts alone, whereas the natural lawyer thinks that it necessarily follows that its existence and content are ultimately determined by moral facts as well. This dispute is far more than a disagreement about labels.

My point here again is that many of the questions that lawyers truly care about simply *cannot* be answered in a philosophical vacuum. Philosophical theories about the nature of law provide necessary truths about the law that are crucially relevant for adjudicating particular disputes about legal authority and interpretation. Before I go on to explore this claim in subsequent chapters, I would like first to clarify it in a couple of ways. First, I am not suggesting that it is *impossible* to answer a legal question correctly unless one is also fully in possession of a correct philosophical theory about the nature of law. Most legal questions can be answered simply by asking a lawyer, reading a hornbook, or typing the query into Google. Nor do lawyers normally need the assistance of philosophers either. Lawyers have a basic understanding of the fundamental ground rules of legal practice, which give them a working knowledge of how to answer garden-variety legal questions. Even when their knowledge runs out, it is likely that the answers to their questions will not depend on any particular view about the nature of law. It is probable, in other words, that both positivism and natural law theory will give the same answers to many of these questions. My claim is rather that the answers to *some* questions do depend on which view about the nature of law is correct. And in these cases, knowing the nature of the law is indispensable.

Second, while it is true that an inquiry into the nature of law has implications for practice, it does not follow that the legal philosopher's task is to answer legal questions. The legal philosopher's job is to identify *the proper method for determining the content of the law;* the lawyer's job is to put that method into practice. Last, it is entirely possible that the correct method for determining the content of the law will indicate that there is no correct legal answer to certain types of legal questions. Just because one might want an answer to the question "What is the law?" does not mean that there is one patiently waiting in the wings.

The Truism of Trust

My aim in this chapter was to unpack the question "What is law?" and to show how we might begin to answer it. I also tried to suggest that some of the antipathy and skepticism that such a question provokes may derive from simple misunderstandings. In particular, I have tried to make clear that philosophical inquiry into the nature of law is *not* an exercise in lexicography; it extends far beyond the issue of whether an unjust rule is a law; and it is of more than merely academic interest. To understand the nature of law is to figure out the principles that structure our social world and, as we have seen, these principles have profound implications for how we ought to engage in legal practice.

There is, however, one grievance that lawyers have toward legal philosophy that I do think is valid. Many legal practitioners have complained that jurisprudence as it is currently practiced is too removed from the everyday activity of lawyers and judges. Their point is not that legal philosophy is irrelevant to practice but rather that the theories of law expounded by philosophers do not seem to reflect the activity of actual legal institutions. In particular, lawyers often complain that legal philosophers ignore considerations of institutional competence in developing their accounts of law, and especially their theories of legal interpretation.[30]

To get a feel for the disconnect between lawyers and philosophers in this regard, consider the way that interpretive debates proceed in the "real" world. When judges, lawyers, and law professors argue for one interpretive methodology over another, they routinely justify themselves by referring to the degree to which certain members of the group can be trusted to act competently and in good faith. Textualists like Justice Antonin Scalia, for example, believe that judges should be constrained to follow the plain meaning of the statute because they do not trust judges to look beyond the text. They fear that judges will insert their own personal political views in the name of effectuating legislative purpose. Other textualists such as Judge Frank Easterbrook reject the search for purpose because they do not trust legislators to fashion public-interest legislation. Statutes, on this view, are built on compromises between opposing interest groups, not unified visions of the general welfare developed by altruistic public servants that can be extended to unanticipated cases. Purposivists such as Henry Hart and Albert Sacks, on the other hand, presumed legal officials to be people pursuing reasonable ends reasonably and thus accorded judges broad powers to delve into the "spirit" of the statute when its letter produces results that strike them as objectionable.

But in contrast to the important role that practicing lawyers attribute to trust relations when assessing interpretive method, the concept of trust almost never figures in philosophical discussions of legal interpretation. Ronald Dworkin's theory of legal interpretation is a case in point. As we will see, Dworkin argues that interpreters should always interpret legal texts in a way that will present these texts in their best moral light. But Dworkin never considers in any meaningful way whether such a methodology is appropriate for participants with normal cognitive and moral capacities. On the contrary, Dworkinian interpretation presupposes a tremendous trust in the philosophical abilities of group members and in their good will for carrying out such rigorous intellectual exercises. If, as is reasonable to suppose, most individuals are not particularly adept at, or likely to engage in, philosophical analysis, it seems imprudent to demand that they interpret the practice as a moral or political theorist would.

Dworkin's disregard for considerations of trustworthiness is not unique to him; it is a pervasive feature of modern analytical jurisprudence. Jurisprudential theorists have tended to approach issues of legal interpretation through the lens of traditional philosophical concerns, such as linguistic meaning, political morality, and conceptual analysis. And in keeping with this, their work has been marked by a striking enthusiasm for debates about the proper semantics of words like "vehicle" and "cruel," the relation of justice to fairness, and the conceptual preconditions of law's claim to legitimate authority.

This indifference to institutional considerations such as trust is not only irritating to lawyers but deeply ironic, given that it flies in the face of a core assumption to which most philosophers of law subscribe. As we have seen, an inquiry into the nature of law treats the considered judgments of informed individuals as the object of explanation. This means that legal philosophers are supposed to listen to the claims that legal participants use to defend and justify their actions. They study the actual practice of legal reasoning and argumentation in an effort to determine the law's nature.

Most of the accounts of law that legal philosophers have proposed nevertheless fall conspicuously short of this standard and seldom reflect the actual structure of legal argumentation. In stark contrast to legal practitioners, legal philosophers rarely take questions of competence and character seriously. And their failure to take these questions seriously is one of the reasons legal participants do not take legal philosophers seriously either.

I hope to address this oversight in the pages that follow. My aim will be to develop a theory of law in which considerations of competence and character are central to the understanding of legal institutions and the structure of legal reasoning and argumentation. Before I begin to advance this new account, however, I want first to look at some of the jurisprudential accounts that have already been formulated, paying attention not only to their logical coherence but also to the extent to which their representations of legal practice are faithful to the shared understanding of legal participants.

2

CRAZY LITTLE THING CALLED "LAW"

The Invention of Law

Thomas Hobbes famously claimed that the state of nature—that is, the social condition without law and government—would be "a war of all against all" in which life would be "solitary, poore, nasty, brutish and short."[1] Without a recognized authority for settling disputes, with each person acting as judge, jury, and executioner, conflict and competition for scarce resources would constantly threaten to erupt in violence. Hobbes was very clear, however, that he understood the state of nature to be a largely fictional construct: at no time had everyone lived entirely outside of the law, although he thought that some civilized peoples had emerged from the state of nature and that "the savage people in America" were living in that wretched condition. Hobbes's point was not that life *was* intolerable without law, but that it *would be,* and that, rather than risk such a fate, people who were fortunate enough to live under stable governments, even tyrannical ones, should not attempt to overthrow them: on the contrary, they should obey their leaders in almost all circumstances.

It turns out that Hobbes was doubly wrong. His first mistake was relatively minor. Anthropologists now believe that humans mostly lived without law for the vast majority of their time on earth. Archeological evidence and extrapolation from ethnographic observation of present-day hunter-gatherers suggest that, until 12,000 years ago, most humans lived in groups called "bands."[2] Bands are small collections of individuals that are generally mobile, have a relatively fluid membership, and subsist through hunting and gathering. They lack formal authority structures and are governed mostly by tradition, consensus, and persuasion by elders. Those who live in bands, in other words, don't have law.

35

Hobbes's second, more serious mistake was to assume that the state of nature was a state of war. Although almost certainly brutish and short, human life, at least within bands themselves, does not appear to have been especially solitary or nasty.[3] Human beings are social creatures and as such they worked together more or less peacefully in groups to collect food, raise children, and protect one another from outside predators. These groups also seem to have been governed by rules that regulated the bare essentials of social life: sharing of food, selection of mates, forbearance from physical aggression, and so on.

In other words, cooperation and order have not only been possible throughout human prehistory: they have been the norm. Prehistoric society was anarchic only in the strict, literal sense that it did not have what we now call "law." It is probably true that people cannot coexist in groups without rules. But they can, and have, lived together for millennia without legal systems. Contrary to Hobbes, therefore, the state of nature is not a philosophical fantasy, but a historical reality experienced by countless generations of human beings. Indeed, it is plausible to suppose that law is a comparatively recent invention, postdating the wheel, language, agriculture, art, and religion.

Hobbes *was* right when he claimed that without law there would be "no culture of the earth; no navigation, nor use of the commodities that may be imported by sea; no commodious building; no instruments of moving, and removing, such things as require much force; no knowledge of the face of the earth; no account of time; no arts; no letters; no society."[4] Civilization is possible only with a very high degree of social cooperation and interdependence, which, in turn, is possible only when a community has the ability to regulate social relations efficiently and effectively. Law was a revolutionary invention precisely because it permitted this regulation. Humans could now use it to create, modify, and apply rules, and thereby manage the myriad aspects of social life without having to rely solely on custom, tradition, persuasion, or consensus.

How Is Law Possible?

We have no way of knowing, of course, whether the first society to have law intentionally set out to create an efficient method of social regulation, or whether they simply stumbled upon it by accident. But in creating law, they produced a technology that has remained, along with organized religion, popular morality, and social convention, an invaluable tool for communal control.

Yet for all our certainty that legal institutions were created at some point in prehistory, and that those responsible had good reason for doing so, we remain puzzled by how the law could have been invented. Just as first-time job seekers often find themselves in the awkward position of needing job experience in order to be able to get job experience, acquiring legal authority too seems to involve a catch-22: in order to *get* legal power, one must already *have* legal power.

So that I can say more about this puzzle, let us engage in a philosophical fantasy. Imagine that law was first invented in a small agricultural village in the Fertile Crescent on January 1, 10,000 B.C. On that day, the village elder, Lex, had an idea and called a communal meeting to discuss it. He addressed his people thus: "Many of you have approached me recently to complain about the increasing divisiveness of village life. We now spend a great portion of our leisure time in village meetings, hearing complaint after complaint, discussing the merits of each grievance, endlessly deliberating about how much help each family must give to other families during planting and harvesting time, how much each family is to contribute to the winter storage, which boys are allowed to marry which girls, whether cows should be allowed to graze in the village square, where to dump our garbage, and so on. Year after year, as our village grows, the situation becomes worse. You will all recall that we were unable to resolve the tithing issue last year, and as a result we ran out of grain before the harvest. And the village commons is almost totally barren from overgrazing, which you might say is a tragedy.

"In order to remedy the situation, I propose the following course of action: I will come up with a set of rules that address the pressing issues of our time. You will know when I have made a rule when I issue a command while sitting under the big palm tree in the village square. I will also be available to resolve disputes about the right way to apply the rules I have made. My judgments will be final and no one may challenge them. Finally, when I die, all of my rules will remain in force, and one of my two children will take over as the official leader of the village. My chosen successor, of course, may change the rules if he so wishes."

Virtually everyone in the village liked Lex's proposal. They respected his wisdom and character immensely and trusted him to make good rules. They also recognized the enormous benefits that would come from

Lex's leadership. With Lex in charge, they would not have to waste time deliberating and trying to reach consensus on every single communal problem. Having rules laid down in advance would prevent feuds from starting and help coordinate behavior so as to produce goods from which all could profit.

Only one villager objected to Lex's plan: Phil, the village philosopher. "Lex, your proposal sounds nice, but it will never work. You see, in order for you to have the power to make, change, and apply rules for our village, there has to be a rule that empowers you to do so. But no such rule yet exists. If you try to make a rule under the palm tree without a rule empowering you to do so, it will have as much force as if I try to make a rule, which is to say 'None.'"

Lex pondered the objection for a short time before responding: "Phil, couldn't I just make a rule that empowered me to make a rule for the community?" Phil shook his head wistfully and said, "Unfortunately, that won't work either. Since there is no rule empowering you to make an empowering rule, your attempt to make such a rule will similarly be null and void."

Lex tried again: "Well, couldn't everyone just vote to empower me to create rules for the village?" Phil replied, "The same problem that arose for you will arise for them as well. Since there is no rule empowering them to empower you to make rules, their act of empowerment will be null and void."

Still Lex wasn't convinced. "You are right to say that I can't create any rules unless there is a rule that empowers me to do so. But why are you so sure that no such rule exists?" "That's easy to show," Phil answered. "In order for an empowering rule to exist, it would have to be created by someone empowered to do so. That would require a preexisting rule empowering that person to create empowering rules. But, by the same logic, this rule would have to be created by someone empowered to do so, which would mean that there would have to be a rule empowering that person to create rules empowering others to create empowering rules. We can go on like this forever. Unless you want to postulate an infinite number of rules and an infinite number of acts that brought them about, I think it is pretty clear that there are no such empowering rules."

"But by your reasoning," Lex concluded, "no one can ever make or change rules for the community." Phil replied, "Yes, that's true. I'm sorry."

Lex and the rest of the village did not listen to Phil. Even in prehistoric times, it seems, people tended to ignore philosophers. Lex started making rules and the rest of the community followed them. And thus, law was born.

Despite the fact that the villagers disregarded Phil's admonitions, his argument is powerful. Basic logic seems to dictate that Lex's assertion of legal power could not have been true. And if Lex's assertion was not true, then he did not have legal authority; hence, law was not created at the time we are supposing.

In fact, Phil's argument can be used to show that no assertion of legal power could ever be true. Consider the claim that Congress has the power to regulate interstate commerce. To justify this claim, one would presumably refer to Article I, Section 8 of the United States Constitution: "The Congress shall have Power To . . . regulate Commerce with foreign Nations, and among the several States."[5] Clearly, this claim presupposes that the United States Constitution is valid law. But what would justify that claim? The natural response would be that the Constitution was ratified by three-fourths of the original thirteen states. But we can then ask: what rule conferred authority on the states to ratify the Constitution?

One might be tempted at this point to mention Article VII of the United States Constitution. It states: "The Ratification of the Conventions of nine States, shall be sufficient for the Establishment of this Constitution between the States so ratifying the Same."[6] But this answer won't do, insofar as Article VII is *part of* the United States Constitution. It cannot confer authority on the ratifiers to ratify the Constitution before the Constitution is itself ratified. To argue otherwise is to engage in viciously circular reasoning.

The only option in this case is to identify some other norm that confers power on the ratifiers to ratify the state constitution. But who created that norm, and where did they get their authority to do so? Again, any answer to this question will simply prompt a new question about the new answer. Trying to find the top of the chain of authority, it would seem, leads us either in a circle or to an infinite regress. Yet, it is precisely this kind of ultimate authority that must be found in order for claims of legal authority to be true.

Note that this paradox is a classic "chicken-egg" problem. On the one hand, all chickens must hatch from chicken eggs. On the other, all chicken eggs must be laid by chickens. These two principles in combination suggest that neither chickens nor chicken eggs can exist in a finite universe, for the existence of one presupposes the existence of the other.

Our puzzle about the possibility of law has the same structure. Imagine that norms that confer legal power are the "eggs," and those with power to create legal norms are the "chickens." The Egg and Chicken principles can be rendered as follows:

> *Egg:* Some body has power to create legal norms only if an existing norm confers that power.
> *Chicken:* A norm conferring power to create legal norms exists only if some body with power to do so created it.

To see why these two principles render legal authority impossible, assume that A_1 has power to create a set of legal norms. By the Egg Principle, a norm exists which confers that power on A_1. Call that power-conferring norm n_1. By the Chicken Principle, some body with power to create n_1 actually created it. We now ask: who created n_1 which confers power on A_1? The answer cannot be "A_1" because he did not have the power to create any norms until n_1 existed. In other words, it would be viciously circular to argue that A_1 granted himself legal power, because n_1 had to exist *before* A_1 could have created it. So a different authority, call her A_2, must have created the norm that conferred power on A_1. But where did A_2 get her power to create n_1? Again, if we want to avoid a vicious circle, the only possible answer is that A_2 got her authority from some other body, A_3. But there is no end to this line of reasoning. Even if A_3 exists, there must be an A_4, A_5, A_6, A_7, and so on. This line of argument purports to show that no assertion of legal authority is compatible with the Chicken and Egg principles without resorting to vicious circles or infinite regresses.

A Note on Norms

The careful reader will have noticed that in the last section I switched terminology in midstream. When I told the story of Lex and Phil, I spoke of "rules." However, in formulating the Chicken and Egg principles and setting out the formal version of the puzzle, I used the term "norm." Why the change?

When constructing a narrative, the reason not to use the word "norm" is that ordinary people don't "normally" use that word, at least in the context in which it is used in the story. We might say, for example, that sending a thank-you note after getting a gift is "*the* norm," but not that there is "*a* norm" to that effect. In a nonacademic context, we would say that "there is a rule to send a thank-you note after receiving a gift," or perhaps more simply, "the rule is that one sends a thank-you note after receiving a gift."

"Norm," on the other hand, is a philosopher's term.[7] One reason that philosophers use it, instead of "rule," is that rules are necessarily general. If Congress enacts legislation that imposes a one-time tax on Acme Corp., it has not created a rule, because the law is individualized and particularized; it applies only to Acme and for one time only. Philosophers need a word to refer to individualized and particularized directives, as well as general ones, so they employ "norm" for that purpose.[8]

The benefit of using a term like "norm" is that one can cast one's net as widely as possible. To formulate the Egg Principle in terms of "rules" arbitrarily restricts the principle to generalized standards of conduct. There is a downside, however, to using a technical term like "norm," which is that philosophers deploy it in many different ways, often without explicitly specifying which particular one they are using in a given instance.

In what follows, I will use the term "norm" to denote any standard—general, individualized, or particularized—that is supposed to guide conduct and serve as a basis for evaluation or criticism.[9] Strict rules, rules of thumb, presumptions, principles, standards, guidelines, plans, recipes, orders, maxims, and recommendations can all be norms. Furthermore, moral, legal, religious, institutional, rational, logical, familial, and social standards are norms as well.

Norms should be distinguished from the sentences that represent them. "No vehicles in the park" is a sentence that describes the no-vehicles-in-the-park norm and hence cannot be the norm itself. Nor are the texts that *create* norms themselves norms. When the sergeant says "Clean the latrine," he creates a norm to clean the latrine, but the utterance itself is not the norm created.

As their name suggests, norms are "normative," not descriptive. They don't purport to tell their subjects what they will or might do; rather, they purport to tell them what, in some sense, they are entitled to, ought to, or may do. For this reason, it is possible to violate a norm without canceling its validity, as would be the case if one acted contrary to a strict behavioral generalization. Many people jaywalk in New York City, even though jaywalking is against the law.

Finally, as I will be using the term, norms need not be valid. Norms always *purport* to tell you what you ought to do or what is desirable, good, or acceptable, but whether they actually succeed at this task is another matter entirely. A norm that tells you to do something that you shouldn't do is an invalid norm. It is a bad norm, not a nonnorm. Norms, in this sense, are like names. Names always purport to refer, although they sometimes fail to do so. "Santa Claus" is a name, despite having no referent.

Possible Solutions

The puzzle I set out in this chapter—a puzzle that I will refer to in what follows as the "Possibility Puzzle"—challenges the idea that legal authority is possible. In this section, I plan to sketch several possible solutions to this puzzle. The point of this sketch is not to exhaustively describe each solution and evaluate its merits. It is rather to familiarize the reader with the possible range of responses available to the legal theorist and thus to provide a road map for the remaining discussion.

Let's start with the big picture. As we saw in the previous sections, the Possibility Puzzle arises because it appears that any body with power to create legal norms must derive its power from some norm, while any norm that could confer such a power must itself be created by someone with the power to do so. But in order to show that law is possible, we have to stop this threatened regress. There are two obvious ways to do this. First, we could reject the Egg Principle by finding a body whose power does not derive from some norm. Call such a body an "ultimate authority." If an ultimate authority can be located, we can solve the puzzle by showing that any authority in a particular legal system will have derived its power from this ultimate authority. There will be no danger of an infinite regress because the ultimate authority does not derive its authority from some other norm.

Alternatively, one can thwart the paradox by finding a norm that confers power to create legal norms, but which was not itself created by someone with a similar power. Call this norm an "ultimate norm." Ultimate norms, if they exist, halt the regress by rejecting the Chicken Principle. The legal power of any body in a particular legal system would be traceable to some ultimate norm that exists without having been posited by anyone else.

Throughout the history of jurisprudence, different legal theorists have opted for different strategies. One popular strategy is to take God as the Ultimate Authority. Thus, on the classical natural law view, God created the natural law, which confers the legal right on rulers to rule. God's moral authority, in other words, is both necessary and sufficient to create legal authority. One benefit of this approach, of course, is that, if God exists, She is a good candidate for the position of Ultimate Authority. At least on "voluntaristic" conceptions of theological ethics, God does not derive moral authority from some other norm or power, but is the unmoved mover of all rules and authority, legal and otherwise.

As one might also imagine, modern natural law theorists have *not* relied on God in order to solve the Possibility Puzzle. They have tended, rather, to look to certain political communities' moral right to determine the terms and direction of social cooperation. On the standard post-Enlightenment view, for example, the People have the moral authority to direct their communal lives as they see fit. This sovereign right does not derive from God: it derives from the rules or principles of political morality. And because the rules of political morality are ultimate—no one has created them—there is no worry about infinite regresses. The People receive their authority to affect the legal process from these ultimate norms, and thus have the power to transmit legitimacy to democratically selected rulers.

This is not to say that modern natural law theorists are committed to reserving the label "law" exclusively for democratic legal systems. They are willing to credit other regimes with such power in certain circumstances. What they do insist, however, is that legal authority must ultimately derive from some moral norm. Put slightly differently, on the natural law view the existence of legal authority ultimately rests on moral facts. It is the moral fact that God or the People (or possibly a benevolent dictator) has the moral authority to empower others to act that invests these bodies with legal authority.

The next two possible solutions are "positivistic," in that they ground legal authority not in moral but in social facts. The simplest option in this vein is to argue that legal authority ultimately rests on brute power—that "might" ultimately makes legal "right." On John Austin's view, as we will see, the sovereign derives his legal authority not from some other existing norm, but from his ability to coerce others into conforming to his will. The sovereign is an ultimate authority, in other words, because his power to create legal norms rests merely on the social facts that his will is habitually obeyed by the political community and that he habitually obeys no one else.

Another positivistic solution would be to argue that all instances of legal authority are ultimately traceable to a social rule. On this view, for example, the People in democratic countries have the legal power to select their rulers not because they are morally entitled to do so, but rather because courts and other legal officials follow rules mandating deference to their choices. On H. L. A. Hart's view, for example, these rules come about not through the exercise of normative power—courts do not have the legal authority to create a legal system. They are simply products of an established practice of deference. In other words, the fundamental rules of the legal system are ultimate norms that rest purely on social facts.

Ultimately

As I have described the debate in legal philosophy, the legal positivist maintains that the law is ultimately determined by social facts alone, whereas the natural lawyer believes that moral facts play a crucial role as well. It is important to caution the reader not to take this description too literally. The legal positivist does not seriously mean that the law is *ultimately* determined by social facts alone, for the simple reason that almost no one believes that social facts are among the ultimate constituents of the universe. That certain members of a group think and act a certain way is not a bedrock fact akin to the location of a quark in space-time. Many philosophers believe, for example, that social facts are reducible to facts about individual psychology and action. Some maintain that social facts are reducible to moral facts. Likewise, many philosophers believe that moral facts are reducible to other, more basic, nonmoral facts. Indeed, some even maintain that moral facts are reducible to social facts of certain kinds.

For our purposes, however, these deep metaphysical questions will largely be ignored. We will draw a methodological line at the social and the moral and treat social and moral facts as though they were ultimate. Our taxonomy of legal philosophers, therefore, will only consider those "above the line" positions. We will, for example, count people as legal positivists as long as they think that legal facts are determined by social facts alone, regardless of whether they also believe that the social facts that ground legal facts are *further* reducible to moral facts.

Hume's Challenge

No doubt some will regard the Possibility Puzzle as a cute little riddle, the sort of thing philosophers love to thrash out, but one that holds little interest for those who are not as enamored with brainteasers. Others might even regard it as an irritating, or exasperating, philosophical stunt, the jurisprudential equivalent of "How do we know we are not dreaming?" Since we know that law is possible, just as we are convinced that we are not dreaming, it is useless to spend so much time trying to refute a proposition that, to use the pragmatist Charles Peirce's phrase, does not pose "a real and living doubt."[10]

However, as I mentioned in the previous chapter, philosophers often use puzzles as analytical devices for solving important philosophical problems. Riddles enable them to isolate deep, and hence often unexamined, assumptions underlying our conception of a certain area or subject matter and show that these presuppositions clash in some fundamental way. Engaging with the puzzle allows philosophers to test the validity of these assumptions and root out those deemed to be mistaken.

The Possibility Puzzle, therefore, is best seen as an analytical device that legal philosophers can use to determine the foundations of legal systems. The unvarnished question—"On what does legal authority ultimately rest, social facts alone or moral facts as well?"—is simply too abstract for anyone to make significant headway. Asking the same question in the form of a puzzle about the possibility of law, however, gives us a better handle on how to resolve an issue about which there are real and living doubts. It allows philosophers to look at the question from a different angle, thus suggesting new approaches to resolving these issues. It prompts us, for example, to consider the various types of ultimate norms and authorities that exist and whether legal authority can be founded on any of them.

Insofar as the Possibility Puzzle concerns the ultimate foundations of legal systems, its resolution has great practical significance as well. For if the positivist solutions are correct, and the law rests on social facts alone, then the only way to definitively determine the fundamental rules of a particular legal system and its proper interpretive methodology is to engage in sociological inquiry. However, if the natural lawyer is correct, and the law rests on moral facts as well, then these legal questions can be conclusively answered only by engaging in moral argument. The Possibility Puzzle, therefore, is not a glorified version of crosswords or Sudoku.

Solving it is a matter of particular urgency for all those who care about legal doctrine.

Positive vs. Natural

As we have seen, the solution to the Possibility Puzzle has important implications for legal reasoning. Because legal judgments must track legal facts, a theory that tells us which facts ultimately determine the content of the law will be essential for a theory that tells us how to *discover* the content of the law. (As a philosopher might say, the metaphysics of law has a direct bearing on its epistemology.)

Once the connection between the solution to the Possibility Puzzle and legal reasoning is made apparent, however, an obvious problem arises for the legal positivist position. To see this, let us return to our fictional first legal system thirty years on. Lex was on his death bed and needed to decide which of his two children, "Positive" and "Natural," should succeed him. Since Positive was a bit smarter than Natural, Lex appointed Positive as his successor. Naturally, Natural resented this decision and grew to hate Positive.

A few years into his reign, Positive changed the tithing rule so as to increase the amount of grain each member of the group must contribute to the communal storage. Since no one was happy with this decision, Natural saw an opening to challenge Positive's power. During the next village meeting, Natural stood up and announced that he would not abide by the new tithing rule. "But Natural," Positive protested, "I am the ruler and you are legally obligated to listen to me."

Natural had been hanging out with Phil and picked up a few of his tricks. In response to Positive's protest, Natural laid out the same puzzle about the possibility of legal authority that Phil had sprung on his father decades earlier: how can Positive have the legal authority to create rules, when rules are required to confer such authority and authority to create such rules? Positive, however, had heard this puzzle from his father many times before and had thought up an answer. Now he had the opportunity to try it out on everyone.

Positive argued that legal authority ultimately rests on political power. Since he has the ability to punish anyone who does not tithe, he has the legal right to impose an obligation on them to obey. But Natural had a reply: "The mere fact that you can punish me is just a descriptive fact about the world. Your statement simply reports what *is* the case. However, in order for me to be legally obligated to listen to you, you must demonstrate that you legally *ought* to be obeyed. Since no one can derive an ought from an is, it follows that I cannot be legally obligated to listen to you."

Positive conceded that Natural was correct but tried another idea he had been kicking around his head. Legal authority, on this alternative view, derives from the practice of deference among members of the group. Positive has legal authority to obligate because everyone takes him to have that authority. But Natural offered the same response: "To say that everyone thinks you have the right to tell them what to do is just to make a descriptive statement about the world. On the other hand, to infer that you actually have a legal right is to draw a normative conclusion. Normative statements can never be deduced simply from descriptive ones." Positive saw Natural's point and thus did not know what to say. So he did what rulers throughout the ages have done to dissidents who make sense: Positive executed him.[11]

Not only did Natural have good responses to Positive's attempts to solve the Possibility Puzzle and legitimate his rule, but we can generalize his objections so that they apply to all forms of legal positivism. According to the legal positivist, the content of the law is ultimately determined by social facts alone. To know the law, therefore, one must (at least in principle) be able to derive this information exclusively from knowledge of social facts. But knowledge of the law is normative whereas knowledge of social facts is descriptive. How can normative knowledge be derived exclusively from descriptive knowledge? That would be to derive judgments about what one legally *ought* to do from judgments about what socially *is* the case. Legal positivism, therefore, appears to violate the famous principle introduced by David Hume (often called "Hume's Law"), which states that one can never derive an ought from an is.[12]

Because this is an extremely serious challenge to legal positivism, we will spend a fair amount of time examining how different positivists have tried to solve it. First, though, I want to set out the challenge itself in greater detail.

Nino and Dino

Suppose I go up to a child and say "Pick up your toys!" The child looks puzzled and responds, "Why should I listen to you?" I say, "Because I said so." At this point, the child complains, "But why should I listen to you just because you said so?" When I say, "Because I am your father," my child replies, "But why should children listen to their fathers?" When I say, "Because children always listen to their parents," my child shoots back, "Yes, but the fact that children always listen to their parents does not mean that they should listen to them."

Note that even though my child is being impudent and imprudent, strictly speaking he has a point. He is right to say that my telling him to pick up his toys, that I am his father, or that children always listen to their parents cannot by themselves, or all together, give him a reason to listen to me. These facts are merely descriptive ones and, as Hume's Law states, no normative conclusion can follow from statements that report them. In order to justify my claim to authority, I must produce a principle that "bridges" the descriptive-normative divide. I have to say something like "You should listen to me because children should respect their parents," or "If you don't listen, I'll punish you and punishments are bad."

Because normative conclusions cannot be derived exclusively from descriptive premises, normative reasoners must conform to a certain pattern of inference: they must ensure that their reasoning takes a normative judgment as input if a normative judgment is the output. Call this "normative in, normative out" pattern of inference a "NINO" pattern. Hume's Law is violated, therefore, if a normative judgment comes out but only descriptive judgments went in. Call this offending sequence a "DINO" pattern.

The worry about legal positivism, we might say, is that it violates Hume's Law by licensing DINO patterns of inference. Suppose a legal reasoner wants to answer some question that requires knowledge of the fundamental rules of the legal system. Perhaps he wants to know whether the president has the power to declare war or whether the death penalty is constitutional. To obtain the answer, the positivist requires the reasoner to take note of certain social facts. Thus, the positivist allows the reasoner to derive normative judgments about legal rights and duties from descriptive judgments about social facts. Normative judgments come out, but none have gone in. Call this objection to legal positivism "Hume's Challenge."

Natural law theory, of course, is untouched by Hume's Challenge because it insists on solving the Possibility Puzzle by referencing moral facts, not social ones. To answer questions that require knowledge of fundamental legal rules, the legal reasoner must form moral judgments and use them as premises to derive legal conclusions. Since both legal and moral judgments appear to be normative, the natural lawyer respects NINO. Normative judgments about the law may come out only because normative judgments about morality have gone in.

Pick Your Poison

One might think that legal positivism is so damaged by Hume's Challenge that it should be rejected in favor of natural law theory. But the natural law solution to the Possibility Puzzle has its own serious problem. By insisting on grounding legal authority in moral authority or moral norms, natural law theory rules out the possibility of evil legal systems. As we remarked in the last chapter, it is a truism that the Soviet Union had law even though the leadership of the Communist Party was not morally legitimate.

Call this the "Problem of Evil." Just as theologians have struggled to explain how evil is possible given the necessary goodness of God, the natural lawyer must account for the possibility of evil legal systems given that the law is necessarily grounded in moral facts. Positivists, on the other hand, have no such difficulties. The Soviet Union had a legal system either because Soviet legal officials had the power to coerce the Soviet population into compliance or because Soviet officials recognized Soviet authority. In either case, the legal authority of evil regimes can be explained by appealing to certain social facts, as opposed to moral ones.

Choosing a starting point for our inquiry, therefore, is very much an exercise in picking our poison. For it would not be an understatement to say that both jurisprudential positions are highly problematic. Indeed, the debate between legal positivists and natural lawyers is so interesting, and has lasted for so long, precisely because it seems as though neither side can be right. On the one hand, if we follow the natural lawyer and try to solve the Possibility Puzzle by ultimately grounding the law in moral facts, then we preclude the possibility of morally illegitimate legal systems. Yet if we eschew the appeal to moral facts completely and follow the positivist in founding the law on social facts alone, we solve the Possibility Puzzle only on pain of violating Hume's Law. Legal philosophers, therefore, face a terrible dilemma: they are damned if they do ground the law in moral facts and damned if they don't.

In the next few chapters, we will examine the responses that legal positivists have offered to these puzzles and challenges, starting with John Austin's theory of law and then moving on to consider other positivistic accounts. I want to begin with the positivists not because the objections to the natural law approach are more damning, but rather for the simple reasons that the objections to the positivistic position are more interesting and enjoy logical priority. For consider how natural lawyers must respond to the Problem of Evil: they must (1) deny that they are flouting a truism or (2) claim that their truism-flouting is not nearly as bad as the problems the positivists face. The first part of this response may be correct (though I doubt it), but it is not a very interesting argument. After all, it amounts to no more than the defiant declaration that evil legal regimes are not possible. Once this tack is taken, it is not clear where the conversation can go from there. And while the second part of the natural law response is philosophically interesting, its cogency can be assessed only once we have determined the force of the objections against the positivists. Thus, we can know which poison to pick only once we have assessed the toxicity of the positivistic one first.

3

AUSTIN'S SANCTION THEORY

Child's Play

To get a feel for how difficult it is to come up with a plausible jurisprudential theory, try to explain law to a smart five-year-old. Five-year-olds are good for testing such theories because even though they have attained a degree of mastery over certain normative ideas like RULE, SHOULD, and WRONG, they possess almost none of the distinctively legal concepts. Their conceptual naiveté blunts our temptation to describe the law as, say, "those rules made by legal authorities," because the typical five-year-old has no idea what legal authorities are. Five-year-olds also don't have mastery of sophisticated normative concepts like PRACTICE and INSTITUTION, so any description of the law would have to explain legal practice and institutions in more basic terms.

If you are like me, you are probably tempted to offer something like the following explanation: "The law consists of those rules that if a grown-up breaks them, a police officer can punish the grown-up, by forcing him or her either to pay some money or to get a time-out in a place called 'jail.' " This description, however, is not quite satisfactory, not only because police officers don't usually punish rule breakers, but because it makes reference to police officers, and hence uses a legal concept (albeit one of the very few legal concepts that children partially grasp). So one might try again and say: "The law consists of those rules that if a grown-up breaks them, people whose job it is to catch and punish rule breakers can catch and punish the grown-up, by forcing him or her either to pay some money or to get a time-out in a place called 'jail.' "

This description, of course, is incomplete. It does not tell us, for example, where legal rules come from; nor does it specify how these rules should be interpreted. The sketch, however, is not meant to be a complete theory of law—it is supposed to convey in one sentence the identity of law, namely, the property or properties of law that make it the thing that it is and distinguish it from other rules and social practices. And at first glance, at least, the description does not do a bad job. First, the description makes reference to simple, relatively unproblematic normative concepts: RULE, JOB, and PUNISHMENT. Five-year-olds understand these concepts pretty well. Second, it is reasonably good at singling out the law as a social practice. Children are often punished by having something valuable taken away or by being given a time-out, but adults are not. These occurrences are extraordinary: when they do happen, only certain people are allowed to exercise force to ensure compliance with legal rules. Third, the description reveals why many care about what the law is. They care because they don't want to be punished. Again, this motivation is clear to any five-year-old.

In this chapter, I will discuss a family of jurisprudential theories that elaborate on this basic description. Because these accounts take sanctions to be central to the nature of law, I will refer to them as "sanction theories of law." As we will see, while sanction theories are intuitively appealing, they are nevertheless seriously flawed and cannot represent plausible theories of law.

Austin's Theory

The most familiar "sanction" theory is the one presented by John Austin in *The Province of Jurisprudence Determined,* a collection of lectures published in 1832. In these lectures, Austin tried to simplify and develop the ideas of his friend and mentor Jeremy Bentham. Tragically, Austin's lectures were met with widespread indifference during his lifetime, and he seemed to have suffered greatly as a result. After his death in 1859, his widow arranged for the republication of *Province,* hoping to "vindicate . . . him from the charge of indolence or indifference to truth."[1] This time Austin's theory met with great celebration. As the Victorian judge James Fitzjames Stephen wrote in his review of the second edition: "Austin's propositions on jurisprudence have as much precision, and will in all probability be seen hereafter to have as much importance, as the propositions of Adam Smith and Ricardo on rent, profits, and value."[2] With its new lease on life, Austin's theory of law came to dominate English jurisprudence for nearly a century.

In this section I will briefly outline Austin's account of law and try to show why it deserved to be taken as seriously as it was. As we will see,

Austin's theory not only is extremely simple, but it provides a noncircular account of legal institutions, has important implications for legal practice, and generates clean solutions to the Possibility Puzzle and Hume's Challenge. In the remainder of the chapter, I will go on to examine in great detail why this theory, and those like it, ultimately proved disappointing, and why a new account would eventually replace it.

Law = Rules + Sovereignty

Austin's version of the sanction theory is best understood as being composed of two parts. The first half consists of his theory of rules, the second of his theory of sovereignty. Since for Austin a law is (1) a rule (2) issued by the sovereign, an account of rules plus an account of sovereignty equals a complete theory of law.[3]

Let's start, then, with a brief outline of Austin's theory of rules. According to Austin, all rules are commands. A command is the expression of a wish, backed by a threat to inflict an evil in case the wish is not fulfilled, issued by someone who is willing and able to act on the threat. Austin calls the evil resulting from the violation of a command a "sanction." Simply telling my daughter to pick up her toys, therefore, is not a command in Austin's sense. Only if I sincerely threaten to sanction her if she fails to listen and am able to carry it out have I *commanded* her to pick up her toys.

For Austin, someone is under an obligation when another expresses a wish that she act or refrain from acting, and the expresser is willing and able to inflict an evil if the wish is not fulfilled. Thus, when I command my daughter to pick up her toys, she becomes *obligated* to comply. It follows from these definitions that all commands impose obligations.

Finally, according to Austin, all rules are general commands. They are general in the sense that they express a wish that a class of actions be performed. A command, for example, that prohibits the importation of corn is a rule, but one that prohibits the importation of a specific shipment of corn is not.

Having characterized the genus of rules, Austin proceeds to delimit the species of law. For Austin, only the rules of positive law are "law simply and strictly so called." Positive law consists of those rules issued by the sovereign. What make the sovereign the sovereign are two things: first, the sovereign must be habitually obeyed by the bulk of the community and, second, the sovereign cannot habitually obey anyone else. Austin took the King-in-Parliament to be the British sovereign because the bulk of British society habitually obeyed it, while it habitually obeyed no one else.[4] In the American context, Austin thought that sovereignty resides not in the president or the Congress, but in the People. They exercised their sovereign powers when they ratified and amended the Constitution and selected representatives during elections.[5]

This, in a nutshell, is Austin's account of the identity of law: what makes the law *the law* is its being the general commands issued by someone who is habitually obeyed by the bulk of the population and habitually obeys no one else.

The Gunman Writ Large

Any philosophical theory that can be summarized in little over a page is not only uncommon but welcome. Philosophy can be a frustratingly difficult subject, and it is a rare pleasure to discuss a philosophical account so easily explainable that even a smart five-year-old can get it. Perhaps it would not be too unfair to say that the ease with which Austin's theory can be presented and understood greatly contributed to its popularity and acceptance.

This is not to imply that Austin's theory has no merits other than simplicity. As mentioned at the beginning of this chapter, one of its considerable virtues is that it provides an analysis of law in exclusively nonlegal terms. Austin's theory is a reductive account, one that shows how legal concepts are analyzable into more basic notions.

The analytical success of this reduction can best be brought out by running it, as it were, in reverse, namely by building an Austinian legal system from scratch and demonstrating that no legal concepts were employed or introduced during the construction process. To do so, we will follow Hart's presentation of Austin's theory in *The Concept of Law*. Hart invites us to imagine a lone gunman who threatens to shoot unless we hand over our money, and shows how to modify this scenario until something resembling a legal system eventually emerges.[6]

Let us begin, therefore, with the gunman. Clearly, he is not a legal official, nor is his threat law. What is missing? As Hart points out, the law does not usually regulate conduct directly through individualized instructions like a gunman's threat, "give me your money now or else I will shoot you." It doesn't address me explicitly and tell me what I must do instant by instant. Rather, it regulates behavior by setting out general standards of conduct that all are required to apply to themselves and obey. Moreover, the law is durable in a way that the gunman's threat is not. The threat of the gunman loses its impact once he is no longer in his victim's presence, but the law remains in force long after the sovereign has spoken.

In order for the gunman to resemble law more closely, Hart asks us to imagine that the gunman issues general threats, for example, "give me a percentage of your income every April 15 or I'll shoot those who don't." These threats are general in two senses: they address *classes* of individuals (for example, all income producers) and direct them to do *types* of acts (for example, pay taxes every April 15). Hart further invites us to suppose that the gunman's threats are not only in force when made but have a "standing" quality to them. Threats are standing, as opposed to ephemeral, when the victims believe that they are at risk of harm even when they are outside the gunman's presence and remain so until his threats are withdrawn.[7]

With the addition of general and standing threats, we start to approach something that looks more like law and less like a random act of coercion. And notice that the construction has taken place without smuggling in any unanalyzed legal concepts. The concepts GENERAL and STANDING routinely occur outside legal contexts and hence are not distinctively legal.

We are not at law yet, however. While the souped-up threats now look like legal rules, the threatener doesn't look much like a legal official. The gunman appears to lack three properties of legal authority. First, legal systems have stability and relative permanence—they do not flit in and out of existence. Threateners who merely have temporary power over others lack the longevity that legal authorities possess. Second, in every legal system, there are individuals or bodies that have *supreme* authority, which is to say their authority trumps the authority of all other subordinate members. But in the gunman scenario, there may be others in the territory that have as much or more power than our gunman. Third, the supreme authorities of any legal system are *independent* of the authorities of other legal systems. The Queen-in-Parliament, for example, is sovereign over a different legal system than are the American People. Yet our gunman may also be subject to the control of more powerful individuals, and hence not independent in the requisite sense.

In order to reproduce these qualities of legal authority, Hart asks us to imagine that the gunman is so powerful that the bulk of the population he threatens is in the habit of obeying him. Because habits are settled dispositions, the fact that the bulk of the population habitually obeys the gunman would lend him and his regime a degree of stability and permanence.

In order to generate supreme and independent authority, we are invited to suppose that, in addition to being obeyed by the bulk of the population, the gunman is not in the habit of obeying anyone else. This absence of a habit of obedience to anyone in the threatened population might then be thought to confer supreme authority on the gunman, and the lack of a habit of obedience to any other population would seem to secure the gunman's independence from any other authority.

As in the first phase, the second stage of the construction takes place without the covert use of any legal concepts; HABIT, the main notion used, is clearly nonlegal. Thus, Hart shows how to construct an Austinian legal system that is describable in purely nonlegal terms.

The Implications of Identity

In Chapter 1, I argued that theories about the identity of law are interesting not only in their own right but also for their ability to help us derive further information about the nature of law. Another virtue of Austin's theory is the ease with which his answer to the Identity Question allows us to respond to the Implication Question.

Consider, for example, the existence conditions for a legal system in an Austinian framework. Because laws are nothing but general commands issued by the sovereign, it follows that a legal system exists in a certain community just in case a sovereign exists within that community and has issued at least some general commands that have not been retracted. Britain has a legal system, on this account, because the bulk of the population habitually obeys the Queen-in-Parliament, the Queen-in-Parliament habitually obeys no one else, and the Queen-in-Parliament has issued at least one general command that has not yet been retracted.

The membership conditions of a legal system are also trivial consequences of Austin's account of identity. An Austinian legal system necessarily consists of all and only those general commands issued by the sovereign. The Defense of Marriage Act and the Patriot Act are both laws of the United States, according to Austin, because they were both commanded by the American People through their elected representatives.

Most significantly, Austin's theory of identity allows us to work out which facts ultimately determine the content of the law. Consider, for example, a claim about legal obligation. Someone is under an obligation, according to Austin, just in case he might suffer harm as a result of not obeying the command that imposed it. Furthermore, an obligation is a legal one just in case the command that imposed the obligation was issued by the sovereign. It follows that the conclusive way to discover one's legal obligations is to establish the likelihood that one will be harmed if one disobeys a threat issued by someone who is habitually obeyed by the bulk of the population and habitually obeys no one else. In other words, in order to determine one's legal obligations, one need only know certain social facts, for example, whether certain wishes were expressed, the likelihood of harm as retaliation for disobedience, habits of obedience, and so on.

It turns out, then, that Austin's theory of law is a version of legal positivism. For on his account, legal facts are necessarily determined by social facts alone. Moral facts are simply irrelevant to Austinian law because they play no role in determining the existence of sovereignty or the attachment of obligations.

The practical implications of this philosophical position, of course, are enormous. If Austin is correct, then in order to figure out the law, a lawyer needs access to sociological data. She must know about the detailed operations of legal institutions and how enforcement of the law will impact her client. Moral philosophy, on the other hand, will do her absolutely no good. Even if she were privy to its secrets, she would be no closer to knowing the law, and hence in no better position to advise her client.

The Chicken Came First!

Austin's theory is not only simple, noncircular, and useful; it also provides a clean resolution to the Possibility Puzzle. On Austin's view, the sovereign is the sovereign not because any rule confers such authority, but because the sovereign has the ability to coerce others to abide by his or her wishes. Austin, in other words, rejects the Egg Principle: the power to create legal norms need not always be conferred by a norm. Because sovereignty rests on habits of obedience, there is no need to postulate a further authority that created a rule conferring sovereignty. In this way, Austin's theory stops the infinite regress dead in its tracks.

Note that Austin's solution to the Possibility Puzzle is a positivistic one. Since sovereignty is constituted by habits of obedience, Austin manages to ground all law in social facts alone. Note further that Austin's positivistic solution does not run afoul of Hume's Law. This is so because the concepts of sovereignty and obligation, on Austin's account, are not normative but descriptive. To say that someone is sovereign is to produce a descriptive statement; it is to make a claim about the existence of habits of obedience. Similarly, to say that someone is under an obligation is to make an assertion about the likelihood that she will be harmed if she fails to comply with a command. These claims do not issue in, or express, prescriptions about what should be done. Rather, they merely describe an aspect of the social state of the community.

Concluding that someone is the sovereign or is under an obligation, therefore, does not involve illicitly deriving an ought from an is. Since the conclusions merely report what is the case, the premises need only represent what is the case as well. On Austin's account, in other words, legal reasoners do not conform to the offending DINO pattern of inference. Only descriptive judgments go in, but only descriptive judgments come out. "DIDO" patterns do not violate Hume's Law because this injunction applies only to inferences that output normative, not descriptive, conclusions.

Because the concepts of sovereignty and obligation are descriptive on Austin's account, there is no conceptual connection between the items that fall under those concepts and actions that one ought to perform. For example, it cannot be inferred from the fact that one is obligated to pay one's taxes that one ought to pay one's taxes.[8] Similarly, if one is commanded to perform an immoral action by the sovereign and threatened with a sanction for failing to do so by someone who is willing and able to carry out the threat, one will be legally obligated to perform an action that one ought not to do.

On Austin's theory, therefore, legal authorities do not tell you what you ought to do; rather, they tell what you are obligated to do. And therein lies the reason why Austin's solution to the Possibility Puzzle does not violate Hume's Law: habits of obedience establish only the power to *obligate*—they do not establish the power to tell others what they *ought* to do. And since for Austin the concept of obligation is descriptive, as opposed to the concept of ought, which is normative, there is no risk of deriving an ought from an is.

At first glance, the decoupling of obligation from ought is very attractive, at least in legal contexts. The law, after all, traffics in "must"s and "mustn't"s. It does not alert us to the fact that we "ought" to pay our taxes. It *demands* that we pay our taxes. In this way, law differs from morality and religion. While both morality and religion impose obligations, they also purport to tell us what we ought to do. Morally speaking, we ought to give our bus seat to pregnant women. But we are not morally obligated to do so. Some religions recommend chastity, but they don't mandate it.

By contrast, there is something peculiar about saying that we legally "ought" to pay our taxes. Rather, we would say that we are legally "obligated" to do so. Moreover, it would be strange to claim that, legally speaking, we ought to perform some action but are not obligated to do so. If we are not legally obligated to give up our seat on the bus (that is, we are legally permitted to keep our seat), then it is not true that we legally ought to give up our seat.

Duty and Power

I would like to bracket for the time being the question of whether Austin's theory lives up to its promise and is able to provide a satisfying answer to the Possibility Puzzle without falling afoul of Hume's Law. For even if it can deliver on that score, it is clear that Austin's theory falls short in so many other ways that it cannot possibly be an adequate theory of law.

Our examination of Austin's theory of law will begin with a critique of his theory of rules. We will see that this account fails in two major respects. Contrary to Austin, not every legal rule (1) imposes an obligation or (2) is a command. Having cast doubt on Austin's theory of rules, the next part of this chapter will critique his theory of sovereignty.

I should warn the reader at the outset that this chapter might seem to quickly degenerate into an exercise in overkill. After the first few objections, it may appear that I am flogging a dead horse. This protracted critique is nevertheless useful, I believe, because Austin's theory of law presents us with a tremendous learning opportunity. As we will see, his account is not only flawed but flawed in a number of interesting ways, and dwelling on them at this stage will prove invaluable when we go about constructing our own theory of law later on in the book.

Conferring Power

Austin's theory fails most spectacularly with respect to its analysis of rules. As mentioned, legal rules for Austin are general commands issued by someone able and willing to carry these threats out. Since for Austin people are under an obligation to perform some action if they have been commanded to do so, it follows that all legal rules impose obligations.

Austin's theory might be thought to work tolerably well for the rules of the criminal law. The criminal law does impose obligations to act or to refrain from acting in certain ways, for example, not to assault other people, pass bad checks, possess certain drugs, and so on. And when we fail to live up to our obligations, the law renders us liable to punishment, that is, the evil that the law threatens in order to motivate us to conform to the rules. Tort law also appears to fit Austin's model. According to standard tort principles, we are under an obligation to exercise due care toward those around us, and the failure to do so constitutes a breach of duty and renders us liable to pay damages to those whom we have harmed.

As Hart points out, however, not all legal rules impose obligations.[9] Consider the rules related to the formation of wills. These rules do not impose obligations on people to make wills; rather, they confer the *power* to do so. They do this by specifying a set of conditions that some person (usually called the "testator") must meet in order to dispose of his property after death. Typical statutes, for example, require, at the very least, that wills be in writing and witnessed by two or more people. When these conditions are met, a valid will is formed and the executor is under a legal obligation to comply with its directions after the passing of the testator.

The fact that rules related to the formation of wills grant powers to testators, rather than impose obligations on them, can be seen by comparing the different expressions lawyers use when discussing the failure to conform to these rules. If a testator fails to get his will attested before two witnesses, he hasn't "broken" the law, acted "illegally," committed an "offense," or "breached" a duty and is not "guilty" of disobedience. Rather, he has merely failed to comply with the rules, and his actions have no legal effect. The will, as lawyers say, is "null and void." It is "invalid," not "illegal."

The law abounds with what Hart calls "power-conferring" rules. In every modern legal system, there are rules for determining who has, and how they may exercise, the power to form contracts, acquire and dispose of property, initiate lawsuits, marry, incorporate businesses, and so on. Unlike the rules of tort or criminal law, these rules don't tell us what we must or must not do. Rather, they tell us what we are required to do *only if we want to accomplish a certain end*. In most cases, it is up to us whether to take advantage of the abilities bestowed on us by the law.

The law not only confers private powers to make wills, form contracts, and get married, but it grants public powers as well. Indeed, most of the rules of constitutional law are power conferring. Article I, Section 8 of the United States Constitution, for example, specifies the powers of Congress ("The Congress *shall have Power* To lay and collect Taxes, Duties,

Imposts and Excises, to pay the Debts and provide for the common Defense and general Welfare of the United States . . .”). Rules that define the jurisdiction of courts, the regulatory scope of administrative agencies, and the authority of the chief executive all confer public powers as well.

It is crucially important not to conflate rules that define valid exercises of power with rules that impose obligations to exercise these powers only in certain ways. For example, in many jurisdictions a marriage is valid only if there has been solemnization by some person authorized by the state. Without the ceremony officiated by the right person, the marriage is a nullity—it has no legal effect and the parties will not enjoy the rights normally accorded to married couples. Contrast this rule with one that forbids incestuous unions. If someone attempts to marry his sister, this act constitutes a breach of duty and renders the marriage not merely invalid but also illegal. This distinction between limitations of power and prohibitions on the exercise of power is usually flagged in legal codes. For example, the rules about solemnization of marriage are often grouped in sections on “Valid Marriages,” whereas the rules about incest are usually placed in sections called “Illegal Marriages” or “Prohibited Marriages.”

Legal rules, however, don't always come prelabeled. For example, a statute may simply state that a contract has been formed between two parties when there has been an offer, acceptance, and bargained-for consideration. Although this statute does not say that it confers the power on parties to make contracts, it obviously does. Now compare this statute with one that states that murder is the purposeful killing of a human being without adequate justification. This statute clearly does not confer a power on individuals to commit murder; rather, it specifies a duty not to purposively engage in unjustified criminal homicide. Why are we inclined to see a power conferred in the first instance, but not in the second, despite the similarity in the way that the statutes are drafted?

The reason for our conflicting reactions stems from the different functions that power-conferring and duty-imposing rules are meant to play. To see this, let us begin by distinguishing between two different aspects of freedom. The first aspect of freedom is negative in character. We are negatively free to the extent to which no one stops us from acting on our desires. I am negatively free to touch my nose because no one will prevent me from doing so. But there is another, more positive aspect of freedom, which is the ability to do certain actions. I enjoy positive freedom to the extent to which I have the ability to pursue those ends that I want to pursue. Someone can enjoy negative freedom, but have very little positive freedom. I am negatively free to buy a beautiful condominium on Park Avenue (no one is stopping me from bidding on the apartment), but I am not positively free to buy it because I don't have the money. I am *free from* external constraint, but I am not *free to* do what I want.[10]

Using this distinction between different aspects of freedom, we might say that the function of duty-imposing rules is to limit our negative freedom. The rules related to physical assaults, passing bad checks, paying taxes, and so on are designed to prevent us from doing actions that we might want to do. Their purpose is to place constraints on our actions. By contrast, power-conferring rules are designed to increase our positive freedom. They exist in order to provide us with the ability to pursue valuable ends. Rules related to the formation of wills, for example, allow property holders to do something they ordinarily would not be able to do. Testators can ensure that certain items get distributed to the appropriate parties *after they die*. This exercise of control from beyond the grave would be unavailable absent the rules conferring power on testators.

We classify rules of contract formation as power conferring, therefore, because we recognize that their function is to increase our positive freedom. By guaranteeing the enforceability of conforming agreements, they allow us to make offers credibly and to rely on the commitment of others. On the other hand, rules defining various forms of criminal homicide are not aimed at increasing the freedom of would-be killers, either positive or negative. Quite the contrary: their function is to limit negative freedom. They place impediments in the way of our abilities by giving reasons, moral as well as prudential, for not engaging in certain types of killings.[11] Because the point of the duty-imposing rules is so obvious, we are never tempted to talk about the "power" to commit murders or describe attempted homicides as "invalid" murders.

Response One: Nullity as a Sanction

Austin was fully aware that his theory of rules did not appear to fit power-conferring rules very well. Nevertheless, he tried to shoehorn this type of rule into his general theory. His strategy was to claim that even the rules governing contract or will formation are actually backed by threats of sanctions. The threat in these cases is the withholding of legal recognition from acts that fail to conform to the rules. If a testator, say, does not reduce his will to writing, his actions will be null and void. Nullity, in other words, is the "sanction" that attends deviation from the rules. Like the threat of a fine or jail, the function of the nullity is to motivate people to conform to the law.

Hart's response to Austin's move is to point out an important disanalogy between nullities and sanctions.[12] In the case of the criminal law, for example, it is possible to subtract the sanction from the rule and still have an intelligible standard of behavior left over. Rules against murder, for example, would still prohibit murder, even without specifying any punishment for their violation. These rules might not be followed as attentively without the threat of punishment, but they would nevertheless remain standards that could guide conduct and by which one could evaluate other conduct.

In the case of a power-conferring rule, by contrast, it is not possible to delete the threat of a nullity without also deleting the rule as well. Suppose a rule requires that a valid will be in writing and witnessed by two people. Now if we subtract the threat of a nullity in cases where the will is not in writing or doesn't have two witnesses, no standard of conduct survives, for everything that the testator does (or does not do) results in a valid will (whatever that would mean). Clearly, it is absurd to call something a rule if one cannot help but conform to it. Rules must be capable of guiding conduct. Subtracting nullities from power-conferring rules nullifies their ability to guide conduct by making every act or omission legally successful.

My sense is that Austin would not have been terribly moved by Hart's response. For a fervent supporter of the sanction theory would simply deny that one can subtract a sanction from a rule of the criminal law and still have a law. Legal rules, on the theory, are commands and commands are expressions of wishes backed by threats; expressions of wishes without the backing of threats, therefore, are not commands and hence not law. Hence, nullities are no different from fines or jail time in the most important respect: it is not possible to scrub either kind of sanction and still end up with a law.

Before I say why I think Austin was wrong to treat nullity as a sanction, let me begin by pointing out what is attractive about his suggestion. Austin was right to note that sanctions and nullities have the same basic function: they both are *negative incentives*. The law threatens jail time in order to motivate people not to steal. Similarly, it warns that it will not recognize oral wills in order to encourage people to put their wills in writing. In both cases, the law attempts to guide behavior by specifying certain unwanted consequences that will follow from certain actions.

But the fact that both sanctions and nullities are negative incentives does not mean that they should be lumped together under the same rubric. In nonlegal contexts, for example, we normally distinguish between different kinds of unwanted spurs to action. If I say to my employee that he must make it to work by 9 A.M. or lose his job, I am clearly threatening to impose a cost on him if he fails to arrive by 9. Yet, if I tell him that I will pay him time and a half to make it to work by that time, I am not warning him about a *sanction* that I will inflict on him if he arrives too late. If he doesn't make it to work by 9, I will simply be refusing to confer a *benefit* on him.

Not every time, then, that we present another with a choice between desirable and undesirable states of affairs are we threatening to impose sanctions. Whether the undesirable option should be understood as the imposition of a cost or the refusal to bestow a benefit depends on the status quo. If the undesirable state makes the other worse off than she would have been absent the intervention, then we are likely to see it as a sanction. On the other hand, if the undesirable state is the status quo, then we will see the choice as presenting the possibility of a benefit. If I say that I will fire you if you don't arrive by 9, I am threatening to make you worse off than you would have been absent the threat. But time and a half presents the prospect of making you better off than the status quo and hence will be understood to be a promise of a benefit.[13]

Sanctions such as fines and jail time are like firings. They are costs imposed in order to make certain behavior less desirable than it ordinarily would be. By contrast, the law's decision to withhold legal recognition from, say, oral bequests is not designed to make them less desirable than they otherwise would be in the absence of wills law. For it is not as though oral bequests would be valid if there were no rules related to will formation; in such a world, there would be no valid wills. By withholding legal recognition from oral wills, the law simply refuses to confer a benefit on those who fail to put their testamentary wishes on paper. We might say, therefore, that whereas sanctions that attend duty-imposing rules are costs, nullities are merely the absence of benefits.

For this reason, I think Austin was wrong to claim that power-conferring rules are *threats;* rather, they are more akin to *offers*. The gunman threatens to shoot because he seeks to make his victims worse off than they would have been had they never met him. In this sense, the threat of jail is a true threat: the law warns that it will impose certain costs if one breaks the rules. However, in the case of an oral bequest, the law is not threatening to make the testator worse off than he would have been had the law not conferred any testamentary powers. Rather, the law is offering to confer a benefit if wills are put in writing, and refusing to lend its assistance otherwise. Power-conferring rules, in other words, are offers to confer benefits, in contrast to duty-imposing rules, which are usually backed by threats to impose costs.

The equation of nullities and sanctions falters in another respect as well. The threat of jail time is designed to operate at all times—it is a *continuous* incentive to conform to the rules. In no circumstances should we murder, steal, pass bad checks, and evade our taxes, and, as a result, the law threatens unpleasant consequences in the hope that we never engage in such behavior. By contrast, the law does not withhold legal recognition of unwritten wills in order to get me to put my will in writing *right now*. Nor does it deny validity to unsolemnized marriages in order to motivate bachelors to run out to the justice of the peace and get married. Whether we write valid wills or get married may be a matter of complete indifference to the law. If I don't want to arrange my financial affairs or become a husband, the withholding of legal recognition to certain possible actions is not meant to affect my behavior in any way. Nullities operate as incentives to conform to power-conferring rules only when the power holder has an interest in exercising a power, not before or after. They are meant to be intermittent, rather than continuous, incentives.

Austin's attempt to treat power-conferring rules as threats by assimilating nullities to sanctions, therefore, fails for two reasons. First, the refusal to accord legal recognition to some act is not the imposition of a cost, like throwing someone in jail. It is rather the refusal to confer a benefit. Second, nullities are not designed to encourage compliance with the rules at all times, like the sanctions of the criminal law. Rather, they are intermittent incentives whose motivational force only comes into play when the power holder desires, or deems it proper, to exercise the specific power in question.

The disparities between nullities and sanctions are ultimately traceable to the basic difference between power-conferring and duty-imposing rules. Power-conferring rules, as we said, are designed to increase positive freedom. As such, they are attempts to confer benefits that were previously unavailable. And they motivate action when the power holder views the exercise of the power as a benefit. By contrast, duty-imposing rules seek to limit negative freedom. Accordingly, the law imposes costs on that freedom in order to discourage its exercise at all times. The ultimate problem with Austin's theory, we might say, is that it ignores this basic distinction between the functions of different kinds of legal rules.

Response Two: Fragments of Rules

As we have seen, Austin's strategy for accommodating power-conferring rules within his theory of law was to expand the concept of sanction to include nullities. Hans Kelsen takes a different tack. Instead of extending the notion of sanction, he restricts the notion of a rule. On Kelsen's view, power-conferring rules are mere fragments of complete legal norms. What appears to be a whole rule conferring a power is really only part of a much larger rule that ultimately directs a legal official to impose a sanction.

Consider the rule conferring power on testators to create valid wills if they are in writing and attested by two witnesses. On Kelsen's account, this rule merely specifies some of the conditions under which courts will sanction executors who fail to execute a written and attested will. Properly speaking, the rule should be formulated as follows: "If and only if a person signs a will and two witnesses attest to it and . . . the executor fails to execute the will, then a court is under a duty to sanction the executor." The ellipsis in the formulation is a placeholder representing the many other conditions that must be satisfied before the court is obligated to impose sanctions on a noncooperating executor. For example, the testator has to die, the will must be brought to probate in a court with the right jurisdiction, the beneficiaries have to file the right sort of claim in the probate court, the beneficiaries must respond to any objections filed by the executor, the court has to rule in their favor, the executor must be within the jurisdictional reach of the probate court, the executor has to be given notice, he must be legally competent, and so on. Thus, the complete norm relating to wills, on Kelsen's scheme, is a very long conditional.

Actually, this is not quite right. On Kelsen's view, the power-conferring norms of constitutional law are not complete laws either, but mere fragments of other norms. In fact, Kelsen thinks that they are part of every norm of their system. Properly formulated, then, every complete law includes all of constitutional law as antecedent conditions. The complete law about wills, therefore, is an unimaginably long conditional that contains not only the power-conferring rules about will formation but those having to do with the constitutional powers of every institution in the legal system.

There is no doubt that Kelsen's account of power-conferring rules is highly counterintuitive. Constitutions and legal codes *never* look like extremely long conditionals. But we should be careful not to conclude that Kelsen is wrong simply because his theory departs so greatly from the formulations given in legal texts. For we must not confuse norms with the language that creates them. Despite the fact that power-conferring rules are formulated like complete rules, their surface grammar might be misleading. It is possible that their true nature is best revealed by a Kelsenian reformulation.

Reconceptualizing power-conferring rules as mere parts of other duty-imposing rules, however, distorts the distinctive way in which these norms function in social life. As I hope to show, power-conferring rules are best thought of as instruments that are meant to be used self-consciously by the holders of power. They are directed at those they empower, not those who are subject to the exercise of such power.

This point may be brought out by contrasting the law's conferring of power on legal actors to Homeric gods helping their favored mortals. When the gods provide assistance, they typically do so without the contemporaneous knowledge of their beneficiaries. Paris is able to kill Achilles because Apollo intercedes after the arrow leaves the quiver and guides it to the vulnerable heel. Odysseus is made aware only at the end of the *Odyssey* that Athena has been constantly manipulating the environment so as to help him overcome many obstacles and arrive safely at Ithaka. By contrast, the law always "wittingly" helps power holders by informing the power holders beforehand that they have certain abilities. When the law confers a power on someone, it alerts the power holder of the consequences of certain of her actions, so that the power holder may self-consciously bring about these consequences if she so chooses. For this reason, power-conferring rules always come with instructions for their use. When a wills statute states that valid wills must be signed in front of two witnesses, it is not merely stating a necessary condition for the imposition of duties on probate courts. The statute is *instructing* the testator (or his attorney) how to create a valid will and hence how to impose duties on probate courts.

The problem with Kelsen's reformulation is that it ignores the self-conscious role that power holders play in the exercise of legal power and instead treats them as though they were at the mercy of the legal version of Homeric gods. When the testator signs a will in front of two witnesses, officials do not operate quietly behind the scenes and contrive to divide the testator's estate according to his wishes. Nor are wills prayer sheets that legal officials deign to fulfill. Rather, they are devices that testators use for imposing duties and changing legal relations. Will statutes treat testators like legal officials and give them power to direct others, including actual legal officials, how to act. We might say, then, that power-conferring rules are not primarily for guiding officials on how they can help power holders; rather, they are for *instructing power holders on how they can help themselves.* Thus, in the case of will formation, the addressee of the norm is the testator. The testator, after all, is the one who needs instruction. She needs to know which steps to take in order to ensure that the desired people receive their portion of the estate after her death.

Treating officials as the primary audience of every legal rule, then, misconstrues the way in which certain rules guide conduct. Power-conferring rules are mini self-help manuals, which not only confer abilities but instruct power holders on their proper use. To be sure, power-conferring rules are of great interest to legal officials as well. Judges need to know when, say, wills are valid and hence enforceable. But Kelsen's account lets the tail wag the dog. While wills law imposes duties on legal officials, it does so merely as a means to helping testators effectuate their wishes. The ultimate goal of will-formation rules is to guide the actions of testators beforehand so that they will take the right steps and thereby successfully exercise their legally enforceable powers.

The same general point applies to constitutional law. The purpose of constitutional law is to guide the behavior of legislators, judges, ministers, and police officers so that they may know how to create, apply, and enforce legal rules. Constitutional norms exist, therefore, as they appear in constitutions, namely, not simply as fragments of other rules but as plans directed at certain individuals and bodies specifying the manner in which they may successfully regulate the community.

Are Laws Commands?

Our criticisms thus far have focused solely on Austin's claim that all laws impose duties. We have seen that this aspect of his theory is unable to account for the existence of rules that confer powers. In contrast to duty-imposing rules, the function of power-conferring rules is not to place obstacles in the way of individuals acting on their wishes; rather, their aim is to provide people with the ability to further those wishes. Treating power-conferring rules as though they were backed by threats of sanctions, therefore, misrepresents the very point of having such rules.

Nothing we have said, however, challenges Austin's assertion that, at least with respect to duty-imposing rules, laws are best understood as expressions backed by threats of sanctions. The function of the criminal law, after all, *is* to place obstacles in our way. Are these duty-imposing rules accurately represented by Austin's model?

The Good Citizen

It is tempting to reject Austin's theory simply by noting that many people do not conceive of the criminal law as merely the expression of wishes backed by threats of sanctions. They don't, in other words, view the law as the gunman writ large; rather, they understand it to consist of legitimate standards of conduct that give reasons to comply over and above the penalties associated with disobedience. If asked why they should pay their taxes, for example, they would say that it is every citizen's moral obligation to pay their taxes. To be sure, they recognize that they have other reasons, such as those penalties threatened by the criminal law, for complying with the rules. But they don't see the law as composed *merely* of threats—the threats, rather, back up legitimate demands that the rules impose on us.

Similarly, many legal officials do not conceive of themselves as gunmen. They think that they possess the legitimate authority to tell others what to do or to use coercion in order to enforce lawful demands. That they regard themselves as having the moral right to rule and coerce can be seen from the way they react to those who break the law. Unlike the gunman who may simply become enraged when disobeyed, officials often feel the moral sentiments of recrimination, betrayal, and blame and, as a result, regard the imposition of sanctions as the meting out of *punishment*, namely, as suffering that is the justified response to wrongdoing.

While these sociological observations are certainly suggestive, they do not yet amount to a good argument against Austin's theory of duty-imposing rules. For Austin can accept that many people regard the law as legitimate, but rightly note that these sentiments do not falsify his theory. When Austin claimed that duty-imposing rules are merely the expression of wishes backed by threats of sanctions, he did not mean that they have no other properties. Rather, he meant that *what makes them duty-imposing rules* is simply that they are general commands. Whatever other properties duty-imposing rules possess are not essential to their identity, any more than my wearing sneakers today is essential to my being me. Hence, Austin can accept that legal rules are often deemed morally legitimate without thinking that their legitimacy, or the belief therein, plays any role in their identity.

While this response is correct, as far as it goes, I think it is possible to sharpen the objection to show why the existence of good citizens is a serious challenge to Austin's theory of duty-imposing rules. Let us begin by clearing up a possible confusion. When we say that some members of the community accept the legitimacy of the law, we are not merely saying that people often think that they have moral reasons to act as the law instructs. We are, rather, making a stronger claim: to accept the legitimacy of the law is to accept that one has moral reasons to obey the law *because the law requires obedience*. Virtually everyone thinks that theft is morally wrong, but only some think that theft is morally wrong, at least in part, because the law has prohibited it. Only the latter—the good citizens—accept that the duties imposed by the rules are separate and independent moral reasons to act.

The problem with Austin's theory of duty-imposing rules is that it effaces the existence of the good citizen. For as we have seen, when someone responds to their Austinian obligations, they are not reacting to the moral reasons created by the law. They are motivated, rather, by the desire to avoid sanctions. The good citizen, on the other hand, takes the obligations imposed by the law as providing a new moral reason to comply. The rules are taken as reasons quite apart from the sanctions that would attend their violation or the moral considerations that independently apply to the actions required.

What makes a duty-imposing legal rule *duty-imposing* cannot, therefore, be the fact that sanctions attend its violation. For when the good citizen recognizes and responds to her legal duties, she is decidedly not being motivated by the painful consequences of disobedience. She does not, in other words, treat the duty-imposing rules as simply setting out the conditions under which the law will not harm her. Rather, she takes the distinctive contribution of the rules to be something else entirely: the creation of new moral reasons to act, which arise simply by virtue of the fact that the law has demanded that these rules be obeyed.

Austin's analysis of duty-imposing rules would be considerably more plausible if the law cared only about the proverbial "bad man," namely, someone who does see the law as the gunman writ large and is motivated by law only insofar as it can affect his self-interest. For the bad man, the only normative contribution that the law makes is its threat of sanctions. While the law certainly cares to control the bad man, and for this reason normally threatens sanctions, it also wishes to guide the behavior of the good citizen.[14] Not only are sanctions not needed to control those who respect the power-conferring rules of the system and impute legitimacy to those who act pursuant to them, but they are terribly expensive. Motivating good citizens by imposing legal duties on them is far more efficient than credibly threatening them. Indeed, a regime whose only means of persuasion was force would quickly bankrupt itself.

Sanctions, in other words, are only one kind of tool that the law may use to motivate behavior. Duties are another; rewards yet a third type. A general theory about the nature of law must adequately represent all of the techniques that the law has at its disposal and not myopically privilege one to the exclusion of all others.

Knowing What You Commanded

Austin's account is often described as an "imperative" theory of law, owing to the fact that he treats all laws as imperatives, that is, as commands. We have seen, however, that his specific version of this theory is unacceptable. Duty-imposing rules cannot merely be commands in Austin's sense, that is, expressions of wishes backed by threats of sanctions. Nevertheless, our critique leaves open the possibility that all laws are commands, where commands are understood in some non-Austinian way, either as something more, less, or different than mere expressions of wishes backed by threats of sanctions.

To explore this possibility, let us begin by noting that, on any plausible view, commands are issued by acts of communication. Someone commands another when the commander expresses her intention that the subject perform or refrain from performing some act.[15] Like asserting, questioning, and requesting, one can command only if one knows that one is commanding and what one has commanded.

Austin was correct to claim that some legal obligations do arise imperatively. When the traffic cop tells the motorist to pull over, this communicative act creates a legal obligation to comply. And a judge may order the defendant to pay the plaintiff damages at the end of the litigation, which again will create a legal duty to heed the order.

Most law creation, however, does not take place in so intimate a manner. It is not as though each and every congressperson reads each piece of recently enacted federal law on television to the entire population of the United States and collectively orders them to comply. For law to be created, it is enough for legislators to vote for some proposal according to the appropriate legal procedures. Indeed, as Hans Kelsen noted, lawmakers might not even know which laws they are creating.[16] Modern legislation is often packaged in documents hundreds of pages long—it would be impossible for legislators in such cases to know the legal effects of all of their actions. Furthermore, legislators might not even intend to make the law they make. If they mistakenly say "yea" instead of "nay," or think that they are voting for the repeal of some measure while the bill mandates its reenactment, they will create law nonetheless. Unintentional lawmaking is possible, but unintentional commanding is a contradiction in terms.[17]

The imperative theory fails because it misconceives the *impersonal* nature of legal regulation. As just mentioned, it is rare for legal officials to give face-to-face instructions. Legal authorities usually regulate conduct by promulgating standards that all are required to learn and apply to themselves. In this respect, the law is responding to the obvious pressures that result from the regulation of mass populations: it simply cannot afford to personally instruct everyone about the rules.

Imperative theories also suffer from another flaw. Commands are, by their nature, bilateral. Superiors command subordinates—commanders cannot command themselves. It is a consequence of Austin's theory—one, incidentally, that Austin fully embraced—that the sovereign must necessarily be above the law. For if the laws are commands and commanders cannot command themselves, the law cannot apply to the chief commander, namely, the sovereign.

However, as Kelsen observed, laws often apply to those who create them.[18] Senators, as well as ordinary citizens, are required to pay their income taxes and are forbidden from possessing marijuana. The fact that they are the authors of these laws does not preclude their being the subjects as well.[19] Indeed, constitutional regimes are celebrated precisely because the rulers are constrained by law. It is the rule of law, not the rule of men, that prevails. Imperative theories, however, preclude the existence of such regimes as a conceptual matter. They cannot account for the reflexivity of law.

Kelsen also noted that imperative theories cannot explain the existence of customary law.[20] Although not a significant source of law in modern legal systems, customs can be legally binding under certain circumstances. However, customs are obviously not commands. No one, for example, has commanded common law courts to abide by judicial precedents; yet the principle of *stare decisis* ("maintain what has been decided") is obviously legally binding.

Austin was aware of this problem but suggested that customs become law through the "tacit" command of the sovereign. When courts apply custom in cases, the rules become law when the sovereign accepts the courts' actions and does not overrule them. In such cases, the sovereign can be said to tacitly order the customary rule to be followed and hence for it to be assimilated into the legal order.

But as Hart pointed out, there is a significant problem with Austin's response. In order to say that the sovereign tacitly ordered compliance with legally valid customary rules, the sovereign would have to know about each and every customary rule applied by courts, for, as we noted earlier, one cannot issue commands unless one is aware of doing so or of which commands have been issued. However, it is unrealistic to suppose that this requirement of knowledge will be met in legal contexts: surely most sovereigns have no idea what happens in the day-to-day operations of their courts.[21]

Habits and Rules

We have seen that the first part of Austin's theory—his account of rules—is fatally flawed. Contrary to his claims, not all laws are duty imposing, merely the expressions of wishes backed by threats of sanctions or issued imperatively. Let us move on, therefore, to the second half of his theory, namely, to his account of sovereignty, and examine how successfully it accounts for the possibility of legal authority.

Continuity, Persistence, and Limitability

As we saw at the beginning of the chapter, Austin's theory of law not only provides a noncircular analysis of legal sovereignty but also affords a simple solution of the Possibility Puzzle. The sovereign is the sovereign, on his view, simply because the bulk of the population habitually obeys him and he habitually obeys no one else. Austin, therefore, did not need to postulate any norms that confer sovereignty precisely because sovereignty is not conferred by norms.

Clearly, this solution will be plausible only if habits of obedience to an individual, and the absence of reciprocal habits from that individual to anyone else, can create legal authority. Unfortunately, habits of obedience are not up to this task. For as Hart conclusively shows, Austin's theory of sovereignty is unable to account for three essential features of every legal system. These properties are so central to our concept of law that no theory can afford to rule them out.

The first feature Hart calls the "continuity of law-making power."[22] To illustrate this property, Hart asks us to imagine a regime ruled by the king Rex. After a long and glorious reign, Rex dies and his eldest son and appointed successor, Rex Jr., immediately becomes the king. As Hart notes, this change in leadership involves no interruption in law-making power. Rex II (as he will now be called) has the power of the sovereign straightaway after the death of his father, Rex I. In the words of the traditional proclamation: "The King is dead! Long live the King!"

This continuity of law-making power, however, cannot be explained by Austin. For on his account Rex II can become sovereign only after a habit of obedience has been formed. But since habits consist in repeated behavior, they cannot materialize instantaneously. Rex II cannot, therefore, ascend the throne straightaway because he cannot be the object of habitual obedience from the get-go. Indeed, it follows from Austin's theory that there can never be a juridically seamless transition of power; every change in leadership must result in a revolution.

The second property that Austin's theory cannot explain Hart calls the "persistence of law."[23] If Rex I makes a law, say, prohibiting dueling, that prohibition would remain in effect even after Rex I dies. Rex II might choose to repeal the law in question, but he would have to do so in order to eliminate it. Legal rules, we might say, are extremely hardy creatures. Unless they contain a sunset clause calling for their own demise, or the system in question subscribes to a doctrine of desuetude, laws will persist across changes in the identity of the sovereign until they are actively retracted.

The normative inertia of law, however, is inexplicable on Austin's theory. Since Austinian laws are commands of the sovereign backed by a threat that the *sovereign* will sanction those who disobey, it follows that Austinian laws cannot survive their makers. Dead men neither tell any tales nor act on their threats. By tying the nature of law so firmly to mortal entities, Austin ruled out the possibility that laws might persist from ruler to ruler.[24]

Finally, Austin's theory cannot explain the "legal limitability" of sovereignty.[25] As we mentioned, sovereigns in constitutional regimes are limited by law. The United States Constitution, for example, constrains the power of the American people in a number of ways: it establishes a very onerous procedure for amending the document and places certain provisions out of reach of that amendment process.

Yet, an Austinian sovereign is, as a matter of necessity, legally unlimited. Since sovereignty is not created by norms, but rather by habits of obedience, there can be no rules that curtail the sovereign's power. This model might be able to represent the British legal system, with its principle of absolute parliamentary supremacy, but it cannot do justice to other regimes, such as the American one, in which sovereignty is controlled and limited by law. While President Richard Nixon famously said that "when the president does it that means that it is not illegal," it should be remembered that Nixon was forced to resign in disgrace for acting on such a view.

Austin's inability to explain the continuity, persistence, and limitability of law stems from his excessively personal understanding of legal authority. The sovereign is the sovereign for Austin because of his personal qualities: it is his power to compel compliance that underwrites his authority. Yet, as we previously argued in our critique of imperative theories, legal authority is impersonal. The authority of the president of the United States, for example, emanates from the *office* of the president. It is because President Obama is the president, not because he is Obama, that accounts for his power to impose legal obligations and confer legal powers.

To account for the continuity, persistence, and limitability of the law, a theory of law must distinguish, in a way that Austin's does not, between an impersonal office and its personal inhabitant. The presidency of the United States is an office. It endures from term to term and its normative character does not change merely because one president vacates and a new inhabitant assumes power. Presidents come and go but the presidency remains. Because the office of the president is continuous over time, each new inhabitant immediately assumes the power conferred on him or her by the office. Moreover, because obligations of obedience run impersonally to the office of the president, not personally to its inhabitant, the rules made by previous presidents have the same authority as those made by current presidents, provided, of course, that they have not actively undercut their predecessor's rules. Finally, the holder of an office enjoys only those powers that attend to the office. If certain powers are denied the officeholder, as they typically are, the power of the inhabitant will correspondingly be limited.

Of course, the existence of legal offices depends on the existence of power-conferring rules. These rules confer on certain individuals that satisfy certain qualifications the power to impose obligations and confer other sorts of powers. It should come as no surprise, therefore, that Austin's theory of law overlooks the impersonal nature of sovereignty. For one can recognize the impersonality of legal authority only if one appreciates the role that power-conferring rules play in the law. But, as we have seen earlier in this chapter, Austin's theory of rules is too impoverished to recognize these sorts of rules. We can now see that his theory of sovereignty suffers as a result.

The Intelligibility of Law

Austin's theory of sovereignty is not only unable to explain certain basic features of sovereignty. It is even incapable of accounting for the very intelligibility of claims of and thoughts about legal authority.

To see this, let us return to our observation that some members of a community regard the law as legitimate. Is it possible within Austin's framework to understand this person's deference to legal authority as motivated by a belief that the sovereign has the legal right to rule? Clearly not. Habits, Hart points out, are not necessarily normative activities.[26] Someone who engages in habitual behavior need not try to act according to that routine. She need not take the habit as a standard of conduct and attempt to conform to it. Indeed, she may not even be aware that she has such a habit. Nor need she criticize herself for failing to act in a habitual manner. Except in bizarre circumstances, people do not say to themselves, "I should have said 'um' more often today." By contrast, those who defer to the sovereign are guiding their behavior by norms. They recognize that there are standards that designate certain people as having special status and they deem these standards to be legitimate. For them, the sovereign is one who has not only the ability to coerce compliance but the legal *right* to do so.

The same point may be made with a nonlegal example. Suppose my wife tells my daughter to clean her room. When I find that she has not listened and reprimand her by saying, "You were supposed to clean your room," I am not following an uncritical habit of supporting my wife in household affairs. Rather, I am expressing my commitment to a norm that entitles parents to tell their minor children what to do. Thus, if my daughter challenges me to explain the basis of my criticism, I might say, "You were supposed to clean your room *because your mother told you to do it."*

Similarly, insofar as some people are committed to following the law, they must, on pain of incoherence, also believe that rules exist that privilege the pronouncements and decisions of certain people. A theory of sovereignty like Austin's that does not admit of norms, or their acceptance, thus does not render comprehensible the way these people think about their actions. The fact that Austin's theory has this implication must disqualify it as a plausible account of law. For any theory that privileges habits and sanctions over norms not only gives a poor explanation of the actions of some citizens but, more importantly, fails to account for the coherence of their thoughts. It cannot explain the fact that they think that the sovereign has the legal *right* to rule, that the exercise of that power generates legal *obligations,* that it would be legally *wrong* to disobey, and that those *guilty* of breaking the law *should* be *punished* for their *offense.*

Clearly, Austin's cure for the Possibility Puzzle is worse than the disease. Habits cannot account for basic properties of legal authority, namely, its continuity, persistence, and limitability. Nor can it render legal thought intelligible. Solutions that reject the Egg Principle (that is, the power to create legal norms must always be conferred by norms) appear to be nonstarters. Sovereignty must be conferred by norms or else it would not be sovereignty.

Nor is Austin's attempt to comply with Hume's Law any more successful. Recall that Austin tried to avoid deriving an ought from an is by treating legal concepts, and the statements and judgments in which they are embedded, as descriptive. Because claims of obligation and right are descriptive, not normative, they may be derived from premises about habits and likelihoods of obedience that are purely descriptive as well.

However, severing the connection between the concepts OBLIGATION and OUGHT has disastrous consequences. For it would be hard to see how statements that deploy purely descriptive concepts could be used in their normal way, namely, in the service of justification and evaluation. When we tell people that they are obligated to perform some action, we are trying to state a *reason* for them to do it. Similarly, when we criticize people for violating their obligations, we are presupposing that they *ought* to have acted differently. We say that they have acted "wrongly" and are "guilty" of an "offense." If any concepts are normative, these are; to borrow a phrase from Wilfrid Sellars, they are "fraught with ought."[27]

To be sure, we normally don't speak of what we legally ought to do. But this should not be taken to mean that the concept OUGHT has no role to play in legal thought. Rather, its less frequent use in a legal context merely signals that OUGHT is weaker than OBLIGATION. To talk about what one legally ought to do is often misleading because we normally assert the strongest proposition we believe. It is not merely that we ought to pay our taxes—we are obligated to pay our taxes! What is salient about the law is that it does not simply presume to tell us what we *should* do; rather, it arrogates to itself the power to tell us what we *must* do. That we focus on the stronger statements of obligation must not blind us to the fact that the weaker statements of ought are necessarily true by implication.

If we are to preserve the coherence of legal thought and discourse, we cannot treat the legal concepts of sovereignty and obligation descriptively and divorce them from the concept of ought. Austin's proposed solutions to the Possibility Puzzle and Hume's Challenge, therefore, must fail.

4

HART AND THE RULE OF RECOGNITION

Rules about Rules

Let's return to our five-year-old. Does the law consist of just those rules for which adults get fined or jailed if they break them? I hope it is clear by now why such a description is both incomplete and misleading. To treat the law as simply the expression of wishes backed by threats of sanction presents a cramped conception of its social function. While certain legal rules are designed to place obstacles in our way, others exist precisely in order to remove them. Power-conferring rules are tools that enable members of the community to realize their plans and projects. These rules are not enforced through the threat of sanctions; rather, the failure to comply is simply met with the refusal to confer benefits that the law offers only according to certain terms.

Ignoring the existence of power-conferring rules distorts our understanding of more than the law's function. As we have also seen, power-conferring rules are necessary to account for many of the formal features that legal systems normally possess. They explain how law can be created impersonally and unintentionally; how laws can apply to their creators; how legal authority can remain continuous over time; how laws normally survive their makers; and how sovereignty may nevertheless be limited by law.

Perhaps the biggest defect of our pithy explanation is that it equates legal authority with the physical power to punish disobedience. But as became evident at the end of the last chapter, legal thought and discourse are unintelligible in so impoverished a framework. The idea that certain people have the legal right to tell others what to do and punish them if they fail to live up to their obligations only makes sense when there are legal rules that confer these rights and impose these obligations. Naked power and uncritical habits may, as a psychological matter, be sufficient to motivate people to act in certain ways; but they are incapable of generating rights and duties and hence cannot provide the appropriate grounding for law.

This chapter examines a more sophisticated and so, alas, less child-friendly theory of law. According to H. L. A. Hart's celebrated account, the law is not only composed of rules that impose duties as well as confer powers, but founded on them as well. In particular, Hart claims that at the foundation of every legal system lies a social rule that sets out the criteria of legal validity. This master rule, which Hart calls "the rule of recognition," determines which power-conferring and duty-imposing rules are valid in the system.[1]

The postulation of the rule of recognition was a great advance in legal theory. As we will see, Hart's theory is able to account for many of the commonplace features of modern legal systems that were mysterious or inconceivable in Austin's account. It also renders legal thought and discourse intelligible by showing how legal concepts and terminology are ultimately rule based in nature.

In philosophy, however, answers usually beget more questions. If the law consists not only of rules that impose duties and confer powers but also of rules about those rules, then the Possibility Puzzle reappears. Recall Phil's objection to Lex in Chapter 2. If the law contains rules that regulate the manner of its own creation, how are these rules created? If legal systems must have rules about rules, must they also have rules that are about the rules that are about rules?

In this chapter, we will see how Hart responded to this puzzle. In short, Hart's strategy was to reject the Chicken Principle: while authority must be conferred by norms, norms can be created by those lacking the authority to do so. As Hart argued, groups are capable of creating social rules simply by engaging in a social practice. The reason that groups can accomplish such a feat is that, for Hart, social rules *are* social practices. Thus, the rule of recognition is generated through the convergent and critical behavior of official identification of certain rules because the rule of recognition is nothing but this practice among officials.

Because Hart's account of social rules is crucial to his showing that legal authority is indeed possible, we will examine his account in the second half of the chapter. As I will argue, Hart's identification of social rules with social practice is not only incorrect but confused. Rules and practices occupy different metaphysical realms and hence one can never be reduced to the other. Nor can Hart's account be salvaged by weakening his claim. Once we reject the equation of rules and practices, we will see that Hart's solution to the Possibility Puzzle simply collapses.

The Rule of Recognition

In the last chapter, we examined Hart's reconstruction of Austin's theory of law as the gunman writ large. According to this story, Austin began with the temporary power of the gunman over his lone victim and progressively increased his muscle until the gunman became the dominant influence in the community. Despite its initial appeal, we have seen that the reconstruction errs at outset. Its original sin is to conceptualize the gunman as a protosovereign and the coercion he exercises over his victim as an embryonic form of an authority relation. On the contrary, legal right can never be equated with naked might, regardless of extent or degree. Any assertion of authority necessarily requires the one asserting it to follow rules conferring rights to demand compliance.

For this reason, Hart does not begin the construction of his own legal system with brute force or uncritical subservience. He starts instead by considering a community that does not have a legal system but does follow rules. He then ponders the various social problems that would arise in that group and how the introduction of additional rules (among them, the rule of recognition) would resolve these problems. How and why this point of departure matters will become clearer as we go along.

Problems of the Pre-legal World

To begin the construction, Hart has us imagine a small pre-law society, such as the fictional one described in Chapter 2. Although such a community does not have a legal system, its members nevertheless follow certain rules. Hart supposes that these rules prohibit the free use of violence, theft, and deception and require members to perform certain services that contribute to communal maintenance.

In this community, Hart further imagines, there are no institutional mechanisms for creating rules. The only rules that exist are customary ones.[2] A rule exists in such a community just in case most members take what Hart calls the "internal point of view" toward the rule. They must, in other words, be committed to act according to the rule and to evaluate conduct in accordance with it. Thus, a group has a customary rule requiring men to bare their heads when entering a sacred place just in case most men bare their heads when entering a sacred place, and those men who do not bare their heads are criticized for doing so (using statements such as "You ought to take off your hat in sacred places" or "It was wrong of me not to take off my ostrich hat last Sunday").

Hart then considers what would happen should some doubt or disagreement arise within the group about proper behavior. Imagine that some members believe that revenge killings are permissible, whereas others think that they are prohibited. Since the only property that this group's rules share is acceptance by the group, there will be no other common mark to which members can point (an inscription in some authoritative text, declaration by some official, and so on) in order to resolve their controversy.[3]

Hart claims that this normative uncertainty would be unproblematic in a small group united by bonds of kinship and inhabiting a stable ecological niche.[4] Presumably, relatively few doubts and disagreements would arise in such groups, and those that did could be overcome through either headcounting to determine existing custom or some combination of persuasion, deliberation, and negotiation. However, as groups expand and become more heterogeneous, or when environmental conditions are highly fluid, uncertainty will likely proliferate and these techniques will become more costly or less effective. Given that the need for dispute resolution is bound to be great within such a group, the insecurity engendered by these doubts and disagreements will be distressing, perhaps even crippling.

Normative uncertainty is not the only problem facing such groups; customary rules also possess a "static character" that renders them defective tools for regulating all but the smallest human communities.[5] Suppose there is sudden need for the group to act in a certain manner, for example, to increase the amount of grain that each family contributes to communal storage as a result of drought. The simplest and quickest response would be for some members of the group to deliberately change the rules of the group to amend the tithing requirements. However, in a group governed solely by custom, this option is unavailable. In such a group, rules cannot be changed at will: customary rules vary only through a slow process of growth and decay. The urgent need of the group to respond to the drought will likely go unmet.

Finally, Hart considers the "inefficiencies" associated with this simple regime of customary rules.[6] Suppose there is a clear rule about how land is to be acquired. It is accepted custom, say, that the first person to stake his claim is the rightful owner. What happens, though, when there is factual disagreement about who the first claimant is? Since the regime contains no mechanism for determining the satisfaction or violation of any of the rules, the attempt to settle who actually staked the claim first will likely be costly and could even turn ugly.

Law as the Solution

Hart suggests that the fundamental rules of legal systems solve the various defects of pre-legal, customary societies. Legal systems address the problem of uncertainty by providing a rule that determines which rules are binding. By referring to this rule about rules—what Hart calls the "rule of recognition"—normative questions can be resolved without engaging in deliberation, negotiation, or persuasion.[7] If there is a doubt about, say, whether revenge killings are permissible, the rule of recognition can direct the parties to the authoritative list of rules on the rock in the town square, the past pronouncements of the village elder, the practice of other villages, and so on to determine the answer.

The static character of customary norms is overcome by what Hart calls a "rule of change."[8] A rule of change confers power on a person or institution to create, modify, or extinguish rules and may also specify the procedures to be used in exercising that power. Since the rule of change empowers certain persons or bodies to amend the rules, behavior may be shifted in the desired direction through the exercise of legal authority. A group facing a drought can, for example, deliberately change its tithing rules and hence address the dire circumstances in an expeditious manner.

Finally, the problem of inefficiency is solved by what Hart calls a "rule of adjudication."[9] This rule confers the power on certain bodies to apply the rules, that is, to determine whether a rule has been satisfied or violated on a particular occasion, and specifies the method to be followed in adjudication. In our example of first claimants, the body identified as the authoritative adjudicator would have the power to determine who first claimed the land and hence is the rightful owner.

Hart's Doctrine of the Rule of Recognition

We are now in a position to state Hart's doctrine of the rule of recognition in a more abstract manner. According to Hart, every legal system necessarily contains one, and only one, rule that sets out the test of validity for that system. The systemic test of validity specifies those properties the possession of which by a rule renders it binding in that system. Any norm that bears one of the marks of authority set out in the rule of recognition *is a law of that system,* and officials are required to recognize it when carrying out their official duties.

In the course of setting out the criteria of legal validity, the rule of recognition also specifies orders of precedence among sources of law. In the United States, for example, the rule of recognition mandates that federal law trumps state law, federal constitutional law trumps federal statutory law, and constitutional amendments made in accordance with Article V trump earlier constitutional provisions.[10] Hart calls tests such as the one set out in Article V "supreme" criteria of legal validity, because they specify those legal rules (for example, unamended constitutional provisions) that are not trumped by any other legal rule.[11]

The most salient property of the rule of recognition is that it is a *secondary* rule. It is a rule about other rules, that is, the primary rules. The rule of recognition is also a *social* rule. It is "social" in two different senses. First, the rule of recognition exists and has the content it does because, and only because, of certain *social facts.*[12] In particular, its existence and content is determined by the fact that members of a group take the internal point of view toward a certain behavioral regularity and use it to evaluate the validity of norms that fall within their purview.[13] Second, the rule of recognition is social in the sense that it sets out a *group-wide* standard. Members of this group do not regard it as an idiosyncratic or personal rule that others are not required to follow, but rather treat the standard it sets out as the official way to determine the law in their community.[14]

The rule of recognition is also an *ultimate* rule.[15] It is ultimate in the sense that it does not exist by virtue of any other rule. Its existence is secured simply because of its acceptance and practice. The primary rules of the legal system, by contrast, are not ultimate because they exist by virtue of the rule of recognition. The rule of recognition validates, but is not itself validated.

Last, the rule of recognition is a *duty-imposing* rule. It imposes a duty on legal officials to apply rules that bear certain characteristics. For example, the British rule of recognition requires British officials to apply the rules enacted by the Queen-in-Parliament.

Although the rule of recognition is a duty-imposing rule, Hart often presents it as though it were a test of whether a rule is binding within a certain jurisdiction. For example, he states that the British rule of recognition is: "What the Queen in Parliament enacts is law."[16] It might be wondered, then, why Hart presents the rule of recognition as a test of legal validity when in reality it is a duty-imposing norm. The answer, I believe, is that, according to Hart, the law of a particular system consists of all the norms that legal participants of that system are under a duty to apply in their official capacities. In other words, the rule of recognition sets out the criteria of legal validity, and hence picks out the set of legal rules for a particular legal system, because *the law of a particular system just is the set of rules that officials of a certain system are under a duty to apply, and the rule of recognition sets out the content of this duty.*[17]

It is important to keep in mind that for Hart the rule of recognition is necessarily directed at officials. Ordinary citizens can follow it in the sense that they can use it to ascertain what the law in their community is. But they don't follow the rule of recognition in the sense of complying with it because they are not, strictly speaking, its audience. Citizens are only under a duty to follow *primary* rules; officials, on the other hand, are required to follow the *secondary* rules, a duty that requires them to evaluate the conduct of citizens according to the rules these citizens are obligated to follow.

The Rule of Recognition and the U.S. Constitution

Since the rule of recognition is a duty-imposing rule, it follows that the vast majority of the text of the United States Constitution does not set out the United States' rule of recognition. Article I, Section 8, for example, begins: "The Congress shall have Power To lay and collect Taxes, Duties, Imposts and Excises . . ."[18] This provision formulates part of the federal rule of change insofar as it confers a power, not imposes a duty, on Congress. Articles V and VII are also part of the rule of change, for both provisions confer power on state legislatures and conventions to ratify and amend the Constitution and specify the procedures to be used. Similarly, most of Article III is best understood as part of the federal rule of adjudication, for it confers power on the Supreme Court (and on any lower federal courts that Congress should happen to create) to decide certain cases, and partially specifies the method that courts should follow when engaged in adjudication.

Indeed, the text of the United States Constitution has no provision that explicitly sets out the duty-imposing portion of the U.S. rule of recognition, at least as it pertains to federal judges, legislators, and executive branch officials.[19] Strictly speaking, Article III only *empowers* courts to decide cases that arise under constitutional and federal law, without *mandating* that they decide cases according to these rules. The closest the text of the Constitution comes to imposing duties on federal judges is the requirement that all federal and state officials take an oath to support the Constitution.[20] Requiring judges to take an oath to support the Constitution is not quite the same as requiring them to support the Constitution. Nevertheless, even though not explicitly mentioned in the text, it is part of federal constitutional law that judges are under such a duty because officials accept this mandate from the internal point of view. Indeed, the obligation of federal officials to apply federal law in performing their official duties is so obvious that it goes without saying.

It follows that the text of the United States Constitution does not constitute a complete description of the fundamental rules of the American legal system. The basic duty of federal judges, legislators, and executive branch officials to apply federal law appears nowhere in the text. Indeed, many aspects of modern legal practice have no textual source whatsoever. For example, the administrative branch of the United States government, the so-called fourth branch, is not mentioned in the Constitution. On the Hartian model, the modern administrative state is nonetheless "constitutional" despite the lack of any textual justification because officials accept the legitimacy of administrative practice from the internal point of view and act accordingly.

The Need for Secondary Rules

In this section, I will try to explain why Hart's postulation of the rule of recognition, as well as the secondary rules more generally, constituted a major breakthrough in legal theory. As we will see, his idea is as powerful as it is simple. The elegant reconceptualization of a legal system as the union of primary and secondary rules not only overcame the many difficulties that bedeviled Austin's theory, but provided the critical element missing from previous characterizations of the identity of law and hence set the terms on which all research in legal theory has since proceeded.

Continuity, Persistence, Supremacy, Independence, and Membership

Recall that Austinian sovereignty is created by asymmetrical habits of obedience. To Austin, the sovereign is the one who is habitually obeyed by the bulk of the population and who habitually obeys no one else. However, as we saw in the last chapter, habits of obedience cannot account for many of the properties of legal sovereignty. Habits, for example, cannot establish the continuity of legal authority. Rex I's successor, Rex II, will be the sovereign from the moment he takes office, even though Rex II has yet to be the object of habitual obedience. Nor can habits establish the "persistence" of law. Rex I's laws will be legally valid after his death despite the fact that the dead cannot be obeyed in any manner, let alone habitually.

Hart argued instead that sovereignty is created by rules, not habits.[21] The sovereign is the sovereign because the secondary rules make her so. In this way, Hart was able to account for the seamless transition of legal power. Rex II has the power to legislate from the moment of Rex I's death because the legal system contains a rule of change giving Rex and his rightful successors the power to rule as soon as they ascend to the throne. This explanation may also be put in the terminology of the previous chapter: the rule of change establishes the continuity of legal authority by creating *the office of the king* and empowering its inhabitants as soon as they assume the office.

The persistence of law is guaranteed in a similar manner. Rex I's rules are valid even after his death because the rule of recognition requires officials to apply all the rules made by Rex or his rightful successors that have not yet been repealed. (Alternatively put, the rule of recognition requires officials to apply all unrepealed rules made by a king.) As long as the same secondary rules endure from regime to regime, legal authority and the rules made pursuant to it that have yet to be repealed will endure as well.

Hart also shows how secondary rules explain the supremacy of the sovereign. In contrast to Austin's account, according to which Rex is supreme because of an asymmetry in habitual obedience, Hart credits the rule of recognition. Rex is supreme, according to this approach, because the supreme criterion of legal validity set out in the system's rule of recognition requires officials to privilege Rex's will above all others'.[22]

A critical advantage of this account of supremacy is that it does not imply that the sovereign is necessarily "above the law."[23] In a constitutional regime, the secondary rules limit the supreme powers of the sovereign. Although the American people are sovereign in the United States and have the power to amend the Constitution, the Constitution nonetheless limits their power to do so, both by making certain provisions unalterable (such as depriving a state of its equal representation in the Senate without its consent) and prescribing an extremely onerous procedure that must be followed before an amendment is ratified (amendments must be proposed by at least two-thirds of the members of both houses of Congress or two-thirds of state legislatures and ratified by three-quarters of all state legislatures or conventions).[24] In this way, the secondary rules simultaneously account for the supremacy of sovereignty as well as its legal limitation.

The rule of recognition is also able to explain the independence of legal systems. Multiple legal systems can coexist because rules of recognition can have different contents. Rex's legal system is separate from, say, Lex's system because the rule of recognition of Rex's legal system deems Rex's, not Lex's, enactments to be binding.

In general, the rule of recognition determines the membership, or content, of particular legal systems: the rule of recognition of S determines all and only the laws of S.[25] Thus does Hart explain how laws with the same content may nonetheless belong to different legal systems. The New York Statute of Frauds, for example, may be word-for-word identical to the New Jersey Statute of Frauds, yet one belongs to the New York legal system and the other to the New Jersey legal system. The Hartian explanation for this phenomenon is simple: the New York Statute of Frauds is a law of the New York legal system because the statute was created by the New York state legislature and hence is in accordance with the requirements of the New York rule of recognition and not in compliance with the New Jersey rule of recognition.

Similarly, Hart is able to explain how laws made by different sovereigns can nevertheless be part of the same legal system. The Patriot Act of 2003, for example, is part of the same legal system as the Federal Trade Commission Act of 1916 because both are validated by the same rule of recognition. Austin's theory cannot account for this mundane legal fact because two rules are part of the same legal system on his view only if they are issued by the *same* sovereign.

Reflexivity, Auto-limitation, Custom, and Power

Austin's theory of sovereignty falls short not only because it grounds legal authority in habits; it also suffers from overemphasis on the imperatival nature of legal regulation. For Austin, all laws are commands, and since it is impossible to command oneself, he cannot explain how laws can reflexively apply to their makers or how sovereignty can be legally limited.

By contrast, Hart does not insist that all laws are commands, and thus is in a position to explain their reflexive character. Since Hartian validity does not arise from the fact of command, but rather from validation by the rule of recognition, there is no reason that a rule cannot apply to the ruler. Senators, for example, are required to pay taxes on their income because the rules they validly create impose a tax on all income. In general, then, a rule can apply to its creator just in case the rule of recognition validates rules made by the creator and the rule in question actually requires, forbids, permits, authorizes . . . the creator to perform some act.

As we saw in the previous section, Hart is also able to explain legal auto-limitation by noting that sovereignty can be limited by virtue of restrictions set out in the secondary rules. The American people cannot change the number of senators per state because their rule of recognition does not recognize constitutional amendments that attempt to increase or decrease the number of senators per state.

Imperatival theories also have trouble explaining the validity of rules—such as customary ones—that arise outside the channels of legal sovereignty. Hart's theory of validity, by contrast, enables him to explain in a straightforward manner how legal rules can be created without being commanded. A custom will be legally valid in a particular jurisdiction just in case the jurisdiction's rule of recognition requires officials to apply customary norms of that type.

Moreover, because Hart does not insist that all laws are commands, he is able to countenance the existence of power-conferring rules. The rules that confer power on testators to create enforceable wills, we have seen, cannot plausibly be understood as commands. Testators are not "commanded" to dispose of their assets using a will; they do nothing wrong if they die intestate or fail to follow the correct procedures and hence render their actions a legal nullity. They simply miss out on their chance to dispose of their assets after death in a desired way. Only by broadening the category of rules to include noncommands can a theory of law make sense of laws like these, which do not impose duties but rather confer the power to create, modify, or extinguish duties.

Validity

The rule of recognition is not only responsible for the existence of customary rules. It accounts for the existence of all the primary rules. To see this, let us return one last time to Hart's pre-law society. As we have seen, all of its rules are customary ones. A rule exists in such a group only if it is accepted and followed from the internal point of view. Legal systems, on the other hand, can, and typically do, contain some rules that are not themselves practiced by members of the group. Jaywalking, for example, is prohibited in New York City even though most everyone engages in it.

According to Hart, a primary legal rule exists just in case it is validated by the system's rule of recognition. Thus, the rule prohibiting jaywalking exists because it is validated by the New York City rule of recognition that requires legal officials to heed rules enacted in a certain fashion. For Hart, then, the rule of recognition secures the existence of all primary rules. As long as a rule bears the characteristics of legality set out in the rule of recognition, it exists and is legally valid. Indeed, Hart claimed that the concept VALIDITY is used precisely in those contexts where the existence of rules does not depend on their being practiced.[26] To say that a rule is valid is to express a judgment that it is binding because it passes the test of some other existing rule, not because it is accepted by its audience from the internal point of view. For this reason, the rule of recognition is never valid—it exists by virtue of being practiced.

Because the rule of recognition is ultimately responsible for the existence of every primary rule, legal justification is complete only when the chain of validity is traced back to it. If asked why a certain norm n_1 legally ought to be followed, a person might point to another norm n_2 which legally requires that n_1 be followed. Unless n_2 is the rule of recognition, it is always open to ask in turn why *it* legally ought to be followed. Such questions must end, however, once the responder adverts to the system's rule of recognition. Once one reaches this norm, one has run out of legal reasons; one has simply hit legal bedrock.

To be sure, there are other kinds of questions that one can ask about the rule of recognition. Someone might wonder, for example, whether a certain norm *is* the rule of recognition. One answers this question by reference to social practice. If officials of a certain system are committed to following the tests of validity set out in the norm, then it is in fact the system's rule of recognition. Moreover, one might question whether a system's rule of recognition is morally legitimate, and hence whether it should be followed. To establish the moral justification of the rule of recognition, one must obviously point to elements besides social practice.

In the moral sense, then, the rule of recognition is not self-justifying. The existence of the rule of recognition never gives anyone a moral reason to follow it. To establish the moral obligation to obey it, one must justify the rule, as it were, "from the outside," that is, by using the extra-legal principles of political morality. In the legal sense, however, the rule of recognition *is* self-justifying. By law, officials ought to follow the rule of recognition for the trivial reason that the rule of recognition ultimately defines what the law is.

Law as the Union of Primary and Secondary Rules

As we have seen, Hart's simple and elegant hypothesis about the existence of secondary rules enables him to account for many of the formal properties that legal systems normally possess (the continuity of legal authority, persistence of legal rules, supremacy and independence of sovereignty, reflexivity of law, legal auto-limitation, validity of customary rules and the primary rules more generally . . .), and hence to overcome the many problems that beset Austin's account. As I would now like to show, the rules of recognition, change, and adjudication also play a major role in answering law's Identity Question.

Recall that the inquiry into the identity of law seeks to identify those properties the possession of which distinguishes legal systems from kindred phenomena. According to Hart, the existence of secondary rules is a distinguishing mark of legality. While games, etiquette, and popular morality all consist of primary rules, legal systems also contain rules *about* their primary rules. According to Hart's famous dictum, the "essence" of law is that it is "the union of primary and secondary rules."[27]

In characterizing the law as the "union" of primary and secondary rules, Hart means to emphasize the *systematicity* of legality. In a legal system, every primary rule is linked to every other rule by virtue of their common validity under the rule of recognition. In this regard, compare the law to rules of etiquette. Insofar as etiquette consists just in those norms of politeness that members of a group accept, there is no one rule that is responsible for the existence of all others. The rules of etiquette, therefore, are not systematically interconnected; they simply form a set of *separate* standards. By contrast, legal systems are *systems:* the existence of any primary rule can always be traced to a common validating source.

While Hart thinks that systematicity distinguishes law from related phenomena, he does not go so far as to claim that it is unique in this regard. For it is clear that other normative systems also contain secondary, as well as primary, rules. Corporations, for example, have rules about who can change the rules of the corporation, and rules about which rules corporate officers must recognize when doing their job. Corporate bylaws are thus systematically interconnected in the same way as legal rules, yet corporations are not legal systems. At best, the existence of secondary rules provides only a partial answer to the Identity Question. It constitutes the "essence" of law in the ordinary meaning of the term, that is, the main idea or gist, rather than the technical, philosophical sense we have been using, that is, the complete set of properties the possession of which makes the object in question the thing that it is and not something else.

Notice that Hart rejects Austin's and Kelsen's idea of sanctions as constituting the "essence" of law. Hart, of course, recognizes that the law's use of coercion to enforce its demands is a very important fact about existing legal institutions. Nevertheless, he maintains that a law would still be a law even if officials were not empowered to punish noncompliance. For even a sanctionless rule would still represent a standard of conduct, and thus could guide behavior accordingly. Indeed, Hart claims that a regime could still have a legal system even if there were no law enforcement institutions. By contrast, a community in which no one had the right to determine authoritatively whether members had complied with the rules would not be one that had law.

Because he deemphasized the importance of sanctions in defining law, Hart was not led to make the same mistakes as his predecessors. He was not forced to treat nullities as sanctions, to represent power-conferring rules as fragments of duty-imposing rules, or to maintain that the sovereign is necessarily above the law. Nor was Hart pushed to adopt a restricted view of human motivation. He understood that people have many different reasons for obeying the law, among them an abiding respect for legal institutions. To be sure, a legal system exists only if its rules are generally obeyed. But not everyone who obeys the rules does so solely from fear of punishment; many may, and in stable regimes typically do, regard the law from the internal point of view, namely, as setting a legitimate standard of conduct and which imposes an obligation on them to comply.

Indeed, Hart argues that a legal system does not exist unless its officials take the internal point of view toward its secondary rules. While the bulk of the population must simply *obey* the primary rules for whatever reason, the rules of recognition, change, and adjudication exist only if they are accepted by legal participants as legitimate standards of conduct. According to Hart, then, we can say that a legal system exists for a group G just in case (1) the bulk of G obeys the primary rules *and* (2) officials of G accept the secondary rules from the internal point of view and follow them in most cases.[28] Rex is the sovereign, therefore, not simply because he is obeyed by the bulk of the population, but because he is also deemed to have the right to rule by the officials of his regime.

Intelligible Reduction

Hart's account of law as the union of primary and secondary rules not only provides an intuitive criterion for distinguishing legal systems from other normative phenomena but, as the constructivist strategy shows, it does so in a noncircular fashion. Recall that in the first phase of Hart's construction of a legal system, a pre-legal community follows simple duty-imposing rules. A duty-imposing rule, according to Hart, is a social rule that imposes a duty; in turn, a social rule is a behavioral regularity that is accepted and practiced by a group from the internal point of view. To understand a duty-imposing rule, then, one need only understand four basic concepts: GROUP, BEHAVIORAL REGULARITY, DUTY, and INTERNAL POINT OF VIEW. Quite obviously, none of these concepts is distinctively legal—each of them occurs outside the law as well.

In the second phase of Hart's construction, the rule of recognition is created to resolve questions in the community about the content and scope of duty-imposing rules. Since the rule of recognition is itself a duty-imposing rule, it is possible to understand it without the use of any uniquely legal concepts. In the final two rounds, the rules of change and adjudication are formed so as to overcome the static and inefficient nature of social rules. Since these secondary rules are power conferring, and power can be understood in terms of obligations (roughly, as the ability to create, alter, or extinguish an obligation), Hart has shown how to generate a legal system using nonlegal concepts.

One might doubt that Hart's construction is truly reductive insofar as it helps itself to the concept OFFICIAL. After all, the group that accepts the secondary rules from the internal point of view consists of the officials of the system. And, it might be thought, the notion of an official *is* a distinctively legal concept.

This objection fails, however, for two reasons. First, the concept OFFICIAL is not distinctively legal, because it routinely occurs in nonlegal contexts. The dean, for example, is a university official; likewise, an umpire is an official of the game. Second, what makes an official an *official* is that the rules that create the office occupied designate the occupant as having certain powers. Thus, once we understand the concepts of a rule of change and a rule of adjudication—concepts that we have seen can be reduced to nonlegal ones—we are in a position to understand the idea of a legal official.

Having established the reductive nature of Hart's account, let us briefly compare it to Austin's effort. As we saw in the previous chapter, Austin is able to produce a noncircular account of law by reducing legality to wishes, expressions, evils, habits, and obedience. The problem with this reduction, as we also saw, is that it renders legal thought and discourse incoherent. The idea of an obligation, let alone a legal obligation, simply makes no sense without the concept of a rule. To say that one is obligated to pay one's taxes logically implies the existence of a standard that identifies the paying of taxes as an action that is to be done. Likewise, legal authority is incomprehensible without the notion of a rule that identifies the utterance or decision of a person and privileges it over the utterances or decisions of others.

It was a mistake, then, for Austin to have started his construction with the naked power of the gunman. Hart shows that it is far better to begin with social rules. The germ of legality, on this account, is that of a group's commitment to a standard of conduct that all are required to heed. Law comes into existence whenever the social rules in question make reference to other rules. From this simple idea, the concepts that are distinctively legal may then be understood.

The Practice Theory

In the past section, we saw the numerous functions of secondary rules in Hart's theory of law. They resolve uncertainty about which rules are obligatory within a community, render the law an agile and efficient normative institution, and account for many of the formal properties possessed by all legal systems. The secondary rules also largely explain the identity, intelligibility, and reducibility of legality.

It is here, however, that the Possibility Puzzle rears its ugly head. If secondary rules must exist, what accounts for *their* existence? Must there be tertiary rules that validate the secondary rules that, in turn, validate the primary rules?

Hart's answer to this last question is "No." The secondary rules of a legal system are social rules, and social rules are brought into existence simply by virtue of being accepted and practiced by members of a group. Just as a secondary rule need not exist in order for the social rules of a pre-law society to exist—for example, men simply need to accept that taking off their hats in a sacred area is appropriate and act accordingly in order to create the head-baring customary rule—tertiary rules need not exist in order to validate the rules of recognition, change, and adjudication.

Yet it will surely be objected that Hart hasn't so much dispelled the mystery as magnified it. Our question about the rule of recognition applies equally to all social rules. How does the head-baring rule come into being simply by being accepted and practiced? This seems like magic.

Hart tries to demystify the creation of social rules by reducing them to social practices. In other words, social practices generate rules because these rules *are nothing but* social practices. Thus, when men regularly take off their hats in sacred places because they take the internal point of view toward this sort of behavior, the behavioral regularity is itself a rule. Similarly, the practice of recognizing Lex's commands generates the rule of recognition because the rule of recognition is nothing but the practice of recognition. Call this the "Practice Theory."[29]

The Practice Theory enables Hart to solve the Possibility Puzzle by rejecting the Chicken Principle. To create a social rule, those involved need not be authorities; rather, they need only engage in a social practice. For according to the Practice Theory, social rules are just social practices. And by rejecting the Chicken Principle, Hart stops the infinite regress: while legal authority must always be conferred by norms, legal norms may be created without authority.

Notice further that Hart's solution to the Possibility Puzzle is a positivistic one. The existence of legal authority need not depend on the moral legitimacy of the body claiming power. Nazis had law because Nazi officials engaged in a social practice of recognizing the pronouncements and decisions of the National Socialist regime. The Practice Theory thus enables Hart to show how legal facts can ultimately be determined by social facts alone.

The Internal Point of View

In one sense, then, Hart's solution to the Possibility Puzzle is similar to Austin's. Both of these positivists ground the law completely in regularities of group behavior. For Austin, the regularity is a social habit of obedience; for Hart, it is a social practice of rule recognition.

Their solutions diverge, however, at a critical point. On Austin's account, the habit of obedience need not be motivated by a commitment on the part of the group to the regularity in question. Each member of the group need obey only because they think that the self-interested implications of each act of obedience are better than those of disobedience. They need not, in other words, be following any *general rule* to the effect that the law ought to be obeyed. On Hart's account, by contrast, legal officials must be motivated by a commitment to a general standard of conduct. They must comply because they judge compliance with the law as proper irrespective of the sanctions that might attend disobedience. Only when participants take the internal point of view can behavioral regularity be transformed into social practice and, thus, a social rule.

We must be careful, however, not to conflate the internal point of view with the *moral* point of view. According to Hart, one can accept a rule for any type of reason, even a nonmoral one. A judge might accept the rule of recognition because it is in his long-term self-interest. He might want to advance his political career, or simply make a living. The judge need not, in other words, believe in the moral legitimacy of the regime in order to commit himself to applying those rules that are applied by his fellow judges. What is crucial is that the judge treat the rule of recognition as a *rule,* that is, as a general standard of conduct that forbids him to depart from its strictures, whether because in a particular case it is in his self-interest or for any other reason. The internal point of view is the attitude of *rule acceptance,* and it precludes its bearer from engaging in this short-term, case-by-case analysis.

It is not hard to see why Hart opted for this rather capacious conception of the internal point of view. For it seems not only possible, but highly likely, that at least some officials in every legal system will be alienated from their jobs. These officials can declare legal rights and wrongs despite judging that, from a moral point of view, citizens have no reason at all to heed their declarations. A theory that insisted that judges accept the fundamental legal rules for moral reasons would be unrealistic—it would assume that legal officials are necessarily true believers, when they often have their own personal reasons for going along with social practice.[30]

Creating a Hartian legal system, therefore, demands far greater psychological sophistication than creating an Austinian one. To habitually obey another merely requires the ability to act reliably in one's own short-term self-interest. Household pets are no doubt capable of such responses. Engaging in a social practice, on the other hand, demands the psychological capacity to commit to a general standard of conduct, apply it in a particular case, and follow through on it—even when doing so is contrary to one's own interests. Participating in legal practice is even more taxing: it requires the further capacity to commit, apply, and follow through on a rule that requires the application of other rules to the applicable persons. As smart as dogs and cats are, it is doubtful that they are capable of such demanding psychological feats.

Legal Facts and Legal Judgments

As we have seen, Hart's solution to the Possibility Puzzle is a scrupulously positivistic one. Legal systems, on his view, are necessarily founded on social practices, never on moral principles. His theory, therefore, must grapple with the problem that all positivistic accounts of law face, namely, Hume's Challenge. How can normative judgments about legal rights and obligations be derived from purely descriptive judgments about social practices?

Curiously, as central as this question is to the success of Hart's jurisprudential project, he does not openly address it. In all of his many writings, he never explicitly explains how his positivistic theory is compatible with Hume's Law. This is not to say, of course, that he ignored or overlooked the problem; in fact, I believe that he was acutely aware of the challenge, and self-consciously fashioned a novel theory of normative judgments and statements to address it.

If there is an explanation for why Hart did not address the problem head on, it is probably that his ideas were so revolutionary that he lacked the terminology and techniques for expressing them. A full elaboration of this theory would have to await developments in the field of philosophy known as "metaethics." In the discussion that follows, I will take advantage of some of these advances to present an interpretation of his theory of normative judgments and statements, and show how this account enables him to address Hume's Challenge.[31]

Theoretical and Practical Engagement

Hume's Challenge to Hart's theory of law may be formulated as follows. According to Hart, the rule of recognition is constituted by a social practice. To recognize that a rule of recognition exists, therefore, is to form a descriptive judgment about the existence of a descriptive fact. Since the rule of recognition validates the primary legal rules, and these rules confer powers and impose duties, the judgment that a rule of recognition exists licenses the formation of judgments about the existence of legally valid rules, legal rights, and legal obligations. But since these latter judgments are normative ones, Hart's theory permits one to derive normative judgments from purely descriptive ones. Legal reasoning would sanction a DINO pattern of inference, a clear violation of Hume's Law.

Hart's insight was to realize that descriptive facts are not limited to being the objects of descriptive judgments; rather, they may be the objects of normative judgments as well. To see this, consider the pain of a pinprick. That the pinprick causes pain is a mundane descriptive fact about the world. One can, therefore, form a judgment about the causal effects of pinpricks, namely, that they cause pain. Yet, one can also treat the pain of a pinprick as *something to be avoided*. That is, one can orient oneself toward this descriptive fact in a practical fashion by assigning it a certain weight in one's deliberations.

According to Hart, it would be a mistake to think that there are two facts in the world, a descriptive fact that pinpricks cause pain and a normative fact that pinpricks are to be avoided. There is only *one* fact: the descriptive one. One can engage with this fact, however, in one of two ways. One can engage with it "theoretically" by apprehending its existence. This theoretical orientation is a descriptive or scientific one; it issues in descriptive judgments that report the state of the world. Alternatively, one can engage with a descriptive fact "practically" by committing oneself to treating it in a certain way. This practical engagement issues in normative judgments, which are commitments to treat descriptive states of the world as having certain weight in one's deliberations about what to do.

Normative judgments on this view do not take normative facts as their objects; indeed, according to Hart, there are no normative facts at all. The judgment that pinpricks are bad, therefore, does not purport to represent the normative fact that pinpricks are bad. Rather, it is nothing more than the practical commitment to give the avoidance of pinpricks great weight in one's deliberations. Similarly, normative statements do not purport to represent normative facts (unlike descriptive statements, which do purport to represent descriptive facts). Rather, the function of normative statements is to express one's practical engagement with descriptive facts. To say that pinpricks are "bad" and that one has a "reason" to avoid them is to articulate one's commitment to desire the avoidance of pinpricks.

Following current usage, let us call theories such as Hart's "expressivist" ones. This label reflects the idea that the function of normative terminology is expressive, not representational: it *expresses* states of mind; it does not represent states of the world. Thus, claims of obligation and right express the internal point of view, that is, the normative attitude of commitment to a social rule.[32] When one claims, say, that one is obligated to keep one's promises, one is expressing one's commitment to the social promise-keeping rule, not asserting the existence of a normative fact requiring one to keep one's promises.

Engaging the Law "Legally"

Now consider the rule of recognition. Its existence is a descriptive fact. On Hart's view, therefore, it is possible to engage with this fact in one of two ways. The social scientist can engage with the rule of recognition in a theoretical fashion and form a descriptive judgment about the existence of the social practice. Hart calls reports of these judgments "external statements," because they reflect the point of view of the external observer who is content simply to record behavioral and attitudinal regularities. "In England, they recognize what the Queen-in-Parliament enacts as law" is an external statement because it reports the existence of a social practice.

It is possible, however, to orient oneself toward this social fact in a practical way as well. That is, one can take the internal point of view toward the practice and treat the pattern of conduct as a standard for the guidance and evaluation of conduct. And once one forms a normative judgment concerning the propriety of following the rule of recognition, one can derive further normative judgments about legal validity, rights, and obligations. Hart calls expressions of these judgments (such as "It is the law that . . ." or "X is legally obligated to . . .") "internal statements" because they articulate the internal point of view.[33]

To understand Hart's theory of law, therefore, we must distinguish sharply between legal facts on the one hand and legal judgments and statements on the other. According to Hart, legal facts are nothing but descriptive facts about social groups, that is, facts about people thinking, saying, and doing certain things in particular environments. But this does not mean that legal judgments and statements are descriptive judgments and statements, representing and reporting the existence of these descriptive facts from a theoretical point of view. Rather, they are normative—they are constituted by and express a practical orientation to these social facts. Thus, to say that one is legally obligated in the United States to pay federal income tax is not to describe the operations of Congress, the federal courts, or the Internal Revenue Service. It is, rather, an internal statement expressing a commitment to a rule that regards these official actions as standards for the guidance and evaluation of conduct.

According to this interpretation of Hart's theory, Hume's Challenge is premised on the erroneous assumption that there is only one kind of attitude that one can form vis-à-vis descriptive facts. It presumes, in other words, that since legal facts are social facts, one can engage with them only theoretically and descriptively. If this were true, it would indeed be mysterious how legal judgments could be derived from purely descriptive attitudes, given that, as we saw in our critique of Austin's response to Hume's Challenge, legal judgments have normative content.

On Hart's account, however, one can not only recognize the existence of a social practice but also take the internal point of view toward it. In England, for example, those who respond to the rule of recognition practically will form a normative judgment expressed as follows: "What the

Queen-in-Parliament enacts is law." From this normative judgment, other normative judgments can be inferred (such as judgments expressed as "It is British law that . . .").

Legal reasoning, therefore, does not follow the offending DINO pattern. To discover the content of the law, one must begin by approaching social facts in a practical vein and forming normative judgments. And because the legal reasoner starts with normative judgments, she can end with normative judgments. The social scientist, on the other hand, can never figure out by himself what the law is because he does not take a practical orientation toward the social practice he observes. His theoretical reasoning follows the DIDO, not NINO, pattern. Without accepting the rule of recognition, he can only form judgments that describe the world, and cannot express a commitment to treat its various features as reasons for action.

Legal and Moral Concepts

It might be thought that Hart's solution to Hume's Challenge raises a serious problem for the positivist: if legal judgments are normative, then how is it possible to acknowledge legal authority and obligations but deny the corresponding moral authority and obligations? For centuries positivists have argued that the existence of the law is one thing, its moral merit and demerit quite another.[34] But it would seem that Hart's account casts legal judgments in such a way that one cannot affirm them while rejecting the corresponding moral judgments.

Hart's way out of this problem was simple: although he regarded legal concepts such as AUTHORITY and OBLIGATION to be normative concepts, he did not think that they were *moral* ones. On this view, therefore, to judge that people have a legal obligation to pay taxes is not to judge that they have a moral obligation to do so. Indeed, one can think that people have a legal obligation to pay their taxes but coherently deny that they have a reason to comply. Thus, by distinguishing legal from moral concepts, Hart thought he could explain the coherence of affirming the existence of a legal obligation but denying the corresponding moral obligation to comply.

But if legal judgments are normative, nonmoral judgments, what are they exactly? According to Hart, to judge that someone is legally obligated to perform some act is to judge it proper to demand and extract performance.[35] In other words, when a judge claims that the defendant is legally obligated to pay the plaintiff damages, she is not talking about the defendant's reasons for action; rather, she is talking about her own. She is claiming that *she* may demand compliance from the defendant and extract performance if necessary.

On Hart's view, then, the term "obligation" has a different meaning in moral and legal contexts. If X is morally obligated to do A, then it follows that X ought to do A. But if X is legally obligated to do A, it does not follow that X ought to do A, or even has a reason to do A. It merely entails that some legal official is authorized to demand that X does A and extract performance if X is not willing to comply.

Rules and Practices

Having set out Hart's solutions to the jurisprudential puzzles, I would now like to assess their cogency. This examination, as we remarked in Chapter 2, is crucially important both as a philosophical and practical matter. For if Hart is correct, and social practices explain how legal systems are possible, then legal reasoning must always be traceable to a social rule of recognition. Arguments about who has authority to do what, what rights individuals have, which legal texts are authoritative, and the proper way to interpret them must ultimately be resolved by reference to the sociological facts of official practice. It would never be sufficient to point out that so-and-so is the morally legitimate authority, that people have inalienable rights, that certain texts are sacred, or that a given interpretive methodology produces the best results from the perspective of public policy. For on the Hartian theory, moral facts are utterly irrelevant to determining the ultimate criteria of legal validity in a particular jurisdiction.

In this section, we will address Hart's proposed solution to the Possibility Puzzle. Can the infinite regress be stopped by reducing social rules to social practices, as the Practice Theory claims?

Category Mistake

Hart's solution to the Possibility Puzzle, as we have seen, rests on the cogency of the Practice Theory. If social rules are reducible to social practices, then social rules are ultimate norms whose creation does not presuppose the prior exercise of authority. On the other hand, if social rules are something other than social practices, then Hart has no justification for rejecting the Chicken Principle, and hence has no way of stopping the infinite regress.

Unfortunately, the Practice Theory is fundamentally unsound, for it commits the type of error philosophers call a "category mistake."[36] Social rules cannot be reduced to social practices because rules and practices belong to different metaphysical categories. Rules are *abstract objects*. They are like games, numbers, plots, propositions, and concepts—they are objects of thought, not entities that exist within space and time. You can't see, hear, or kick a rule; a "No Smoking" sign is a formulation of a non-smoking rule, not the rule itself (much as the numeral "7" represents, but is not identical to, the number seven). Practices, on the other hand, are *concrete events*. They take place within the natural world and causally interact with other physical events.

Because rules are abstract objects, they have a potentially infinite domain. The head-baring rule has the following logical form: "For all objects O, places P, and times t, if O is a man and P is a sacred place and O is at P at t, O is to bare his head at t." The rule, therefore, governs all objects in the universe at all times. On the other hand, practices are finite activities. They are simply the complex of past singular events involving the actions in question under certain circumstances.

Because rules and practices are different kinds of things, one cannot be reduced to the other (much like the abstract number seven cannot be identified with the concrete numeral "7" or seven apples). Indeed, our way of talking about practices and rules confirms this distinction. We say that practices *exemplify, embody, conform to, are structured by,* and *are grounds for* rules. This strongly suggests that rules are standards that guide conduct, not the conduct itself.

At this point, Hart might want to weaken his claim. He might concede that social rules are not literally social practices, while still maintaining that social rules are exclusively determined by social practices. Just as some philosophers (often called "nonreductive materialists") deny that the brain and the mind are identical, but claim that the brain necessarily brings the mind into being, Hart might admit that social rules are not reducible to social practices, but claim that social practices necessarily generate social rules in their wake.

The problem with this version of the Practice Theory is that the metaphysical relation it claims exists simply does not obtain: social practices do not necessarily generate social rules. In baseball, for example, third basemen typically draw toward home plate when a bunt is suspected.

Moreover, if they fail to draw near they would be criticized for not doing so. Drawing near, in other words, is a Hartian social practice. Yet, there is no rule that *requires* third basemen to draw near when a bunt is suspected. Contrast this practice with batters retiring after three strikes. The latter activity is rule governed.[37]

In fact, many (if not most) of our social practices fail to generate social rules. Among the professional class in the United States, for example, it is now generally accepted that people ought not to smoke even when no one else is affected. Smokers are routinely criticized by nonsmokers. Smoking, they say, is "stupid," is a "dirty habit," and sets a "bad example." Moreover, these nonsmokers are not criticized by other nonsmokers for engaging in such criticism. Yet there is no social rule against smoking alone or with other smokers. Members of this group simply believe that there are excellent reasons not to smoke, reasons that exist independently of the practice and which the practice is supposed to promote. Similarly, there are no social rules requiring that people save for their retirements, that acquaintances say hello to one another, that drivers lock their cars at night, and that people comb their hair, despite the fact that nearly everyone accepts these practices from the internal point of view.

Since it is false that social practices necessarily generate social rules, Hart's solution to the Possibility Puzzle collapses. His solution, we have seen, depends essentially on the idea that the social practice of recognition among officials is sufficient to generate the fundamental rules of the legal system. Prior authority is not needed to produce these rules; groups are capable of creating them by engaging in a practice from the internal point of view. Yet it turns out that many practices fail to produce such results. Hart cannot, therefore, simply assume that social rules will be generated just because officials regularly engage in a practice of rule recognition in every legal system.

At this point, Hart might weaken the Practice Theory even further. He might concede that while social practices do not necessarily generate social rules, a certain subset of these practices do. Call these special practices "practices*." The Possibility Puzzle is solved by claiming that the practice of recognition by officials is a social practice* and hence generates a rule of recognition.

I have no doubt that this watered-down version of the Practice Theory is true. As we will see in the next section, some social practices do generate social rules. Unfortunately, this weakened theory is insufficient to solve the Possibility Puzzle, for if we do not know which practices are practices*, we have no way of knowing whether the social practice of rule recognition is one of them. The natural lawyer, of course, will argue that these regularities are no different from third basemen drawing near for bunts, that is, practices that fail to generate rules. On this view, officials regularly recognize the rules that they do because they think that moral rules require the actions in question, and they accept *those* rules from the internal point of view. Because Hart cannot rule out this possibility, he cannot be said to have solved the Possibility Puzzle.

Coordination Conventions

As we have seen, the Practice Theory cannot help solve the Possibility Puzzle because social practices do not necessarily generate social rules. While some practices might give rise to rules, not every practice does.

Such considerations have led latter-day legal positivists to search for the set of social practices that necessarily generate social rules—those we have called "practices*." The aim of this strategy is to show that the social practice of rule recognition in every legal system is a practice*. If such a showing could be made, the Possibility Puzzle would be solved. For the existence of convergent behavior among officials would generate a regress-stopper, an ultimate social rule that validates the other rules of the system.

The most promising attempt to amend the Practice Theory in this manner has been to argue that the fundamental rules of legal systems are generated by what philosophers and game theorists call "coordination conventions"—they are, if you will, the "rules of the road" for legal practice.[38] Their function is to coordinate the behavior of officials so that everyone defers to the same set of authorities. Because coordination conventions are constituted purely by social facts and necessarily generate social rules, the thought is that they can serve as a positivist foundation for every legal system. In this section, we will explore whether this strategy can be used to salvage Hart's practice-based solution to the Possibility Puzzle.

Coordination Problems

The positivist strategy we will explore begins with the observation that one of the most important functions that legal authorities serve is to solve recurring coordination problems. Roughly speaking, a coordination problem is a situation where every individual involved strictly prefers that every person act in a uniform manner.[39] A recurring coordination problem is a repeated situation where each event poses a coordination problem.

For example, motorists want to drive on the same side of the road as all other motorists who are driving in the same direction. However, because both the left and right sides are equally good choices, they will have problems knowing on which side of the street others will drive and, hence, on which side they should drive. Authorities are able to solve coordination problems by designating one of the strategies as the choice for all to follow. By marking one of the combinations as binding on all, authorities focus everyone's expectations on that combination, and the problems of incomplete information are overcome. Motorists know that they should drive on the right side of the road because the law has selected this side by imposing a rule requiring it. A motorist should drive on the right side because he knows that others will drive on the right, given that they expect him to do likewise.

The ability of authorities to solve coordination problems does not stem from any expertise. When the law designates the right side of the road as the proper way to drive, it does not do so because the right side is better than the left; indeed, the law was needed precisely because the right side was as good as the left.

Given that expertise is not necessary to solve a coordination problem, there will be many different sets of authorities that are able to perform such a task. The appropriateness of an authority will be determined in large part by whether members of society already look to it as a solver of coordination problems. It appears, therefore, that the choice of an authority structure is itself a recurring coordination problem. Members of a society will prefer that every member follow the same set of authorities just in case *almost* everyone else does. On this account, everyone in the United States prefers that everyone always heed the United States Constitution just in case almost everyone does. And everyone in the United States also would prefer that everyone always heed, say, the French Constitution just in case almost everyone consults it instead.[40]

The claim that the choice of an authority structure is a recurring coordination problem does not imply that everyone will prefer that everyone else follow the same authority structure *no matter the structure*. Some people need not prefer heeding the Constitution of the Third Reich even if every one else does. Rather, the claim is that there will always be a set containing more than one authority structure such that everyone would prefer universal conformity to any member of the set over unilateral defection. While reasonable people would not prefer heeding the Constitution of the Third Reich under any circumstances, they would be happy to heed the United States or, say, the French Constitution—depending on what everyone else did.

Coordination Conventions

The next step in the argument relies on the work of the philosopher David Lewis. Lewis famously argued that conventions are commonly used to solve recurring coordination problems. When a convention exists, the fact that everyone acts according to this convention renders conventional behavior "salient," thereby giving everyone a reason to continue acting according to that convention. The fact that drivers generally drive on the right side of the road gives drivers reason to believe that the other drivers will continue to drive on the right side, thereby making it rational for them to continue to drive on the right side.[41]

Note that coordination conventions generate social rules. If there is a convention to drive on the right side of the road, then it makes sense to say that there is a *social rule* that one ought to drive on the right side of the road. Coordination conventions, in other words, are practices*. Their presence necessarily brings a corresponding rule into existence.

Having identified a set of practices*, the positivist now argues that the social practice of rule recognition among legal officials is a practice*. It is a practice* because it is a coordination convention. It is a coordination convention because it solves the recurring coordination problem of settling on an authority structure. On this interpretation, then, the fact that most officials generally heed the United States Constitution is a coordination convention, because it gives most everyone else reason to expect that most everyone else will continue to heed the United States Constitution, and thus lead them to prefer continuing to heed the United States Constitution. Call this the "Coordination Convention Interpretation" of legal practice ("CCI").

The positivist is now in a position to solve the Possibility Puzzle. Since the social practice of recognition among officials is, according to the CCI, a practice*, it necessarily generates a social *rule* of recognition. This rule, therefore, can serve as a regress-stopper because its creation does not presuppose prior authoritative assistance. Just as drivers do not need authority to create and sustain a convention to drive on the right side of the road, officials do not need authority to create and sustain conventional legal practice. They need only face a recurring coordination problem and treat any regularity in which they engage as a reason to continue the regularity in question.

Alienation and Convention

The construal of the social practice of rule recognition as a coordination convention represents an ingenious attempt to amend Hart's Practice Theory so that it may solve the Possibility Puzzle. Despite its promise, however, the CCI falls short. As I would like to show, the interpretation of legal practice as a coordination convention can only succeed by unjustifiably restricting the types of motivation that legal officials may have for engaging in legal practice.

Let us begin by noting that coordination conventions exist only when the participants are motivated to conform for certain reasons. In particular, they must abide by the convention *for the reason that others also abide by the convention.* For only when they act as others do (for example, when everyone drives on the same side of the road) can they coordinate their behavior accordingly.

This motivational requirement effectively precludes the possibility of widespread official alienation. Suppose most judges accept their appointment to the bench simply in order to collect their paychecks. They have absolutely no interest in whether others follow the rule of recognition as well; they simply care about whether they themselves follow the rule, for only in that way will they be compensated. Since these alienated officials are not motivated by the desire to conform their behavior to that of their colleagues, they cannot be engaged in a coordination convention. They are like third basemen who draw near for bunts: each of them recognizes that he has reasons to do what he does that are quite independent from whether others do likewise.

Proponents of the CCI, therefore, must maintain that a legal regime largely staffed by alienated officials is impossible. For if it were possible, the social practice of rule recognition that structured such a regime would not be a coordination convention, and hence not a practice*. Yet precluding the existence of this kind of regime is ad hoc: it is motivated solely by the desire to save the theory and not by any other independent consideration.

Arbitrariness and Convention

As we have seen, the CCI unjustifiably rules out the possibility of widespread alienation among officials. Paradoxically, it also precludes as conceptually possible regimes on the opposite end of the motivational spectrum. As I would now like to show, social practices involving fundamentalists of a certain stripe might also fail to be coordination conventions.

Let us begin by noting a special feature of all coordination problems, which is that their solutions are arbitrary.[42] They are arbitrary in the sense that individual preferences that all act on a certain solution can always be "flipped" to some other solution simply by changing the background behavioral assumption: if everyone prefers that everyone act on some combination of choices (because almost everyone acts this way), everyone would prefer that everyone act on some different combination under the supposition that almost everyone acts in this different way instead. For example, preferences for everyone riding on the right could always be changed to the left if it were supposed that almost everyone rides on the left instead.

According to the CCI, the choice of an authority structure is a recurring coordination problem. As a result, the CCI is committed to the view that all officials will see the solutions as arbitrary in the sense just described. But is this assumption plausible? Is it true that in every legal system, everyone's preference for heeding some set of authorities would change if it were supposed that everyone acted differently? This, I think, is rather doubtful. Consider, for example, the Ancient Hebrews. They absolutely believed that the Old Testament was the literal word of God. Surely many, if not most, would not have preferred to follow a different text just in case everyone else did. Indeed, this thought would have been heretical!

In fact, I am not even sure that most Americans would view the United States Constitution as an arbitrary solution to a recurring coordination problem. My guess is that many would believe that the text of the Constitution is sacred and that they had a moral obligation to heed it, regardless of what everyone else did. Many officials would probably also share such an attitude. If most officials suddenly abandoned the United

States Constitution, this would not lead all others to similar action. Some would resign in protest, while others would continue applying the rules validly enacted under the United States Constitution. To be sure, if the French Constitution had been ratified instead, these judges would prefer following the French, instead of the United States, Constitution. But since the United States Constitution was ratified, they prefer to follow it and it alone.

I am not denying that many individuals in many legal systems regard their authority structure as arbitrary in some way and hence prefer agreement on such structures to disagreement. The point is that it does not seem to be conceptually necessary that such an attitude be universally held. The CCI, of course, must deny that a regime of fundamentalists of the kind I have described is possible. For in those (possible or actual) legal systems where individuals do not view selected authority structures as arbitrary, the selection of an authority structure will not constitute a recurring coordination problem, and hence the convergence on one such structure will not constitute a coordination convention. The positivist adherent of the CCI would therefore give us no reason to believe that every social practice of rule recognition is a practice*, thereby undermining their solution to the Possibility Puzzle.

As we have seen, the Coordination Convention Interpretation unduly restricts the types of reasons that officials may have for accepting the rule of recognition. It cannot countenance regimes largely staffed by alienated hacks or constitutional fundamentalists. In this respect, the Coordination Convention account represents a jurisprudential step backward. As we saw, Hart's original theory is ecumenical with respect to the reasons officials have for accepting the rule of recognition. Judges can take the internal point of view simply in order to pick up their paychecks, or they might believe that their practice is perfect and would accept no substitutes. The CCI has no justification for ruling out these possibilities.

Legal, Normative, Moral

As we have seen, Hart's Practice Theory cannot help solve the Possibility Puzzle. The original version fails for the simple reason that being a social practice is neither identical to being, nor sufficient to generate, a social rule. The modified form of the theory, which treats the social practice of rule recognition as a coordination convention, is also flawed, because it indefensibly restricts the kinds of motivation that officials may possess for engaging in legal practice.

Having rejected Hart's solution to the Possibility Puzzle, we should examine his response to Hume's Challenge. Since the latter is largely independent of the former, and constitutes a fascinating philosophical position in its own right, it behooves us to consider it seriously. Can Hart's expressivist theory save legal positivism from the charge that it derives an ought from an is?

In this section, we will see that it cannot. The problem with Hart's expressivism is that it cannot account for certain features of legal thought and discourse. Even when people do not accept the law from the internal point of view, it is always possible for them to figure out the content of the law and to describe legal rules using the familiar normative terminology of "obligation," "rights," and "validity." The fact that even the bad man can engage in legal reasoning, despite his alienation from legal practice, strongly suggests that legal judgments can be made without taking the internal point of view. If so, then the bad man will have derived a normative judgment from purely descriptive ones, and will have violated Hume's Law in the process.

We will also see that Hart's attempt at preserving the distinction between legal and moral thought stakes out a middle ground that is unstable and unsupportable. For once it is admitted that legal concepts are normative, it becomes difficult to deny, as Hart did, that they are moral as well. The claims of law are far too serious to accept the possibility that they are amoral in nature.

The Redescribability of Law and Openness of Legal Reasoning

According to Hart's response, Hume's Challenge erroneously assumes that there is only one way to orient oneself toward a social practice. It assumes, in other words, that social facts can be approached only theoretically, as the object of a descriptive judgment. As Hart argues, this objection ignores the possibility of approaching social facts practically, as reasons for action. Normative judgments, on this view, are not apprehensions of normative facts, but rather commitments to giving descriptive facts certain weight in one's deliberations. Thus, one may take the internal point of view toward the social practice of rule recognition and, in so doing, treat it as a standard for guidance and evaluation. The normative judgments that are formed through this practical engagement with social practice can then be used to derive other normative judgments about legal rights, obligations, and validity. Legal reasoning in a positivistic framework does not, therefore, violate Hume's Law, insofar as legal judgments are derived only from other, similarly normative judgments.

Hart's solution to Hume's Challenge, we can see, depends critically on the assumption that legal reasoners always engage practically with the social facts of legal practice when deriving legal conclusions. Unfortunately, this account fares no better than the Practice Theory. For as I will show, legal judgments can be coherently formed and expressed even when the judger does not take the internal point of view toward the system's rule of recognition.

Consider the bad man. For him, the law provides the same basic reason to act that the gunman generates, namely, the avoidance of sanctions. He follows the law out of rational self-interest, because he is "obliged" to do so. Note, however, that the bad man is able to recharacterize the law using an alternative vocabulary. While the bad man may describe the law in the same terms that he would use vis-à-vis a mugging—"I was obliged to hand over the money"—he can also accurately *re*describe the former using the language of obligation. He might say not only that the law obliges him to pay his taxes, but also that he is *legally obligated* to do so. That is, he can describe the tax laws not only as the expression of wishes backed by threats of sanctions, but also as rules that impose legal duties.

Call this law's "redescribability." Even when the law is no better than the gunman, it is always possible to accurately redescribe its content using normative terminology. This is so even when the asserter does not take the internal point of view toward the secondary rules of the system. The bad man does not accept these norms but can nonetheless truthfully redescribe the law in terms of obligations, rights, and legal validity.

The bad man not only can talk the talk; he can think the thought. He too can "think like a lawyer." Legal reasoning, we might say, is a remarkably open process. Even those who judge the law morally illegitimate, or reject it for self-interested reasons, can figure out what the law demands of them. Indeed, it would be bizarre if the only people who could understand the law were those who accepted it. The law claims the right to demand compliance from everyone, even those who reject its demands.

Unfortunately, Hart cannot explain either the redescribability of the law or the openness of legal reasoning. On his expressivist theory, the law can be described as imposing obligations, conferring rights, and validating rules only when the asserter accepts the system's rule of recognition. However, the bad man can redescribe the law using normative terminology, even though he takes the external point of view. Similarly, legal reasoning makes sense in a Hartian framework only when the reasoner accepts a particular rule of recognition. But the bad man does not engage with the law in a practical manner, yet he is still able to derive the content of the law. On Hart's account, legal reasoning turns out to be a highly discriminatory process: only good people can engage in it.[43]

That Hart's theory cannot account for the bad man's behavior seriously undermines his response to Hume's Challenge. Insofar as the bad man is *bad,* he does not engage practically with the regularity among officials. This practice of recognition is merely the object of a descriptive judgment, not a normative judgment to treat it as a standard of conduct and evaluation. Despite the lack of practical engagement, he is able to figure out the law of his jurisdiction and characterize it using standard legal terminology. He is able, in other words, to derive a normative judgment from a purely descriptive one. Since the reasoning of the bad man follows the DINO pattern, it violates Hume's Law.[44]

An Unstable Compromise

As we saw, Hart's response to Hume's Challenge threatens to efface the distinction between the legal and the moral. If legal judgments and claims are normative judgments and claims, how is critique of the law possible? Hart's solution is to regard legal concepts such as AUTHORITY and OBLIGATION as normative, but not moral. To judge that someone is legally obligated to pay taxes is not to judge that she has a moral obligation to do so. Likewise, he thought that the corresponding normative terms, that is, "authority" and "obligation," have different meanings depending on their context. By claiming that law and morality do not share the same stock of concepts and words, Hart thought he could explain how someone can impute legal obligations to others despite denying that they are morally obligated to act accordingly.

Unfortunately, this compromise is unsustainable. For the same argument that compels us to treat legal concepts and terminology as normative, not descriptive, demands that we regard them as moral as well. As we pointed out at the end of last chapter, legal concepts and terminology play a characteristic role in social life: they are used to guide and evaluate conduct. Legal concepts are used to make demands, issue recommendations, state reasons, assess behavior, and justify punitive action. Since descriptive concepts and terms are used to represent the way things are, rather than the way they ought to be, they cannot play such a justificatory and evaluative role. Hence, we concluded, legal concepts and terms cannot be descriptive in nature.

But once we recognize the social role that legal concepts are typically made to play, it becomes hard to resist the conclusion that these concepts must be moral as well.[45] For concepts such as AUTHORITY and OBLIGATION are characteristically employed in contexts where moral notions are uniquely apt, namely, where the conduct being guided and evaluated is contrary to our self-interest, requires considerable sacrifice, significantly affects the lives of others, and subjects the actor to punishment and censure for failure to comply. Thus, claims of legal authority and obligation are not merely used to guide conduct; they are used to make demands that materially constrain freedom. They are not used simply to assess behavior; they are employed to assess guilt, blame the guilty, and ground coercive and punitive responses. In other words, we are not talking here about demands to go to jail in Monopoly, stand up when an elder enters the room, or avoid splitting infinitives. In legal contexts, we require people to pay their taxes, join the army, pass difficult licensing exams before practicing a profession, and testify in a criminal trial, under the threat of jail or heavy fines. Only moral concepts have the heft to make such serious claims.

The striking fact that law and morality use many words that sound the same, therefore, is not a sheer coincidence. As we have just seen, treating this overlap as a shared vocabulary and conceptual scheme makes sense of legal thought and discourse. For only moral terms and concepts enable law-abiding citizens and officials to make the claims and form the thoughts that are appropriate to the context.

Indeed, similar considerations also defeat Hart's particular account of the normative nature of legal concepts and terms. According to Hart, to judge that X is legally obligated to do A is to judge it proper to demand X to do A and to extract performance from X in case of disobedience. However, as Joseph Raz has noted, Hart's account seems like a throwback to Kelsen's theory.[46] For both treat the law as primarily concerned with the propriety of official behavior, rather than the actions of subjects. As a result, Hart's account is subject to the very same criticism that he leveled against Kelsen, namely, that it misconstrues the intended audience of the law. Subjects, not officials, are the primary objects of legal guidance and evaluation. Thus, when officials guide and evaluate conduct, they form judgments and make claims about the conduct their subjects should perform. Statements about X's legal obligations to do A are statements about *X's* reasons to do A, not the official's reasons for demanding that X do A.

We can see that Hart's attempt to distinguish the legal from the moral is seriously flawed. For once we focus on the role that legal judgments and claims play in social life, it becomes hard to deny that they are constituted not only by normative concepts and terms, but by moral ones as well. Ironically, then, Hart's solution to Hume's Challenge actually undermines the positivistic project. For if legal judgments are normative judgments, they must be moral judgments as well. And if they are moral judgments, then the critique of the law whose very possibility positivists hoped to secure would forever be beyond their reach.

Where Now?

One of the principal lessons of Hart's jurisprudential theory is that legal systems are not only composed of rules, but founded on them as well. For as he painstakingly showed, we cannot account for the way in which we talk and think about the law—that is, as an institution that persists over time despite turnover of officials, imposes duties and confers powers, enjoys supremacy over other kinds of practices, resolves doubts and disagreements about what is to be done in a community, and so on—without supposing that it is at bottom regulated by what he called the secondary rules of recognition, change, and adjudication.

While Hart was plainly correct in emphasizing the importance of the secondary rules, and thus greatly advanced our understanding of law, he was unfortunately less successful in explaining how these secondary rules are brought into existence. His attempt to solve the Possibility Puzzle by reducing the fundamental rules of a legal system to the social practice of legal officials fails for the simple reason that rules and practices belong to different metaphysical categories. Nor, as we have seen, can his practice-based theory be amended in a suitable way. For not all social practices give rise to social rules, and those that do, such as co-ordination conventions, are nonexistent in regimes where legal officials have certain kinds of motivations.

Nor was Hart more successful in explaining how his positivistic theory of law survives Hume's Challenge. By arguing that a descriptive fact may be the object of a normative judgment, he did manage to show how the good person can engage in legal reasoning within a positivistic framework. Unfortunately, Hart could not perform a similar service for the bad man. For the bad man does not accept the norms of legal practice and hence, according to Hart's theory, should not be able to figure out the content of the law.[47]

Moreover, Hart's attempt to preserve the distinction between legal and moral thought and discourse ultimately results in an unstable compromise. For once we concede that legal judgments are normative, we should admit that they are moral as well. In the legal sphere, where demands, sacrifice, coercion, and blame are commonplace, there are no amoral concepts of authority and obligation and hence no middle ground between the descriptive and the moral that positivists can call their own.

While I have argued in this chapter that Hart's particular solutions to the Possibility Puzzle and Hume's Challenge must be rejected, I do not mean to suggest that we have nothing to learn from his efforts. Quite the contrary, I believe that the basics of the Hartian approach are sound. For Hart was right to claim that the fundamental rules of a legal system come into being by virtue of the *commitments* of legal officials. And he was correct to claim that the judgments formed by legal officials are, in some important sense, *evaluations* and that these evaluations need not reflect the officials' own moral point of view.

The problem with Hart's solutions to the jurisprudential puzzles lies not in these core insights, but in the specific ways he tried to elaborate them. Thus, Hart's solution to the Possibility Puzzle assumes that any generic commitment to a standard of conduct by members of a group is sufficient to generate a social rule, a premise we have seen is unfortunately false. Likewise, Hart concluded from the facts that legal judgments are evaluations and not moral endorsements that they must be normative, but amoral, judgments. We have seen that this idea is also mistaken.

If legal positivists are to offer plausible solutions to the jurisprudential puzzles, they must find a way to work out these core Hartian insights differently than Hart did. They must pinpoint the specific kind of commitments that generate social rules and show how legal judgments can be constituted by moral concepts without requiring the legal reasoner to morally endorse the judgments formed. Whether this strategy can be vindicated is a matter to which we will now turn.

5

HOW TO DO THINGS WITH PLANS

A Fresh Start

From childhood on, we are taught that there is a crucial difference between that which others think is right or wrong and what *is* right or wrong. Just because everyone does it does not mean that we should do it. We are repeatedly told that the rules of ethical behavior apply to us regardless of whether other people accept them as well.

But in the realm of law, the legal positivist claims, this admonition is out of place. What is *legally* right or wrong *does* depend on other people and certain other people in particular. According to H. L. A. Hart, if judges accept a rule requiring you to jump off the proverbial bridge, then it is legally wrong for you *not* to plunge into the icy waters below.

This claim follows from the positivist's picture of morality and law as distinct domains with correspondingly distinct ground rules. According to this picture, the proper way to establish the existence of moral rules is to engage in substantive moral argument. It is never enough simply to say, "That's what we do around here."[1] While a convention may of course be morally relevant, it is because some moral fact ultimately deems it to be so. In the case of law, on the other hand, rules must satisfy the specific criteria for legal validity, and these criteria can only be discovered through empirical observations of the relevant legal communities. To divine the set of legally valid rules, in other words, one must know what legal officials think, intend, claim, and do. For the legal positivist, it is simply irrelevant to point out that these criteria of validity are morally illegitimate, or that they sanction undesirable rules. Regardless of the merits, the law is just what certain people think, intend, claim, and do around here.

In the past two chapters we rehearsed various arguments legal positivists have used to buttress their story and found them lacking. In the

118

next two chapters, I want to present an alternative to these arguments, which I believe captures the power of the positivistic picture of law while also addressing the important limitations we noted earlier. My strategy is to show that there is another realm whose norms can only be discovered through social, not moral, observation, namely, the realm of *planning*. The proper way to establish the existence of plans, as I argue below, is simply to point to the fact of their adoption and acceptance. Whether I have a plan to go to the store today, or we have a plan to cook dinner together tonight, depends not on the desirability of these plans but simply on whether we have in fact adopted (and not yet rejected) them. In other words, positivism is trivially and uncontroversially true in the case of plans: the existence of a plan is one thing, its merits or demerits quite another.

As I hope will become clear in what follows, my purpose here is not to draw an analogy between laws and plans but to flesh out an implication. The existence conditions for law are the same as those for plans because the fundamental rules of legal systems *are* plans. Their function is to structure legal activity so that participants can work together and thereby achieve goods and realize values that would otherwise be unattainable. For that reason, the existence of legal authority can only be determined *sociologically*: the question of whether a body has legal power is never one of its moral legitimacy; it is a question of whether the relevant officials of that system accept a plan that authorizes and requires deference to that body.

I am going to argue here that understanding fundamental laws as plans not only vindicates the positivist conception of law but provides a compelling solution to our earlier puzzle about how legal authority is possible. For the picture that emerges is one in which the creation and persistence of the fundamental rules of law is grounded in the capacity that all individuals possess to adopt plans. As I attempt to show, this power is not conferred on us by morality. On the contrary, it is a manifestation of the fact that we are planning creatures. As the philosopher Michael Bratman has shown in his groundbreaking work on intention and action, human beings have a special kind of psychology: we not only have desires to achieve complex goals, but we also have the capacity to settle on such goals and to organize our behavior over time and between persons to attain them.

Building on Bratman's insights, I want to show that understanding the law entails understanding our special psychology and the norms of rationality that regulate its proper functioning. For that reason, I am going to spend a significant amount of time describing the activity of planning, the structure of plans, the motivation for creating plans, and the rationality constraints that attend this activity. I will begin by constructing simple hypotheticals involving one person planning his own actions and then move on to more complicated examples, such as group planning in hierarchical and nonhierarchical contexts among both small and large numbers of people.

One of my main goals in this chapter is to show that planning is a surprisingly diverse activity. Not only can it be carried out in very different ways, but it comprises many distinct stages. In fact, multiple individuals can engage in the very same planning process: one person can formulate a plan, another can adopt it, and a third can apply the plan. Plans are also complex entities: they have a rich structure and assume diverse forms. As our hypotheticals will illustrate, planners are able to combine different kinds of plans to construct new and sophisticated technologies of planning, which enable participants in shared activities to navigate complex, contentious, and arbitrary environments.

In the next chapter, I want to develop my central argument that legal activity is best understood as social planning and that legal rules themselves constitute *plans,* or *planlike* norms. I realize that this claim is not self-evidently true, and the relationship between legality and planning is not yet apparent. But as the nature of planning becomes more explicit, and our examples become more complex, the connection between the two phenomena will become clearer. Or at least that is the plan.

Individual Planning

The Partiality of Plans

I am sitting at my desk in my office and thinking about what to do for dinner tonight. Should I eat out or cook dinner at home? Since I feel a bit guilty about having frequented restaurants so often lately, I decide on the latter option. I now have a plan, namely, to cook dinner at home tonight. Admittedly, it is not much of a plan, because I have no food at home to cook. So the question with which I started—where to eat?—has been replaced with a new query: where should I get food to cook?

I respond to this new query by forming an intention to buy the food from a supermarket. And so I now have two plans: one to cook dinner tonight and one to buy food at the supermarket. These plans are clearly related to one another. Buying food at the supermarket is a means to cooking dinner at home tonight. When one plan specifies a means for accomplishing, or a way of realizing, the end fixed by another plan, we will say that it is a "subplan" of the second. Thus, the plan to buy food at the supermarket is a subplan of the initial plan to cook dinner tonight.

Of course, by adopting these two plans, I have also created a third plan, namely, the plan to cook dinner *by* buying food at the supermarket. This larger plan, we might say, has two parts to it: the first is the plan to cook dinner tonight and the second is the plan to buy food for dinner at the supermarket. These parts are related as means to end: the second part is a subplan of the first.

As Michael Bratman has shown, planning typically involves the creation of these larger plans.[2] When I initially form my intention to cook dinner tonight, my plan simply identifies my end goal. But if my plan is going to work—that is, if it is to organize my behavior so that I may attain the goal I set for myself—I have to specify the means as well. I must decide which meal to make, what kind of food to buy, where and when to buy it, whether to make enough for leftovers, which knife to use when preparing the food, and so on.

Bratman notes that these larger plans are typically partial. They begin as empty shells and, as more details are added, they become more comprehensive and useful. Plans are almost never exhaustive because there is rarely a need for a full specification of every step necessary to achieve a goal. My plan to cook dinner tonight will not specify the correct way to hold the knife when I cut the food because I can accomplish the task without deliberation or reflection.

As plans are filled in, they thus naturally assume a nested structure. My plan to make dinner tonight specifies the overall goal I wish to achieve. My plan to buy food from a supermarket, as we mentioned, is a subplan of the overall plan of making dinner. My intention to buy chicken at the supermarket after work is, in turn, a subplan of the plan to buy food at the supermarket and, thus, a sub-subplan of the overall plan to cook dinner tonight.

The nested structure of plans explains how past deliberation shapes present planning. When constructing my plan, I take my prior decisions about means and ends as given. These plans and subplans are settled and not up for reconsideration. Rather, my present deliberation is confined solely to those options that are not ruled out by past decisions. If I have decided to go to Stop & Shop to buy food, I figure out how to get there, not whether it might be better to go to Pathmark instead.

As Bratman points out, plans not only organize our behavior, they also organize our thinking about how to organize our behavior.[3] The planner sets ends to be achieved and determines which means are best suited to achieve those ends. Once selected, these means are treated as new ends and lead the planner to determine which new means ought to be adopted. By fleshing out plans in this manner, the planner ensures that, according to his beliefs, he will perform all the necessary actions in the right sequence and thus realize the overall ends of the plan.

Planning Ahead

Clearly, if we did not seek to achieve complex ends, there would be no need to engage in planning about the future. Planning is a core component of human agency because we have desires for many ends that demand substantial coordination. But there is another aspect of our psychology that compels us to plan, namely, that our rationality is limited. If we were like chess computers, able to look ahead millions of moves on each turn and choose the best play among the myriad alternatives, we might have little use for planning. Since we are not, however, mentally omnipotent, and rational deliberation is costly, we must conserve our energies. I cannot spend every second of the day thinking about what to do and reviewing every one of my past judgments or I would never get anything done. It is often far more efficient to decide on a course of action beforehand and follow it when the time for action arrives.

Planning ahead is not, however, solely an economizing measure; we often plan out of a lack of trust in our future selves. Deliberation is a risky endeavor. If I were to engage only in on-the-spot reasoning about what I ought to do, I would almost certainly find myself at times in a poor state to make decisions. I would lack the composure, energy, and will either to think through all of the possibilities or to resist temptation. Making up my mind well in advance allows me to compensate for the lack of trust in myself: I can pick a good occasion for reflection, one that provides ample time to puzzle things out, and use the opportunity to choose the best course of action.

We have good reason, therefore, to be planners: planning guides and organizes our behavior over time, enabling us to achieve ends that we might not be able to achieve otherwise. As Bratman has argued, this pragmatic rationale for planning suggests that the activity is subject to several different norms of rationality.[4] Suppose that having decided to make dinner at home tonight, I do not give that decision any more thought. I do not contemplate how I am going to pull off this feat, for example, where to get the food, what to eat, and when to cook. These omissions would be irrational because I would not be able to achieve the end that I set for myself. I cannot just *cook dinner*. Cooking dinner is not a simple action like raising my arm—it is a multistep process, requiring that I make preparations, string numerous actions together, and perform them in the proper order.

When we set ends for ourselves, rationality thus demands that we flesh out our plans. Of course we need not settle all outstanding issues at once. While I should soon decide when to buy the food for dinner, I can probably wait until I arrive at the supermarket to decide what to make and how much to cook. And I certainly can wait until I get to the kitchen before settling on which knife to use. Indeed, there is a pragmatic argument for leaving certain aspects of plans open until the time for action nears. Settling on a course of conduct far ahead of time in the absence of complete information is a risky thing to do. By leaving our plans for future actions somewhat sketchy, we provide the measure of flexibility necessary to enable us to fill in the details as our visibility substantially improves.

Strictly speaking, rationality does not demand that the planners formulate courses of action *themselves*. Others may tailor the means and communicate the plan to the person committed to the end in question. My foodie friend may tell me what food to buy and how to cook it. Rationality does not forbid taking instruction from others; indeed, it requires it when they are more reliable or when doing so is economical. When we say that planners are rationally obligated to "fill in" their plans, we mean they are required to *adopt* the means to their ends, not that they are required to figure out what those means are themselves.

Rationality not only demands that we fill in our plans over time; it also counsels us to settle on plans of actions that are internally consistent and consistent with each other. In this respect, plans are different from desires. Desires may conflict, but plans must not. There is nothing irrational about wanting both to lose weight and to have dessert, but it is incoherent to go on a no-dessert diet and, at the same time, order dessert. In the same way, one's plans must be consistent with one's beliefs about the world. One should not adopt a plan that one believes cannot successfully be carried out. Again, these consistency demands are supported by the pragmatic rationale for planning: consistency within plans is necessary if we are to achieve the ends of the plan; consistency between plans is necessary if we are to achieve the ends of all our plans; and consistency with one's beliefs ensures that the plans we have adopted can be achieved in the world in which we find ourselves.

Finally, if planning is to compensate for our limited cognitive capacities and reduce deliberation costs, our plans must be fairly stable, which is to say that they must be reasonably resistant to reconsideration. Suppose on my way home from the office I ask myself, "Should I eat out or at home?" After thinking about the issue, and weighing the ease of dining out against the economy of eating in, I settle on the same option I chose earlier, namely, cooking dinner at home. My reconsideration of the issue of where to eat, therefore, rendered my prior decision moot. I did not derive any benefit from my earlier planning, for I ended up engaging in the same thought processes that I followed earlier.

To be sure, choosing a plan does not set it in stone. Reconsideration is rational when, but only when, there is good enough reason for it. If I find out, for example, that the power is off at home, then I *should,* of course, reconsider my earlier decision. If nothing much has changed, however, it would be irrational to upend my earlier judgment. It would defeat the purpose of having plans if I were to review their wisdom without an otherwise compelling reason to do so.

Top-Down vs. Bottom-Up Planning

As we saw in the last section, planning never occurs in a vacuum. Past decisions form a framework that constrains and guides present deliberation. When a rational planner contemplates whether to pursue a certain end, she attempts to determine whether the goal can be achieved in a manner compatible with this framework of prior decision making.

In fleshing out her plans, the planner may pursue one of two options: "top-down" or "bottom-up" planning. In instances of top-down planning, the planner starts with the overall action to achieve (cook dinner) and breaks it up into a few major tasks (buy food, cook food, clean up). She then refines each major task into its component parts (buy food: drive to store, select food, buy food, load car, and drive home). The planner continues this process of refinement at each step until she reaches a point at which the relevant actions can be accomplished without further planning (get in car, start car, make right at State Street, and so on).

In cases of bottom-up planning, the planner starts with a vague sense of the goals to be achieved (I want soup for dinner though not sure what else to eat) and proceeds to think through the lower-level tasks in great detail (make the stock: fill pot with water; throw in carrots, celery, onions, and chicken; skim when it boils; simmer for one hour). Any decision to carry out a simple task in a certain way constrains how other simple tasks will be carried out (making chicken stock requires going to a market that sells chickens). Once other basic tasks are planned, she attempts to combine them to see whether they fit together. They might fail to connect up for two reasons: either they are inconsistent with each other (it may not be possible to get to Safeway and cook the soup in the available time) or they are consistent, but insufficient, to accomplish any higher-level task (something more must be added to the stock to make soup). In the first case, consistency must be restored through fiddling with one or both of the conflicting tasks (go to Pathmark instead). In the second case, new lower-level tasks must be added to achieve the necessary effect (add rice to stock). Once the subplans are adjusted, the new higher-level tasks are then combined to see whether they fit together (is there enough time to make the rice? is soup enough for dinner?). The process of planning ends when all the tasks settled on are sufficient to achieve the ultimate goal.

Bottom-up planning is especially useful when the planner is unsure which tasks she must undertake or how they all will hang together. In such cases, she cannot start from her main aim and methodically work her way down the planning tree because she lacks an abstract appreciation of how the various tasks connect up. By starting with lower-level tasks whose contours she understands, her detailed planning of one part of the project constrains how the closely related tasks must be performed. She can proceed to fill in adjacent slots, moving slowly across and up the planning hierarchy and eventually establishing a coherent and complete plan of action.

The downside of bottom-up planning is that the ordering of tasks is not informed by a full sense of the overall structure of the activity. Too much attention to low-level detail may unwittingly cause the planner to lose the forest for the trees and result in plans that are riddled with inconsistencies, gaps, and redundancies. By contrast, if the functional shape of the project is well understood, a top-down approach is usually more appropriate. To be sure, planning in real life usually combines elements of both top-down and bottom-up planning, with the best mix determined by how well the planner understands the nature of the activity she intends to perform.

Applying Plans

There would be no point in making plans if we did not use them to guide our conduct. If my cooking plan is to be useful to me, it is not enough to formulate and adopt it: I must apply it as well.

As I employ the term, to "apply" a plan means to use it to guide or evaluate conduct. A plan is applied prospectively when it is used to determine which actions are required, permitted, or authorized in the circumstances; a plan is applied retrospectively when it is employed to assess whether an action conformed, or failed to conform, to the plan in question. (A note of caution: sometimes, when we say that we are "applying" a plan, we mean that we are carrying it out. Thus, I apply my chicken-on-sale plan when I actually buy the chicken because it is on sale. When I speak of "applying" plans, however, I will be referring to the use of plans to guide or evaluate action, reserving "carrying out" for the process of following through on them.)

Applying a plan is a three-step process. The plan applier must determine (1) the content of the plan, (2) the context of its application, and (3) how to conform to the plan in that context. Thus, if I apply my plan during the afternoon, I must decide what that plan is ("to cook dinner tonight"), what the world is like (for example, do I have enough food to cook?), and what I should do to execute the plan at that point (must head out soon to buy food). The planner might find out that the plan is not applicable to a particular situation, in which case there is nothing that the plan requires, permits, or authorizes the subject to do or not to do.

Just as someone need not formulate a plan she adopts, she need not apply it herself either. If I ask the butcher for a pot roast at the supermarket, my friend might say to me, "Wait, I thought you told me that you were going to buy the chicken if it's on sale, and look, it's on sale." My friend, thus, applied my plan for me.

Regardless of who applies the plan, rationality requires that the plan adopter make sure that *someone* does. To adopt a plan and not use it, or use it incorrectly, is irrational. In other words, a planner is subject to criticism when she forgets that she adopted a certain plan, cannot figure out the content of the plan, does not bother to find out what the world is like, fails to use her beliefs to determine the application of the plan, uses these beliefs incorrectly, or simply does not carry out the plan that she believes applies.

In order to determine the content of the plan, the planner must be careful not to engage in deliberation about its merits. As we have seen, the value of a plan is that it does the thinking for us. If in order to determine the content of my cooking plan I had to deliberate about whether I should cook dinner tonight, then adopting my plan would have been useless. Plans cannot do the thinking for us if, in order to discover their counsel, we are required to repeat the same sort of reasoning.[5]

Plans and Norms

Let me end this section on individual planning by saying a few words about what I mean by the term "plan." By a "plan," I am not referring to the mental state of "having a plan." Intentions are not plans, but rather take plans as their objects. For my purposes, plans are abstract propositional entities that require, permit, or authorize agents to act, or not act, in certain ways under certain conditions.

In Chapter 2, I characterized a norm as an abstract object that functions as a guide for conduct and a standard for evaluation. In keeping with this characterization, plans too are norms. They are guides for conduct, insofar as their function is to pick out courses of action that are required, permitted, or authorized under certain circumstances. They are also standards for evaluation, insofar as they are supposed to be used as measures of correct conduct, if not by others then at least by the subjects of the plans themselves.

When a person adopts a personal plan, she thus places herself under the governance of a norm. This power of self-governance is conferred on her by the principles of instrumental rationality. Planning creatures, in other words, have the rational capacity to subject themselves to norms. Indeed, this capacity explains the efficacy of planning. Planning psychology is unique not only because it enables planners to form mental states that control future conduct but insofar as it enables them to recognize that the formation of these states generates rational pressure to act accordingly. Thus, when an individual adopts a self-governing plan, the disposition to follow through is not akin to a brute reflex; it is instead mediated by the recognition that the plan is a justified standard of conduct and imposes a rational requirement to carry it out.

While all plans are norms, not all norms are plans. The laws of logic and the principles of morality, for example, are norms but they are not usually considered plans. Plans are "positive" entities—they are created via adoption and sustained through acceptance. By contrast, logical and moral norms exist simply by virtue of their ultimate validity. They are not created by anyone. Plans are also typically partial norms that are supposed to be fleshed out over time, whereas it makes no sense to talk about incrementally developing the laws of logic or morality.

Plans are also purposive entities. They are norms that are not only created, but are created *to be norms*. I adopted a plan to cook dinner tonight precisely so that it would guide my conduct in the direction of cooking dinner. Customary norms, on the other hand, may exist even though they were not created in order to be used in decision making. The practice of eating turkey on Thanksgiving, for example, may have arisen spontaneously and not for the purpose of getting people to choose to eat turkey on Thanksgiving.

In general, we can say that a norm is a plan as long as it was created by a process that is supposed to create norms. In the case of individual planning, the process is the psychological activity of intending. In institutional contexts, however, as we will see in the next chapter, a plan may be created even though the one who adopted it did not intend to create a norm. As long as the institutionally prescribed procedure is followed, he will be acting in accordance with a process that is supposed to create norms and will therefore be capable of adopting a plan.

While all plans are positive purposive norms, not all positive purposive norms are plans. Threats are created by human action, and are created to guide action, but they are not typically structured norms: unlike plans, they are not characteristically partial, composite, or nested. More importantly, these norms are not meant to guide conduct by settling questions about how to act, nor do they purport to settle such questions. Threats are merely supposed to be, and purport to be, one factor among many to be considered. It shows no irrationality or disrespect to deliberate about whether to capitulate to a threat—the gunman, after all, gives you a choice: "Your money or your life." By contrast, when one has adopted a plan, for oneself or for another person, the plan is supposed to preempt deliberations about its merits, as well as purporting to provide a reason to preempt deliberations about its merits.

Finally, a norm is a plan only if it is created by a process that disposes the subjects of a norm to follow it. If I plan to cook dinner tonight, I will be disposed to cook dinner tonight. This does not entail that I *will* cook dinner, only that under normal conditions I will. It follows then that decisions that do not instill dispositions in their subjects to comply do not generate plans. If a madman "plans" to withdraw the United States Army from Iraq, no withdrawal plan exists because the madman's decisions have absolutely no effect on troop movements.

To conclude, a plan is a special kind of norm. First, it has a typical structure, namely, it is partial, composite, and nested. Second, it is created by a certain kind of process, namely, one that is incremental, is purposive, and disposes subjects to comply with the norms created. Third, it is supposed to settle, and purports to settle, questions about what is to be done.

Planning for Small-Scale Shared Activities

My Part and Your Part

Having decided that I will cook dinner at home, it occurs to me that it would be fun to cook with someone else. I therefore call up my friend Henry, invite him over to cook together, and he agrees. We now have a plan: that is, to cook dinner together tonight.

Of course, this plan won't be of much use to us unless we fill it in. But here matters become complicated. Whereas I was previously able to resolve all issues regarding cooking by myself, I must now consult Henry, at least with respect to the major tasks. It would be unfair, not to mention rude, to decide unilaterally what we are going to eat, when we should start cooking, and so on. In addition, we have a new set of questions that must be answered, such as who should get the food, who should cook which part of the meal, who should clean up, and so on. Planning for two involves organizing behavior not only across time but between persons as well.

Let's say that Henry and I decide to cook fish and make a salad. I opt to get the fish and he opts to get the ingredients for the salad. How many plans do we now have (or, as I will sometimes say, how many plans do we now *share*)? Again, the answer depends. In one sense, we have adopted five plans: we cook dinner together tonight; we cook fish together tonight; we make a salad together tonight; I get the fish before dinner; you get the salad ingredients before dinner.

In another sense, we share only one plan, namely, the plan to cook dinner together tonight. Cooking fish and making salad together are subplans of the overall plan of cooking dinner together. We cook dinner together *by* cooking fish and making salad together. Likewise, my purchasing the fish before dinner is a subplan of our cooking fish together tonight, Henry's procuring the salad ingredients before dinner is a subplan of our making salad together, and each is a sub-subplan of the overall plan of cooking together tonight.

As the foregoing suggests, the structure of shared plans is similar to that of individual plans. Shared plans too are typically partial: they are developed over time, beginning with a settling of ends and a progressive divvying up of steps each member is to take. Shared plans are also normally composite: they have parts that are themselves plans. Our plan to cook dinner, for example, includes plans to buy and cook the food. Finally, shared plans are usually nested: they identify the overall end to be achieved by the group and specify in their subplans the parts that everyone is to take. When fleshing out how we are to cook dinner together, we take our cooking together as settled and deliberate only about which courses of action each of us should take so that our combined activity adds up to tonight's dinner.

Planning for the Group

Although planning for a group can be a complicated affair, especially when it is also performed *by* a group, the benefits of planning normally outweigh the costs. As with individual planning, participants in a group activity will not always be able to ponder the optimality of their next move. Since Henry and I are not high-tech deliberation machines, programmed for precisely this purpose, we need to map out some of our actions beforehand so that when the time for execution arrives we can each consult our respective parts of the shared plan and proceed accordingly.

There are, nonetheless, reasons to plan for the group that are quite independent of these benefits of planning ahead. To see what they are, let us begin by considering the advantages of acting together. According to David Hume, "When every individual person labours a-part, and only for himself, his force is too small to execute any considerable work; his labour being employ'd in supplying all his different necessities, he never attains a perfection in any particular art; and as his force and success are not at all times equal, the least failure in either of these particulars must be attended with inevitable ruin and misery."[6] As Hume points out, individual effort is often too feeble, amateurish, or risky to accomplish many of the ends we wish to accomplish (think of building a house all by yourself). By pooling efforts in an orderly fashion, we are able to supplement our energies, engage in specialization, and minimize the risk of failure.

In a shared activity, then, the actions of the participants must be coordinated with one another in order to benefit from the pooling of talent. The utility of any course of action cannot be evaluated in isolation but only as part of a total vector of concerted effort. Rational deliberation in a shared activity is, therefore, inherently strategic: what one person ought to do depends on what others will do.

We can imagine two basic ways in which participants in a shared activity might attempt to order their affairs. The first way is completely improvised: at each moment, each person assesses the various options open to him based on his predictions about how the others will act and chooses the option that he judges to be best. When an activity is completely improvised, no guidance is provided to any participant; each is left to his own deliberative devices.

While this kind of improvisation is effective in many contexts, such as leisurely walks, doubles tennis, and jazz riffs, there are a number of reasons why it cannot be a universal method for coordinating shared activity. First, participants might not always be able to rely on one another to make the right decisions: some participants might be less informed and mistakenly judge certain choices to be the best; some might have all the necessary information, but become overwhelmed at the moment of choice and pick the wrong option; or some might have different preferences and, as a result, choose courses of conduct that work at cross-purposes. Without some method for correcting or guiding behavior, information asymmetries, cognitive incapacities, and divergent preferences threaten to plunge joint ventures into chaos.

Second, improvisation of this kind might also fail to coordinate behavior due to problems of predictability. Since rational deliberation in shared activities is strategic, improvisers must be able to predict what their fellow improvisers will choose. Predictions, however, may be hard to come by. Participants cannot assume that others will do what they want them to do because the others may not know what to do or may have different wants. Although participants might be able to predict behavior if they knew what everyone believes and desires, they will not typically have that sort of information, and even if they did, it might be very time-consuming to figure out what everyone will do by calculating what it would be sensible for them to do given everything they believe and want.

The problems of predictability are especially acute when the group faces a coordination problem. Recall that in these strategic situations, the solutions to the games are arbitrary. When solutions are arbitrary, each player's preferences are determined exclusively by their expectations of what the other players will do. For example, I may not care whether I get the fish and Henry the salad ingredients or he gets the fish and I the salad ingredients. He may be similarly indifferent. The right strategy for each of us, therefore, depends entirely on which strategy the other chooses. Unless we have some basis for predicting each other's choices, our attempt to coordinate our actions is likely to be thwarted.

Unconstrained improvisation is not a robust method for coordinating shared activities because it is appropriate only when there is a very high degree of trust, commonality of interest, and predictability among participants. When any of these breaks down, some form of advance planning will be the preferred strategy. Thus, if I have worries about Henry's abilities or preferences, I should raise them with him prior to action. For if I can convince him that it would be best for him to choose one option and me another, or bargain to some form of compromise, we can settle on the same joint strategy and implement a good plan when the time for action rolls around.

Planning in the context of shared activities, thus, serves a crucial control function. It enables some participants to channel the behavior of others in directions that they judge to be desirable. The need to guide the behavior of the other members will be pressing whenever members do not trust each other's intelligence, character, or knowledge or when their preferences significantly diverge. In such circumstances, participants cannot simply assume that others will be able to coordinate their behavior properly. They must use plans to compensate for their distrust or disagreements so that their fellow participants will act in the way that they want them to or believe they should.

Planning in group contexts also alleviates problems of predictability. The adoption of shared plans by members of the group obviates the need for high levels of competence or detailed knowledge about everyone's beliefs and desires. I don't have to *know* that Henry wants to choose some option in order to be able to expect that he will choose it. Notice here that the function of planning is not to improve choices, but rather to render them legible to others. By having a common blueprint that each of us accepts, each of us can reasonably forecast that the others will do their part. In these circumstances, it is better to settle for a decent plan than to hope for the best solution.

Complex, Contentious, Arbitrary

As we have seen, group planning is unnecessary for shared activities when it seems clear that the members of the group, if left to their own devices, will end up coordinating their behavior effectively. However, if participants harbor reasonable worries that order will not appear extemporaneously, or that it will be significantly defective, then they ought to formulate and adopt shared plans. Such fears will naturally arise in three kinds of scenarios: when the activities to be shared are complex, are contentious, or possess arbitrary solutions.

In the absence of guidance, *complex* activities demand significant knowledge and skill, tax cognitive capacities, and consume precious mental resources. Completely improvised attempts at coordination are thus bound to lead participants to distrust their own judgments or those of their fellow group members. Plans aim to compensate for this lack of trust by greatly simplifying the decision-making procedure. Instead of having to arrive at an all-things-considered judgment about what to do, participants can focus on the same few variables and, as a result, make better choices, or at least ones that cohere well with those of others.

In the case of *contentious* activities, there is a threat that, without planning, some participants will choose poorly or worse, act at cross-purposes. The contentiousness of an activity might stem from its complexity, or from the simple fact that the members of the group have different preferences or values. In either case, it is crucial that potential conflicts be identified and resolved ahead of time. The function of planning here is to settle disputes correctly and definitively before mistakes are made and become irreversible.

Finally, the *arbitrariness* of many aspects of shared activities generates coordination problems that render the behavior of the other participants difficult, if not impossible, to predict. Plans pick one solution out of a multiplicity of options, enabling the group to converge on that solution and hence to coordinate their actions successfully.

To be sure, a shared activity may be *so* complex that planners may be unable to map out a sequence of events that will lead to the desired outcome. A standard critique of planned economies, for example, is that allocation decisions are so intricate that no central body can gather all the necessary information, process it correctly, and optimally direct production and consumption.[7] This does not however mean that planning plays no role in market economies. Indeed, the rules of property, contract, and tort can be understood as general plans whose function is to create the conditions favorable for order to emerge spontaneously. Rather than acting as visible hands directly guiding economic decisions, they provide market actors the facilities to carry out their own profit-maximizing plans so that overall economic efficiency will be maximized in the process.

Similarly, if a shared activity is too contentious, participants will be unable to agree on a common plan to order their affairs. Imagine, for example, trying to use the political process to distribute food, shelter, education, child care, sneakers, books, shampoo, laptops, iPods, DVDs, beer, candy bars, paper clips, and so on. Aside from being impossibly complicated, questions about optimal levels of production and fair distribution are simply too contentious to be resolved in a collective manner. The plans that structure market interactions, on the other hand, allow individuals who fundamentally disagree with one another to place values on goods and services and to engage in mutually advantageous trades. The benefits that are unavailable through collective action can thus be had through the spontaneous interaction of group members following their own conceptions of the good life.[8]

Shared Plans and Shared Agency

In the last section, we saw why a group would want to converge on a common plan when engaged in a shared activity. We said that the value of planning stems not only from its ability to lower deliberation costs and compensate for cognitive incapacities, but also from its power to coordinate the participants' behavior. Insofar as the utility of an individual action is a function of the choices made by other participants, it is imperative that the behavior of the group members be channeled in the right direction and made predictable to one another. In complex, contentious, and arbitrary environments, however, doubts and disagreements about the best way to proceed thwart the prospect of coordination through complete improvisation. Shared plans resolve these doubts and disagreements, harnessing and focusing the individual efforts of the participants so that they may accomplish together what they could not achieve separately.

Having argued for the importance of plans in joint ventures, we might ask how exactly groups have or share plans. For example, what makes our plan to cook dinner tonight *our* plan?

Clearly, when we speak of a group sharing a plan, we don't mean that the group has a collective mind that has adopted a plan. A plan is shared by a group only if each of the members of the group in some sense "accepts" the plan. Henry and I would not share a plan to cook dinner if both of us did not accept the plan to cook dinner.

By the same token, two people cannot be said to share a plan simply because each intends to engage in the same generic activity. I intend to cook dinner tonight and my neighbor intends to cook dinner tonight, but my neighbor and I do not share a plan to cook tonight. To say that a group has a plan to do A is to say more (and, as we will soon see, sometimes less) than that each member of the group plans to do A.

One reason that Henry and I can be said to share a plan, but my neighbor and I cannot, is that Henry and I designed the plan for ourselves, and not for my neighbor. This suggests that a group shares a plan only if the plan was designed, at least in part, with the group in mind, as a joint activity constituted by each member's individual actions.[9]

The requirement that shared plans be designed for members of the group does not however require that every member play a role in the design of the plan. One group member could take the lead and design the plan for others. In fact, someone who is not even a member of the group could take on this role. My wife could plan for Henry and me to cook dinner tonight for all three of us. Henry and I would then share a plan in part because it would have been designed with Henry and me in mind.[10]

But simply designing a plan for a group is not enough for plan sharing. For even though my neighbor might have designed a plan with me in mind, my neighbor and I do not yet have a plan unless I agree to it. In order for a group to share a plan, then, each member of the group must accept the plan. And "acceptance" of a shared plan does not mean simply that each member accepts *her* particular part of the plan. To accept a plan entails a commitment to let the other members do their parts as well. Thus, if our plan requires that I cook the fish and Henry make the salad, I am committed to acting in a manner consistent with his making the salad. If he needs the big knife to cut the carrots, I must at some point during our cooking let him have it. The acceptance of a plan does not require that the participants actually know the full content of the shared plan; the commitment may simply be to allow others to do their parts, *whatever they happen to be.*

Because a plan can be shared only if it is accepted by all participants, shared plans may be quite incomplete. I can plan on Henry making the salad without having any commitment to let him use the big knife first. In this case, the shared plan will specify only who makes what, but not who uses the knife first. In fact, there may be no accepted plan apart from the commitment to engage in the joint venture, in which case the shared plan will be virtually blank. "We cook dinner tonight" can be its only content. Wherever the shared plan is unspecified in this way, participants may be required to design individual subplans in order to execute the plan itself. Unless these subplans come to be accepted by others, these parts will not be shared and may be contested some time in the future. If these problems are anticipated, prudence dictates that efforts be undertaken to resolve them ahead of time by negotiating and accepting new provisions to the shared plan.

Thus far, we have said that a group shares a plan only if the plan was designed, at least in part, with the group in mind and the group accepts it. It seems nevertheless that one more condition is required. Because a plan that is completely secret cannot be shared, it should be insisted that a shared plan be at least "publicly accessible," namely, that the participants could discover the parts of the plan that pertain to them and to others with whom they are likely to interact if they wished to do so.

At the same time, it should also be noted that plan sharing does *not* require that members of the group *desire* or *intend* the plan to work. Let's say I want my house painted and hire my two sworn enemies, Dudley and Stephens, to paint my house. I offer $1,000 dollars to Dudley if Dudley does what I tell him to do. I offer Stephens the same terms. Dudley and Stephens both agree because they need the money. I then tell Dudley to scrape off all the old paint and Stephens to paint a new coat on the scraped surface. Despite the fact that Dudley and Stephens hate me and loathe the idea that my house will be freshly painted, and, as a result, do not intend that the house be painted, they nevertheless share a plan, namely, one that directs Dudley to scrape and Stephens to paint.[11] They share a plan because I designed the plan for them, it is accessible to them, and they accept it.[12]

Acting Together

In the last section, we tried to explain why Henry and I shared a plan to cook dinner, but my neighbor and I did not. We said that in the former case, the plan to cook dinner was designed with Henry and me in mind, we accepted it, and the plan was accessible to us. In the latter case, however, none of these conditions obtained. No plan was designed to enable my neighbor and me to cook dinner together. And since there was no such plan, we could not accept it and it could not be publicly accessible.

Suppose now that Henry and I cook dinner together. One might ask: why is it the case that Henry and I cooked dinner together but my neighbor and I did not? A plausible response is to say that Henry and I acted together because we shared a plan to cook dinner and this plan enabled us to cook dinner, whereas my neighbor and I did not share such a plan. Shared agency, that is, acting together, is distinguished from individual agency, that is, acting alone, by virtue of the plans of the agents. Even if my neighbor used my kitchen to cook and cooked his meal at the same time as Henry and I cooked, and even if we cooked the same food, our cooking was distinct from his cooking because we did not share a plan to cook with him and he did not share a plan to cook with us. Shared plans, we might say, bind groups together.[13]

Shared plans are constitutive of shared agency because they explain how groups are able to engage in the activity.[14] By appealing to them, group members are relieved, at least partially, from deliberating about proper action. Shared plans do the thinking for the group, enabling participants to know what they should do and what others will do. They not only coordinate the behavior of each participant, they organize their further planning, directing them to fill in their subplans in a manner consistent with their own and other participants' subplans.

But while sharing a plan is necessary for shared activity, it is clearly not sufficient. For even if Henry and I shared a plan to cook dinner, we will not have cooked dinner together unless we acted on the plan and successfully carried it out. This suggests that a group intentionally acts together only when all members of the group intentionally play their parts in the plan and the activity takes place because they did so. Henry and I cooked together because we played our respective parts in the shared plan and, in so doing, managed to cook dinner.

In addition to sharing a plan, acting on the plan, and achieving it, there seem to be two more conditions that are necessary for a group to act together. First, the existence of the shared plan must be common knowledge. We could hardly be said to have acted together intentionally if it were not plain to each of us that we shared the same plan. Second, members of a group intentionally act together only if they resolve their conflicts in a peaceful and open manner. If Henry and I disagree with one another about who gets to use various pots and knifes and, instead of talking our problems out, we wrestle each other over, or hide, every piece of cooking equipment, our activity would be more competitive than cooperative. Force and fraud not only destroy trust, but they render shared intentional activities impossible as well.

Reducing Planning Costs

As we have seen, the function of shared plans is to guide and coordinate the behavior of participants by compensating for cognitive limitations and resolving the doubts and disagreements that naturally arise in strategic contexts. Indeed, shared activities are partially constituted by the acceptance of shared plans precisely because the existence of shared plans explains how agents can work together in complex, contentious, or arbitrary environments.

However, many of the same reasons that make shared plans necessary for shared activities also make them costly to produce. If shared plans are needed to regulate behavior in complex and contentious environments, it is likely that they will be expensive to create ahead of time through deliberation, negotiation, or bargaining. Fortunately, it is often possible to reduce these costs. As we will see, policies, customs, and hierarchy are three ways in which shared plans can be forged without the members of the group having to engage in the time-consuming process of plan formulation and adoption.

Policies

Having enjoyed our collaboration, Henry and I decide to invite several of our friends over to cook with us. Cooking in this larger group turns out to be even more entertaining and, as a result, we start to make dinner together every week. We call ourselves the "Cooking Club."

Initially, we find planning these culinary events the least fun part of the process. Each week we make many phone calls and send numerous e-mails to club members trying to work out the details of our get-together: the day, time, and location of our dinner, what we will make, who is to get what, who is to cook what, and so on.

Slowly, though, we start to learn ways to avoid having to consult each other on every issue. In particular, we begin developing "policies," that is, general plans. For example, instead of selecting the menu each week, we decide instead to follow the recipes set out in the Wednesday edition of the *New York Times*. This general plan radically cuts down on our deliberation and bargaining costs. We simply follow this subpolicy of our shared plan every week and know what each of us should and, hence, will do.

Policies have their downsides, however. While planning every week was tiresome, at least it allowed our choice to suit our then-current tastes. By deciding to follow the recipes in the *Times*, we tie ourselves to courses of action that may be less than ideal. In this respect, adopting policies involves a tradeoff: planners must decide whether the risks of suboptimal outcomes by following a plan outweigh the costs of repeated deliberation and bargaining.

Customs

Another way planning costs are reduced in ongoing shared activities is through the development of customs. When we began the club, for example, we chose a different person's house to cook the dinner every week. Once we went through the entire club roster, we followed the same pattern again. Eventually, we begin to treat this pattern as the norm. In other words, the group regards the choice of venue for our cooking as settled and, thus, not something normally up for reconsideration. Likewise, because everyone always agreed to make three courses for dinner—appetizer, main course, and dessert—we eventually take this pattern as the standard for our dinners and act accordingly.

These customs turn out to be quite beneficial. We do not have to deliberate, negotiate, or bargain about these matters in order to apply our shared plan. The customs, in other words, coordinate our behavior spontaneously. My subplans about venue and menu are consistent with my friends' subplans about venue and menu because we always fill out our shared plans in the customary way.

It is tempting to say that our past practice has led us to adopt a "plan" for venues and menus. After all, we regard alternating houses and three-course meals as the right way to cook dinner together. But this temptation should, I believe, be resisted, since our customs were not created *for the purpose* of settling questions about proper conduct but instead emerged spontaneously. Each of us independently found it advantageous to act in accordance with the pattern set by past practice and eventually took the matter as settled.[15]

When customary standards that purport to settle what is to be done arise in a nonpurposive manner, I will not refer to them as "plans," but rather as "planlike" norms.[16] Despite the fact that they did not arise through the process of planning, they are planlike because they do what plans are normally supposed to do: they economize on deliberation costs, compensate for cognitive incapacities, and organize behavior between participants. Like plans, and unlike other norms such as the rules of morality and logic, they are created and sustained by human action. Moreover, they are also typically partial and hierarchical. Our custom to alternate houses does not specify the time that we are supposed to show up at each others' houses. And if we were to fill in this custom by setting a time, this decision would act just as a subplan, that is, specifying the means by which we carry out the end of alternating houses. Finally, customary norms purport to do what plans purport to do, namely, settle what is to be done.

Although some customary standards may only be planlike, I will nevertheless consider them as eligible to be part of shared plans. Shared plans, then, need not contain only plans but may incorporate planlike norms as well. These norms are part of a shared plan just in case they are accepted by the members of the group and are seen as specifying the means by which they are to engage in the shared activity.

Introducing Hierarchy

While adopting policies and developing customs did lessen some of the burden associated with planning our dinners, we were nevertheless forced to engage in extensive deliberation and negotiation each week to set up our club meetings. In order to reduce the costs of planning more radically, we decided to let one person take charge of planning the whole meal for the rest of us. The "head chef" for the week would direct the "sous chefs" on what to make and buy; where, when, and how to cook the food; and so on. We decided to select our leader randomly: the head chef for the next week is the one who draws the longest straw at the end of each week's dinner.

As expected, most of our planning problems disappeared. When I am head chef, I am able to plan the shared activity without having to worry about winning an argument, striking a deal, or forging a consensus. Regardless of whether my friends agree with me, I can get them to do what I think they should do straightaway. That is, I can *order* them to do so. Similarly, when I am the sous chef, I need not enlist the others in filling out our shared plan. I can just sit back and take instruction from the head chef. To be sure, this scheme does not totally relieve me of responsibility for planning. The head chef never completely plans out my actions and hence I am required to fill in the gaps of the shared plan that apply to me.

When the head chef orders a sous chef to perform some action, we might say that she "adopts a plan" for the sous chef. By issuing the order, the head chef places the sous chef under a norm designed to guide his conduct and to be used as a standard for evaluation. Moreover, the head chef does not intend her order to be treated as one more consideration to be taken into account when the sous chef plans what to do. Rather, she means it to settle the matter in her favor. And because the sous chef accepts the hierarchical relationship, he will adopt the content of the order as his plan and revise his other plans so that they are consistent with the order. He will treat the order as though he formulated and adopted it himself and, as a result, will be disposed to apply and comply with it.

In setting up our hierarchy, therefore, we "vertically" divide our labor. Instead of everyone deliberating and negotiating with each other, we entrust one person with the responsibility to fashion the shared plan for us. When accepting the role of sous chef, club members thus surrender their exclusive power to plan. Put somewhat more precisely, when accepting their subordinate position, the sous chefs *use* their power to plan to outsource various stages of planning to the head chef. Instead of formulating and adopting their own plans, they accept a plan to defer to someone else's planning. In turn, when one of us assumes the role of head chef, we agree to play the role of planner for other members of the group. Instead of simply planning our own affairs, we plan to formulate and adopt plans for others.

In this context, it is possible to see hierarchy as a major technological advance in behavioral organization. By dividing labor between those who plan and those who follow through on such plans, group members are no longer limited to arduous deliberations and unpleasant squabbling on the one hand and precarious attempts at improvisation on the other. When doubts or disagreements arise with respect to the proper way to proceed, superiors can resolve these conflicts quickly and cheaply by issuing orders and thus changing the shared plan that subordinates are required to follow. Leaders are useful, in other words, because they are efficient "planning mechanisms." They can simplify complexity, settle controversy, and disambiguate arbitrariness without having to engage in costly deliberations, negotiations, or bargaining.

Self-Regulating Shared Plans

But hierarchy is not only an efficient tool for producing shared plans; it is often the product of shared plans as well. In the cooking case, for example, part of our shared plan authorizes one member of the group to adopt plans for the others. Thus, the reason I become the *head chef* after drawing the longest straw is that our shared plan authorizes the longest-straw drawer to do the group's planning.

In a shared activity involving hierarchy, then, shared plans are self-regulating, that is to say, they regulate the manner of their own creation and application. Parts of the shared plan authorize certain members of the group to flesh out or apply the other parts of the shared plan. These "authorizations" are accepted when members of the group agree to surrender their exclusive power to plan and commit to follow the plans formulated and applied by the authorized members. Thus, when someone authorized by the shared plan issues an order, she thereby extends the plan and gives members of the group new subplans to follow.

The fact that someone adopts a plan for others to follow does not, of course, mean that, from the moral point of view, those others *ought* to comply. The plan might be foolish or evil and, thus, unless there are substantial costs associated with nonconformity, the subjects morally should not carry it out. However, if the subject has accepted the shared plan that sets out the hierarchy, then, from the point of view of instrumental rationality, he is bound to heed the plan. For if someone submits to the planning of another, and yet ignores an order directed to him, he will be acting in a manner inconsistent with his own plan. His disobedience will be in direct conflict with his intention to defer.

While acceptance of a subordinate position within a hierarchy creates rational requirements of obedience, it may of course be the case that participants were irrational for acquiescing to the shared plan in the first place. Their superiors may be ignorant, unethical, or irresponsible. Nevertheless, there are often good reasons to defer. For example, others might know more than the subordinates do about what the group should do and can be trusted to point them in the right direction. As we have also seen, the complexity and contentiousness of shared activities increases not only the benefits of planning, but also its costs. By vertically dividing labor between those who adopt plans and those who apply and carry them out, participants are able to resolve their doubts and disagreements without having to engage in costly deliberations or negotiations. It should also not be overlooked that individuals might accept a subordinate role in a shared activity because they have no other viable option. They might desperately need the money or fear that they will be harmed if they do not. Even in cases of economic or physical coercion, once individuals form an intention to treat the superior's directives as trumps to their own planning, they have transformed their normative situation and are rationally—if not morally—committed to follow through unless good reasons suddenly appear that force them to reconsider.

Planning for Massively Shared Agency

While concentrating the power to plan in the hands of a few is often useful for small-scale shared activities, it is absolutely indispensable when large collections of individuals act together. On the one hand, the complexity, contentiousness, and arbitrariness of shared activities grow with the size of the group participating, leading to a corresponding increase in the need for and cost of planning. Without economical methods for adopting and applying plans, it is unlikely that the members of the group will be able to organize themselves through sheer improvisation or group deliberation and bargaining. Even more importantly, hierarchy is necessary because of the need to hold members of the group accountable. If an activity is to be shared in a group of considerable size, those who are committed to the success of the activity must have some way of directing and monitoring those who fail to share their enthusiasm.

As we will see, the simple forms of planning and hierarchy we have been exploring are insufficient for these larger-scale tasks. To manage instances of massively shared agency, it is imperative to divide labor horizontally, develop a dense network of plans, and erect sophisticated planning structures so that the participants can navigate their way through unfamiliar and challenging terrain and others can chart their progress.

Plans and Alienation

The Cooking Club has been going strong for so long that one day one of us suggests that we open up a catering company. Why not make money doing something that we enjoy doing for free? We all find the idea appealing and thus decide to turn the Cooking Club into The Cooking Club Inc.

Our initial venture into business turns out to be hugely successful. Word of mouth spreads the news quickly, and soon we can no longer meet the demand for catering services. We know that we must hire more workers to help us with our business. Expanding the business in this way, however, requires us to change the way that we run it. Because the new workers know little or nothing about the complexities of the catering business, we must provide them with detailed instructions if they are to be productive.

But lack of catering experience is not the only reason forcing us to plan for them. Unlike the founders and owners of The Cooking Club Inc., a large percentage of these workers are not committed to seeing the business prosper. Many are aspiring actors waiting for their big break and care only about picking up their paychecks. Relying on them to organize themselves, therefore, would be foolish. If they get paid as long as they merely appear to help, there is no reason to think that they will in fact be helpful. Given their alienation from the activity, they will not do what really needs to be done if doing it is too demanding.

The natural solution is for those who care about the success of the endeavor to direct the actions of those who do not. Having all read Adam Smith and knowing about the gains to productivity that the division of labor enables, we decide to assign to each worker separate roles, for example, cook, dishwasher, waiter, driver, bartender, bookkeeper, and so on. The benefits of specialization, we anticipate, will be considerable: instead of teaching the staff how to perform every single task, we can simply train each to do one job well; because each worker performs only one job, they are able to perfect their skills; given that workers stay at their posts, they waste no time shifting and retooling from one task to another; and since each staff member is assigned a specific task, we are able to determine who is responsible, and should be held accountable, for shortfalls in performance.

In order to divide the labor in the horizontal direction, we adopt policies that direct staff members to act, or not act, in certain ways. For example, the bartender policy states: "During a job, the bartender is to stand behind the bar and prepare the drinks that the guests request." In addition to these role specifications, we also adopt company-wide directives, such as "Waiters, cooks, and bartenders must wear the Cooking Club Inc. uniform" and "All employees must wash their hands after using the restroom."

Since the policies allocating roles are highly general, we adopt further policies to help guide the staff in applying them. For example, we provide the bartender a book of drink recipes. These recipes stipulate the "right" way to mix various drinks. When a guest requests, say, a Bloody Mary, the bartender is required to carry out the bartender policy by using the Bloody Mary recipe as his guide. If the bartender does not use that recipe, he will not have performed his job correctly.

Call these types of policies *stipulations*. Stipulations do not demand that their subjects believe the stipulated propositions to be true; rather, they are merely required to *treat them as true* for the purpose of applying certain plans. Suppose that the Bloody Mary recipe uses mango nectar. The bartender need not believe that Bloody Marys should be made with mango nectar. Rather, he should regard the stipulated recipe as the right way to make a Bloody Mary only for the purposes of preparing drinks for the guests. Another stipulation is that the customer is always right. Regardless of whether the customer is actually justified on some matter, workers are required to treat what she claims as correct for the sake of doing their job.

In addition to stipulations, we promulgate *factorizations*. Factorizations specify the factors that should be taken into account when planning how to act. For example, we direct the staff to be cost conscious. This plan directs the staff to give weight to the cost of various actions and adopt plans in part based on this consideration. Like stipulations, factorizations do not require that their subjects actually value the factors specified by the plan; rather, they merely direct them to *treat these factors as valuable* for the sake of doing their jobs.

In addition to plans that direct planning and action, we also introduce *permissions*. Permissions are best understood as "antidirectives": they do not direct the staff to do, or not do, any action; rather, they inform their addressees that they are *not* required to perform, or refrain from performing, some action. Thus, the permission to take home leftover food instructs the staff members that they are not required to leave leftover food, which is useful to know if one is concerned that taking food home may be forbidden.

These general plans, stipulations, factorizations, and permissions constitute subplans of the shared plan to engage in the catering business together. Their function is to guide and organize the behavior of the group. Instead of staff members having to design a shared plan themselves, each can simply appeal to the parts of the shared plan formulated and adopted for them. The promulgated policies also serve a crucial monitoring function. Once they have been adopted and disseminated, the lines of responsibility become clear, rendering it difficult for workers to shirk or blame failure on ignorance. If they do not perform their assigned role or carry it out in the manner specified by the plans, they can be held accountable for any omissions, mishaps, or abuses that result from their waywardness.

Decentralized Planning Mechanisms

Assigning roles to the staff partly compensates for the distrust we feel toward them, but it is by no means sufficient. While the adopted directives set out the basic division of labor, most of the operational details are left unresolved. Moreover, given the staff's indifference to our success, we need a way of checking that they are indeed doing their jobs. Unfortunately, we cannot organize and oversee day-to-day operations because there are simply too many problems to solve and there is too much activity to supervise. We are able to allocate roles and set broad institutional objectives but our group is too slow and unwieldy to effectively run the day-to-day aspects of the business.

As a result, the owners develop a more elaborate vertical division of labor. First, we empower individuals whom we deem trustworthy to adopt detailed plans for the day-to-day operations of the company. They are authorized to determine whom to staff on which job, where trucks should be parked at catering sites, when the soup gets served during the meals, and so on. Second, we direct them to supervise the staff. They are, in other words, to "apply" company policies to the staff to see whether they are carrying them out properly. If they are not, we direct the supervisors to notify the staff members of the shortfall and respectfully insist that the job be done correctly.

By appointing these supervisors, we *decentralize* the process of group planning. Instead of direction coming exclusively from the center, multiple planning mechanisms are available to create and administer the company's shared plan on a distributed basis. When the supervisors create new plans for daily operations, they are engaged in decentralized plan adoption; when evaluating staff behavior using existing company policies, they are engaged in decentralized plan application. Because of decentralization, doubts and disagreements about the best plans to adopt or the proper way to apply existing plans need not make their way to us. Nor must we supervise every aspect of the business. Local supervisors who are close to the action and are deemed trustworthy can resolve conflicts and monitor behavior in an agile fashion.

To decentralize our planning hierarchy, we adopt various *authorizations*. Thus, the authorization that empowers supervisors to apply plans to others can be formulated as follows: "Supervisors have the power to apply those company plans that are directed to staff members." By accepting this authorization, staff members commit themselves, for the purpose of applying company plans, to treat as correct their supervisors' judgments about the applications of company plans.

We also adopt plans that specify how supervisors are to exercise their authorized powers. For lack of a better term, I am going to call plans of this sort *instructions*. One instruction, for example, requires the supervisor to issue a warning before she docks a staff member for failures to comply with company policies. This plan has the following form: "In order to dock pay from a staff member, a supervisor must first issue a warning." The instruction does not actually require the supervisor to issue a warning; rather, it specifies the proper procedure that the supervisor is to follow if she wishes to validly exercise the power to dock pay. Thus, if the supervisor fails to issue a warning, the worker cannot be denied wages.

Authorizations, instructions, stipulations, and factorizations are special types of plans. Unlike the bartender directive or the smoking permission, which regulate *action,* these types of plans guide *planning.* Authorizations specify *who* is to plan, while instructions, stipulations, and factorizations specify *how* to plan. We might say that these plans are "plans for planning." They constitute the self-regulating parts of shared plans that specify the manner in which the shared plan is to be formulated, adopted, applied, and enforced.

With the creation of this new hierarchical structure, our shared plan now has a dual function: it not only compensates for our lack of trust in the staff, but also capitalizes on our trust in the supervisors. By empowering the supervisors to plan for the staff, we are able to focus on other aspects of the catering business, secure in the knowledge that trustworthy individuals are minding the store.

Affecting Plans

One of the powers conferred on supervisors is to hire and fire employees. But this power is not the same as the power to adopt or apply any plan. If a supervisor fires a waiter for being rude to a patron, she is not directly telling anybody to do anything: she is simply letting the waiter go.

Of course, by firing the waiter, the supervisor affects the applicability of numerous company plans. For example, the bookkeeper is no longer required to pay the fired employee, and other employees are not permitted to let him into the kitchen. We might say, therefore, that the authorization to fire employees involves the power to *affect* certain preexisting company plans.

At the risk of some artificiality, I will consider the exercise of an authorization to affect plans to be a form of planning. For although affecting plans does not involve the creation of any new plans, it is the functional equivalent. When someone affects plans in an authorized manner, she generates the same normative consequences as if she adopted a new set of plans herself. Indeed, affecting preexisting plans is typically a more efficient way of organizing behavior than adopting new plans. Instead of separately directing the bookkeeper not to pay the waiter, the employees not to let him back into the kitchen, and so on, the supervisor can accomplish the same ends by simply firing the waiter.

Modernity and Massively Shared Agency

As we have seen, we respond to the challenge of managing a large group of inexperienced and unmotivated individuals by requiring them to hand over vast amounts of planning power to us. By accepting the shared plan, they not only assume certain roles but transfer their powers to adopt and apply plans when their plans conflict with the planning of the supervisors. This dense horizontal and vertical division of labor channels the behavior of the staff in such a way that they eventually end up doing what we want them to do. The beauty of the scheme is that the workers themselves need not care a whit about helping us; their interest can lie simply in earning enough money to make it to the next audition. Nor do they have to understand how the whole enterprise hangs together. As long as they do what they are told, our business prospers.

That individuals can be made to work together in pursuit of ends that they do not value is critically important in understanding how the modern world is possible. For the world that we encounter in day-to-day life is distinguished by the enormous scale of social life. Business corporations, consumer cooperatives, trade unions, research universities, philanthropic organizations, professional associations, standing armies, political parties, organized religions, governments and legal systems, not to mention the collaborative ventures made possible by the digitally networked information and communication technology, such as Wikipedia, massively multiplayer online games (MMOGs), open-source software, and the World Wide Web itself, all harness the agency of multitudes in order to fulfill certain objectives. The modern world, we might say, is one defined by "massively shared agency"—the agency of crowds.

Because the modern world is also characterized by diversity, it is extremely unlikely that large-scale ventures can be staffed with individuals who are all committed to the same goals. The Cooking Club Inc., for example, simply could not find enough truly dedicated people to staff our services. Ultimately, we had to rely on others who were willing to do what was demanded of them but no more. In the modern world, alienation and massively shared agency usually go hand in hand.

As we have seen, shared agency is indeed possible in the face of alienation. In order for a group to act together, they need not intend the success of the joint enterprise. They need only share a plan. That plan, in turn, can be developed by someone who does intend the success of the joint activity. As long as participants accept the plan, intentionally play their parts, and resolve their disputes peacefully and openly, and all of this is common knowledge, they are acting together intentionally.

To be sure, some participants may be so apathetic, lazy, selfish, misguided, rebellious, or, in some cases, honorable that they will not be committed to acting on their part of the plan or letting others do likewise unless they are forced to do so. In such cases, the only alternative is to direct others who are trusted to enforce the group policies against those who are not.

The prevalence of alienated participants in massively shared agency does, however, require that we modify our account of shared agency in one further respect. The proposal offered above requires that *all* participants accept the plan in order for the plan to be shared. Yet, only shared activities involving the smallest groups could pass a test of universal acceptance, even when some participants are prepared to enforce the plan against others. The only requirement that should be imposed is that *most* members who are supposed to participate according to the shared plan accept it. The "most" is intentionally vague, as the concepts being explicated are vague in just this way.

Although alienation does not confound the possibility of shared agency, the case of The Cooking Club Inc. illustrates that its existence presents difficult logistical problems for planners. Because alienated participants are not usually committed to the success of the joint activity, it is likely that they will have to be given detailed guidance on how to act. It may also be necessary to create hierarchical structures so that conflicts are resolved and performance monitored. Finally, those in supervisory positions might need to be authorized to enforce the group's policies through the imposition of sanctions. Plans, we can see, are powerful tools for managing the distrust generated by alienation. For the task of institutional design in such circumstances is to create a practice that is *so thick with plans and adopters, affecters, appliers, and enforcers of plans that alienated participants end up acting in the same way as nonalienated ones*. The fact that activities can often be structured so that participants intentionally achieve goals that are not *their* goals accounts for the pervasiveness of massively shared agency in the world around us.

Living Together

We began this chapter by exploring individual planning and why we need it. We saw that human beings plan their individual actions because they typically pursue ends that can only be achieved by taking several, sometimes myriad, different actions over time sequenced in just the right order. Our desire to achieve complex ends outstrips our capacity to deliberate continuously and arrive at the optimal choice for every moment. We compensate for this cognitive failing by thinking through the best course of action in advance, settling on it, and then relying on this judgment when the time comes to carry it out.

We then proceeded to explore why and how small groups plan their shared activities. Aside from the deliberative demands that complex activities place on us, we saw that shared activities require constituent action to be coordinated in certain ways. When complex, contentious, or arbitrary activities are involved, it is unlikely that completely improvised attempts at ordering will result in synergistic patterns of behavior. Group planning is an improvement over simple improvisation insofar as it enables participants to control behavior and render it predictable to others. By having a common blueprint to guide them, members of groups need no longer guess what parts they should play.

While shared plans are often essential to the success of shared activities, we also saw that they are costly to produce. We, therefore, went on to examine several strategies that participants normally use to reduce their planning costs. Adopting policies enables participants to guide their conduct over a whole class of cases; developing customs permits groups to take advantage of planlike norms in order to settle questions about how to act without anyone formulating or adopting them for the group; and consolidating and concentrating planning power in the hands of a few circumvents the need for the many to deliberate, negotiate, or bargain about how to conduct their shared activity.

We also considered the challenges posed by massively shared agency. We saw that the complexity, contentiousness, and arbitrariness of shared activities tend to increase with group size to the point that planning and hierarchy becomes not only desirable but absolutely indispensable. But massively shared agency brings with it a pressure for planning not typically present in the small case. As a group enlarges, the odds that some members will be alienated from the joint activity grow. Developing a dense network of plans and empowering trustworthy individuals to be decentralized plan adopters, affecters, and appliers are essential to supplying distrusted participants with correct instructions for how to proceed as well as standards for holding them accountable. In the end, massively shared activity is possible only because shared plans are capable of capitalizing on trust as well as compensating for distrust.

I would like to end this long discussion of planning by noting one other occasion in which members of groups plan for one another. Most roommates, for example, have policies about how they are to behave in their shared dwelling. These policies usually prohibit playing loud music late at night; require certain cleaning duties and responsibilities; specify who must buy communal items such as toilet paper, butter, and beer; identify the proper place to put the key when they leave the house; and so on. While some of these plans regulate shared activity (for example, stocking the house with essentials), others concern solely individual pursuits (for example, playing music in one's room late at night).

There is no mystery about why plans are needed to regulate individual actions in communal settings. When people occupy the same space and share a common pool of resources, certain courses of action will result in clashes between individual pursuits, while others will avoid them. Planning is often necessary to ensure that those who live together do not undermine each other's ends.

As with cases involving individual and shared agency, plans that regulate individual pursuits in communal contexts aim to harness the benefits of thinking ahead. First, plans enable the group members to figure out the best ways to avoid conflict and hence eliminate the need to deliberate at every turn about how to steer clear of trouble. Second, they allow group members to anticipate possible mistaken choices that negatively affect others and to prevent them before they happen.

As we saw with shared activities, plans are also useful in communal settings because they are capable of coordinating behavior in complex, contentious, and arbitrary environments. Social life presents numerous ethical quandaries about personal and social rights and responsibilities. People not only have doubts about the proper way to live together but, more perilously, often find themselves at odds with one another about how such doubts should be resolved. The contentiousness of living together, not to mention its complexity, increases the costs of deliberation, negotiation, and bargaining and threatens to generate additional emotional and moral costs should the parties fail to talk through their problems.

Plans are vital for groups because they are capable of resolving many of the ethical problems of communal life. Members of the group who live together and face conflict need not litigate every dispute, disagreement, or perceived act of disrespect. Nor need they try to overpower or deceive each other in order to circumvent the difficulty. They may rely instead on plans that were adopted in anticipation of the conflict. Prior planning allows the community members to treat questions of fairness and what they owe to each other as settled, as matters not up for reconsideration. And in this way they are able not only to economize on costs and increase predictability of behavior, but also to facilitate an ethic of respect among the entire community.

6

THE MAKING OF A LEGAL SYSTEM

The Idea of Social Planning

The twentieth century was not very kind to the activity often referred to as "social planning." Any list of social engineering projects of the past hundred years tends to read like a veritable Who's Who of Unmitigated Human Disasters, for example, the collectivization of Russian agriculture after the Bolshevik revolution, the command economy of the Soviet Union, the Great Leap Forward, the deurbanization of Cambodia under the Khmer Rouge, the villagization of Tanzanian farmers after independence, the totally planned city of Brasilia, and so on.[1] At the very least, it seems safe to say that the social planners responsible for these tragedies—Lenin, Stalin, Mao, Pol Pot, Julius Nyerere, and Le Corbusier, have fared far worse in history's estimation than their critics—Karl Popper, Friedrich Hayek, George Orwell, Jane Jacobs, and, depending on your politics, Rosa Luxemburg and Ronald Reagan.

But, in truth, there is no reason that these notorious large-scale public projects should be taken to represent and thus discredit the practice of social planning in general. As we have seen, planning is an excellent, often indispensable, method for guiding, coordinating, and monitoring behavior in social settings. What the above list *does* bring into disrepute is a very specific mode of social planning. What distinguishes these disastrous political experiments is the hubristic and coercive use of an untested ideology to radically transform communities purely through directives issued from the center. These social planners conducted themselves as experts whose monopoly on superior scientific, technological, and ethical knowledge entitled them to ruthlessly impose their vision of society on everyone else.

154

Most social planning, however, is not revolutionary, centralized, top-down, and directive in nature. In fact, most attempts at group planning in general, and social planning in particular, combine centralized and decentralized mechanisms for progressive and conservative ends; use bottom-up, as well as top-down, practical reasoning; and rely on authorizations in addition to directives. As Hayek himself complained, socialists hijacked the term "social planning" to suggest that socialism is the "only rational way of handling our affairs."[2] But as Hayek reminded us, liberals engage in social planning as well. "The dispute between the modern planners and their opponents . . . is not a dispute on whether we ought to employ foresight and systematic thinking in planning our common affairs. It is a dispute about what is the best way of so doing. The question is whether for this purpose it is better that the holder of coercive power should confine himself in general to creating conditions under which the knowledge and initiative of individuals are given the best scope so that *they* can plan most successfully; or whether a rational utilitization of our resources requires *central* direction and organization of all our activities according to some consciously constructed 'blueprint.'"[3]

Hayek's point here is uncontroversially right. Socialism is hardly unique in advocating that the state engage in social planning. With the exception of certain extreme forms of anarchism, *all* political theories do so to some degree. What distinguishes these various theories is *how* they understand the planning process: to whom they allocate planning authority, the moral ends of planning, and which activities should be subject to social planning in the first place.

In this chapter I will begin to develop the central claim of the book, namely, that legal activity is a form of social planning. Legal institutions plan for the communities over which they claim authority, both by telling members what they may or may not do, and by identifying those who are entitled to affect what others may or may not do. Following this claim, legal rules are themselves generalized plans, or planlike norms, issued by those who are authorized to plan for others. And adjudication involves the application of these plans, or planlike norms, to those to whom they apply. In this way, the law organizes individual and collective behavior so that members of the community can bring about moral goods that could not have been achieved, or achieved as well, otherwise.

In order to motivate these claims, I begin with the oldest trick in the book. I return to the Cooking Club narrative I began in the previous chapter, drop the club members into the "state of nature" and describe their various reasons for creating a legal system. As I show, communal life generates a need for social planning. Those who live together must be able to organize shared activities, solve coordination problems, settle disputes, and ensure that individual pursuits do not thwart one another. As the group attempts to cope with these pressures, they develop simple social planning mechanisms. The success of these mechanisms, nevertheless, inevitably leads to population growth and hence the need for further planning. In order to meet this increased need, simple techniques give way to more complicated and efficient structures of planning. The end result is the creation of a highly sophisticated planning organization, otherwise known as a legal system.

I should emphasize, of course, that I am not making an empirical claim about the evolution of legal systems or why they were originally created. The state of nature is an analytical device for running a philosophical thought experiment, one that is designed to draw our attention to certain features of law that we might otherwise overlook. By focusing on a group of people who have a perfect understanding of their predicament and have the wherewithal to correct it, the hope is to shed light on our own often imperfect appreciation of the social world. For as we will see, the pressures to create a legal system are hardly unique to this particular fictional setting. Any human community of modest size will experience similar needs for social planning that can only be met by highly sophisticated technologies of plan adoption and application. We may not self-consciously value law for the same reasons they did, but the narrative will enable us to see that we do so implicitly, or at least that we should.

My aim in what follows is also to build on the discussion in the previous chapter by demonstrating that *technologies of planning,* even the highly complex ones that are mobilized by the law, *can be constructed through human agency alone.* In other words, to build or operate a legal system one need not possess moral legitimacy to impose legal obligations and confer legal rights: one need only have the ability to plan. The existence of law, therefore, reflects the fact that human beings are planning creatures, endowed with the cognitive and volitional capacities and dispositions to organize their behavior over time and across persons in order to achieve highly complex ends.

Private Planning

The Cooking Club Inc. eventually becomes so successful that Wall Street approaches us with an offer to take the company public. Unable to resist the lure of obscene wealth, we agree to turn our business over to the public markets. We will still participate in the business at the management level, but our cooking days are over.

As it turns out, however, the thrill of being executives in a multinational corporation nevertheless proves to be extremely short-lived. None of us went into the catering business in order to push paper in a corporate office. We soon decide to sell our shares, move to an uninhabited island in the South Pacific, and start a new community. Alienated by our brief experience of corporate life, we plan to live off the land, treat each other with equal concern and respect, eschew coercive means of social control, and live happily ever after.

The island that we purchase, and rename "Cooks Island," appears to be an ideal location for hunting and gathering. It is inhabited by wild boar, deer, and game birds and has a wide variety of fruit trees, numerous species of wild grains and cereals, and a natural lagoon filled with fish, crab, and edible seaweeds. We move to Cooks Island in the spring, finding plenty of food to eat and abundant materials with which to build huts.

From the outset, small-scale group planning is crucial to our ability to live peacefully and productively together. The main features of our lives—building shelter, collecting fuel, finding food, preparing meals, raising children, playing, and entertaining—are shared activities, and so we need a way to organize them. The hunters among us must decide where to go, what to hunt, who should flush, shoot, gut, and so on. We will also need designated caretakers to look after the children while the hunters are on an expedition. Since everyone has plenty of time on their hands, group members are free to negotiate with one another about who will perform which tasks. In instances of group planning such as this, no one has the authority to tell everyone else what to do: each individual decides which course of action to take and then finds ways to coordinate his or her chosen course of action with those who wish to join them.

Group planning is not always necessary, however; in some cases, order is spontaneously generated. Coordination problems such as where to dispose of our refuse or which side of the road to ride our bikes on are usually solved through the emergence of coordination conventions. We find others disposing of their refuse in a certain location or riding on one side of the road and we simply follow suit. No one plans for this result—it simply happens through "spontaneous ordering."

In this respect, we might say that Cooks Island is an *unplanned* community. All issues concerning how members should act are resolved solely through the unilateral decisions of individuals or small subgroups. Questions about which individual and shared activities ought to be required, prohibited, and regulated are not resolved on a community-wide basis, either through unanimous consensus or exercises of authority, but rather exclusively through private ordering. In other words, while there is plenty of *group* planning, there is no *social* planning.

Internalizing Costs

Notwithstanding the absence of social planning, members of our unplanned community are able to work and live together in harmony throughout the spring, summer, and fall. Winter, however, is a different story. Many of the animals hibernate for the winter and the game birds migrate north. The fish move farther offshore in order to take advantage of richer feeding grounds. The fruit trees bear fruit only in the spring and summer, and the wild grains refuse to germinate in the winter. Each of us anticipates this shortage to some extent by privately storing smoked meat and surplus grain, but there is not nearly enough food to feed us all. We are ultimately able to survive only by importing food from the mainland.

After this first difficult winter, we all recognize that hunting and gathering is not a sustainable way of life and that community-wide action is necessary if we are to survive on the island. In keeping with this, the community decides to pool its resources and buy domesticated grains and livestock from the mainland. Together we clear large portions of the island to plant the domesticated strains of grains and cereals and graze our newly purchased sheep, goats, and cows. We abandon hunting and gathering and take up farming and ranching instead.

Before we are able to embark on this new agricultural lifestyle, however, we have to make an important choice. Until now, the island has been treated as common property. All were entitled to harvest the game animals, lagoon fish, wild berries, fresh water, and hardwood timber and use them in any way they saw fit. Now we must decide whether to maintain common ownership of resources, holding the new livestock, crops, and pastures as joint owners and engaging in a shared activity of farming, or whether we should instead create a system of private property in which a share of animals, seeds, and land is allocated to individuals in order that they will be able to grow food for themselves.

Since all of the inhabitants of Cooks Island have taken basic economics, we know what economists would advise us to do in this situation. In a collective property regime, there is always a danger of free riding. If each islander must work the fields in order to produce food for all, the economist warns, each is likely to be tempted by the following calculation: to do my fair share is to work very hard; if I do not do my fair share, there will be a little less to eat; I would rather eat a little less and not work very hard than eat a little more but work very hard; therefore, I ought not do my fair share. But, of course, if each islander reasons in this way and acts accordingly, everyone will starve.

The economically efficient decision is to switch from a system in which each enjoys the benefits of others' labor to one in which each gains only from his own efforts. In economic terms, the socially optimal decision involves instituting an arrangement whereby each "internalizes" the costs and benefits of his actions. If I benefit from my labor alone, and not from anyone else's, then I have no incentive to be lazy. For if I do not work, I will be the one to starve.

In an effort to make good on this economic insight, we assemble and engage in another act of social planning. We agree as a community to allocate the newly arable land, seeds, and livestock on the basis of family size. The larger the family, the greater the share received. This allocation is accomplished through the adoption of stipulations of the form: "For the purposes of complying with island land use policies, Family X is to be deemed the owner of Plot A, Seed lot B and Livestock lot C."[4] In addition to these specific plans, we also adopt several general policies that govern the use of the allocated land. For example, one policy permits owners to use and enjoy the property as they see fit, while another forbids a nonlandowner from taking the grain or livestock of another without the owner's consent. A third policy permits anyone to cross another's field in order to reach the village square, but a fourth one requires that anyone who does so must compensate the landowner for the destruction of any crops or injury of any livestock on that property.

A principal purpose of these plans is to force each member of the group to internalize the costs and benefits of his or her actions. The first policy, for example, permits owners to enjoy the fruits of their labor, while the second one attempts to avert free riding by directing nonowners not to benefit from the agricultural labor of owners without their permission. The third and fourth policies permit nonowners to use another's land when the alternatives are particularly costly but encourage them to exercise reasonable precautions by requiring them to pay for what they damage. Insofar as a major aim of these policies is to prevent free riding, it is imperative that the policies govern the activities of the whole community. That is to say, in order to be effective, they must be *social* plans.

We also adopt plans that allow for the transfer of property rights. A fifth policy, for example, authorizes owners to alienate their property, whereas a sixth instructs the owners of movable property on how to exercise this power. It states that in order for ownership to pass, there must be physical delivery and acceptance, unless the parties agree otherwise. These policies, in other words, confer power on owners to affect the previous four policies. By alienating property in the proper manner, owners affect who falls within and without these preexisting policies and hence who may use and enjoy the alienated property.

Planning for Spontaneous Order

Fortunately, our shared plan fulfills its intended purpose. The new property regime leads to a substantial crop yield and livestock supply and provides the community with plenty of food to eat and store for the winter. In fact, each of us has more goods than we can possibly use. And, as a result, markets emerge in which the islanders trade their surplus goods.

Not surprisingly, the participants in these markets are able to adjust their production to aggregate demand and their consumption to aggregate supply without engaging in social planning. Our group does not, for example, decide in advance that the cheese makers will make more or less cheese. The cheese makers instead take their cues from the demand they find in the market. If more cheese is demanded, more cheese is supplied. If the amount of cheese demanded cannot be met, the cost of the cheese goes up until the amount of cheese demanded equals the amount of cheese available.

To say that market decisions about supply and demand proceed in the absence of social planning should not be taken to mean that the existence of the market itself is independent of social planning. For the regime of private property that makes our market possible—the allocation of ownership rights to members of the group, the policies for how to treat the items allocated, and the power to affect these policies through voluntary exchange—is the product of plans developed *by us for us*. That group members can only procure one set of goods by trading them for another, and cannot simply appropriate them without permission, is a requirement imposed by our shared plan. This plan seeks to boost agricultural output by creating the conditions favorable for spontaneous order to emerge.[5]

Nevertheless, as more goods are produced and traded, the possibility of economic loss through mishaps grows. These accidents raise numerous questions of responsibility. Let's say that my cow wanders from my pasture and eats some of your crops. Am I responsible for the damage? Or should you bear the costs of not having built a fence?

Even though our group has no shared plan about liability in these circumstances, the various parties find themselves able to resolve the conflict through private deliberation and bargaining. Each person relies on a sense of fairness and neighborliness in determining how to reach a just settlement. For example, neighbors normally choose to overlook small damage to their crops caused by grazing livestock. Because they are aware that their own animals probably inflict similar damage to their neighbor's property, they figure that it all evens out in the long run. As for large losses, which tend not to net out over time, livestock owners generally feel obligated to compensate their neighbors for the damage.[6]

The Supply and Demand for Plans

The Need for Social Planning

Although our shared plan solves important social problems, it generates new ones as well. For it turns out that the move to a system of private property exponentially increases the range of matters over which we can quarrel. When property was held in common, all were permitted to plan their own actions on any aspect of island life. The land, water, air, animals, fruit, grains, and so on were freely available to all. The private property regime changed all that, rendering previously abundant resources instantaneously scarce. Our shared plan has rendered most of the land, and the goods it yields, inaccessible to almost everyone. Moreover, while the incentives to create and innovate that were generated by the new property regime increase the overall production of goods, the prevailing system of ownership dictates that these goods are under the exclusive control of only certain members of the group.

As a result of our shared plan, therefore, questions of rights become extremely urgent and, at the same time, increasingly contentious as well. For we now have an incentive to dispute which objects we own and what we are permitted to do with them. Thus, we bicker about whether islanders are authorized to acquire new land and, if so, how they can or should do so. Owners who live upstream assert the right to use the water for irrigation, even if this means that there is less water for downstream farmers to use. Downstream farmers hotly contest this claim. Those who find fresh water on their property assert exclusive control over this precious resource, while the bulk of the group denies their right to do so. The merchants claim that the islanders should have the ability to condemn private property for public purposes, such as building roads, while another portion of the group, mainly the farmers, vehemently rejects this position.

Our private property regime has not only rendered our communal life more contentious but also greatly increased its complexity. For in an effort to innovate economically, we start to unbundle the property rights allocated to each family under the original shared plan and recombine them with various promises to create new packets of claims and duties. In this way, gifts, leases, easements, bailments, consignments, life estates, loans, assignments, mortgages, partnerships, trusts, wills, negotiable instruments, and other types of contractual and property arrangements are formed. But, while successful in certain respects, these new measures once again raise further questions about the content and scope of the normative relationships created. For example, if a farmer enters into an agreement with, say, the baker to supply a certain quantity of wheat at harvest and then, due to bad weather, the crop fails, does the farmer owe the baker damages and, if so, what kind? If one farmer sells a cow to another but, unbeknownst to both, the cow is barren, can the purchaser get his money back? And what if someone builds a hut for someone else but fabricates the roof of that hut out of an inferior material that makes it less durable than the other huts in the village? Can the purchaser insist on a better roof? Can a creditor foreclose on property if the debtor goes bankrupt? In what circumstances can a tenant refuse to pay rent and, if those circumstances do not obtain, at what point can a landlord evict a tenant?

Not only have our private transactions become more complex and contentious, but our public projects have done so as well. For example, our new economy has generated much material prosperity but it has also skewed its distribution. As a result, we are eager to institute a program of income redistribution. Unfortunately, however, this particular shared activity turns out to be too complicated and presents too many coordination problems for us to be able to bring it about exclusively through improvisation or planning in small groups. Furthermore, while we all agree on the broad outlines of the redistributive program, we disagree about its precise implementation, thus increasing the costs of resolving our conflicts through private deliberations and negotiations.

It is important to note at this point that the doubts and disagreements that arise on Cooks Island are entirely sincere. Each of us is willing to do what we morally ought to do—the problem is that none of us knows or can agree about what that is. Customs cannot keep up with the evolving conflict because they develop too slowly to regulate rapidly changing social conditions and are too sketchy to resolve complex disputes and coordinate large-scale social projects. While private negotiation and bargaining are able to quell some conflicts, this process can be very costly, not only in terms of time and energy but emotionally and morally as well. With many more ways to interfere with one another's pursuits and many more goods to fight over, there is a danger that disputes will proliferate and fester, causing the parties to refuse to cooperate in the next communal venture or, worse, to become involved in ongoing and entrenched feuds. Some projects, such as income redistribution, are so complex, contentious, and arbitrary that they are simply not feasible through private planning alone.

To compensate for this failure of private ordering, we revive our earlier experiment in social planning and regularize it as an ongoing shared activity. We get together several times a week to discuss how best to handle the social issues that arise within our group. We discuss not only how to structure our interactions in the market but also how to collect and redistribute wealth, educate our children, protect ourselves against droughts, hurricanes, and wild animals, and so on. Though our deliberations and negotiations are sometimes long and protracted, dealing as they do with weighty matters of political morality and group morale, we eventually settle on morally sensible plans that we believe will enable us to live together on the island for the foreseeable future.

Failure of Consensus

The disadvantages of social planning via consensus nevertheless become apparent very quickly. Not only is it time-consuming and emotionally draining, but it is extremely unstable. For the plans are useful only so long as they are accepted by almost everyone. As soon as people start to reconsider their wisdom, the plans lose their ability to guide behavior and settle conflict, and the group must start deliberating and negotiating once again.

Eventually, as the island economy booms and its population multiplies, this consensual method of governance becomes intolerable. Economic prosperity makes it possible to sustain a greater number of people, and family size increases along with this new capacity. At the same time, people from the mainland immigrate to the island in search of the good life. More people engage in more interactions, more interactions lead to more doubts and disagreements, and more doubts and disagreements generate higher planning costs.

The increase in conflict is not only a function of the increased number of interactions. Population growth also entails a more intricate division of labor, with group members engaging in ever more complex activities (the cheese maker, for example, recently hired ten workers and incorporated his business, with the bread maker and meat smoker as the chief equity investors). Simply relying on untutored judgments of fairness and neighborliness tends to be a poor method for resolving the complicated disputes that arise from these arrangements. And the expansion of the population makes it increasingly unlikely that these untutored judgments will be shared among the contestants or that losses from any particular interaction will balance out in the long run. Social life has become extremely complex and more contentious as well. Community-wide shared activities are less and less amenable to large doses of improvisation.

On the one hand, then, population growth enhances the need for plans in order to guide and organize the behavior of the islanders. This *increased* demand for morally sensible shared plans, however, coincides with a corresponding *decrease* in our community's ability to supply them through consensus. We simply can no longer get everyone to agree to particular solutions to many social problems and, when we can, the time and expense incurred in the course of forging a consensus is enormous.

Nor do our difficulties end here. Experience has shown us that the mere existence of shared plans is not a panacea. For in order for a plan to resolve doubts or disagreements, the relevant parties must agree about how to implement it. Not only has the number of disputes unregulated by prior plans increased, so have the number of disputes about the application of prior plans. Yet, as the demand for adjudication has increased, so, once again, has the cost of supplying it. If the parties must agree on the application of plans in order to settle their disputes, the expense of conflict resolution will rise with the quantity and complexity of the disagreements.

The Solution: Hierarchy

Recognizing that our need for morally sensible plans and adjudication exceeds our ability to generate them, the inhabitants of Cooks Island converge on the idea of *hierarchy*. At one of our weekly meetings, we decide to divide the social labor vertically by outsourcing various stages of social planning to a small group of trusted islanders. First, we identify three people who will be the chief plan adopters for the island. They will act together as a unit to develop social plans for our community. Second, we identify three islanders who serve as plan appliers for the Island. When a dispute arises between islanders as to the proper application of some social policy and one of the parties wants the dispute resolved, he or she may ask one of these appliers to do so. The plan applier will determine by herself which course of action is required by the island policies and her decision will be binding on both parties.

In addition to this vertical division of labor, which delegates the social planning to a small group of islanders, our newly hierarchical approach also distributes the planning labor horizontally among those few designated social planners. The new plan authorizes three people to *adopt* plans for the islanders and three other people to *apply* these norms whenever a conflict arises and their services are sought. Our hierarchy, in other words, involves a separation of planning powers. Moreover, the plan centralizes plan adoption, but decentralizes plan application: the adopters must act together in order to make plans, but the appliers can resolve conflicts on a solo basis. Only one body can adopt plans, but multiple bodies can apply them.

Notice that the plan that establishes the hierarchy for the island is a shared plan: it has been designed for the social planners, it is accessible to them, and they accept it. This shared plan regulates the activity of social planning. It guides and organizes the behavior of the social planners so that each knows which part they are to play in the shared activity. *It is a shared plan for social planning.*

Notice further that since the shared plan was designed for the handful of social planners, it is they who share the plan, not the islanders as a whole. This means that it is not necessary for the community to accept the shared plan in order for it to obtain—though, as a matter of fact, we do approve of the plan. Since we consider the social planners to be morally legitimate, we plan to allow the adopters and appliers to adopt and apply plans for us. For this reason, we consider the shared plan to be the "master plan" for the group.

As expected, the master plan does solve many of the planning difficulties we encountered earlier. Now social policies can be adopted simply by the adopters proclaiming that such-and-such shall be the case—no one has to agree with the wisdom of the policies themselves. As a result, we have an agile protocol for guiding and organizing our community's behavior and for resolving any disputes that might arise. When one of the designated appliers determines that a policy has been satisfied or violated, his or her judgment does not need to be regarded as wise or right by anyone involved. It is binding simply because it was applied by the authorized individual.

The newly adopted plans prove to be durable as well. In our revamped system, the persistence of plans does not depend on whether members of the community accept their wisdom. As long as they are approved in accordance with the requirements of the shared plan, the plans will be deemed binding, both by the planners and by the islanders generally, and followed accordingly.

The Office

Unfortunately, our saga does not end here. For while the islanders find that their original master plan drastically reduces the costs of social planning, it is nonetheless a crude prototype that suffers from several significant flaws.

It turns out that the plan's *most* significant flaw is that it is limited to a particular set of individuals. The plan specifies those who are currently authorized to plan for the community (that is, "Bob, Ted, and Jane have the power to adopt plans for the residents of Cooks Island") but says nothing about who is to succeed them if they step down, become physically or mentally incapacitated, or die. As a result, when one of them vacates his or her post, we have to deliberate again about whether we want hierarchy and, if so, who should possess the power to plan for others. What we learn from this frustrating duplication of effort is that it would be far more convenient to devise policies that create an abstract structure of control and specify in impersonal terms who should occupy which role at which time. In this way, when one planner quits, another person can assume his or her structural role but the master plan itself will remain unaffected.

With this in mind, we develop new policies that define various structural roles and identify their occupants in less personal, and more general, terms. With respect to the adopters, for example, three new policies are adopted: an authorization of the form: "Adopters have the power to adopt plans for residents of Cooks Island"; a directive of the form: "Appliers are required to apply the plans adopted by adopters in cases that arise before them"; and a stipulation of the form: "A person shall be deemed an 'adopter' if and only if he or she has lived on the island for more than a year and receives the most votes in the latest island election."

This hierarchical structure establishes what is otherwise known as an "office." The office of "adopter," for example, carries with it various rights and responsibilities, all of which persist over time and attach to whoever happens to occupy the office at the given moment. Because the authorization to adopt plans does not single out planners by name, but rather defines a class of individuals who meet the appropriate qualifications (for example, they were elected by a majority of islanders), the master plan does not need to be amended each time a new person seeks to acquire the power to plan for the island. As long as such persons satisfy the impersonal qualifications associated with the office, they will immediately inherit all of its powers as determined by the relevant parts of the master plan.[7]

And we soon discover another advantage of offices. Instead of requiring succeeding adopters to readopt every plan adopted by their predecessors, the master plan is amended to mandate that the policies of past holders of the office are to be followed whenever a new occupant takes over, unless and until the new occupants change the policies in question. In this way, the plans of previous officeholders acquire a normative inertia that renders them even more durable.

Institutionalizing Plans

But while the introduction of offices does depersonalize our hierarchy, we soon find that it is still not impersonal enough. For example, when the adopters wish to adopt a plan, they must gather us in the village square and issue proclamations of the form: "We hereby direct all farmers to erect fences on their land no lower than two meters" or "In order to discharge debts, debtors must use clamshells." These proclamations are commands that direct the community to comply with the proclaimed policies.

Needless to say, this face-to-face mode of social planning proves to be tedious for all, and so the adopters eventually switch to a less intimate system. This process involves writing down their plans and deliberating on the proposed edict before them. If at the end of the deliberations all of the adopters form an intention to settle the matter in favor of following the order, then the edict is valid. The document is then posted in the village square as a written record for all to see.

The problem with *this* method is that it ties the validity of an edict to the private mental state of the plan adopters. An edict is binding only if the adopters *intend* for the edict to settle the matter in its favor and for others to guide their conduct by it. In many cases, however, the islanders have legitimate concerns about whether the posted decree truly represents the will of the planners, for example, when the plan is long and complex, or contains provisions that lead to absurd recommendations. These doubts lead some residents to question whether they are in fact required to follow certain of the posted orders.

In an effort to make the plans more robust, the master plan is amended to include new provisions that specify the formal conditions for the exercise of planning power. For example, in order to enact a new plan, the master plan merely requires that a majority of the adopters say "Aye" when polled. The master plan, in other words, does not mandate that the plan adopters *intend* that others follow the plan. Instead, plan adoption has become *institutionalized:* the adopters' votes have normative significance for the islanders regardless of the specific intentions with which they were carried out.

By institutionalizing our social planning in this way, the governance system of the Island attains a very high degree of impersonality. Not only can those who hold the office of adopter adopt plans outside the earshot of the islanders, they can do so regardless of the intentions with which they performed their actions. As long as they follow the procedures set out in the master plan, their actions will have binding force. And so the islanders no longer need to divine the intentions of the planners in order to know which plans they must follow.

Law as Social Planning

Sanctions?

At this point, it seems safe to say that Cooks Island has developed a legal system. The planners are the legal officials; the plan adopters are the legislators; and the plan appliers, the judges. The master plan is the constitution that defines their offices. The plans created and applied by these officials pursuant to the shared plan are the laws of the system: the policy directives are the duty-imposing rules and the authorizing policies are the power-conferring ones. Finally, the islanders all act according to plan. They are law-abiding citizens.

Some might object and deny that Cooks Island has a genuine legal system because its plans do not impose penalties in cases of disobedience. It seems to me a mistake, however, to consider sanctions to be a *necessary* feature of law. There is nothing unimaginable about a sanctionless legal system; in fact, we have just imagined one.[8] The Cooks Island legal system makes no provisions for sanctions but it has a constitution, a legislature, and judges. It has norms that confer powers and impose duties. It maintains order, redistributes wealth, protects the moral rights of parties, provides facilities for private ordering, solves coordination problems, and settles disputes. This legal system is sanctionless not because it could not impose sanctions; after all, to impose sanctions merely requires that certain types of plans be adopted. Rather, it does not impose sanctions because its designers did not think them necessary. The islanders all accept the legitimacy of the group plans and, as a result, abide by them. And when they make mistakes, they voluntarily make amends. Sanctions would simply be otiose in such a setting.[9]

Sanction-oriented theorists often discount the possibility of sanctionless legal systems because they cannot imagine *why* such a legal system would exist. What would be the point of a community having law if its members are willing to listen to the existing social or moral norms regardless? The story of Cooks Island rebuts this concern.[10] The islanders' decision to develop a legal system was not motivated by fear of antisocial behavior. They had no problem relying on one another to follow the policies they created. Their problem was that they could not create enough policies to follow.

As we saw, the Cooks Islanders were motivated to develop a legal system as part of their effort to break a potentially destructive dynamic.

On the one hand, population growth on the island led to an increase in the need for morally sensible policies to guide and coordinate behavior. Yet, the same growth also amplified the cost of producing and applying such policies. At some point, the costs associated with improvisation, spontaneous ordering, private bargaining, and communal consensus became so great that the demand for policies outstripped the island's ability to supply them. In an effort to radically reduce the costs of planning, the islanders sought to capitalize on the trust they had in certain members of the group by constructing a hierarchical, impersonal, and shared form of social planning. In doing so, they were able to create the policies they needed and thereby solve the moral problems that more expensive or risky methods of planning could not.

The Circumstances of Legality

The residents of Cooks Island may be atypical in their level of communal spirit and moral virtue, but their social problems are hardly unusual. For it is plausible to suppose that any modestly sized community will face similar questions about ownership, contractual obligations, duties of care to one another, proper levels of taxation, limitations on public power, legitimacy of state coercion, and so on. Moreover, like the islanders, it will find that resorting exclusively to nonlegal forms of planning is an inefficient or inadequate way of resolving these questions. To settle the doubts and disagreements of its members in a cost-effective manner, or even at all, requires sophisticated techniques of social planning such as those provided by legal institutions.

I am going to refer to the social conditions that render sophisticated forms of social planning desirable as the "circumstances of legality."[11] The circumstances of legality obtain whenever a community has numerous and serious moral problems whose solutions are complex, contentious, or arbitrary. In such instances, the benefits of planning will be great, but so will the costs and risks associated with nonlegal forms of ordering behavior, such as improvisation, spontaneous ordering, private agreements, communal consensus, or personalized hierarchies. Indeed, the costs and risks of nonlegal planning may be so large as to be prohibitive. Communities who face such circumstances, therefore, have compelling reasons to reduce these associated costs and risks. And in order to do so, they will need the sophisticated technologies of social planning that only legal institutions provide.

Although the circumstances of legality emerged on Cooks Island due to its system of private property, we can easily imagine similar conditions cropping up in a system of common ownership as well. In fact, in a collectivist regime where mass mobilization of the community is needed to produce the necessities of daily life, the value of sophisticated technologies of social planning will be especially great. Massively shared activities, as we saw in the previous chapter, can be managed only through the development of a dense network of plans and planners. Relying solely on nonlegal methods to coordinate collective action on such an immense scale will eventually prove to be inferior to legal forms of social planning.

Once we recognize the extent to which even modestly sized human communities require sophisticated methods for guiding, organizing, and monitoring conduct, we can begin to see legal institutions in a new light. According to what I will call the "Planning Theory of Law," *legal systems are institutions of social planning and their fundamental aim is to compensate for the deficiencies of alternative forms of planning in the circumstances of legality.* Legal institutions are supposed to enable communities to overcome the complexity, contentiousness, and arbitrariness of communal life by resolving those social problems that cannot be solved, or solved as well, by nonlegal means alone.

Of course, the aim of the law is not planning for planning's sake. If legal systems were merely supposed to adopt and apply plans regardless of method or content, the task would be better served by flipping a coin. Rather, the law aims to compensate for the deficiencies of nonlegal forms of planning by planning in the "right" way, namely, by adopting and applying morally sensible plans in a morally legitimate manner. Legal systems are improvements over alternative forms of planning, and hence fulfill their mission, whenever the total reduction in the costs of planning more than offsets any increase in the moral costs engendered by the switch. The task of institutional design, therefore, is to ensure that the legal process does not render mistakes so likely, or use methods that are so unsavory, that the moral benefits of switching to law vanish. Indeed, as we will see later on, legal systems are sometimes designed to *increase* the cost of adopting plans so as to *decrease* the risk that bad plans will be adopted. The worry here is that social planning may be *too* easy and, thus, overly responsive to the momentary passions of the electorate or self-interest of politicians. Throwing some sand in the gears may slow down the legal process enough to improve its ultimate reliability.

The Planning Theory of Law's central claim—that the law is first and foremost a social planning mechanism whose aim is to rectify the moral deficiencies of the circumstances of legality—is supported by two considerations. First, it explains why we consider law to be valuable. It is, for example, a widely shared assumption of political theories that agree on virtually nothing else that the law is an indispensable social institution in the modern world. This belief is of course entirely sensible when we consider the benefits and costs of various methods of planning in such settings. Given the complexity, contentiousness, and arbitrariness of modern life, the moral need for plans to guide, coordinate, and monitor conduct are enormous. Yet, for the same reasons, it is extremely costly and risky for people to solve their social problems by themselves, via improvisation, spontaneous ordering, or private agreements, or communally, via consensus or personalized forms of hierarchy. Legal systems, by contrast, are able to respond to this great demand for norms at a reasonable price. Because of the hierarchical, impersonal, and shared nature of legal planning, legal systems are agile, durable, and capable of reducing planning costs to such a degree that social problems can be solved in an efficient manner.

On the other hand, when the net savings in planning costs engendered by the switch to law are low or nonexistent, we tend not to judge legal institutions to be necessary or even desirable. For example, it would be odd to criticize or pity simple hunter-gatherer groups for not having law. Simple hunter-gatherers, after all, usually need very few rules. Since they do not cultivate land or domesticate animals, they have no need for a fixed system of property rights in real property. Moreover, because the food collected is perishable, hunter-gatherers accumulate little or no surplus and hence have no need for rights in personal property as well. Rules for the voluntary transfer of property and compensation for its damage are not terribly useful to them. Not only are the benefits of social planning normally low but so too are the costs. For when hunter-gatherers require rules, they can either rely on custom or create them straightaway. They can deliberate among themselves about how they ought to live and arrive at some consensus or, failing that, the discontents can separate and merge with other groups. Determining whether the rules have been broken is easy both insofar as there are very few of them and collective deliberations are possible. And when a rule has been violated, communal responses are not difficult to organize. In short, simple hunter-gatherer groups usually do not need law because they do not typically face the circumstances of legality and, hence, have no compensatory need for sophisticated technologies of social planning.[12]

Attributing a compensatory aim to law is further supported by the observation that legal systems can be criticized for being not only evil, but also poorly designed. The Articles of Confederation, for example, were roundly condemned for their inability to regulate interstate commerce, impose taxes, raise an army, establish a system of federal courts, and so forth. They were also assailed for their amendment procedures, which required unanimous consent to change any article. In other words, the former colonists considered their legal system defective precisely because it was an inadequate response to the circumstances of legality. Confederation following Independence generated so much complexity, contentiousness, and arbitrariness that the system could not meet the nation's new demands for social planning.

Law as a Universal Means

According to the Planning Theory, then, the fundamental problem to which law is a solution is not any *particular* moral quandary. Rather, law is an answer to a higher-order problem, namely, the problem of how to solve moral quandaries *in general*. A community needs law whenever its moral problems—whatever they happen to be—are so numerous and serious, and their solutions so complex, contentious, or arbitrary, that nonlegal forms of ordering behavior are inferior ways of guiding, coordinating, and monitoring conduct.

In this sense, laws, like intentions, are "universal means."[13] Just as there are no specific ends that intentions are supposed to serve, there are no substantive goals or values that laws are supposed to achieve or realize. They are all-purpose tools that enable agents with complex goals, conflicting values, and limited abilities to achieve ends that they would not be able to achieve, or achieve as well, without them.

The Problem of Bad Character

It is worth noting at this point that the Planning Theory contrasts sharply with a more conventional view of the law, famously expressed by James Madison in Federalist 51, when he wrote that "if men were angels, no government would be necessary."[14] Following this popular view, the function of the law is to solve a particular social problem, namely, *the problem of bad character*. Legal institutions are created not as general purpose technologies of social planning but rather as antidotes to the infirmities of human nature that inevitably lead people to transgress existing social or moral norms.

The problem of bad character is perhaps the most salient theme running through the classical social contract theories of the early modern period. Hobbes argued, for example, that the state of nature is a state of war because men are greedy and vain.[15] In their desire to dominate others as well as protect themselves, they inevitably disregard their covenants of nonaggression and launch preemptive attacks against those who might attack them first. Locke also thought that individuals in the state of nature would act aggressively.[16] Unlike Hobbes, however, he did not think they would do so out of callous disregard for the natural law but rather as a result of self-deception. Since people are often biased in their own favor, each side in a dispute will judge themselves justified and hence be unwilling to yield. Unable to settle their conflicts peacefully, individuals in the state of nature will resort to violence, leading to destructive cycles of feuding. Similarly, Hume believed that, in the absence of government, people will tend to ignore the principles of justice.[17] Hume attributed this noncompliance largely to irrationality: people often heavily discount the future and seek to maximize short-term benefit over long-term gain. As a result, they routinely fail to recognize the benefits of abiding by the principles of justice.

For each of these three political theorists, the state of nature is undesirable because human nature is corrupt in some way. And, correspondingly, the law is a necessary social institution precisely because it compensates for the infirmities of human nature by ensuring that individuals abide by the existing norms. For Hobbes and Hume, the law secures compliance by threatening coercion and sanctions whereas, for Locke, it acts as a third-party adjudicator, providing impartial resolution of disputes for those who consent to its authority.

In view of our earlier discussion, however, this general account of the law is obviously flawed. For if the principal aim of law is to solve the problem of bad character, we would expect law to be deemed unnecessary in situations where everyone has good character. But as we saw in the last section, legal institutions can be highly desirable even though everyone in the community is willing to abide by the existing norms. The residents of Cooks Island, for example, were committed to following their shared plan and acting in accordance with morality. The complexity and contentiousness of these normative questions, however, rendered that task difficult and costly to accomplish. Moreover, the complexity and arbitrariness of many large-scale shared activities rendered it impossible for members of the group to do what they had good ethical reasons to do. Even when they knew what moral problems they ought to rectify, they could not figure out how to coordinate their behavior so as to resolve these problems. Their sterling characters did not, in other words, diminish their need for law.

The Plan Is Mightier than the Sword

Following the Planning Theory, it is a mistake to suppose that the function of the law is to solve the problem of bad character or any other particular social or moral quandary. As a contingent matter, of course, the law serves a number of important social aims. It builds roads and bridges, educates the population, finances and organizes communal self-defense, sets up markets, regulates imports and exports, controls the money supply, standardizes weights and measures, collects and redistributes wealth, arbitrates and mediates disputes, constitutes national identity, and so on. It also ensures that people listen to its rules. Indeed, it would be absurd to deny that, in the modern world at least, social deviance caused by vicious character is one of the reasons why law is an indispensable social institution. It is indeed likely that life would be poor, nasty, brutish, and short without legal systems maintaining order through threats of coercion.

The essential point, however, is that whenever the law properly addresses a particular social problem, it does so because, given current social conditions, alternative methods of planning are somehow deficient. Thus, when the law is needed to combat bad character, it is because, and only because, *coercion in the absence of sophisticated forms of social planning would be expensive, ineffective, or dangerous*. To appreciate this, it is important to remember that law enforcement is a shared activity and, in modern states, a quite massive one. In some cases, the roster of officers who are engaged in enforcement—police, judges, magistrates, bailiffs, clerks, wardens, guards, and lawyers—contains millions of names. It is hard to imagine such groups acting together in such complex and contentious environments without an extensive network of social plans to regulate their behavior. These inherent problems can be further aggravated when alienated participants are asked to play roles that they cannot be trusted to perform in the absence of guidance and monitoring. Add to these difficulties the enormous number of coordination problems that arise in such large-scale contexts and it becomes evident that improvisation, spontaneous ordering, private planning, and simple forms of social planning are not adequate to guide, organize, and monitor such activities.

Kelsen once described law as an "organization of force."[18] Although I disagree with this claim that the law necessarily uses force, I agree that, when the law does use force, it is always organized. Both to maximize its effect and control its power, the law organizes a coercive response to social deviance through an interlocking set of social plans. The master plan that regulates all official conduct controls the procedural aspects of coercion: it selects those whose role it is to enforce the law and the procedures that they must follow in order for coercion to be permissible. The directives that are created pursuant to the master plan concern the substantive aspects of coercion: they identify those actions that warrant a coercive response. Legal officials know which behaviors to punish because other officials have issued directives informing members of the group of their rights and obligations. When enforcement personnel follow this dense network of social plans, they are able to act collectively to subdue members of the community. Thus, despite the fact that legal officials are almost always a small minority of a population, the shared agency made possible by social planning harnesses and magnifies their power, thereby enabling them to enforce the will of the law.

The Primacy of Social Facts

As we have seen, the Planning Theory not only maintains that legal activity results *in* planning; it maintains that it results *from* planning as well. Legal institutions are structured by shared plans that are developed for officials so as to enable them to work together in order to plan for the community. These norms set out the vertical and horizontal divisions of social labor, specifying who is authorized to formulate, adopt, repudiate, affect, apply, and enforce the plans and instructing them about how to engage in these various stages of social planning. These shared plans can be thought of as *the law's plans for planning*.

Once we recognize the central role that shared plans play in the law, we can begin to address the question with which we began the last chapter. Why might one claim—as legal positivists do—that law and morality do not share the same basic ground rules? Why is the determination of legal validity a matter of a sociological, rather than moral, inquiry?

I hope that my answer to these questions is now apparent: namely, that the fundamental rules of a legal system constitute a shared plan and, as we have seen, the proper way to ascertain the existence or content of a shared plan is through an examination of the relevant social facts. A shared plan exists just in case the plan was designed with a group in mind so that they may engage in a joint activity, it is publicly accessible, and it is accepted by most members of the group in question. As a result, if we want to discover the existence or content of the fundamental rules of a legal system, we must look only to these social facts. We must look, in other words, only to what officials think, intend, claim, and do around here.

Notice further that the existence of the shared plan does not depend on any moral facts obtaining. The shared plan can be morally obnoxious. It may cede total control of social planning to a malevolent dictator or privilege the rights of certain subgroups of the community over others. The shared plan may have no support from the population at large; those governed by it may absolutely hate it. Nevertheless, if the social facts obtain for plan sharing—if most officials accept a publicly accessible plan designed for them—then the shared plan will exist. And if the shared plan sets out an activity of social planning that is hierarchical and highly impersonal and the community normally abides by the plans created pursuant to it, then a system of legal authority will exist as well.

The crucial point here is that the determination by social facts is not some necessary, but otherwise unimportant, property of shared plans. Shared plans must be determined exclusively by social facts *if they are to fulfill their function*. As we have seen, shared plans are supposed to guide and coordinate behavior by resolving doubts and disagreements about how to act. If a plan with a particular content exists only when certain moral facts obtain, then it could not resolve doubts and disagreements about the right way of proceeding. For in order to apply it, the participants would have to engage in deliberation or bargaining that would recreate the problem that the plan aimed to solve. The logic of planning requires that plans be ascertainable by a method that does not resurrect the very questions that plans are designed to settle. Only social facts, not moral ones, can serve this function.[19]

The purpose of the master plan, we have said, is to guide, organize, and monitor the shared activity of legal officials. It seeks to overcome the enormously complex, contentious, and arbitrary problems associated with arranging a system of social planning. Because reasonable (and unreasonable) people can have doubts and disagreements about which social problems to pursue and who should be trusted to pursue them, it is essential to have a mechanism that can settle such questions, creating a mesh between legal officials and leading them all in the same direction. To seek to discover the existence or content of such a mechanism by looking to moral philosophy, as the natural lawyer recommends we do, would frustrate the function of the master plan. It would require members of the community to answer the very sorts of questions that the master plan aimed to circumvent.

This argument for legal positivism might helpfully be put in a slightly different way. Consider a theory called "plan positivism." Plan positivists believe that the existence and content of plans never depend on moral facts. Plan positivism is uncontroversially true. No one believes that there are moral constraints on the existence of plans; even natural lawyers are willing to concede that evil plans are still plans. Terrorist plots, for example, exist even though there are no moral facts that justify their existence; rather, they exist just because terrorists share certain plans. Indeed, as I have just argued, plan positivism must be true if plans are to fulfill their function. Plans can do the thinking for us only if we can discover their existence or content without engaging in deliberation on the merits.

The claim, then, is that plan positivism, in combination with the Planning Theory, guarantees the truth of legal positivism. Since plan positivism claims that the existence and content of plans are never determined by moral facts, it follows that the existence and content of the master plan that grounds all law cannot be determined by moral facts either. Moreover, since the identity of this plan as a *legal* plan does not depend on its moral legitimacy—its status as law depends, rather, on possessing certain formal features such as being shared, regulating the activity of social planning, and generating highly impersonal positions of power—it follows that all law is grounded in a norm whose existence, content, and identity are determined by social facts alone.

The Possibility of Legal Authority

I argued in Chapter 2 that a crucial test for any jurisprudential theory is its ability to solve what I have called the Possibility Puzzle. Recall that the Possibility Puzzle purports to show that legal authority is impossible. On the one hand, legal authority must be conferred by legal norms; yet, on the other, legal norms must be created by legal authority. From these two assumptions, we get a classic chicken-egg paradox. Any time we try to establish a claim of legal authority, we either enter into a vicious circle (the authority created the norm that conferred the power on the authority to create that very norm) or an infinite regress (the authority got his power from another authority, who got his power from another authority, and so on).

In this final section, I want to show that the Planning Theory does indeed provide a convincing solution to this apparent paradox. Before I can do so, however, I need to say a bit more about how legal authority is generated by the plans of a legal system.

The Ability to Plan

According to the Planning Theory, someone has legal authority only if he is authorized by the master plan of a particular legal system. But while authorization is necessary for legal authority, it is clearly not sufficient. The reason is simple: if legal authority entails the ability to plan for others, as the Planning Theory claims, then the norms adopted and applied by legal authorities must be plans. Plans, as I have argued, are special kind of norms. They are not only positive entities that form nested structures, but they are formed by a process that disposes their subjects to comply. As a result, unless the members of the community are disposed to follow the norms created to guide their conduct, the norms created will not be plans.

Thus, being authorized to plan for others does not entail that one actually has the *ability* to plan for others. A group of poor deluded souls can share a plan authorizing one of them to plan for the withdrawal of U.S. forces from Iraq. But the one authorized will not have the ability to adopt a plan for U.S. forces because he cannot dispose them to act in accordance with his directives.

The disposition instilled by the legal process is obviously not a brute causal one; it must be tied in some way to human motivation. Legal authorities have the ability to plan for others, in other words, only if they are able to motivate their subjects to obey under normal conditions. Of course, not every official with legal authority need be able to instill this disposition; rather, he must be part of a group of individuals who, by planning together in accordance with the master plan, can dispose most of the people to comply with most of the plans most of the time.

When members of the community consider legal authorities to be morally legitimate, encouraging compliant behavior will be relatively straightforward. By designating a standard as *the* standard to be used to guide and evaluate conduct, their subjects will take themselves to have reasons to defer and, in the normal course, will obey. If members of the community are less cooperative, legal authorities can dispose them to comply through various forms of intimidation. When these threats are strong and credible enough, even those who do not accept the law's moral authority will nevertheless be motivated to follow the adopted plans.[20]

Legal Authority and Planning Authority

As we have seen, the Planning Theory claims that a body has legal authority in a particular legal system when two conditions are met: (1) the system's master plan authorizes that body to plan for others, and (2) the members of the community normally heed all those who are so authorized. Legal authority will be possible, therefore, just in case it is possible for both of these conditions to obtain. Let us, then, consider each of these two conditions in turn.

First, is it possible that a shared plan authorizes some body to plan? Of course it is! As we have seen, shared plans exist when certain social facts obtain. A shared plan can authorize some person to plan for another just in case some person or persons designed the plan, at least in part, for a group; part of the plan authorizes some body to plan for another; the plan is publicly accessible; and the members of the group accept it. When these conditions obtain, a shared plan will be created and will authorize some to plan for others.

On this account, the question of how Lex can be the ruler is no more perplexing than the question of how my friend can be the head chef during a meeting of our club. My friend is authorized to adopt plans for club members because we have committed ourselves to defer to him. Similarly, Lex is legally authorized to plan for others because officials of his regime have accepted a shared plan that authorizes him to play a certain role in adopting legal policies and, hence, requires them to defer to him in the circumstances specified in that plan.

In the end, shared plans are able to authorize legal officials to plan for others because human beings are planning agents and are capable of guiding and organizing their actions both over time and across persons. Not only can we figure out how others should act in order to achieve some complex goal, but we can form intentions to do what we are instructed to do. In other words, we are able to create law because we are able to create and share plans.

Notice that the Planning Theory is able to secure the existence of fundamental legal rules without generating vicious circles or infinite regresses. Legal officials have the power to adopt the shared plan that sets out these fundamental rules by virtue of the norms of instrumental rationality. Since these norms that confer the rational power to plan are not themselves plans, they have not been created by any other authority. They exist simply in virtue of being rationally valid principles.

Having shown that shared plans authorizing bodies to plan for others are possible, we should consider the second condition of legal authority, namely, whether those so authorized can motivate their subjects to comply under normal conditions. As we have just seen, there is nothing perplexing about this condition obtaining either. Members of the group might all accept a general policy to obey the law or deem those in authority to be morally legitimate. In such cases, the adoption of plans by legal officials will induce a rational requirement for those individuals to comply. Even when members of the group are not predisposed to conform to the law, the commitment of officials to carry out parts of the shared plan that direct punishment in case of disobedience may be sufficient to motivate ordinary citizens to obey.

The Normativity of Legal Authority

According to the Planning Theory, legal authority is possible because certain kinds of agents are capable of (1) creating and sharing a plan for planning and (2) motivating others to heed their plans. Legal systems are possible, in other words, because certain states of affairs are achievable, namely, those that underwrite the existence of a legal system's master plan and those that account for the disposition of the community to comply with the plans created under normal conditions.

In this section, I consider an important challenge to this solution to the Possibility Puzzle. According to this objection, planning agency merely establishes that certain individuals are capable of planning for others. It does not establish that these individuals have *legal authority*, for to have legal authority entails the ability to impose legal obligations or confer legal rights. But individuals can have the ability to create obligations or rights, according to the objection, only if they have normative power over others—namely, the power to change what others, in some sense, ought to do—and to render them criticizable if they fail to comply. Moreover, in light of the discussion in Chapter 4 where we concluded that legal concepts such as OBLIGATION and RIGHT are moral concepts, it would seem that this normative power must be a *moral* power. The Planning Theory cannot establish the possibility of legal authority, therefore, because capacities to plan and motivate others to comply do not necessarily render the ability to plan for others morally legitimate and hence cannot generate the moral power to impose obligations or confer rights.

This objection may be brought out in another way. Some natural lawyers might accept the core idea behind the Planning Theory. They might regard the fundamental rules of a legal system as forming a shared plan for social planning. Their only quibble would be that this plan is a special kind of plan, namely, a *morally legitimate* one. Shared plans that are morally illegitimate certainly exist, they will happily concede, but they don't count as law. They don't count as law because only morally legitimate plans can empower individuals to impose legal obligations or confer legal rights and hence to have legal authority. The possibility of legal authority requires more than the social facts necessary to establish the existence of plans—it requires moral facts as well.

I will begin my response to this objection by conceding that the normativity of the master plan of a legal system is of a very limited sort. While legal officials are rationally required to conform to their shared plan, it is also true that those who do not accept the law are not similarly bound. Furthermore, the master plan of a legal system may be morally illegitimate and hence not capable of imposing a moral obligation on anyone to obey.

I will argue, however, that the objection is mistaken in concluding that the normative limitations of the master plan preclude its ability to ground claims of legal authority. For once we appreciate the distinctive role that the word "legal" plays in discourse about the law, we will see that moral powers are not necessary to render legal statements true. Legal authority, rights, and obligations are possible, it will turn out, simply because highly impersonal shared practices of social planning are possible.

The Inner Rationality of Law

Let us begin our discussion of the normativity of the master plan by briefly comparing the Planning Theory with Hart's model. According to both accounts, the fundamental rules of a legal system exist only if legal officials adopt an attitude of acceptance toward them. Hart called this attitude "the internal point of view," which is the acceptance of a rule as a guide to conduct and standard of evaluation.

The Planning Theory also requires officials to accept the fundamental legal rules as a condition of their existence. But since the Planning Theory regards the fundamental rules as elements of a shared plan, the acceptance in question is a more complex attitude than Hart's internal point of view. For as we have mentioned in the previous chapter, acceptance of a plan involves more than just committing to do one's part; one must also commit to allow others to do their parts as well. Moreover, to accept one's part is to *adopt a plan*. In other words, to accept one's part does not merely commit oneself to following the plan; one also commits to filling out the plan, to ensuring consistency with one's beliefs, subplans, and other plans, and to not reconsidering it absent a compelling reason for doing so.

Since acceptance of the fundamental legal rules involves the adoption of plans, the distinctive norms of rationality that attend the activity of planning necessarily come into play. Thus, an official who accepts her position within an authority structure will be rationally criticizable if she disobeys her superiors, fails to flesh out their orders so that she may take the means necessary to satisfy their demands, adopts plans that are inconsistent with these orders, or reconsiders them without a compelling reason to do so. Because these rationality requirements apply whenever legal systems exist, we might say that they constitute the "inner rationality of law."[21]

The inner rationality of law, of course, is a limited set of constraints because the rational norms of planning only apply to those who accept plans. The bad man, therefore, cannot be rationally criticizable for failing to obey legal authorities insofar as he does not accept the law. On the other hand, since most officials do accept the master legal plan, they are criticizable for disobeying the law absent a compelling reason to do so.

Adjectival vs. Perspectival Claims

While rational requirements of obedience necessarily attend the existence of any legal system, I do not think the same holds true for moral requirements. For there is no reason to think that the master plans of every possible legal system will be morally legitimate. Though the master plan of Cooks Island set out a commendable system of governance affirmed by all, it is easy to imagine distributions of legal rights and responsibilities that would be unfair, inefficient, or monstrous and rejected by everyone except legal officials. Remember that the existence and content of shared plans are determined by social, not moral, facts. It is doubtful, then, that the social facts necessary for the existence of a shared plan will always generate morally acceptable legal arrangements.

We might analogize the law to a game.[22] If one has no reason to play a game, one has no reason to respect its rules. Likewise, if one has no moral reason to participate in or support a particular legal system, one has no moral reason to recognize its demands. As a result, the authorization of a master plan and the ability to dispose others to comply cannot by themselves confer moral legitimacy on the one authorized. Unless the master plan sets out a morally legitimate scheme of governance, those authorized will merely enjoy legal authority but will lack the ability to impose moral obligations to obey.

Let us revisit the objection with which we began this section. On the Planning Theory, the challenge points out, nothing of moral significance necessarily follows from the claim that X has legal authority over Y. For if the master plan happens to be morally inappropriate, X will have no moral authority to impose a moral obligation on Y. And if X has no moral authority to morally obligate Y, in what sense can X have legal authority to legally obligate Y? Recall our earlier criticism of Hart's theory of legal concepts. We saw there that legal concepts such as OBLIGATION and RIGHT are best understood as moral concepts, for only moral concepts can constitute claims limiting freedom, establishing guilt and licensing punishment. If so, how can the social facts necessary for the existence of social planning establish the ability to impose legal obligations and legal rights? Moreover, if Y does not accept the master plan, there will be no rational demand that he comply either. It follows on the Planning Theory that one can be subject to legal authority even though no normative relation of any sort obtains between him and the alleged authority!

In order to address this objection, we should examine claims of legal authority in more detail: what are we imputing to someone when we say that she has "legal authority"? One possibility is that we are imputing a type of moral authority. On this reading, the word "authority" means the same as it does in moral contexts, roughly speaking, the power to impose moral obligations and confer moral rights, and the word "legal" functions as an adjective, identifying this kind of moral power. We are saying, then, that the person in question has moral authority in virtue of being an official in a legal institution. Call this the "adjectival" interpretation.

It appears that the objection we have been considering interprets claims of legal authority adjectivally. For on the adjectival interpretation, legal authority entails moral authority, and since morally illegitimate shared plans do not confer moral authority they cannot confer legal authority. To be sure, this implication would be devastating for the Planning Theory if we were compelled to accept the adjectival interpretation of legal authority claims as the only possible one. I do not however think we are. The problem with the adjectival interpretation is that it ties legal authority to moral authority and thus precludes the possibility of morally illegitimate legal regimes. Not only are such cases possible, they are actual. Stalin, Hitler, and Mao, to use three paradigmatic examples, all had legal authority but were morally illegitimate. The adjectival interpretation, therefore, cannot provide the exclusive meaning for all claims of legal authority, for it would not permit us to attribute legal authority to those individuals upon which we ordinarily bestow such titles.

Fortunately, there is another interpretation that does permit the ascription of legal authority to morally illegitimate bodies. The key here is to recognize that, although the term "authority" in claims of legal authority refers to a moral power, the word "legal" often does not modify this noun-phrase; rather, its role is to qualify the statement in which it is embedded. When we ascribe legal authority to someone, in other words, we are not necessarily imputing any kind of moral authority to her. To the contrary, we are qualifying our ascription of moral legitimacy. We are saying that, *from the legal point of view,* the person in question has morally legitimate power.[23] Similarly, to say that one is legally obligated to perform some action need not commit the asserter to affirming that one is really obligated to perform that action, that is, has a moral obligation to perform that action. The statement may be understood to mean only that from the legal point of view one is (morally) obligated to perform that action. Call this the "perspectival" interpretation.

To understand the discourse of legality, therefore, one must recognize that it typically plays a *distancing* function. It enables us to talk about the moral conception of a particular legal system without necessarily endorsing that conception. Sure, one might say, sodomy is wrong from the legal point of view. But this assertion does not imply that sodomy is in fact wrong. In some cases, the word "legal" registers our agnosticism: we do not know or care whether the law's normative judgments are correct—we are simply reporting these judgments and, in effect, bracketing them off in a special kind of invisible inverted commas. At other times, the word "legal" signals our alienation from the legal point of view. Sodomy, we can say, is legally wrong, but it is wrong *only legally*. From our own point of view, sodomy is morally permissible.

The Legal Point of View

Perspectival legal claims, we have seen, carry no moral implications. To ascribe legal authority to another on the perspectival reading is not to impute moral authority and hence does not imply, as it would on the adjectival reading, that others are morally obligated to comply and their disobedience would be moral criticizable. Rather, it merely commits one to believing that disobedience is criticizable from the legal point of view.

What, then, is the legal point of view? It is not necessarily the perspective of any particular legal official. No officials may personally accept it, although they will normally act as though they do. The legal point of view, rather, is the perspective of a certain normative theory. According to that theory, those who are authorized by the norms of legal institutions have moral legitimacy and, when they act in accordance with those norms, they generate a moral obligation to obey. The legal point of view of a certain system, in other words, is a theory that holds that the norms of that system are morally legitimate and obligating.

The normative theory that represents a system's point of view is not a complete account of morality. The legal point of view merely asserts that the norms of the legal system are legitimate and binding and hence that moral questions are to be answered on the basis of these norms; it is silent on how to answer moral questions not resolved by these norms. Moreover, this normative theory may be false from a moral perspective. Those authorized by legal institutions to act may be morally illegitimate and their actions may generate no moral obligations to obey. The point of view of a particular legal system may be like the phlogiston theory of combustion: a scientific theory that aimed to be true but missed the mark. In short, the legal point of view always *purports* to represent the moral point of view, even when it fails to do so.

Given this interpretation of claims of legal authority and legal obligation, we can easily see how morally illegitimate shared plans can confer legal authority. For to ascribe legal authority to a body in a particular legal system is to assert that, from the point of view of that legal system, the body in question is morally legitimate. This interpretation of perspectival statements can be rendered as follows:[24]

(1) X has legal authority over Y with respect to subject matter Z in system S ↔ From the point of view of S, X has moral authority over Y with respect to Z.

The point of view of a legal system, I have just said, will ascribe moral legitimacy to a body just in case its norms confer power on that body. Since on the Planning Theory the legal norms that confer legal authority are subplans of the system's master plan, the legal point of view will ascribe moral legitimacy to a body when its master plan authorizes that body to so act. The relation between the legal point of view and the master plan can be rendered like so:

(2) From the point of view of S, X has moral authority over Y with respect to subject matter Z ↔ The master plan of S authorizes X to plan for Y with respect to Z.

It follows from (1) and (2) that a body will have legal authority in a particular legal system just in case the system's master plan authorizes that body to so act.[25]

(3) X has legal authority over Y with respect to subject matter Z in system S ↔ The master plan of S authorizes X to plan for Y with respect to Z.

We can see that, contrary to the objection with which we began this section, the truth of legal authority claims is not dependent on the moral legitimacy of a system's master plan. For legal claims interpreted perspectivally are not moral claims; they are descriptions of a perspective according to which the law is morally legitimate. On the perspectival reading, a body has legal authority in a system just in case it has moral authority from the legal point of view and it has moral authority from the legal point of view just in case it is authorized by the system's norms. Because the norms which authorize bodies are part of that system's master plan, it follows that a body has legal authority in a system because the master plan authorizes it. And, as we have seen, master plans exist regardless of the moral facts; they exist just in case officials have exercised their rational planning capacity in the right sort of way.

It bears emphasizing that, even on the Planning Theory, the master plan of a legal system is insufficient to establish the truth of legal authority claims understood adjectivally. For on this interpretation, legal authorities have moral authority and can have that power only if the principles of political morality concur. The Planning Theory insists, however, that the master plan, and the principles of instrumental rationality that ground it, are sufficient to ground legal authority understood perspectivally. For on this interpretation, legal authority does not entail the power to impose moral obligations to obey and hence does not require the approval of the principles of political morality.

Hume's Challenge Revisited

I hope it is clear at this point how the Planning Theory will rebut Hume's Challenge. For on the perspectival interpretation of the word "legal," statements of legal authority, legal rights, and legal obligations are *descriptive,* not normative. They describe the normative point of view of the law. Statements such as "X has legal authority over Y in S" are true just in case it is true that *according to S's point of view* X has moral authority over Y.

Because legal statements purport to describe the legal point of view, the conclusion of legal reasoning will be a descriptive judgment. Legal reasoning, therefore, follows the acceptable DIDO pattern. From descriptive judgments about the existence of shared plans or the content of the legal point of view, other descriptive judgments about the legal point of view can be derived. The Planning Theory, in other words, conforms to Hume's Law because legal reasoning does not involve the derivation of an ought from an is, but rather an is from an is.[26]

Comparisons

At this point, I want to return briefly to our criticisms of previous positivist attempts to solve the Possibility Puzzle in order to see if the planning solution escapes these same objections. The first attempt I discussed was Austin's attempt to ground all legal systems in habits of obedience. Recall that we made three principal objections to this reduction. First, habits are not normative activities. When someone habitually engages in some activity, he does not necessarily subject his conduct to the evaluation of a norm and/or describe his actions using normative terminology. For this reason, it would be bizarre to describe a judge's hewing to the law as an instance of *habitual* obedience. The judge not only evaluates his own law-applying actions by norms, but expresses his legal judgments with normative-loaded words like "ought," "must," "right," and "wrong." Second, habits of obedience cannot account for the continuity of legal authority. Once Rex I dies, there will necessarily be a lag time before a new habit of obedience to his successor develops. Yet the successor, Rex II, has legal power from the time of the death of Rex I and need not wait until a habit of obedience forms. Third, Austin's reduction to habits cannot account for the persistence of law. The laws made by Rex I carry over into the realm of Rex II even though Rex I can no longer be the object of habitual obedience and Rex II has not reenacted his laws.

Because the planning model replaces habits with plans, it has no problem explaining the normative nature of legal activity. When a judge applies the law, he is following a plan directing him to do so. He takes the plan as settling for him how he ought to proceed. It is natural, therefore, for him to express his actions using normative terminology. For when one follows a plan, one takes the plan as determining what one ought to do. Likewise, plans neatly account for the continuity and persistence of law. The shared plans that underwrite legal systems establish offices and accord power to different inhabitants as soon as they fulfill the requirements for accession to their offices. They need not wait for habits of obedience to kick in. These same plans accord validity to the planning of past inhabitants, hence ensuring the persistence of their plans.

Hart tried to solve the Possibility Puzzle via his practice theory. On the Practice Theory, all social rules are practices. The rule of recognition can thus be brought into existence by being practiced, because it is a social rule and social rules are just practices. We saw, however, that the Practice Theory of social rules is terribly flawed. First, it is a category mistake to identify rules with practices. Rules are abstract entities, whereas practices are concrete events that reside within space and time. Second, not every social practice creates a social rule and, indeed, most do not. If social practices can fail to generate social rules, then Hart gives us no reason to believe that the rule of recognition is brought into existence simply by being practiced.

Following the Planning Theory, however, shared plans are not identical with practices. They are abstract entities that members of a group accept and are thus the objects of their intentions. Furthermore, the Planning Theory does not claim that all social practices generate social rules or shared plans. It merely claims that the social practice that lies at the foundation of law is structured by a shared plan. It is a shared plan because its function is to guide and organize the planning behavior of the group of officials. And since the norm is a shared plan, it must be practiced by that group if it is to exist. They must accept it and it must dispose them to act accordingly.

The last positivist theory we explored was the coordination convention account. On this account, the rule of recognition is like a rule of the road: it is a coordination convention, and coordination conventions are behavioral regularities. The rule of recognition can thus be brought into existence simply by being practiced. This theory, however, suffers from a fatal flaw: it places too many restrictions on the type of motivations that judges must possess. First, coordination conventions arise only when the players deem the game to have arbitrary solutions. However, there is no justification for insisting that most officials in every conceivable legal system must treat their system of government like the rules of the road, as just one out of several acceptable alternatives. Second, coordination conventions require that the players take the fact that others are acting in a similar manner as a *reason* for them to act similarly. This seems to exclude cases of alienated players, those who participate in the practice for no other reason than that it is in their self-interest to do so.

The Planning Theory, by contrast, does not insist that officials have particular beliefs or motivations. They may think that there is one way, and only one way, to structure government and accept the shared plan precisely because they think that the plan has hit on this unique way of engaging in social planning. Or they may think that the shared plan sets out the worst blueprint for social planning but accept it purely for reasons of self-interest. As long as most officials accept the plan, play their part in it, and resolve their disputes peacefully and openly, and all this is common knowledge, it does not matter why they are doing so. A shared plan will exist and their planning pursuant to it will be a shared activity.

Finally, the Planning Theory's response to Hume's Challenge escapes the objections that were made against previous positivistic accounts. As we saw, Austin denied that his positivistic theory permits the derivation of an ought from an is because concepts such as SOVEREIGNTY and OBLIGATION are descriptive in nature (they refer to the existence of habits and likelihood of sanctions). Legal reasoning, on this account, follows a DIDO pattern, issuing from, and in, descriptive judgments. This response fails, however, insofar as statements of right and obligation are used to justify and evaluate action, roles that would be inexplicable if the concepts that these statements employed were descriptive ones.

While the Planning Theory agrees with Austin that legal statements are descriptive, it maintains that the main concepts that they employ are moral and hence normative. Legal statements are descriptive, rather, because they describe the moral perspective of the law. For this reason, statements involving these concepts may be used in justification and evaluation. When claims sans the word "legal" are made, they express propositions with moral significance. To say that you are obligated to pay your taxes, for example, implies that you morally ought to pay your taxes. When the word "legal" is used to preface the use of normative terminology, the speaker might be either employing the adjectival sense of the word and hence expressing her judgment about a moral reason for action (namely, that the reason results from the operation of a legal institution) or exploiting the perspectival interpretation of the word and hence distancing herself from such a claim. In the latter case, the agent is not justifying or evaluating action from her own point of view, but rather that of the law.

Like the Planning Theory, Hart's account treats legal concepts as irreducibly normative; but in contrast to Planning Theory, it conceives of legal judgments as irreducibly normative as well. In response to the charge that positivism permits legal reasoners to derive normative judgments from descriptive judgments about social facts, Hart pointed out that reasoners might practically engage with social practices by taking the internal point of view toward them. From the normative judgment that the social practice of rule recognition ought to be followed, they might then derive further normative judgments about legal rights and obligations. And since, according to Hart, legal concepts such as AUTHORITY and OBLIGATION are normative but amoral, legal judgments are not moral judgments and hence can be accepted by those who morally reject the law. The problem with this general strategy, however, is explaining how the bad man can both redescribe the law in normative terminology and engage in legal reasoning despite not taking the internal point of view toward a particular social practice of recognition. It also has trouble explaining how legal concepts are nonmoral and yet are used to guide and evaluate conduct in settings where the moral stakes are characteristically very high.

The Planning Theory, by contrast, does not require the legal reasoner to take the internal point of view toward the master plan of a legal system. As a result, it has no difficulty explaining how the bad man may discover the content of the law or how legal concepts can be moral concepts. Because the existence of the master plan is a matter of descriptive fact, anyone can acknowledge its existence regardless of their normative commitments. And once a legal reasoner recognizes the existence and content of the master plan, he can begin to make descriptive assessments about the law's perspective on moral rights, obligations, and validity, even if he judges the law's perspective mistaken from the moral point of view.

7

WHAT LAW IS

Flipping the Soul-State Analogy

In *The Republic,* Plato attempted to reveal the nature of justice in the soul by constructing a just state and extrapolating from the latter to the former. He reasoned that it is easier to discern the properties of an entity when it is depicted on a very large canvas. "[I]s not a State larger than an individual? . . . Then in the larger the quantity of justice is likely to be larger and more easily discernible. I propose therefore that we enquire into the nature of justice and injustice, first as they appear in the State, and secondly in the individual, proceeding from the greater to the lesser and comparing them."[1]

In the last two chapters, I have proceeded in the opposite direction. I began by investigating how individuals govern their own individual actions, moved to the case of small shared activities, then to instances of massively shared agency, back to households, and, finally, on to political government. My strategy, in other words, has been to explore familiar forms of human agency, that is, individual and small-scale planning, and then extrapolate to lesser-understood cases, that is, massively shared agency and legal activity.

Thus we began with the simple fact, emphasized by Bratman, that human beings are planning creatures: we not only have the capacity to act purposively, something we share with nonhuman animals, but also the ability to form and execute plans. We saw that our need for planning arises from the complexity of our goals, the limitations of our abilities, and the pluralism of our values and preferences. In order to achieve complicated goals, we must assemble long sequences of actions correctly; in order to act together, we must be able to coordinate many of our actions with one another. Deliberation at the time of action will often be too

193

costly or risky due to the complexity, contentiousness, or arbitrariness of the choice situation. Planning guides and organizes our behavior so that we can accomplish ends that we would not otherwise be able to achieve, or achieve as well.

Just as social creatures with complex goals, conflicting values, and limited abilities require a special kind of psychology, we also saw that they need a special kind of social structure in order to flourish. In any community of modest size, the moral problems and opportunities that arise will not be solvable exclusively through improvisation, spontaneous ordering, private agreements, social consensus, personalized hierarchies, or some combination thereof. Only a sophisticated mechanism of social planning, like the hierarchical, impersonal, and institutional one exemplified by the law, can address these issues in an effective and efficient manner. Laws, we might say, play the same role in social life that intentions play in individual and shared agency: they are universal means that enable us to coordinate our behavior intra- and interpersonally.

By reversing Plato's course and moving from the small to the large, I have tried to show that political government is continuous with the intimately familiar activities we understand so well. I have argued that, far from being an esoteric activity completely divorced from ordinary experience, the law is simply a sophisticated apparatus for planning in very complex, contentious, and arbitrary communal settings.

By returning to the soul-state analogy throughout the rest of the book, I intend to draw on our practical knowledge of planning in order to uncover and explore the identity of law and its implications. I will argue that many vexing jurisprudential puzzles can easily be solved by recognizing that legal activity is the shared activity of social planning and that laws are just plans, or planlike norms. I will also try to make good on the promise made in the first chapter, namely, to show how a philosophical investigation into the nature of law can help us understand the practice of legal interpretation. For if the planning model is right, the interpretation of law is nothing but the interpretation of plans. Knowing how to interpret a plan does not ordinarily require a Ph.D. or J.D.—it is an activity that we do hundreds of times a day. We know how to do this simply because we are planning creatures.

In this chapter, my aim will be to develop and defend the Planning Theory of Law in a systematic and detailed fashion. To do so, I will shift my methodology from the Constructivist Strategy to the Comparative one. Rather than build a legal system from scratch, I will try instead to isolate the distinctive nature of legal institutions by contrasting them with closely related planning phenomena, such as parenting, clubs, organized crime, condominium associations, and so on. I hope to show through this comparative process that legal institutions are planning organizations of a very special kind and that laws are plans or planlike norms created by them. This account will represent the Planning Theory's answer to the Identity Question: it will show what makes the law *the law* and not something else. In the chapters that follow I intend to show the practical implications of this theoretical finding.

The Planning Thesis

The main idea behind the Planning Theory of Law is that the exercise of legal authority, which I will refer to as "legal activity," is an activity of social planning. Legal institutions plan for the communities over whom they claim authority, both by telling their members what they may or may not do and by authorizing some of these members to plan for others. Call this idea the "Planning Thesis."

Planning Thesis: Legal activity is an activity of social planning.

Central to the Planning Thesis is the claim that legal activity is more than simply the activity of formulating, adopting, repudiating, affecting, and applying norms for members of the community. It is the activity of *planning*. In this section, I hope to show that this description is not only justified but illuminating.

The Path of the Law

As we saw in Chapter 5, plans do not normally leap like Athena from Zeus's head, fully mature at the time of birth. Planners usually begin with partial plans and fill in the details over time. Law follows the same route. Schemes of legal regulation are rarely created all at once. They are typically assembled piece by piece, starting off either as broad standards that are refined over time, detailed regulations that are unified by the development of general standards, or a hodgepodge of rules that are supplemented bit by bit as new problems arise.

Consider as an example of legal planning the law of business competition in the United States. The first major piece of federal regulation was enacted in 1890 in the form of the Sherman Antitrust Act. Section 1 of the Sherman Act, for example, provides that: "Every contract, combination in the form of trust or otherwise, or conspiracy, in restraint of trade or commerce among the several States, or with foreign nations, is declared to be illegal." The Sherman Act, however, does not specify which activities are "restraints of trade." It simply sets out a very broad standard, prohibiting any activity of restraining trade that results from a contract, combination, or conspiracy.[2]

Subsequent litigation under the Sherman Act forced federal courts to interpret and develop the limited guidance they had received. In 1911, for example, the Supreme Court held that only "unreasonable" acts that restrain trade violate the Sherman Act.[3] In subsequent cases, the Court clarified this ruling, maintaining that certain acts—price-fixing, bid rigging, and market allocation schemes—are so anticompetitive that they are unreasonable per se and hence illegal.[4] It also held that other activities must be judged according to the so-called rule of reason, that is, on a case-by-case basis to ascertain whether, on balance, the anticompetitive effects of the business activity outweigh any procompetitive effects it may have.

As it turned out, many in Congress were unhappy with the doctrine emerging from the courts. In an effort to overturn certain precedents, as well as provide greater guidance, Congress enacted the Clayton Antitrust Act of 1914. According to Section 2 of the Clayton Act, price discrimination that "substantially lessens competition or tends to create a monopoly in any line of commerce" counts as a "restraint of trade" under Section 1 of the Sherman Act, while according to Section 6, labor activities such as boycotts and strikes do not. Congress provided further direction in 1936 by enacting the Robinson-Patman Act, which specifies in greater detail which activities count as price discrimination under the Clayton Act and, hence, as illegal restraints of trade under the Sherman Act.

In the same year that Congress enacted the Clayton Act, it passed the Federal Trade Commission (FTC) Act, which prohibits all forms of "unfair competition in or affecting commerce." This standard is broader than Section 1 of the Sherman Act, in that all unreasonable restraints of trade are unfair methods of competition but not vice versa. Subsequent legislation by Congress specified which acts are to be considered unfair methods of competition under the FTC Act, such as the misbranding of wool (in the Wool Products Labeling Act), fur (the Fur Products Labeling Act), and textile fibers (the Textile Fiber Products Identification Act). The FTC Act also created a new administrative agency, the Federal Trade Commission, and directed it to promulgate rules prohibiting practices deemed to be unfair methods of competition under the act. Since then, the FTC has promulgated numerous regulations, including extremely detailed rules regulating the branding of wool, fur, and textile fiber products.

Federal antitrust law, therefore, did not come into being all at once. It resulted from multiple acts of planning, following a mostly top-down path: Congress began with broad standards, such as prohibitions on "restraints of trade" and "unfair methods of competition," which were then refined by more detailed standards. These narrower standards, such as those set out in the Clayton Act, the "rule of reason," and the Wool Products Labeling Act, were then further fleshed out by the Robinson-Patman Act and FTC regulations. At times, the planning has gone in the opposite direction, as when Congress broadened the prohibition on unreasonable restraints of trade in the Sherman Act to include all unfair methods of competition as specified in the FTC Act.

The social planning that created antitrust law has also followed a decentralized process. In addition to Congress, the federal courts have played a very substantial role in the development of this body of law. And the grant of administrative authority to the FTC confers on it the primary responsibility for social planning in the area. It is empowered, in other words, to adopt those subplans it deems to best realize the legislative plans set out by Congress.

Because the development of the federal antitrust regime has taken place over many decades involving numerous actors and agencies, social planning in this area has experienced a considerable degree of repudiation and revision. Thus, Congress has overturned Supreme Court precedent, the Supreme Court has reversed decisions of other federal courts and its own earlier rulings, federal courts have struck down administrative rulings through the exercise of judicial review, Congress has repealed and amended earlier legislation, and so on. And, of course, the federal antitrust regime preempted and largely displaced state common law regulation of business competition, which had reigned for several centuries. In this sense, legal regulation differs from ordinary, nonlegal planning, where the shorter life span of plans renders repudiation and revision a less common, though not entirely unusual, phenomenon.

Common Law as Bottom-Up Planning

In contrast to top-down planning characteristic of some forms of legislation, common law reasoning represents the paradigm of bottom-up legal planning. Consider for example the development of the tort of negligence. Until the early part of the twentieth century, courts were mostly content to develop very case-specific rules regarding the civil duties of ordinary care. Duties were classified based on the capacities of the defendant (adult, child, blind, mentally challenged), relationship of the defendant to property (owner, renter, bailee), and the kind of relationship the defendant bore to the victim (defendant as common carrier, manufacturer, salesman, employer, landlord; victim as passenger, customer, employee, renter, stranger). Courts then began to broaden the standards of liability and eventually settled on the modern rule of negligence law, which holds that everyone owes everyone else a duty of reasonable care.[5] These courts, in other words, engaged in bottom-up social planning. By adopting a consolidating standard of liability, they moved up the legal planning tree, converting previous rulings into subplans of a much more general plan.

The bottom-up nature of common law reasoning is motivated by two different institutional considerations. The first is the political conviction that courts are not the appropriate venues for large-scale social planning: duly elected representatives ought to set broad policies in democratic societies, not the courts. This perceived deficit in legitimacy also explains why common law courts are not usually empowered to develop standards with arbitrary elements. Judges may not, for example, enact a rule that requires swimming pool owners to build a fence 40 inches or higher to protect neighboring children from drowning. They are merely authorized to promulgate nonarbitrary standards such as "swimming pool owners must take reasonable precautions in protecting children from hazards on their land." This restriction to principled standards greatly reduces the power of courts to engage in social planning. If no common law rule may contain arbitrary elements (for example, whether a fence should be 40 or 41 inches high), there is an inherent limitation to how specific, and hence comprehensive, judge-made plans can be.

Aside from considerations of political legitimacy, the common law tradition has also been skeptical about the value of abstract moral reasoning.[6] Concrete cases, it has often been thought, provide the rich detail judges need to make good decisions and provide the base from which analogies can be made to other concrete cases. Courts are authorized to take a broader view only when there has been sufficient judicial experience with low-level decision making. Vigorous and prolonged engagement with the concrete implications of various legal rules enables courts to figure out how various aspects of social policy hang together and thus licenses them to consolidate specific rules into more expansive legal standards.

The bottom-up nature of common law social planning is also evident in the power that courts have to "distinguish" precedents. Even when a past case announces a rule framed at a certain level of generality, a court may contract the scope of the rule by holding that it applies only to certain facts of the past decision that are not present in the current case.[7] In distinguishing precedent, courts in essence split general rules into narrower ones that are more closely tied to the facts of each case. The practice of distinguishing manifests yet again the common law's distrust of high-level theorizing and the comparative faith it places in decision making based on concrete and detailed fact patterns.

By claiming that legal planning is an incremental process, I do not mean to suggest, however, that schemes of legal regulation are never created all at once. On certain occasions, especially in civil law countries, legislatures have enacted entire codes, either encompassing the whole field of legal regulation (the Code of Justinian, the Napoleonic Code, the Prussian Civil Code) or subject-specific ones (penal, tax, or bankruptcy codes). In most of these cases, however, these systematic collections of rules simply "codify" existing law, presenting the rules in an orderly manner and resolving contradictions between customary, judicial, and statutory materials.

It is not hard to understand why one-shot comprehensive legislation is generally avoided. As we have seen in the case of personal planning, committing to a course of conduct far in advance of action is inherently risky. Because the future is often unclear and human beings do not have the ability to consider every single contingency, it often makes sense to wait until more information is available before deciding how to respond. Aside from the moral perils of premature planning, there are political risks as well. Enacting a comprehensive regulatory scheme usually requires legislators to make hard choices. By contrast, setting broad policies enables them to take credit for solving social problems without incurring the costs of imposing restrictions on specific individuals and groups. The delegation of planning to judicial or administrative bodies is not only efficient in a large range of cases, but expedient as well.

The Positivity of Planning

By characterizing legal activity as planning activity, my aim thus far has been to highlight the incremental nature of the law's regulatory behavior. But the parallel does not end there. As I would now like to show, legal activity also seeks to accomplish the same basic goals that ordinary, garden-variety planning does, namely, to guide, organize, and monitor the behavior of individuals and groups. It does this by helping agents lower their deliberation, negotiation, and bargaining costs, increase predictability of behavior, compensate for ignorance and bad character, and provide methods of accountability.

Consider laws regulating motorists. Rules that require drivers to be a certain age, pass a test, inspect their cars every year, wear seat belts, buy liability insurance, stop at red lights, ride on the right side, and drive not over 55 mph or under the influence of alcohol are all part of a comprehensive regulatory regime. Their aim is to guide and organize the behavior of many different individuals so as to achieve a very complex and contentious goal, which is safe, fast, and fair driving, in an arbitrary environment. They do so by serving as paternalistic measures that compensate for cognitive incapacities, weakness of the will, and ignorance; coordination devices that render behavior more predictable; and ethically acceptable guidelines that ensure that motorists will not interfere with one another while simultaneously obviating the need to deliberate, negotiate, and bargain about what behavior is reasonable under the circumstances.

Other examples of legal rules that guide and organize the behavior of community members include rules limiting the legal capacity of minors (paternalistic measures that compensate for cognitive incapacity), prohibitions on the use of certain recreational drugs (paternalistic measures that compensate for weakness of will), laws regulating pharmaceuticals (paternalistic measures that compensate for ignorance), rules designating legal tender (solve coordination problems by rendering behavior more predictable), voting laws (enable shared activities to take place by reducing deliberation and negotiation costs and rendering behavior more predictable), business competition laws (forestall shared activities by guiding behavior that is deemed injurious to others), nuisance rules (prevent individual behavior from interfering with others unfairly and, in the process, lower negotiation and bargaining costs associated with ethical conflicts), and contract laws (confer power on persons to plan for others).

Laws are able to perform these functions for exactly the same reason that plans can, namely, they are *positive* norms. By simply referring to norms designated as authoritative, the individuals in question need not deliberate, negotiate, or bargain. They can simply rely on the norm in question to settle their practical doubts or disagreements. Compare such norms to moral rules and principles that have not been similarly marked off as binding by planning or custom. In order to resolve any practical doubt or disagreement, individuals would have to deliberate, negotiate, or bargain, precisely the activities that are circumvented by plans. Moreover, moral norms are not able to solve coordination problems because morality concerns itself with principled action and coordination problems arise because of their arbitrary nature. There are no moral rules telling motorists which side of the road to ride on, whether to use clamshells or silver coins as legal tender, whether the president should be at least thirty-five or thirty-six years old, and so on. Norms that have been designated in advance can solve such problems precisely because human beings have the ability to make arbitrary choices.

Legal Activity as Settling, Dispositive, and Purposive

As I argued in Chapter 5, planning is a process that not only produces norms in an incremental fashion but also (1) produces norms that are supposed to settle, and purport to settle, questions about how to act; (2) disposes addressees to obey; and (3) is purposive, that is, has the function of producing norms. I would quickly like to show that legal activity meets these three conditions as well, and thus the core idea of the Planning Theory, namely the Planning Thesis, is valid.

(1) *Settling:* There is an old joke that goes: "Gravity. It's Not Just a Good Idea. It's the Law!" The joke works not only because it is crazy to admonish people to obey the laws of physics, but equally because it isn't crazy to insist that they heed the laws of political institutions. It makes perfect sense to say, for example, that legislation requiring passengers to wear their seat belts is not "just a good idea." Legal institutions are not in the business of either offering advice or making requests. They do not present their rules as one more factor that subjects

are supposed to consider when deciding what they should do. Rather, their task is to *settle* normative matters in their favor and claim the right to demand compliance. For this reason, deliberating or bargaining with officials about the propriety of obedience normally shows profound disrespect for them, and for the law's authority. Regardless of whether seat belts are a good idea, passengers are required to buckle up—after all, it's the law.

It is important not to overstate the law's claim to authority. That the law is supposed to settle, and purports to settle, normative questions should not be taken to mean that the law demands that its dictates be followed *come what may*. Laws, like all plans, are typically defeasible. When compelling reasons exist, the law will normally permit its subjects to reconsider its direction and engage in deliberation on the merits. The catch here is that the law claims the right to determine the conditions of its own defeasibility. It attempts to settle when the quandaries it has resolved become unsettled. Thus, in jurisdictions that accept a necessity defense, persons are allowed to break the law if doing so is the choice of the lesser evil. The availability of a lesser evil, therefore, is a reason that the law recognizes to be compelling enough to defeat its own mandates.

(2) *Dispositive:* The dispositive nature of legal activity can be seen by attending to the "general efficacy" condition on legal systems. All legal philosophers agree that legal systems exist only if they are generally efficacious, that is, they are normally obeyed. General efficacy does not require that community members actually accept the law's legitimacy; they may comply out of fear of punishment, habit, or peer pressure. But if most fail to conform to the dictates of the regime claiming authority, then such a community cannot be said to have a legal system.

If we accept the correctness of the general efficacy condition, which I think we should, we must conclude that legal activity is dispositive in nature. For according to the general efficacy condition, if an activity did not generate a general disposition to obey in a certain community, then it would not be legal activity.

(3) *Purposive:* Finally, it is clear that legal activity is purposive in nature. The legislative process does not just happen to produce laws as a side effect of its pursuit of some other end. Its very point is to create norms that are supposed to settle questions about how to act. Similarly, the function of adjudication is to apply norms to others. Evaluations are not just happy accidents but what courts are supposed to churn out.

Legal Activity as Social Planning

As I have been at pains to demonstrate in the last few chapters, not every way of guiding conduct counts as "planning." Indeed, planning is a very distinctive way of guiding conduct. For this reason, the Planning Thesis makes a strong jurisprudential claim. According to it, legal activity is not simply the creation and application of rules. It is an incremental process whose function is to guide, organize, and monitor behavior through the settling of normative questions and which disposes its addressees to comply under normal conditions. In this section I hope to have established the plausibility of this position.

To argue that the exercise of legal authority is describable as the activity of social planning is not to say that it can only be characterized in this way, or that this model is the most useful for all purposes. Many legal scholars have argued, for example, that the law is often expressive in nature. Thus, when the law permits people to protect themselves when confronted with deadly force in public even if they could safely retreat, it is plausible to suppose that the law aims to express a judgment about socially proper behavior, namely, that "real men" don't back down from fights.[8] The Planning Thesis, of course, does not preclude this interpretation. It simply points out that when the law serves an expressive function, it does so through *planning*. Thus, the law expresses its attitudes about gender not by relating proverbs about how real men behave or giving sermons, issuing advice, performing ritual dances, and so on, but rather by permitting them to kill even when they could retreat in total safety.

The Planning Thesis does not simply state that legal activity is an activity of planning; it claims that it is an activity of *social* planning. The planning is "social" in three different senses. First, the activity creates and administers norms that represent *communal standards of behavior*. Members of the community are required to conform to these standards and are held accountable by legal officials if they do not. Second, the planning regulates most communal activity via *general policies*. The law's primary mode of address is not naming particular individuals; actors are regulated only insofar as they instantiate the general description set out in the rules. Third, the planning regulates most communal activity via *publicly accessible standards*. Secret plans that satisfy the formal requirements of the system are possible, but if most legal regulation is inaccessible to those to whom it applies, then these plans are not the result of social planning and hence not law.[9]

If legal activity is social planning activity, then it follows that legal authorities are social planners. In other words, they exercise their power by formulating, adopting, repudiating, affecting, and applying plans. Of course, legal authorities often do things other than engage in social planning. Most notably, they support the social planning effort through law enforcement. When the plans do not succeed in guiding conduct, the master plan of the system normally authorizes certain officials to impose costs on the violators.

The Shared Agency Thesis

Virtually everyone would agree that certain aspects of legal activity are shared activities. When Congress legislates, its members are acting together in creating law. Similarly, judges on an appellate panel are engaged in the shared activity of adjudication. The Planning Theory, however, makes a stronger claim. Not only are some aspects of legal activity shared, but so is the whole process. Legal activity is a shared activity in that the various legal actors involved play certain roles in the same activity of social planning: some participate by making and affecting plans and some participate by applying them. Each has a part to play in planning for the community. Call this the "Shared Agency" Thesis.

Shared Agency Thesis: Legal activity is a shared activity.

As I argued in the previous chapters, legal authorities need not intend to engage in the shared activity of social planning in order to do so. He, she, or they may be completely alienated from the process. A legal authority is simply required to accept the shared master plan of the system. This plan specifies the part that each is supposed to play in the shared activity of social planning: who has authority to plan with respect to what subject matter and over whom, and who has the duty to apply and enforce these plans made by these authorities.

The Shared Agency Thesis may be justified by two different considerations. First, it accounts for the core intuition that some legal officials are related to one another in a special way: they are each *members* of particular legal systems. We recognize, for example, that French judges, ministers, legislators, and law enforcement personnel are part of the French legal system, as opposed to the British legal system. Likewise, British officials belong to the same system, but not to the French system. The

Shared Agency Thesis explains these commonsense distinctions. We distinguish between different groups of legal officials because we recognize that different groups are engaged in different collective activities. Furthermore, we sort officials based on the shared activity in which they are supposed to participate: officials of a particular legal system are members of the same system just in case they are supposed to work together in planning for a community. Thus, French legal officials are *French* legal officials because they are supposed to work with each other, and not with British legal officials, in governing their country.

The idea that legal activity is shared activity is also meant to explain how it is that legal systems are able to do what they typically do. For the functions we normally attribute to legal systems—maintaining order, redistributing wealth, protecting the rights of at least some parties, providing facilities for private ordering, settling disputes—are goals that are usually unachievable solely by individual agency. In communities that have legal systems, it is normally not possible for any one person, or a cohort of uncoordinated persons, to establish and maintain control over the entire population, redistribute their wealth, protect their rights, and resolve their disputes. In order to achieve these political ends, collective and concerted action is essential. Members of the group must work together and do so in an organized fashion.

The Design of the Master Plan

It goes without saying that designers of legal systems do not merely intend *that* legal participants plan—they very much care *how* they plan. The framers of the United States Constitution were not, for example, indifferent between democratic, communist, socialist, theocratic, and monarchic forms of government. They were committed to a form of democratic self-rule, and this commitment explains why the United States Constitution has the content that it does.

The design of a legal system will, therefore, be a function of the substantive goals that designers intend to advance. The relation between planning hierarchies and substantive goals may be either intrinsic or instrumental. It is intrinsic when the goals themselves demand that certain individuals be empowered to act in certain ways. The promotion of democratic self-rule, for example, requires that the citizenry have some say in determining the rules of the system. A system designed to further such a goal, therefore, will make provisions such as elections, representation, voting, and protection of free speech so that individuals are empowered to determine the terms and direction of social interaction.

The relation between structure and goal may also be highly instrumental. Federalism, for example, is often justified by the effect that partial decentralization has on the protection of individual liberty. In theory at least, depriving the centralized authority of certain power diminishes its ability to oppress the citizenry. Moreover, by removing barriers to internal migration, the units that make up the federal system are forced to compete for residents, thereby giving them an incentive not to enact abusive regulations. Finally, dividing authority between sets of rivalrous political actors enables the participants in each set to serve as checks to the encroachment of the others.

When legal systems are designed to achieve certain moral or political goals, it is often possible to recover the goals of a system by a close examination of its master plan. For example, a system that made provisions for voting, representation, elections, and some protection for public deliberation would be one in which democratic self-rule was prized. By contrast, an institutional structure that empowered clerics to decide matters of principle and policy and minimized the degree to which secular forces could affect the direction of the law would be a system in which religious values were being promoted.

Reverse engineering, however, is not the only method available for ascertaining the goals of a system. Usually, legal systems are proud of their objectives and proudly proclaim them to the world. Consider for example the preamble to the United States Constitution: "We the People of the United States, in Order to form a more perfect Union, establish Justice, insure domestic Tranquility, provide for the common defence, promote the general Welfare, and secure the Blessing of Liberty to ourselves and our Posterity, do ordain and establish this Constitution for the United States of America."

The preamble sets out, either explicitly or implicitly, the following goals of the federal system: (1) democratic self-rule; (2) political and economic integration; (3) personal security against domestic and foreign threats; (4) promotion of the general welfare; (5) protection of the individual from governmental tyranny. These goals are served by the institutional arrangements set out in the Constitution. For example, the goal of democratic self-rule is furthered by the creation of a dual system of political representation, one based on population (for the House of Representatives), the other based on statehood (for the Senate), the mandate of periodic elections for congressional representatives and for the president, the institution of majority voting to enact legislation, supermajority voting to ratify and amend the Constitution, the protection of freedom of speech and the press, and so on. Political and economic integration is furthered by the creation of a national Congress comprising representatives from every state, the grant to Congress of the power to regulate foreign and interstate commerce, the denial of power to the states to close their borders to other states or impose import duties on them, the grant of power to the Senate and the president to enter into treaties with other countries and the denial of such power to the states, and so forth.

The diversity of goals that legal systems are designed to achieve is actually quite striking. Some legal regimes aim to build "a classless communist society," others intend to advance "the cultural, social, political, and economic institutions of . . . society based on Islamic principles and norms," while still others seek to "secure the right to work, housing and education, and to promote social care and social security and a good living environment."[10]

It is important to note that legal officials can be committed to the substantive political or moral goals of a regime without agreeing on comprehensive worldviews. This, as we have seen, is typical of shared activity: participants may converge on a set of common goals despite differing on more fundamental beliefs and values. One can be a Kantian, utilitarian, Aristotelian, libertarian, Rawlsian, Christian, Muslim, or Jew and still believe in the moral necessity of promoting democratic self-rule and protecting individual rights. But these officials may not even be committed to the aims of the legal system in which they participate. This, we have also seen, is a typical feature of *massively* shared agency: participants may share a plan even though some are not committed to the success of the joint activity.

I do not mean to suggest, of course, that all legal systems have been designed in advance. Historically, certain fundamental aspects of legal systems have arisen purely through custom. The model of shared agency I developed in Chapter 5 accounts for these cases by requiring only that the shared plan be designed "at least in part" with the group in mind. Groups may share plans, in other words, even though parts of their plans have not been planned for the group. A plan is shared if at least *some* part of the plan was designed for the group and group members see the nonplanned parts as means to carry out the ends of the shared activity. Thus, the master plan of a legal system may contain many customary parts, so long as it also contains noncustomary parts and the officials see the customary parts as *subplans* of these noncustomary parts.

To be sure, when large portions of a legal system arise purely through custom, it may turn out that there is no ideology that underlies the system's institutional structure, no coherent set of political objectives at which the shared activity aims. I say that there *may* be no ideology for two reasons. First, convergence in practice is often the product of common beliefs and values. Second, legal officials may theorize previously untheorized customary aspects of a certain system and develop the system in the direction of this new ideology. These officials are then properly seen as designers of the legal system, reworking the crooked timber of custom in the hopes of making it straight.

The Unity of Law

As I argued at the beginning of this section, one reason to accept the Shared Agency Thesis is that it provides an intuitive account of group membership within a legal system. Group membership, on this view, is constituted by the shared activity in which its members are supposed to participate. Just as my friends and I are members of the Cooking Club because we are supposed to cook together, officials are members of the same legal system because they are supposed to participate in the same collective activity of social planning.

The Shared Agency Thesis also provides a natural way to define norm membership in a legal system. We might say that two laws are part of the same legal system just in case they are created and applied by officials of the same legal organization. The *unity* of a set of legal norms is thus derived from the *sociality* of legal participants. What makes it the case that the laws of a particular system are laws of that system is that they are the products of the activity of *one group* sharing a plan and working together in planning for a community.

Put more precisely, the law of a certain system consists in (1) the master plan shared by a group of planners; (2) those plans created in accordance with, and whose application is required by, such a master plan; and (3) those planlike norms (such as customary norms) whose application is required by such a master plan. New York statutory law is New York law, for example, because it was created in accordance with, and its application regulated by, the master plan shared by a certain group working together in governing New York State. Executive orders of the New York State governor are also laws of New York State because the governor shares a plan with the legislature and they both work together in governing New York. On the other hand, New Jersey law is distinct from New York law because New Jersey officials do not share a plan, and hence do not work together, with New York officials.[11]

Offices, Institutionality, and Compulsion

Thus far, I have argued that legal activity is the shared activity of social planning. Unfortunately, this description cannot be considered a complete answer to the Identity Question for law. Consider parenting. My wife and I plan for our family together. We consult with each other about how our children should treat other people, who should set the table, what we will eat for dinner, where we will go on vacation, and so on. We also apply each other's rules and enforce them when necessary.

Yet only in the most metaphorical sense are we "the law." My wife and I have authority within our house, but that power is not legal in nature. Thus, legal activity cannot just be the shared activity of social planning, for there can be such activities that are not legal activities. What, then, is missing?

Official Activity

One reason why my wife and I are not the law is that we are not "officials," that is, we do not occupy offices. Offices are designed to deal with recurring sets of issues and, as such, have long life spans and admit of different occupants. The presidency of the United States, for example, is an office because it persists from term to term and its normative character does not change merely because one president vacates and a new one assumes power.[12]

It is an essential feature of an office, therefore, that holders of power are "fungible," namely, that the rights and responsibilities that attend the office do not depend on the identity of those who inhabit the office. If X and Y are both eligible to occupy office O, then X and Y will have the same rights and responsibilities when they occupy O.

Because offices are meant to serve a recurring set of issues, they normally possess two other properties; neither is necessary but both are typically present. First, offices are typically stable. Rights and responsibilities should not fluctuate over time but remain constant throughout. Second, turnover in occupancy is not only possible but expected.

By these measures, parents do not occupy offices. Although parenthood is fungible, its normative character is not typically stable. The rights of parents decrease over time and, in many cultures, are taken to cease, or nearly so, upon the maturity of their children. Even in societies where parental rights remain constant throughout life, parental responsibilities typically change and diminish as children grow. Nor is parental turnover expected. Although parents may die or have their rights legally terminated and other persons take their place through adoption, such changes are unusual. Parents normally stay the parents of their children—for better or worse.

Because legal activity must be an activity conducted by officials, parental planning cannot be legal in nature. By contrast, legislators, judges, police officers, regulators, and clerks are officials, if any are, and as a result they may properly be thought to engage in legal activity.

Institutional Activity

When my wife or I want to make a rule for our family, we have to do it the old-fashioned way, namely, by issuing a command or granting permission. If I wish to order my daughter to pick up her toys before she goes out to play, I must intend that she pick up her toys at that time and express that intention to her.

Legislatures, on the other hand, can bypass that drudgery. They can get some staff attorney (or lobbyist) to draft legislation and then simply follow some formal procedure, such as raising their hands at a certain time, in order to enact it. They need not intend that those obligated by the rule follow it. Indeed, they do not even have to know which rule they are enacting. As long as they follow the procedures set out in their rules, their acts are legally valid and a new plan will have been created.

As we have seen, the normativity of law is "institutional" in nature, which is to say that the legal relations may obtain between people independent of the particular intentions of those people. This institutionality is made possible by the structure of master legal plans. Master plans contain not only authorizations but instructions as well, namely, plans that specify how the authorized power should be exercised. These instructions will typically set out formal procedures that allow people to exercise power even without the intention to do so. Thus, if part of the master plan of a legal system validates a rule if a majority of legislators simply say "Yea" after the rule is read, then the rule is legally valid if a majority of legislators do say "Yea" after the rule is read. The rule will be valid even if those enacting it had no intention of enacting it or even knew that their actions would lead to enactment. By contrast, my wife and I have no formal rules for how to make rules in our family. If we want to exercise our power, we have no choice but to intend that something happen and express that intention directly to those whom we wish to bind.

The introduction of institutional normativity is a revolutionary advance in social planning. Plans can be adopted without the planners actually intending that the community act accordingly. As a result, the community need not worry about whether the planners had these intentions. They can know that they are legally obligated simply because the planners followed the right procedures. Of course, the institutionality of law is ultimately grounded in intentions. Rules are legally valid because they were created pursuant to a rule that most officials accept. If officials stopped accepting the plan, then the plans created in accordance with it would cease to be legally valid as well.

Compulsory Governance

Let us say that any group that engages in a shared, official, and institutional activity is an "organization." It follows then that legal systems are *planning organizations*. Legal officials constitute such organizations because they are engaged in a shared activity of social planning, occupy offices, and are capable of instituting normative relations irrespective of particular intentions. By the same token, parents are not legal systems because, even though they are shared planners, they do not constitute a planning organization.

There is a sense, however, in which parental authority is closer to legal authority than the powers exercised by other planning organizations. Let us return to the Cooking Club Inc. The hierarchical relationship that exists between the supervisors and any particular staff member is entirely contingent on the will of the staff member. If the staff member no longer wants to work for the company, he or she may quit and, as a result, will no longer be subject to the planning power of the designated supervisor.

By contrast, the parent-child relationship is not terminable at will. At least until maturity, children cannot "quit" their parents and are subject to parental norms even against their will. Parental authority, we can say, is "compulsory" because consent is not a necessary condition for the applicability of its requirements. Legal authority is similar in this regard. Except in rare circumstances, it is not a valid legal defense to claim that one has not consented, or no longer consents, to the authority of the law. Acceptance is virtually, and in some systems totally, irrelevant to the legal validity of official action and to its applicability.

The compulsory nature of the law's authority is clearly central to its efficacy as an institution of social planning. Compliance with the law is often onerous, sometimes extremely so. If one could be relieved from paying one's taxes, complying with military conscription, serving on a jury, driving within the speed limit, and so on, simply by repudiating the law's authority, then one would expect many people to avail themselves of this option, or at least have legitimate concerns that their law-abidingness will be exploited by others availing themselves of this option. Conditioning authority on consent is a luxury that the law normally cannot afford.

The compulsory nature of the law, however, might appear puzzling. Unlike parents, who are more informed and mature than their young children and as a result can bind them even against their wills, how can a plan legally obligate competent adults in so involuntary a fashion? The mystery dissolves once we recall our analysis of legal obligation claims. On the Planning Theory, to say that laws legally obligate is to say (at least on the perspectival interpretation) that they morally obligate *from the legal point of view*. From the perspective of legal institutions, in other words, their plans morally bind regardless of whether those who are bound consent to their authority. Thus, just as I claim the power to morally bind my six-year-old son to clear the table after dinner even if he objects, the law claims the moral power to obligate irrespective of the will of its subjects.

As I have emphasized before, although the legal point of view purports to represent the moral point of view, it may fail to do so. In some cases, it will be unable to morally obligate without the consent of the governed; indeed, if the system is sufficiently unjust, the law may be incapable of morally binding even *with* their consent. Yet, from the law's own point of view, the compulsory nature of its demands is morally legitimate. And this conviction in its own rectitude is expressed by legal officials when they describe themselves as having the *right* to be obeyed and those who fail to comply as *wrong* and as *deserving punishment* for their *guilty* actions.

The Moral Aim Thesis

According to the Planning Theory, the law is not simply a compulsory planning organization—it is a compulsory planning organization with a characteristic aim. As I suggested in the last chapter, the fundamental aim of the law is to rectify the moral deficiencies associated with the circumstances of legality. When a community faces moral problems that are numerous and serious, and whose solutions are complex, contentious, or arbitrary, certain modes of planning such as improvisation, spontaneous ordering, private bargaining, communal consensus, or personalized hierarchies will be costly to engage in, sometimes prohibitively so. Unless the community has a way of reducing the costs and risks of planning, resolving these moral problems will be, at best, expensive and, at worst, impossible. On the Planning Theory, the fundamental aim of the law is to meet this moral demand in an efficient manner. By providing a highly nimble and durable method of social planning, the law enables communities to solve the numerous and serious problems that would otherwise be too costly or risky to resolve.[13] Call this the "Moral Aim" Thesis.

> *Moral Aim Thesis:* The fundamental aim of legal activity is to remedy the moral deficiencies of the circumstances of legality.

To say that the fundamental aim of the law is to compensate for the infirmities of custom, tradition, persuasion, consensus, and promise is not to suggest that the law *never* relies on these other mechanisms. When simpler methods of organizing behavior work, it would be irrational to abandon or overturn them in favor of accomplishing the very same ends through more sophisticated methods. Thus, when customs or contracts solve moral problems, the law will typically let them stand. Indeed, legal systems often rely on custom and contract when they judge these methods of solving moral problems to be superior to legal planning.

Moreover, to say that the law's mission is to address the moral defects of alternative forms of social ordering is not to claim that legal systems *always* succeed in their mission. The law may end up pursuing immoral objectives or simply replace private moral mistakes with public ones. Indeed, the sheer diversity of political objectives that actual legal systems have attempted to secure throughout human history suggests that the law often fails in its primary mission. What makes the law *the law* is that it has a moral aim, not that it satisfies that aim.

By asserting that legal systems have a characteristic aim, the Planning Theory bucks the trend among legal positivists who have been skeptical of such claims.[14] These positivists, of course, do not deny that legal systems pursue particular ends. Rather, they worry that there is no aim that is both universal *and* nontrivial.[15] For consider any particular aim: the defense of human rights, promotion of democracy, protection of private property, redistribution of wealth inequality, and so forth. It always seems possible to find or imagine some legal regime that is not dedicated to such an end. These particular aims are too parochial to play the necessary universalizing role. On the other hand, if we impute an end that is plausibly universal, such as coordinating social activity or guiding conduct, we end up with an empty truism. Of course, the law does those things, but so do games, religion, etiquette, and so on.

The Moral Aim Thesis, however, posits an end that is neither parochial nor empty. It is not parochial because it does not claim that the law is supposed to pursue any substantive end. It is agnostic, in other words, about which particular moral problems and opportunities the law should address. The law, we said, is a universal means, adapted to solve any kind of moral problem. But the aim the Planning Theory attributes to the law is not empty either, for it specifies one that most things do not pursue, namely, the rectification of the moral defects associated with the circumstances of legality. Any normative system coordinates social activity and guides action. But only a legal system is supposed to address those problems that less sophisticated methods of coordinating social activity and guiding action are unable to resolve.

Happy Accidents

As I argued in the last chapter, the Moral Aim Thesis is bolstered by two considerations. First, it explains why we think that law is invaluable in the modern world but not, say, among simple hunter-gatherers. The former is the paradigm of the circumstances of legality, whereas the latter is its antithesis. Second, the Moral Aim Thesis explains why legal systems that are unable to solve serious moral problems are criticizable. No one blames baseball for failing to alleviate poverty or protecting populations from natural disasters, but a legal system that ignores such problems, or addresses them incompetently, is subject to rebuke.

There is a third consideration that supports the Moral Aim Thesis and shows why the end it attributes is central to the law's identity. Consider sophisticated crime syndicates like the Japanese Yakuza or the Sicilian Mafia. These firms are compulsory planning organizations: their members engage in collective planning designed to further shared criminal ends, they occupy offices (for example, the don, consigliores, capos, lieutenants, bodyguards, hitmen, and so forth), their normativity is institutional in nature (for example, the Yamaguchi-gumi of Japan has tens of thousands of members and as a result has an extremely complex hierarchical structure), and they do not require consent before imposing their demands on their victims. Yet, these criminal organizations are not legal systems.

We can see, therefore, that though all legal systems are compulsory planning organizations, not all compulsory planning organizations are legal systems. What, then, distinguishes the nonlegal compulsory planning organizations, such as the firms just mentioned, from the legal ones? I think it is plausible to say that the difference is one of aim. If we want to explain what makes the law *the law,* we must see it as necessarily having a moral aim, an end that criminal organizations do not necessarily possess.

I am not suggesting that organized crime never produces morally good benefits. Indeed, some studies have shown that organized crime arises and flourishes in societies where established legal systems fail to provide adequate levels of dispute resolution, property rights enforcement, and protective services. Criminal enterprises act as black-market entrepreneurs who supply much-needed social services and thereby fill important niches left by weak state institutions.[16] According to the Moral Aim Thesis, the difference between legal systems and these criminal syndicates is not that the former are *in fact* morally better than the latter; rather, the distinguishing factor is that it is in the nature of the former that they are *supposed to be* so. In other words, it is part of the identity of law to have a moral mission, whereas it is not in the nature of nonlegal criminal syndicates to have such a mandate.

There is a sense, of course, in which both legal systems and these criminal organizations are supposed to act in a morally appropriate fashion, namely, as a matter of substantive morality. Morally speaking, everyone should act morally, which clearly includes criminals as well. The claim I am advancing here, however, is a metaphysical, not a moral, one. A legal system cannot help but have a moral aim if it is to be a legal system; whereas a criminal organization that did not have a moral aim would still be a criminal organization, though it would likely be a morally bad one.

Additional support for the Moral Aim Thesis can be gleaned from the diverse reactions we have to situations in which morally good consequences are produced. When organized crime happens to solve moral problems, these occurrences are treated by us as *serendipitous,* as happy accidents. By contrast, the moral benefits generated by a just legal system are not accidental or side effects of legal activity; rather, producing them is the very point of its activity. Legal systems are by their very nature supposed to be morally good, and when they are so they fulfill their aim.[17]

Conversely, when a Mafia don terrorizes a neighborhood, we don't think that he has *abused* his power or has acted in a *corrupt* fashion. It doesn't even make sense to accuse the Mafia of being *unjust,* since the Mafia does not fail at a task that by its nature it is supposed to perform. By contrast, legal systems can be unjust, and when they are, they fall short of their defining mission: unlike the Yakuza or Mafia, they fail not only morally but on their own terms as well.

Representing Moral Aims

According to the Planning Theory, the law has the aim that it does irrespective of the aim of legal participants. Imagine a legal system staffed by officials who merely pretend to pursue noble aims, but are solely after their own material gain. It would nevertheless be true that the aim of legal activity in that system is moral in nature (much as the aim of assertion is to convey true information even though the asserter is lying). It is simply an essential truth about the law that it is supposed to solve moral problems.

This last point, though, raises a substantial concern. If we grant that the law does not derive its aim from any intention of legal participants, what makes it the case that the law has the aim that it does? On what basis do we impute a moral end to legal systems?

It might be thought that the law's aim is taken from the fact that legal officials at the very least pretend to pursue noble ends.[18] Unfortunately, this cannot be the full story either because it is possible to imagine a legal system staffed mostly by alienated bureaucrats who merely follow the rules because it is their job.

Here, I think it is crucial to distinguish legal elites from lower-level functionaries. The law possesses the aim that it does because high-ranking officials represent the practice as having a moral aim or aims. Their avowals need not be sincere, but they must be made. These representations may take many forms, either explicitly in speeches, ceremonial steles, preambles to constitutions, prologues to legal codes, and judicial dicta, or implicitly through the atmospherics of ritual dress and speech, the construction of monumental buildings housing legal activity, and the use of religious or moral iconography in legal settings. Perhaps most importantly, the moral aims of the law are represented through legal discourse. By describing legal demands as "obligating," not merely "obliging," and power as based on "right," not merely "might," elites present their practice as something other than a criminal enterprise or self-interested pursuit of pleasure, profit, or glory. They depict it, in other words, as an activity that is supposed to solve moral problems and should be obeyed for that reason.

The foot soldiers have a role to play here as well. In their official capacities, they must speak their lines, namely, use moral language to describe the law. But the fact that they use moral terminology and concepts does not mean that they personally endorse, or are trying to make others think that they personally endorse, such moral evaluations. They may just be doing their job, one that requires them to evaluate conduct from the legal point of view.

Augustine famously asked: "Justice removed, then what are kingdoms but great bands of robbers?"[19] Morally speaking, the answer may be nothing. But from a conceptual point of view, there is all the difference in the world. The kingdom is a kingdom because the king and his court represent it as having a moral mission. Members of the criminal syndicates we have been considering, by contrast, do not portray their threats as creating obligations and right for their victims. They drop the conceit that they are trying to solve the problems associated with the circumstances of legality—in fact, they realize that they *are* the problems of the circumstances of legality. It is that recognition, and their lack of shame about it, that make them mere criminals and not legal officials.[20]

Self-Certifying Organizations

At first, life at Del Boca Vista, a growing retirement community in South Florida, was paradise. Residents filled their days at this beautiful location by the ocean with swimming, sailing, bingo, shuffleboard, and socializing. When disputes arose, over such things as parking spaces or proper attire at the pool, residents were able to resolve them privately or, on occasion, publicly at community forums through consensual deliberation and bargaining.

As more retirees bought condos in the sprawling complex, disputes between the residents increased, both in quantity and intensity. Life no longer seemed so pleasant. In an effort to reduce the bickering and tension, the residents agreed to form a condominium board consisting of a president, vice president, treasurer, and secretary. They set the task of the board as the enactment of regulations governing the common areas and the resolution of disagreements that might arise under the rules created.

The Condo Board of Del Boca Vista engages in a shared activity of social planning. It creates rules for the residents of Del Boca Vista and applies them in case of disputes. It is constituted by officials and their actions are governed by a complex set of rules that renders the intentions of the board members irrelevant for decision making. Its rules are binding irrespective of consent. And its aim is to solve those moral problems that cannot be solved, or solved as well, through alternative forms of social ordering. But the Condo Board is not the law. Why not?

What Law is Not

Distinguishing between private entities such as the Condo Board and legal institutions turns out to be trickier than it might first appear. For example, one might think that the Condo Board is not the law because it is not supreme within its territory. In cases of conflict, Florida law trumps the condo rules. Since the law must enjoy, or claim to enjoy, supreme authority within a territory or over a group of people, the Condo Board cannot be a legal institution.[21]

This proposal is not sound, however, because supremacy is not a necessary condition for the legality of an institution. For if this were so, Florida would not have a legal system either. According to the Supremacy Clause of the United States Constitution, federal law is supreme over state law. A supremacy requirement would rule out American-style federalism as a potential legal configuration, as well as the very possibility that international law could impose obligations on nation-states.[22]

Another tack would be to claim that legal systems are necessarily comprehensive, that is, they claim the authority to regulate any kind of

behavior, whereas the Condo Board's regulatory authority is highly cir-
cumscribed.[23] The Condo Board, for example, cannot tell people which
foods they may eat in their apartments, which doctors they may see, how
to make a valid will, and so on. Florida law, by contrast, is capable of
regulating any behavior it deems fit to regulate.

This response, however, is doubly wrong. First, the limited scope of the
Condo Board's governance is a contingent matter. We can easily imagine
residents granting the Condo Board a comprehensive police power and
authorizing them to enact any regulation they see fit to make. Even so,
the Condo Board would not be a legal system. Second, although modern
legal systems are comprehensive planning organizations, premodern legal
systems did not enjoy universal scope. In thirteenth century England, for
example, many legal systems coexisted alongside one another, each having
limited subject matter jurisdiction. Manorial law governed feudal estates;
mercantile law regulated commercial interactions among merchants; ec-
clesiastical law concerned church matters, which at the time included
marriages and legitimation of offspring; and the common law and equity
regulated everything else. Subject-specificity and legality are not mutually
exclusive.

Last, it might be argued that the Condo Board is not a legal system because it does not enjoy a monopoly on the legitimate use of force within
its territory.[24] The Florida state police, for example, may use force on the
condo grounds in order to enforce Florida state law. Since all legal systems
must possess such coercive control, the Condo Board cannot be a legal
system.

The problem with this suggestion is obvious: if the Condo Board does
not enjoy a monopoly on the legitimate use of force within its territory,
neither does the Florida legal system. After all, Floridians are permitted
to use force in certain circumstances. Suppose that the president of the
board sees a resident attempting to burn down an apartment building.
Florida law would permit the president to use nondeadly force, and in
some instances deadly force, to restrain the resident. Hence, even the
state of Florida does not have or claim a monopoly on the legitimate use
of force within Florida. Indeed, a legal system that truly cornered the
market on legitimate coercion would be a monstrous thing. To completely preclude others from using force would entail denying them, for
example, the right of self-defense. While it is possible to imagine such a
legal system, I doubt that any such regime has existed on the face of the
earth.

The Presumption of Validity

As we have seen, one cannot disqualify the Condo Board from being a legal system simply by showing that Florida is a superior planning organization. If supremacy were necessary for legality, then Florida would not have a legal system either, insofar as Florida law is subordinate to federal law. U.S. law preempts state law just as state law preempts the rules of the Condo Board.

Nevertheless, there is a crucial difference between these hierarchical relationships that we have thus far overlooked. Although state law must comply with federal law, *federal law automatically presumes that state law complies with federal law*. Federal law, in other words, gives states the benefit of the doubt and thus permits state officials to enforce their law without first demonstrating the validity of their actions. By contrast, the states afford no comparable presumption to private entities such as condo boards. It is not enough for the private actors to be in compliance with state law: in many instances, private actors may not enforce their rules unless they first demonstrate the validity of their actions to some state actor.

To take a concrete example, suppose that the state legislature enacts legislation forbidding skinny-dipping in any pool, public or private. We will assume for the sake of the example that this rule is constitutional and does not conflict with any preexisting federal law. Now imagine that some resident skinny-dips in the Del Boca Vista pool and the state police are notified. In order to enforce this rule, the Florida state police need not file suit in federal court to receive permission to pull the naked offender out the pool. Nor must the state police contact the FBI. They can simply yank the skinny-dipper out of the pool and charge him with the crime of skinny-dipping.

Now suppose that the Condo Board enacts a similar policy forbidding skinny-dipping in the condo pool. How will the Condo Board enforce their rule against the offending resident? Not by physically apprehending the swimmer and ejecting him from the condo premises. For Florida, like many other legal systems, does not permit owners to enforce their property rights (as opposed to their right not to be physically harmed) through this form of self-help. Rather, they must call the police and hope that the police agree that the skinny-dipper is trespassing on their property. Furthermore, they are not permitted to change the locks on the resident's condominium. The Condo Board must leave criminal punishment to the prosecutor, court, jury, and sheriff and await a civil judgment before they are permitted to change the locks.

The Condo Board, we can say, does not enjoy the same presumption of validity that state governments do. Even though both the Condo Board and Florida are required to comply with the rules of superior planning institutions, only Florida is presumed to be in compliance with those rules and, hence, only it is allowed to enforce its own rules without federal permission. But since the Condo Board is not so presumed, it often has the burden of demonstrating to the state that the rules it wishes to enforce are valid under Florida property and contract law. Without making such a showing, the Condo Board violates Florida law, even though it is enforcing legally valid claims.

It might be helpful here to introduce the notion of a "general presumption of validity." X enjoys a general presumption of validity from a superior planning organization Y whenever Y does not require X to demonstrate the validity of its rules before they are enforced. In other words, when X enjoys a general presumption of validity from Y, Y places no "prior restraints" on X's enforcement powers. X may enforce its rules without making a case to Y that its rules are valid.

By contrast, a planning organization X does not enjoy a general presumption of validity when, under some circumstance, the superior organization Y requires X to demonstrate that its rules are valid before they are enforced. In situations where their rules are not presumed valid, these organizations are forbidden to enforce them. They are subject to a rule of prior restraint. If they wish to enforce, or have another enforce, a rule, they must make a case to their superiors demonstrating the validity of their claim and hope that their superiors agree.

Call a planning organization "self-certifying" whenever it is free to enforce its rules without first demonstrating to a superior (if one exists) that its rules are valid. A planning organization, therefore, will be self-certifying whenever it is supreme or enjoys a general presumption of validity from all superior planning organizations. By contrast, a planning organization is not self-certifying whenever it is required to demonstrate that its rules are valid before it may enforce or have another enforce them. A planning organization, therefore, is not self-certifying whenever it has a superior and this superior does not accord it a general presumption of validity.

According to the Planning Theory, the law is a self-certifying planning organization. Even when it lacks supreme legal authority, it enjoys a general presumption of validity from all of its superiors. For this reason, the Condo Board is not a legal institution. In many cases, Florida does not presume that the Condo Board acts validly. The Condo Board cannot, for example, physically remove trespassers from the condo grounds, break into apartments to collect unpaid maintenance fees, or change the locks. To do any of these things, the Condo Board must appeal to some legal official or body, hope that they agree that the Condo Board's legal rights are being violated, and either direct law enforcement personnel to exercise coercion or permit the Condo Board to do so themselves.

It is easy to see why self-certification would be valuable to a planning organization. For when an organization cannot certify the validity of its valid rules, its ability to govern is greatly diminished. It cannot enforce its rules whenever it deems fit: in many cases, it must first submit its proposal to another organization and hope that its superior agrees with its judgment and certifies its claims. This burden of prior restraint not only results in delays, perhaps serious ones, but puts subordinates at the mercy of their superiors. Like being official and institutional, self-certification contributes significantly to the law's nimbleness as a planning organization.

By the same token, it is usually in the interest of the law to deny self-certification to powerful groups within its territory. In not extending the benefit of the doubt to others, the law plays a gate-keeping function: by requiring them to convince a competent legal tribunal that their rules are valid, it ensures that groups that can abuse their power do not do so. Furthermore, denying groups the presumption of validity also reduces the risk that feuding will break out. As Locke emphasized, long-running battles and cycles of revenge often result from the absence of neutral arbiters. If a group cannot take "the law" into its own hands, but must submit its claims to an impartial tribunal, the dangers associated with the state of nature are greatly diminished.

Because self-certification plays an important role in characterizing legal institutions, and since this property has not been previously identified or discussed in the literature, a few clarifications of it are in order. First, a self-certifying organization does not necessarily enforce its own rules. An organization is self-certifying when it is *free* to enforce its own valid rules without first having to establish their validity before some superior official or tribunal (if one should exist). Thus, the medieval Icelandic legal system was self-certifying even though its officials did not enforce the law, because they *could have* enforced it if they so chose.[25]

Whether a legal system avails itself of the freedom to enforce is immaterial to its status as self-certifying.

Second, self-certification does not imply that the organizations that enjoy it are completely free to use any enforcement method they wish. American states, for example, are prohibited by the Eighth Amendment from using cruel and unusual punishment in order to enforce their criminal laws. To claim that an organization is self-certifying is to say that the permissibility of using a certain method of enforcement is never conditioned on the certification of its rules by a superior. Some methods may be forbidden, but those that are permitted are permitted without prior certification. The Eighth Amendment, therefore, does not destroy the states' presumption of validity because this constitutional provision does not impose a prior restraint on the use of cruel and unusual punishment. Rather, it imposes a blanket prohibition on this enforcement method. In other words, the prohibition on cruel and unusual punishment *would have* destroyed the presumption of validity if states had to convince the federal government that their laws are constitutional in order to use cruel and usual punishment or to get the federal government to use such methods. But since no one is permitted to use such methods, the fact that states are so prohibited does not affect their status as self-certifying.

Third, while nonsupreme but self-certifying organizations enjoy a general presumption of validity, this presumption is rebuttable. Plaintiffs, for example, may sue a state in federal court and make the case that the state's behavior violates federal or constitutional law. In such circumstances, the presumption of validity evaporates, thereby shifting to the state the burden of demonstrating the validity of their actions.

Degrees of Legality

Although I have described self-certification as a binary property—either an organization has it or it does not—it is probably best to see it as something that comes in degrees. Some organizations that are not completely self-certifying may be virtually so if they are *almost* always free to enforce their rules without certification by a superior. State legal systems in the United States are virtually, but not completely, self-certifying because under rare circumstances they are required to shoulder the burden of establishing the validity of their rules to a federal tribunal before they may enforce their own rules. Section 5 of the Voting Rights Act, for example, requires certain states (so-called covered jurisdictions) to submit proposed changes in voting procedures to the Justice Department or a federal district court for preclearance before they may enforce these new procedures.[26]

Other properties that are constitutive of legality also come in degrees. Thus, some organizations may be virtually, but not completely, compulsory. Some legal systems, for example, allow certain groups the right to refuse obedience to certain laws out of reasons of conscience. While they are not allowed to "quit" the law entirely, they may quit some part of it under limited circumstances.

Indeed, it is plausible to suppose that legality itself is not a binary property but also comes in degrees.[27] The more self-certifying or compulsory an organization is, the more legal it should be considered. Ordinarily, we call something "law" when it lies toward, but not necessarily on, the end of various spectrums. We think that states have legal systems because they are virtually self-certifying. Preclearance requirements such as those imposed by the Voting Rights Act are actually quite extraordinary, and may even be unique to the voting rights context.

In other cases, the property of legality will be even less fully instantiated, thus creating borderline instances of law. The United States Golf Association, for example, straddles the line between law and nonlaw. On the one hand, it is an organization that regulates the game of golf in the United States and Mexico and its activities are self-certifying (the USGA does not have to go to court in order to award or revoke titles). Thus, it styles itself the "national governing body of golf." On the other hand, it is not fully compulsory. One can, of course, not pay one's dues to the organization and not follow the rules that they impose on members. But it is compulsory in the sense that USGA determines the official rules of golf in the United States and Mexico, and hence one cannot play golf (or at least the official version of golf) unless one follows the regulations they have enacted. One might also question whether USGA has the moral aim characteristic of law. While USGA does solve problems that would be difficult to solve otherwise, and thus improves human welfare, these problems are not of the same moral seriousness as those legal systems typically address. The best we can say about the USGA, therefore, is that it is like a legal system in some senses, but not in others, and leave it at that.

Laws as Plans, or Planlike Norms

Thus far, I have argued that a group of individuals are engaged in legal activity whenever their activity of social planning is shared, official, institutional, compulsory, self-certifying, and has a moral aim. This constitutes the Planning Theory's answer to the Identity Question for law: what makes the law, understood here as a legal institution, *the law* is that it is a self-certifying compulsory planning organization whose aim is to solve those moral problems that cannot be solved, or solved as well, through alternative forms of social ordering.

If legal activity is the activity of planning, then it follows that all norms generated by this activity are plans. Thus, Section 1 of the Sherman Act should be understood as an extremely partial plan: it prohibits combinations and contracts in restraint of trade but does not specify how to avoid restraining trade. Subsequent antitrust legislation constitutes further subplans that flesh out the requirements of the Sherman Act and thus provide business guidance on how to avoid running afoul of these provisions. In particular, the Robinson-Patman Act, the rules related to price-fixing, bid rigging, and market allocation, and the rule of reason are all subplans of Section 1. Similarly, the Wool Products Labeling Act is a subplan of the FTC Act, and the regulations relating to it developed by the FTC are sub-subplans of the FTC Act because they are subplans of the Wool Products Labeling Act. And so on.

Since not all laws are created through legal activity, and thus through the process of planning, it would be incorrect to say that all laws are plans. Customary norms, for example, that form part of a system's master plan are not plans; nevertheless, they are highly planlike in nature. While they might not have been produced by a purposive process, they typically possess all the other properties that plans typically possess, namely, their structures are partial and nested, they purport to settle questions about how to act, and they dispose their addressees to comply. Consequently, if pressed to give an account of the identity of the law—understood here as an indeterminate quantity of legal norms—we should say that what makes laws *laws* is that they are either (1) parts of the master plan of a self-certifying, compulsory planning organization with a moral aim; (2) plans that have been created in accordance with, and whose application is required by, such a master plan, or (3) planlike norms whose application is required by such a master plan.

If this answer to the Identity Question is correct, then we ought to be able to show how different laws can be classified as different kinds of plans or planlike norms. In the next few sections, I would like to briefly show how this may be done.

Directives, Permissions, and Stipulations

The most basic type of legal norm is the directive.[28] A directive enjoins a person, persons, or institutional body to do, or not do, some action, possibly under certain circumstances. A directive that requires some action can be called a "requirement," whereas one that requires that an action not be performed can be called a "prohibition." Examples of requirements include: "Every person conducting the business of auctioneer shall pay a business tax of one hundred dollars for the first day during which he conducts an auction sale, and fifty dollars for each subsequent day"[29] and "If a man put out the eye of another man, his eye shall be put out."[30] Examples of prohibitions include: "No person under the age of twenty-one shall operate a motor vehicle after having consumed alcohol as defined in this section"[31] and "No person shall be held criminally liable for an act which was lawful at the time it was committed, or of which he has been acquitted, nor shall he be placed in double jeopardy."[32]

The law will sometimes explicitly *not* direct some person, persons, or body to forbear from acting in a certain way. Such plans can be called "permissions." For example, the English Criminal Law Act 1967 provides that: "A person may use such force as is reasonable in the circumstances in the prevention of crime." This provision is a plan that permits persons to use reasonable force to prevent crimes.[33]

The examples of directives and permissions I have cited wear their planlike nature on their sleeve. In each case, the laws in question either direct, or do not direct, some person, persons, or body to do, or not do, some action. In other cases, the planlike nature is less clear. For example, the law often expresses its requirements in the passive voice. A New Zealand regulation provides that: "No fruit or vegetables shall be exported from New Zealand unless graded in accordance with or superior to the grade determined to be the minimum grade for export for that fruit or vegetable for the purposes of Part 2 of these regulations."[34] Clearly, this regulation could have been reformulated to make its planlike nature apparent without changing its meaning (for example, "No person may export from New Zealand . . . "). Other times, the law will formulate its directives by describing the purported normative consequences of its enactment. Thus, the United States Code provides that: "The period of service for which an individual *shall be obligated* to serve as an employee of the Federal Aviation Administration is, except as provided in subsection (h)(2), 24 months for each academic year for which a scholarship under this section is provided."[35]

It might be objected that many laws cannot be seen as plans in disguise. Consider the Defense of Marriage Act (DOMA). It states that: "In determining the meaning of any Act of Congress, or of any ruling, regulation, or interpretation of the various administrative bureaus and agencies of the United States, the word 'marriage' means only a legal union between one man and one woman as husband and wife." On its face, at least, this provision does not seem like a plan at all. It does not appear to tell anyone to do, or not do, anything. The provision merely defines "marriage" for the purposes of federal law.

Recall that not all plans direct their subjects to engage in, or not to engage in, some bodily movement. Some concern the activity of planning itself. Stipulations, for example, are plans that specify how to apply another plan or plans in particular contexts. We can say, therefore, that this provision of DOMA is a stipulation. It requires that, for the purposes of applying federal law, the word "marriage" be treated as referring only to the union between a man and a woman. Notice that the one who accepts such a stipulation need not believe that marriage involves only a man and a woman. One can be convinced that same sex unions are also capable of being marriages. But, for the purposes of applying federal law, DOMA requires the bracketing of these convictions and treating a more socially conservative proposition as true.

A Note on the Definition of Crimes

Interestingly, criminal statutes are not usually formulated as directives. For example, statutes that forbid murder are not normally couched as prohibitions of the form: "No person shall purposely and with premeditation cause the death of another human being." Rather, they are formulated as definitions, such as: "A person is guilty of the offense of murder in the first degree when the person purposely and with premeditation causes the death of a human being."

On the Planning Theory, criminal statutes of this sort are composite plans, consisting of both behavioral directives and stipulations. Properly understood, the above definition of murder is a behavioral directive prohibiting acts of murder and a stipulation requiring that the former directive be applied to all acts of purposeful and premeditated killing.

There are two reasons why criminal statutes are not usually formulated solely as behavioral directives. First, as Tony Honore has pointed out, if statutes simply directed persons not to engage in certain kinds of conduct, there would be no way to know from their face whether the conduct is being criminalized or simply constitutes a civil wrong.[36] By stipulating the conduct as an *offense,* the criminal nature of the behavior is made explicit. Second, for every statute criminalizing certain conduct, there is normally another corresponding statute that specifies the punishment that such conduct warrants. If a criminalizing statute did not stipulate, say, what "murder in the first degree" is, but merely prohibited purposeful and premeditated killings, it would be cumbersome to specify the punishment associated with such conduct (as opposed to purposeful but nonpremeditated killing). By defining "murder in the first degree," the criminal law creates an easy method for cross-referencing offenses with their punishments.

Authorizations and Instructions

Another basic type of legal plan is the authorization. Unlike directives, authorizations do not plan action; rather, they confer the ability on others to plan action. Compare, for example, Article II, Section 3 of the United States Constitution: "[The President] shall from time to time give to the Congress Information of the State of the Union,"[37] with Article I, Section 8: "Congress shall have Power To lay and collect Taxes." The first provision directs the President to give the State of the Union address, whereas the second does not require Congress to lay and collect taxes, but rather empowers them to do so.

Authorizations are accompanied by what I earlier called instructions. Instructions are recipes that specify how the authorized person is to exercise the power conferred. Thus, Section 7 of Article I of the United States Constitution sets out the proper procedure for passage of legislation, which roughly amounts to bicameral approval and presentment to the president without a veto, or bicameral approval by two-thirds of each house after a presidential veto. Similarly, much of Article II of the Uniform Commercial Code sets out the instructions for the creation and modification of valid sales contracts. The failure to comply with instructions results not in wrongful conduct, but rather in null and void actions.

Authorizations are also almost always accompanied by corresponding directives. The authorization for testators to create wills, for example, is coupled with directives addressed to probate judges, executors, beneficiaries, and so on, to take or not take certain actions when a valid will has been created and the testator dies. We might say that these directives specify the *force* of the testamentary power insofar as they describe the legal effects that arise when the authorized power is exercised.

It might be wondered, then, why the law bothers to create a separate plan to authorize the testator to create a will when the directives to others would have sufficed. As long as the testator knows that his actions will have certain legal effects on judges, executors, beneficiaries, and so forth, the plan authorizing the testator to take those actions would seem to be otiose.

An analogy might help illustrate the value that authorizations and instructions add to a scheme of social planning. Suppose you wanted to show someone how to bake a chocolate cake. One way would be to teach her chemistry. Using basic principles of chemical theory, she could derive the steps needed to create a cake from scratch. Obviously, the simpler solution would be to give your friend a recipe. Instead of requiring her to figure out from first principles the necessary steps, a recipe would provide this crucial information.

Authorizations and instructions, we might say, are legal recipes. Authorizations indicate who has the power to do which actions; instructions inform the power holder how to exercise these powers. When the law creates authorizations, therefore, power holders need not piece together from other parts of the law that their actions will have certain effects. Rather, they can tell directly from the "recipe" that they have the powers conferred. Thus, while it is true that a testator might be able to figure out that he can dispose of his assets after death by examining the directives to executors and probate courts and noting that their duties are conditional on his actions, there is a simpler way for him to determine that he has such a power, namely, to look up the statutes of wills. In this way, he can know both that he has the power to dispose of his assets after his death and the proper way to exercise this power.

In addition to this informational function, authorizations and instructions play an important signaling role. Couching laws in terms of power demonstrates that their aim is to increase positive freedom, not decrease negative freedom. As we argued in Chapter 3 the point of will statutes is not to prevent testators from creating oral or unattested wills; rather, it is to provide them with the facilities to dispose of their assets after their death (or, put in the language of the Planning Theory, to enable them to *plan* who gets which assets after their death). If wills law were couched only in directives, this characteristic function would be obscured.

Directing and authorizing, of course, are not mutually exclusive activities. In many cases, the law not only authorizes persons to plan for others, but directs them to exercise those powers. Thus, judges in common law systems are not only authorized to decide questions of law, but are under a duty to do so. Other times, the law will authorize persons to engage in certain conduct, but direct them *not* to exercise those powers in a certain way. For example, on one view of jury nullification, juries are authorized to acquit against the weight of the evidence, but are directed not to do so. Should a jury acquit against the weight of the evidence, they will have acted wrongfully but nevertheless will have issued a valid verdict.

The law may also direct authorized persons to exercise their powers by giving various considerations weight in their planning. Thus, as Ronald Dworkin has pointed out, the legal principle respecting freedom of contract does not require that courts always abide by the agreed-upon terms of contracts. Rather, it merely requires that courts give significant weight to the importance of freedom of contract in their deliberations. On the taxonomy I have introduced, this legal principle would be considered a factorization, for it isolates a factor that judges are to use when engaged in planning.[38]

As the above discussion indicates, actions are often regulated by more than one kind of legal plan. The entering of criminal verdicts by a jury, for example, is the subject of an *authorization* that empowers them to enter verdicts, *instructions* for how to enter verdicts, a *requirement* to engage in deliberations, a *permission* to deliberate as long as necessary, *prohibitions* against voting for the wrong reasons, *factorizations* that require the giving of weight to some factors and not to others in deciding guilt or innocence, and a *stipulation* that requires defendants to be presumed innocent before proven guilty. Legal plans also regulate the proper execution of other legal plans: the aforementioned instructions, factorizations, and stipulations regulate the proper exercise of jury authorizations and the deliberation requirement directs the application of criminal prohibitions, requirements, and permissions to the facts of the particular case. We might say, therefore, that a legal system is a massive network of plans, many of which regulate the same actions and many of which regulate the proper execution of each other.

Law, Plan, and Critique

As I have characterized them, plans do not claim moral force. They do not, in other words, state that certain people "ought" to, are "obligated" to, have the "right" to, or are "guilty" if they do not, perform certain actions. Rather, plans simply direct, permit, authorize, or disable people to do, or not to do, certain actions, possibly under certain circumstances.

Since laws are plans, or planlike norms, they do not claim moral force either. Strictly speaking, the directive to pay income tax is best rendered as: "Everyone, pay x percent of your income in taxes!" (rather than: "Everyone is obligated to pay x percent of their income in taxes") and the authorization to Congress to regulate interstate commerce is similarly rendered as: "Everyone, *Congress* regulates interstate commerce!" (as opposed to: "Congress has the right to regulate interstate commerce").

It might be wondered, then, how laws can be subject to moral evaluation. If legal directives simply specify actions to be done, rather than tell us which actions we are morally obligated to do, and if legal authorizations simply tell us who gets to plan for whom with respect to which actions, rather than who has the moral right to do so, then how can we criticize them for getting our moral obligations and rights *wrong?*

Fortunately, this problem is not real. When we evaluate a law from the moral point of view, we assess it based on the actions that it directs us to take, or those whom it authorizes to act. We ask: if this law is obeyed, will a moral problem be solved or will another be created? If we judge that the law specifies the wrong action to take, instructs us not to take some action that is in fact morally permissible, or selects persons who have no moral right to plan for us, then we have reason to think that the law is morally deficient.

By the same token, when we morally endorse a law, we are approving its choice of action or person. Even though the plan itself does not state that we are obligated to act in a certain way or that someone has the moral right to regulate certain conduct, we can determine that its very enactment generates the moral effects it is supposed to generate. Indeed, we can, and frequently do, redescribe a law in these approving terms. We say, for example, that the plan directing us to pay income tax *obligates* us to pay income tax. In doing so, we are redescribing an entity in terms of the moral effects that it is supposed to produce.

Rendering laws as plans, therefore, does not preclude the moral evaluation of legal content. In fact, the freedom to critique the law depends on its moral neutrality. To see this, imagine the difficulty of criticizing a norm whose content was morally inflected. Suppose the content of a law mandating conscription to an unjust war were best rendered as: "All men between eighteen and forty-five are obligated to enlist in the army for the duration of the war against Oceana." It would seem to follow that the law obligates conscription. Yet, since the war is unjust, it is proper to criticize the law and even to deny that men between eighteen and forty-five are obligated to enlist in the army. The would-be reformer finds herself in the awkward, even impossible, situation of conceding in the active voice what she denies in the passive voice. She must say that the law obligates persons to act in a manner they are not obligated to act, which is a contradiction.

On the Planning Theory, by contrast, the law in question is best rendered as: "Men between eighteen and forty-five, enlist in the army for the duration of the war against Oceana!" As opposed to the morally inflected version, it does not follow from the existence of this plan that men of the requisite age are in fact obligated to enlist. Thus, the call for moral resistance can be made out: we can say that the law directs/requires/tells/demands/forces men between eighteen and forty-five to enlist but they are not in fact obligated to do so.

To be sure, the existence of the law ensures that men between eighteen and forty-five are *legally* obligated to enlist in the army (where "legally" gets a perspectival interpretation). But this simply means that from the legal point of view, men of a certain age are morally obligated to enlist.[39] Clearly, there is no contradiction in affirming that men are obligated to enlist from one point of view and denying that they are from another.

The Question of Legal Interpretation

In the last three chapters, we explored the Planning Theory of Law. We saw how it solves the Possibility Puzzle and overcomes Hume's Challenge. We also set out its answer to the Identity Question. In the next part of the book, I try to draw out some of the practical implications of these theoretical reflections. In particular, I ask how the Planning Theory should affect the practice of legal interpretation. If the law is a highly sophisticated planning organization, and laws are plans, or planlike norms, what is the proper way to interpret legal texts?

Rather than tackle this question head on, I will take a more indirect route. I will examine a number of objections that have been raised against standard theories of legal positivism which concern its ability to account for the standard practice of legal interpretation. On these views, legal positivism is deficient for ignoring the vital role that moral considerations play in interpreting the law. The existence and content of the law cannot depend on social facts alone for the simple reason that discovering the law is not merely a sociological inquiry, but necessarily involves moral reasoning.

My aim in proceeding in this fashion is to determine which, if any, of these objections succeeds in showing the deficiencies of standard theories of legal positivism. As we will see, most objections do not. They are either based on certain confusions about the nature of legal positivism or ignore the resources that standard theories have for accommodating the role of moral reasoning in legal interpretation.

Yet, we will see that a certain version of this critique does hit its mark. Current theories of legal positivism do not square with the actual practice of legal interpretation, and they are inadequate for this reason. I will then show how the Planning Theory is able to overcome this objection. In the process of responding to this powerful critique, I hope to develop a theory that not only squares with the actual process of legal interpretation but takes the nature of plans and planning seriously.

8

LEGAL REASONING AND
JUDICIAL DECISION MAKING

The Awful Truth

In my experience, most entering students think the sole educational mission of American law schools is to teach them "the rules." When they take Criminal Law, they imagine that they will spend their time learning the rules of American criminal law. In Constitutional Law, they assume that they will be taught the rules set out in the founding document that forms the basis of the American system of government. They think that their textbooks are filled with these rules and that they will be required to memorize and spit them back on their exams. They further suppose that the law library is packed with these textbooks and they will be taught which parts of the library to go to in order to locate the answers to their questions. Perhaps, if they are lucky, their professors will have written some of these authoritative tomes. And they are confident that when they graduate they will know the rules, or at least know where to find them.

Law students quickly discover, often to their chagrin, that this is not the case. Although they learn some "black letter" law in the first year, the bulk of class time is taken up not with reciting or explaining these rules, but with arguing over what they are. Students are taught to think like lawyers, which involves learning how to argue both sides of a case. First they argue that Rule A is correct and then switch to argue that Rule B is correct. Particularly upsetting to students is that they are usually not told which side is the right one. Classes focus on so-called hard cases, suits where good arguments are made by each of the opposing parties and reasonable lawyers disagree about which side should prevail. Professors are silent on the law not so much because they are "hiding the ball," but because they usually do not know where the ball is either.

The awful truth is that there are limits to legal knowledge. There are many live questions that we would like to be able to resolve with certainty, or at least with a modest degree of confidence, but that we are unable to answer to our satisfaction. Students worrying about being cold-called in class, defendants facing jail time, clients seeking tax advice, and judges deciding a case are not guaranteed to find or receive definitive answers about the law. At best, lawyers can make educated guesses, but the case may be too hard for them to honestly say that they *know* what the law is.

The existence of hard cases is shocking to many, not only because they regard it as unfair to hold people responsible for legal violations (or wrong answers on exams!) when the law cannot be ascertained with confidence. They are also surprised because they did not realize how much of legal reasoning is art, not science. Consider the professorial chestnut: "No vehicles are permitted in the park." Regular cars and motorcycles are clearly forbidden from entering the park, and it takes no skill to figure that out. But what about the ambulance driver who enters the park in order to get a heart attack victim to the hospital quickly? Ambulances are undeniably vehicles. Should ambulances be deemed "vehicles" within the meaning of the statute? And if so, does "No vehicles" mean *absolutely* no vehicles? Or consider the gardener who wants to use a riding lawn mower to cut the grass in the park. Riding lawn mowers are borderline cases of vehicles. Should they be deemed "vehicles" under the statute?

Clearly, these legal questions cannot be answered in a purely mechanical or algorithmic fashion. It is not enough to figure out whether these cases fall within the plain meaning of the statute. Ambulances undeniably fall within the plain meaning of the term "vehicle," yet they might be permitted to enter the park. Riding lawn mowers, on the other hand, fall neither within nor without the plain meaning of "vehicle." Syllogistic reasoning alone, therefore, cannot tell us whether the gardener is legally permitted to use this contraption.

These conundrums are not simply the consequences of crazy hypotheticals concocted by law professors to impress and upset their students; they are the bread and butter of dispute resolution in the appellate courts of actual legal systems. Consider the following cases:

• Congress enacted a statute imposing a five-year minimum sentence on any person who "uses or carries" a firearm during and in relation to a drug trafficking offense. Is a person who seeks to trade a gun for cocaine "using" the firearm and hence subject to the minimum sentence?[1] Is a person who transports marijuana in his truck and has a rifle locked in the glove compartment "carrying" a firearm within the meaning of the statute?[2]

- Under the Tariff Act of 1883, a 10 percent import duty must be levied on "vegetables," but not "fruit." Although tomatoes are botanical fruits, should they be considered "vegetables" within the meaning of the Act?[3]

- A provision of the Massachusetts Constitution ratified in 1780 states that members of the House of Representatives "shall be chosen by written votes." Can state representatives be chosen by modern voting machines that do not record votes on paper?[4]

- A federal statute requires that certain unpatented mining claims to federal land must be refiled every year "prior to December 31." Is a claim filed on December 31 past the deadline and hence invalid?[5]

- According to the common law, injurers can be held liable only for those injuries that they have "proximately" caused. In one case, a man was carrying a package while trying to get onto a train. Believing that the man might fall, a train company employee pushed the man inside the car and, as a result, he lost control of the package. The package happened to contain fireworks and exploded when it fell on the track. Due to the explosion, some scales fell down and hit a woman standing on the other side of the station. Was the employee's shoving the man the proximate cause of the woman's injuries?[6]

- The Representation of the People Act passed by the British Parliament in 1867 extended the franchise to every "man" who met certain qualifications. Did the enactment of the Interpretation Act in 1850, which mandated that statutes using the masculine should be read to include the feminine as well (unless otherwise provided), require the extension of suffrage to women?[7]

- A federal statute made it a crime to transport a stolen "motor vehicle" across state lines. Does the statute apply to someone who flew an airplane which he knew was stolen from Illinois to Oklahoma?[8]

- An 1885 federal law prohibited "the importation and migration of foreigners and aliens under contract or agreement to perform labor in the United States." Was the Holy Trinity Church in violation of this statute when it contracted with an English rector to relocate to New York City and work in its parish?[9]

- A contract is valid only when there has been an offer and acceptance. Is an offer accepted at the time the offeree drops an acceptance letter into the mailbox or when it is actually received by the offeror?[10]

In each of these cases, the relevant constitutional, statutory, administrative, or judicial text does not admit of a clear answer. To figure out what is to be done one must "think like a lawyer." One must consider both sides of the issue and use good sense to pick the best interpretation.

The often murky nature of the law, and the corresponding need for the exercise of judgment, is even starker when legal texts conflict. For example, in the infamous case of *Bush v. Gore,* courts were called upon to resolve several inconsistencies between different Florida statutes that regulated the vote recount procedure. Were county election officials allowed to conduct a manual recount because the Gore campaign requested one before the election results were certified, as one statute seemed to suggest, or was the secretary of state required to ignore the information because it was submitted more than seven days after the election, as another statute appeared to mandate? Or was the matter entirely within the discretion of the Florida secretary of state, as a third statute stated? The difficulties in interpreting the law were compounded, of course, by the question about the constitutionality of manual recounts, namely, whether the Equal Protection Clause of the Fourteenth Amendment prohibits counties from using different methods of discerning the intent of the voters on the theory that disparate procedures distribute voting power unequally.[11]

Finding the law, therefore, involves more than just looking up a statutory provision in a legal code and reading the answer. Legal reasoning is not the same as legal research. Nor is it an impersonal, technical, scientific process. To know the law, one must exercise a considerable degree of *judgment,* which is a mental faculty ungoverned by explicitly specifiable and quantifiable rules and procedures.

The recognition that legal reasoning is highly discretionary has led many jurists to find legal positivism extremely unsatisfying. They cannot reconcile a theory of law that grounds all legal facts exclusively in social facts—that distinguishes the way that the law is from the way it ought to be—with the realities of legal practice. For legal reasoning does not appear to be just a sociological inquiry. In hard cases, normative considerations of one sort or another seem relevant to resolving legal disputes.

Knowing that the city council approved a bill stating "No vehicles are permitted in the park" does not settle whether ambulances or riding lawn mowers are permitted in the park. Many lawyers would say that to know whether an ambulance should be permitted in the park, one has to answer a question of "policy," which is a catch-all term for any consideration that bears, or has been thought to bear, on the issue presented. Thus, a judge would have to decide whether it would be a good idea if ambulances or riding lawn mowers were permitted in the park, or perhaps, whether the same policy that justified excluding cars from the park would also recommend excluding these other wheeled objects as well. Similarly, the debate over *Bush v. Gore* did not appear to be a dispute exclusively, or even primarily, about social facts. Everyone knew that the various statutes clashed. The resolution of that conflict, rather, concerned complex questions of democracy and equality, the rights of political parties and individual voters, the importance of certainty and finality in elections, the value of federalism, and the proper role of federal courts in settling political conflicts.

Legal positivism, the thought continues, is premised on a naive picture of the law worthy only of matriculating law students. If all cases were easy and could be resolved just by looking up one's question in some authoritative rulebook, then it would make sense to think that social facts determine the content of the law. Social conventions would pick out which rulebooks are authoritative, and hence sociological inquiry, linguistic competence, and logical analysis would suffice to answer any legal question.

This discomfort with legal positivism has led many in the legal academy to embrace some version of natural law theory. On this view, moral facts are essential ingredients in determining legal content and must always supplement social facts, such as the provenance of an authoritative text or linguistic conventions that determine the text's plain meaning. To figure out what the law is, therefore, the legal reasoner must take notice of these moral facts. This picture of legal reasoning as a form of moral reasoning provides a natural explanation for why hard cases arise in the law. There are limits to legal knowledge, on this view, because there are limits to moral knowledge. We often find ourselves uncertain about how to proceed from the moral point of view, and reasonable people frequently disagree with one another about their considered ethical judgments. Hard cases cannot be eliminated in the law because their prevalence is an indelible feature of our moral lives.

Of course, none of this should be taken as a knock-down argument against legal positivism. It simply sets out a traditional concern that many have had vis-à-vis positivistic theories, namely, that an account of law that rests exclusively on social facts may be incapable of explaining the role played by normative considerations in the actual practice of legal reasoning. Needless to say, this concern about positivism in general applies equally to the Planning Theory. For as we saw in the last few chapters, the Planning Theory is a positivistic account that ultimately grounds the law in social facts alone. Moreover, it denies that normative premises can appear in a valid scheme of legal justification: legal reasoning, according to the Planning Theory, is a descriptive in, descriptive out process. At least at first glance, however, actual legal practice does not seem to fit this description. There simply is no magic user's manual that sets out all of these so-called plans. Nor does judicial decision making appear to respect the DIDO pattern of reasoning. Judges do not restrict themselves to the available legal texts, but often resort to moral argument in order to resolve disputes. It is far from obvious, therefore, how the Planning Theory can be squared with the realities of legal practice.

To explore whether this concern is fatal to positivism in general, and the Planning Theory in particular, we must sharpen the attack and see whether positivists have any response to it. In this chapter, we will examine one version of this challenge from legal reasoning, reserving others for the following chapters.

The first objection claims that legal positivism is committed to a jurisprudential conception often called "legal formalism." According to legal formalism, modern legal regimes, such as those in the United States and Western Europe, are consistent and complete normative systems. Formalism maintains, in other words, that every legal question has a uniquely correct legal answer, and that the role of the judge is to find and apply it. Judges discover the law by locating a set of principles within the available legal materials and then, using these norms, derive specific answers to legal questions. Legal reasoning, on this view, is solely an exercise in linguistic competence, conceptual analysis, and logical calculation. The model for the formalist judge is the mathematician who derives new truths about geometry from Euclid's assumptions, rather than the legislator who engages in moral reasoning so as to fashion the best rule for the current state of society.

According to this objection, positivism is committed to formalism because positivists maintain that the existence of the law never depends on moral facts. Positivism, in other words, treats legal reasoning as an *amoral* activity and, therefore, denies judges the opportunity to respond to the social imperatives of the case at hand. Like formalist judges, then, positivist judges are prohibited from appealing to considerations of fairness, justice, efficiency, institutional design, and political legitimacy when deciding cases.

Once the connection between positivism and formalism is drawn, however, the fate of positivism is sealed. For the objection rightly points out that formalism is an embarrassing and pernicious theory. A doctrine that denies courts the right to rely on moral considerations in adjudication is not only inconsistent with established practice in the United States and other mature legal systems but could not possibly be true given the pressing need for courts to engage in moral reasoning in order to resolve hard cases. Since positivism is committed to formalism, and formalism is false, the objection concludes that positivism must be false as well.

Insofar as the challenge we will consider in this chapter identifies legal positivism with legal formalism, it will be helpful to begin the discussion with a thumbnail sketch of formalism. My concern here will not be to present a nuanced and historically accurate description of legal formalism; nor will it be to discuss every theory that has been called "formalistic" at one time or by some person. Rather, I intend to set out the "received view" of the doctrine that forms the basis of the challenges to legal positivism.[12] While the discussion may exaggerate certain positions held by actual formalists, my primary aim will be to see whether legal positivism correctly understood can be criticized as being committed to this somewhat caricatured and flawed jurisprudential conception.

Legal Formalism

As I understand it, legal formalism is primarily a descriptive theory about the content of modern legal systems. Roughly put, it claims that in modern regimes there is always a right answer to every legal question, and that it is the responsibility of the judge to find and apply this answer without resorting to moral considerations of any sort. Formalism, therefore, should be distinguished from an empirical theory about how judges actually make decisions. Formalists do not claim that judges always try to find the law and never legislate from the bench or never resort to moral considerations to resolve disputes. Rather, they maintain that judges are legally obligated to find the law, and when judges, say, legislate from the bench, they act in a legally improper fashion.

Formalism's descriptive thesis concerning modern legal systems is often conjoined with a conceptual claim about all legal systems. While formalists accept the possibility that a legal system may be incomplete—that there might not be a right answer to every legal question—they claim that such a system is nonetheless *completable*. In such situations, the legislature is under a legal obligation to fill in the gaps so that the system in question achieves the ideal of complete determinacy.

To ease exposition, I will concentrate mainly on the descriptive thesis of legal formalism. When I speak of the formalists' description of "the law," therefore, I do not intend to refer to all legal systems, but only the paradigmatic modern ones. Moreover, I will set out the version of legal formalism most closely associated with the American school, leaving it open whether Continental jurists would characterize formalism in a different manner.[13]

Four Theses of Legal Formalism

Legal formalism may be understood as an account that is committed to the following four theses:[14]

(1) *Judicial Restraint:* The formalist conception of the judicial role is highly restrictive. According to it, judges are always under a duty to apply existing law. They never, in other words, enjoy the discretion to disregard or correct the rules in favor of their conception of morality or social policy. Only the legislature may amend the law; judges are required to find and apply it whenever it exists.

(2) *Determinacy:* Not only do formalists maintain that judges are obligated to apply law whenever it exists, they think that the law always exists and is available to judges for deciding cases. On their view, the law is completely determinate: for every legal question, there is one, and only one, correct answer. Formalists thus deny that there are factual situations ungoverned by a legal norm, or "gaps" in the law. Nor do they accept the possibility of legal inconsistencies, factual situations governed by two or more mutually unsatisfiable rules. For this reason, judges may never throw up their hands and say there is no law to apply. From the formalistic point of view, there is always one right way to decide a dispute, and judges are required to find and apply it.

(3) *Conceptualism:* If judges are to find the law, formalism must ensure that the law be findable. This consideration precludes the possibility that

the law is composed solely of particular rules governing limited factual situations, for to cover all possible cases the rules would have to be infinite, and hence unknowable. Accordingly, formalists accept a view often called "conceptualism." Conceptualism claims that the mass of lower-level legal rules can be derived from a handful of general principles containing abstract concepts. Examples of these principles include "A contract is not valid unless backed by consideration," "The act does not make a person guilty unless the mind is also guilty," and "A person acting negligently is responsible for all harm to another of which his negligence is the proximate cause."

On this model, the law resembles a squat pyramid. The general principles reside at the apex, and they justify the mass of rules governing specific fact patterns at the base. By knowing a limited number of top-level principles, a judge can derive the lower-level rules, and hence correctly decide which party is legally entitled to prevail. The generality and abstraction of these principles not only secure the determinacy and knowability of the law, but lend legal doctrine a pleasing conceptual order. The bulk of the law can be subsumed under a few general principles, and the fixed abstract concepts that they employ classify the rules in an intelligible fashion.

(4) *Amorality of Adjudication:* According to the formalists, judges must decide cases without resorting to moral reasoning. They must, in other words, be able to discover the general legal principles, derive the lower-level rules, and apply the rules to the facts at hand without resort to moral considerations. Judges are only supposed to use "logic," where logic is broadly construed to include the operations of deduction, induction, and conceptual analysis.

Let us begin with the discovery of principles. On the formalist model, general norms that justify and structure the law are to be found in authoritative legal texts, such as statutes and opinions. When they are enacted by a legislature and set out at the beginning of a code, judges can simply read the legal text to determine the principles at play. Unfortunately, principles are rarely stated explicitly in legislative texts but must be derived instead through a close examination of past judicial decisions. They are drawn, according to the formalists, from the case law much as scientific hypotheses are supported by corroborative observations, namely, through the process of induction. Cases whose rulings exemplify the principle are treated as confirming instances; the principle is treated as valid when a sufficient number of such cases are found.

Having located the applicable general principles, judges must then derive the lower-level rules that decide the case. According to the formalists, this process consists of a combination of conceptual analysis and deductive reasoning. First, the judge should analyze the abstract concepts that these principles employ (for example, PROPERTY, CONSIDERATION, PROXIMATE CAUSE). This analysis will provide the judge with certain necessary truths about the concepts analyzed. Second, the judge should use these necessary truths to derive new lower-level rules. The principles play the role of major premises, and the necessary truths are the minor ones. The lower-level rules are the conclusions of these syllogisms.

Once these more specific rules are derived, the judge can then plug in the facts of the case. At this final stage, the lower-level rules play the role of major premises and the facts are subsumed as the minor ones. The conclusions specify the proper legal disposition of the case.

According to the formalist way of thinking, therefore, legal reasoning in general, and judicial decision making in particular, are completely *amoral* processes. To justify her ruling, a judge cannot advert to a moral judgment: she cannot mention the equity or fairness of a particular ruling, the long-term social and economic effects of creating a certain precedent, or the institutional ramifications of judicial resolution of a dispute. The general principles, particular rules, and actual resolution of cases are to be discovered without the help of social science or first-order moral theories. Economics and justice are for the legislature; logic and legal materials are for the courts.

The Mailbox Rule

This abstract description of formalism may be made more vivid with a concrete illustration.[15] The classic example of formalist legal reasoning is Christopher Langdell's argument against the so-called Mailbox Rule. The Mailbox Rule holds that a contract is formed by an acceptance letter when the letter is mailed, not when it is actually received. Langdell argued that the Mailbox Rule is inconsistent with the general principles of American contract law and hence should be rejected.

Langdell's argument begins with the principle accepted by most American courts at the time, namely, that a contract cannot be formed unless an offer is backed by "consideration." An offer is backed by consideration under two conditions: the offeree either (1) performs the action required by the offeror or (2) merely promises to perform it. Since the

Mailbox Rule concerns cases where an offer is accepted by return promise, the first condition does not obtain. A new rule, therefore, can be derived for acceptance letter cases: contracts cannot be formed by an acceptance letter unless the offeree has promised to perform the action required by the offeror.

Langdell then asked: when does the offeree promise to perform the action required by the offeror—when the letter containing the promise is mailed or when it is received? If the former, the offer is backed by consideration and the contract formed when the letter is mailed; if the latter, the offer is backed by consideration and the contract formed when the letter is received.

To answer this crucial question, Langdell proceeded to analyze the concepts PROMISE and COMMUNICATION. First, he claimed that a promise is not made until it is communicated to the promisee. Second, he claimed that a promise is communicated by letter when the letter is received by the promisee. From these two alleged conceptual truths, Langdell derived a third alleged truth: a promise is made by letter when the letter is received by the promisee. Combining this last conceptual truth with the rule from two paragraphs back, Langdell derived the following low-level legal rule: a contract cannot be formed by an acceptance letter unless the acceptance letter is received.

Thus, Langdell claimed to have shown that the Mailbox Rule is not legally valid in American law. In doing so, he did not rely on policy considerations, such as it being fairer or more efficient to place the burden of learning about acceptance on the offeror. Rather, he consulted the cases to determine the existence of the general principle about consideration via induction, engaged in conceptual analysis, and derived his conclusion via deduction.

The Positivism-Formalism Connection

We are now in a position to see why many have associated positivism with formalism. The thought goes something as follows: legal positivism is committed to the idea that law is a matter of social fact alone, never of moral fact. In order for a judge to decide a case, therefore, she cannot rely on any moral facts. Only social facts are relevant, for only they determine legal content. Social facts, we might say, "crowd out" moral facts in judicial decision making. Like formalism, then, positivism demands that adjudication be a completely *amoral* affair. A positivistic judge cannot rely on moral philosophy in order to decide disputes. She is confined to legal texts and the amoral operations of linguistic comprehension, induction, analysis, and deduction.[16]

This link between positivism and formalism has seemed problematic to many who regard formalism as a seriously flawed theory of judicial decision making. Most Anglo-American lawyers believe judges use more than just logic when resolving legal issues and, more importantly, that they are legally permitted to do so. This sentiment is best captured in the opening paragraph of Oliver Wendell Holmes's *The Common Law,* where Holmes makes arguably the most famous statement of American legal thought: "The life of the law has not been logic; it has been experience."[17] One need only look at the average state or federal appellate opinion to confirm Holmes's observation. Judges are not passive, mechanical appliers of rules or, to use Roscoe Pound's evocative image, "slot-machines" that take in facts and spit out rulings.[18] Their opinions are often long, sprawling documents; rarely are they neat, tidy syllogisms. They include, and are sometimes overrun by, discussions and debates about fairness, justice, social policy, institutional design, and political legitimacy.

The types of moral considerations that appellate courts rely on in their deliberations are numerous and familiar to lawyers. They range from the ethical (what justice requires in a given case, which behaviors and character traits are virtuous and which are vicious, whether a procedure is fair) to the pragmatic (what will the short- and long-term social, economic, and institutional effects of certain decisions be, who can be trusted to implement which policies, which incentives best promote optimal compliance) and, finally, to the political (who has the greatest legitimacy to decide particular questions, which rights do individuals have against the government, how can the aims and values of the system best be promoted). In fact, one of the most important lessons a beginning law student learns is that these considerations are usually at play in any interesting legal case. Thus, they are taught about floodgates, slippery slopes, unclean hands, frustrated expectations, cheapest cost avoiders, loss spreading, deep pockets, transaction costs, unconscionability, undue burden, formal justice, conflict of interest, institutional competence, administrability, accountability, predictability, fair warning, federalism, democracy, autonomy, fundamental rights, and so on.

Moral reasoning is most obviously present in common law cases. Judges often employ moral considerations to determine which conflicting line of cases to follow, how to differentiate holdings from dicta, whether to read a holding broadly or narrowly, and, especially, whether to follow, distinguish, or overrule a precedent. Courts also use moral reasoning when applying legal standards that employ normative concepts, such as REASONABLE, PUBLIC INTEREST, UNCONSCIONABLE, FAIR USE, or OBSCENE. A judge cannot determine how a reasonable person would act, or whether a film has redeeming social value, without engaging in some sort of substantive moral analysis or value inquiry. Likewise, a court engaging in judicial review and applying a multiprong, judicially created test such as the "strict scrutiny" one ("A statute that infringes a fundamental right or discriminates against a suspect class is constitutional only if it is narrowly tailored to effectuate a compelling state interest") will be relying on moral considerations in deciding a case. Other courts employ moral reasoning to determine which of two interpretations of a text is the better one, whether one reading of a statute should be rejected for being "absurd," which of two conflicting rules should be heeded, how to adapt a rule to an unforeseen or novel situation, whether a right is fundamental or is weighty enough to override another right, and so on.

Even if courts never openly engaged in moral reasoning, it would nonetheless be obvious that they were doing so sotto voce. For as we saw at the beginning of this chapter, judges often preside over cases that cannot be settled simply by reference to the authoritative legal texts. Indeed, as comparative lawyers have long argued, the formalist self-presentation of civil law judges can only be a façade, hiding the extensive policy argumentation that is the true basis for many of these decisions.[19] Rule books and syllogisms may dispose of easy cases, but hard cases require more potent stuff.

Formalism is seen as flawed, therefore, because it assumes that judges are prohibited from deciding cases on the basis of moral considerations. It denies that in many cases judges respond, are permitted to respond, and indeed *must* respond to the social imperatives of the case, tempering the law when it gives inefficient or unjust results, adapting outdated rules to new and unforeseen situations, and plugging gaps and resolving inconsistencies when they present themselves.

Our first objection to legal positivism, therefore, amounts to the charge that positivism concurs with formalism about the role of the judge: they both regard judicial decision making as legitimate when, and only when, it is free from the corruption of moral considerations. Since this insistence on amoral adjudication appears to be radically inconsistent with existing legal practice, which permits judges to form moral judgments and use these judgments to decide certain cases, legal positivism must be rejected as a plausible theory of legal reasoning and take its place alongside formalism in the graveyard of failed legal theories.

Core and Penumbra

Like most American lawyers, Hart rejected legal formalism as a flawed theory of legal reasoning and judicial decision making. He was acutely aware that judges in common law systems use more than just "logic" when interpreting the law and resolving disputes. In his writings on interpretation, therefore, Hart sought to distance himself from the formalists. Indeed, he not only denied that positivism is a form of formalism, he argued that it is a form of antiformalism. Positivists reject the complete determinacy of the law and therefore insist that judges rely on moral consideration in at least some cases.

Legal Reasoning and Judicial Decision-Making

Formalism, we have seen, is committed to the amorality of adjudication. A formalist judge never interprets the law or decides a case by engaging in moral reasoning. The objection we have been considering claims that legal positivism is faulty because it is committed to a similarly amoral, formalistic picture of adjudication. Positivists are committed to this conception, on this view, because they privilege social facts in the determination of legal content. Social facts crowd out moral facts and thus render them irrelevant for deciding cases.

Hart began the process of distancing positivism from formalism by pointing out the fallacy in the last inference. Simply because social facts determine the content of the law does not entail that judicial decision making is devoid of moral reasoning.[20] The inference goes through only if one assumes that the law is completely determinate. For if every case is resolvable according to law, and the law is determined by social facts alone, then every case is resolvable by social facts alone. Social facts crowd out moral facts in adjudication, in other words, only on the assumption that the law governs every inch of the normative universe. However, if the law is indeterminate in some cases, then not every question is resolvable according to law. Some disputes, then, will fall through the legal cracks; they can be resolved only by reference to policy considerations.

We might express Hart's point by distinguishing between "legal reasoning" and "judicial decision making." The object of legal reasoning is the discovery of the law;[21] the aim of judicial decision making, on the other hand, is the resolution of a dispute. The positivistic privileging of social facts might indicate that legal reasoning is amoral, but it does not show the same about judicial decision making. This conclusion follows only on the assumption that the law is completely determinate. Only when the law resolves every issue will judicial decision making be entirely taken up by legal reasoning. But when the law has gaps or is inconsistent, a judge who is obligated to rule cannot employ legal reasoning, and therefore has no choice but to rely on policy arguments in order to discharge his duty.

The Limitations of Guidance

As we have seen, the objection is able to connect positivism to formalism only when it smuggles in formalism as one of its premises. Positivistic judges would be forbidden from relying on moral considerations *only on the assumption that the law determines the correct result in every situation.* But if the law were silent in some cases, then social facts would not crowd out moral facts, thereby leaving judges free to rely on them to resolve the legally unregulated disputes.

The next step in Hart's attempt to distinguish positivism from formalism is to argue that positivism is not committed to the complete determinacy of the law. To the contrary, it is committed to the partial *indeterminacy* of the law. This positivistic embrace of indeterminacy, and rejection of formalism, follows from the impossibility of transmitting standards of conduct to others to settle every contingency in advance. Because guidance must always be limited, so must the law.[22]

To demonstrate the inherent limits of human guidance, Hart considered two methods for communicating standards to others: precedent and legislation. In a system of precedent, reference is made to a specific event, and others are told that they are required to act in similar ways under similar circumstances. A father might take off his hat when entering church and tell his son that he is always to act likewise. The obvious deficiency of the method of precedent is that, while the exemplar is identified, the relevant standard of similarity is not. For any two distinct events, there are an infinite number of possible standards of similarity, some of which will rank the two events as similar and others that will assess them as dissimilar. While common sense will eliminate certain similarity standards as inappropriate, there will always be a healthy number of conflicting standards that will seem more or less reasonable. When the father tells his son to take off his hat, does that apply to his daughter as well? Should the son take off his hat reverently or smartly? Should he keep it off for the entire service? Reasonable doubts arise in all of these cases.

Hart was not the first to point out the deficiencies of guidance by precedent. Legal reformers of the eighteenth and nineteenth centuries, especially his positivist predecessors Bentham and Austin, often argued in favor of replacing common law decision making with legislation and codification.[23] The uncertainty and unpredictability engendered by the common law—what Bentham used to call "dog law"—would be resolved through the use of texts containing general classifying terms. The terms in these canonical texts would eliminate doubts about individual cases by specifying directly what is to be done in a general class of cases. If a father were to tell his children, "Males must always remove their hats for the entire time they are in church," his daughter would then learn that she may keep her bonnet on and his son is to remain bareheaded for the time that he is present in church.

Hart credited the American legal realists with puncturing the inflated claims of determinacy often made on behalf of legislation. Although the use of general terms would seem to guarantee certainty as to what is expected, this certitude is illusory. For even though general terms will resolve many doubts about certain cases, borderline instances will remain.[24]

Return to "No vehicles are permitted in the park." While the rule expressed by the statutory text would prohibit a car from entering the park—cars are paradigmatic instances of vehicles—questions arise with respect to riding lawn mowers. A riding lawn mower, for example, shares certain features with a car, but not others. It is neither a vehicle nor not a vehicle. As Hart famously put the point, while cars fall within the "core" of the term, such instances fall within the "penumbra."[25]

According to Hart, penumbral cases can never be eradicated—every general term in natural language is necessarily "open textured." To eliminate linguistic indeterminacy would require the existence of an exhaustive test for determining the application of a general term under every conceivable condition. Clearly, humans cannot formulate or follow such tests. Open texture in natural language is thus a by-product of the cognitive limitations of human beings. While the canons of interpretation might be able to eliminate some of the uncertainty engendered by the open texture of language, it is obvious that they cannot foreclose all doubt. Insofar as the canons are linguistically formulated, Hart pointed out, they too are vulnerable to the open texture of language.[26]

The Limits of the Social

Hart was not content simply to point out the limitations of language as a method of guiding conduct. He thought that this fact had significant implications for the nature of law. According to Hart, the fact that language is partially indeterminate entails that the law will be partially indeterminate. A statute that reads "No vehicles are permitted in the park" will be partially indeterminate, because the extension of the term "vehicle" is not well defined. Insofar as a riding lawn mower is neither a vehicle nor a nonvehicle, the rule neither applies nor does not apply to it. In deciding a case involving the permissibility of bringing riding lawn mowers into the park, then, judges will be forced to exercise discretion. They must look beyond the law and rely on other considerations to decide such cases.

On Hart's view, the formalists' sin consists in denying that judges ever create law. The general principles of the law could not determine the answers to every legal question, for the abstract concepts they contain have an open texture and give indeterminate guidance in some cases. While my punching you in the face is a clear case of action being the proximate cause of another person's injury, the train employee shoving someone who drops a bag of fireworks onto a railroad track causing an explosion that knocks down scales onto a woman on the other side of the platform is a borderline instance. Likewise, the statute that imposes mandatory sentences for carrying a weapon during a drug offense clearly applies to someone who holds a loaded gun in a threatening manner while selling a suitcase full of cocaine, but does not clearly apply to someone who keeps a rifle in his locked glove compartment when driving a truck containing marijuana. Judges must legislate in the penumbra, for in such cases the law runs out.[27] Hart conjectured that formalism arose as an ideological response to the political imperatives of systems with separated powers. If legislatures are the only institutions permitted to make law in a system, then the only way to legitimate judicial decision making is to deny the existence of legal indeterminacy.[28]

By rejecting formalism and acknowledging the relative indeterminacy of the law, Hart was merely following the implications of his own commitment to legal positivism. For according to the positivist, the social facts that determine the content of the law are those that concern *actions that guide conduct*. In the case of legislation and adjudication, the actions that guide are the selection of linguistic texts; in the case of custom, they are repeated conformity to exemplary behavior coupled with a disposition to criticize deviations from this pattern. In both cases, the guiding actions cannot settle every question that might possibly arise about which actions are to be done. The open texture of language guarantees that any finite linguistic text will be silent on a range of possible issues. Likewise, any case is both similar to, and different from, a finite pattern of behavior in an infinite number of ways. Judicial discretion is inevitable because it is impossible for finite beings to guide conduct in ways that resolve every conceivable question. At some point, guidance by social facts, and hence the law, must run out.[29]

Let us call the idea that social facts are incapable of settling what is to be done under every circumstance the "Limits of the Social" argument. Finite beings simply cannot select comprehensive and consistent norms to guide conduct. The Limits of the Social argument explains why the objection to legal positivism we have been considering in this chapter is misconceived. By privileging social facts over moral ones in the determination of legal content, the positivist does not render judicial decision making completely amoral. Quite the contrary, positivism actually requires that, at least in certain cases, judges engage in policy argumentation, which in decent legal systems generally involves the consideration of genuine moral concerns. For if the law crucially depends on social facts, and social facts necessarily run out at some point, then judges will not always be able to rely on them to resolve disputes. In the inevitable penumbra, judges will have to exercise their discretion, for there will be no legal standards left to apply.

While Hart thought that social facts have their limitations, he also cautioned against overreaction. In contrast to the intemperate claims of some legal realists who denied that the law is ever determinate, Hart affirmed the commonsense belief that there are right answers to many legal questions.[30] Guidance offered by legislation is often determinate, because general terms have core instances. Cars are not permitted in the park because cars are clearly vehicles.

Mechanical metaphors, although misleading, are more appropriate for these core cases. In the core, the application of a term to a case seems immediate and obvious. Though the judge must still apply the rule herself—she must determine, for example, that a car counts as a vehicle—the ease with which it is done tends to obscure the fact that judgment of a certain sort is being exercised. If judicial opinions seem rife with considerations of moral principle and social utility, this is due to the types of cases that get litigated and become the subject of appellate decision making. Lawyers and law students study the hard cases, where the law is indeterminate and judges must resort to extralegal considerations to fill the gaps. These cases are the exception, however; in most instances, the rule is clear and the issue is resolved with little or no fanfare.

Watered-Down Formalisms

As a historical matter, Hart's efforts to distance legal positivism from the classical version of legal formalism were highly effective. Thus, it is hard (though not impossible!) to find anyone these days who imputes to positivism the central commitment of legal formalism, namely, the complete determinacy of the law. The Hartian distinction between core and penumbra is an evocative one and seems to have taken hold in the jurisprudential consciousness.

Though legal positivism is no longer equated with the classical version of formalism, the association nevertheless survives in various attenuated forms. In this section, therefore, I would like to examine two of the more common equations of positivism with certain watered-down versions of formalism and show that these interpretations, while understandable, are nonetheless mistaken.

Purposive Interpretation

It is often said that legal positivists are committed to a "formalist" method for interpreting legal texts. According to this interpretive methodology, legal texts must be interpreted in accordance with their plain meaning, never their purpose. For the sake of clarity, let us call this version of formalism "textualism."

The identification of positivism with textualism has been motivated by the following thought: to use the purpose behind a legal text in order to interpret that text is to engage in moral reasoning and, hence, is an activity barred by legal positivism. To keep legal reasoning free of moral considerations, only the linguistic meaning of a text may count. Legal positivism, therefore, is committed to textualist forms of legal interpretation.[31]

Hart's position in the so-called Hart-Fuller debate further encouraged this equation of positivism with textualism. In this famous dispute, which took place in 1958 in the pages of the *Harvard Law Review* and concerned the relative merits of legal positivism over natural law theory, Hart seemed to suggest that when a case falls within the core of the general terms of a text, the judge is obligated to apply the rule.[32] This injunction made it appear as though, for the positivist, linguistic meaning was the sole consideration a judge may take into consideration when interpreting the law.

Lon Fuller responded to Hart by pointing out the absurdity of strict textualism. Suppose someone wants to use a jeep as part of a war memorial in the park. Even though a jeep falls within the core of the general term "vehicle," surely it would not be ridiculous to think that *this* vehicle falls outside the rule. In contrast to Hart, Fuller claimed that the interpretation of statutes must always be informed by considerations of social purpose, not just linguistic meaning.[33] Forbidding jeeps from adorning war memorials would not seem to further any policy that the legislators would have hoped to advance by enacting such a statute, and so it should be considered a legally permissible action.

Fuller took the inevitability of purposive interpretation as a reason to reject legal positivism in favor of natural law theory. Positivism, on his view, could not abide by inquiries into purpose because such investigations into the way the law ought to be would infect the analysis of what the law is. Since positivism requires a strict separation between legal and moral facts, positivists like Hart cannot endorse purposive interpretation but must content themselves with absurd approaches to legal interpretation such as textualism.[34]

It is not hard, however, to detect the fallacy in Fuller's objection to legal positivism. An inquiry into the purpose or policy behind a legislative text need not be an analysis of the way the law ought to be. It may be an investigation into social fact. In the case of the war memorial, for example, a judge might inquire into the reasons that the legislators had for enacting the rule in question. The policies of the rule, in other words, need not be those that are judged to be the morally best ones; they may simply be those that the legislators had in mind during legislation. These purposes have social sources and hence possess the appropriate positivistic pedigree.[35]

Indeed, Hart relaxed his position in response to Fuller's objections, accepting that a system's norms of interpretation might require the purposive interpretation of certain legal texts. The core of a general term would be determined in these cases not solely by linguistic norms, but rather by the purpose the rule is supposed to serve.[36] Thus, on this new view, a jeep may actually fall outside the core of the term "vehicle" when prohibiting it from entering the park clearly does not further the policy underlying the no-vehicles-in-the-park rule.

While Hart accepted the force of Fuller's critique, he did not go as far as Fuller in regarding purposive interpretation as the only acceptable interpretive methodology. Hart thought it a contingent matter whether a legal system opted for a purposive or more strictly textualist approach. The determination of a legal system's interpretive methodology, of course, is itself a matter of social fact. If there is a convention among officials to interpret certain texts in accordance with their purpose, then purposive interpretation is appropriate for that legal system.

One last point is worth noting. Even though reliance on purposes might help resolve certain doubts about the interpretation of a legal text—it is plausible to suppose, for example, that the policy behind the no-vehicles-in-the-park rule would not be violated by allowing ambulances into the park, hence reliance on purpose would resolve this case—it would be a mistake to think that it can render the law completely determinate. First, the subjective purposes of individual legislators might conflict and hence recommend different actions in particular cases. Second, concepts share the same open texture as terms in natural language. Thus, if the purpose behind the no-vehicles-in-the-park rule is to reduce noise pollution, it may be doubted whether banning electric cars, which are 75 percent quieter than gasoline-powered cars, furthers this purpose. Since the concept NOISE is open textured, the reliance on purpose will generate a legal gap in this case. And since all concepts are open textured, a regime of purposive interpretation will inevitably lead to legal indeterminacy, at least in some cases.[37]

Judicial Restraint

Though it is generally acknowledged that legal positivists reject the formalist theory of legal determinacy, it is nevertheless thought they are committed to the formalist conception of the judicial office. On this interpretation, judges are permitted to rely on moral considerations in the penumbra; in the core, however, they are required to apply the law come what may. Positivistic courts, in other words, are supposed to play a very restricted legislative role: though they may add to the law when it is silent, they have no power to revise the law, even when there are compelling moral reasons to do so.[38]

It is likely that Hart's critique of classical formalism contributed to this misinterpretation of legal positivism, or at least did nothing to correct it. For in his discussion of legal determinacy, Hart not only claimed that judges exercise discretion in the penumbra, he made it appear as though they exercise discretion *only in the penumbra*. In the core, he seemed to suggest, judges are legally bound to apply the law.[39] This position simply restates the Judicial Restraint thesis, according to which judges never enjoy the discretion to override the law in the name of compelling moral considerations.

Because many attribute to legal positivism a restrictive role for the judge, they fault it for being unable to account for cases where judges have taken a more active role in amending the law. We are told, for example, that *Brown v. Board of Education*[40] and *Griswold v. Connecticut*[41] are "anti-positivistic" cases, because in these instances the Supreme Court reversed course and reformed the law in favor of judicial conceptions of justice and fundamental rights.[42] The critique here, of course, is not simply that legal positivism is descriptively inaccurate, but that it is morally noxious as well. *Brown* ended racial segregation in education and *Griswold* found a right to privacy in the Constitution. Any theory of law that would uphold Jim Crow or allow the prohibition on the use of contraceptives by married couples, the thought goes, leaves much to be desired.

Indeed, some have gone as far as to hold legal positivism responsible for facilitating gross atrocities. Thus, Robert Cover claimed that legal positivism encouraged antebellum judges to uphold the fugitive slave laws and hence to return runaway slaves to their masters.[43] Similarly, Gustav Radbruch notoriously argued that German positivism led Nazi-era judges to apply, rather than resist, Nazi law.[44]

It is an interesting question whether a jurisprudential theory ought to be rejected simply because its acceptance engenders morally bad consequences.[45] We need not resolve this question, however, because in the present case the issue is moot. Legal positivism, properly understood, does not assign a restrictive role to courts. The legal positivist conceives of the institutional function of a judge as a parochial matter, one regulated by the fundamental rules of the legal system in question. These rules will restrain judges in some systems; in others, they will accord judges substantial discretion to override the law when compelling moral reasons exist. Positivism no more entails a limited legislative role for the American judge than it entails the supremacy of federal law over state law. These are contingent legal positions ultimately determined by social practice.

Moreover, even in systems where judges are *legally* obligated to apply the law come what may, legal positivism does not claim that judges are thus *morally* required to apply the law come what may. To the contrary, this inference is mandated by natural law theory. Legal positivism, as we have seen, is predicated on the conceptual distinction between legal and moral obligation and denies that there is always a moral obligation to obey the law. A good positivist judge, therefore, would not confuse the constitutionality of the fugitive slave laws with its moral validity and would resist the authoritarian demand to heed the law simply because the law said so.

Is the Truth So Awful?

We began this chapter with the awful truth about legal knowledge. Because the law is not always cut and dried, smart and capable lawyers are sometimes unable to say for sure what the law is. I hope we can now see that this problem may be overstated. In many instances, the best explanation for why lawyers do not know the law is that there is no law to know. They may find, for example, that their case falls within the penumbra of a rule. Or one statute may say one thing, while another statute says something else. The uncertainty on how to proceed in these cases, then, will not reflect their ignorance of the law; it concerns their doubts about how the law ought to be developed or how a court will eventually rule.

No doubt, those whose fortunes lie in the balance will find little comfort in this more accurate description of their predicament. It does not matter to them whether their anxieties are about the present state of the law or its looming future. For them, the issue is purely semantic.

As upsetting as uncertainty is for those vulnerable to the coercive power of the state, it is nevertheless clear that the world would be far worse if no such doubts ever arose. For suppose that, *per impossibile*, legislators could draft a rule whose text either was infinitely detailed or contained terms that were completely well defined. In order to produce such a comprehensive rule, these legislators would have had to settle how to act in a range of cases that they could not have anticipated. They would have had, in other words, to rule in a *blind and arbitrary* fashion and thus would have had no way of knowing whether the law will do more good than harm.[46]

Formalism, therefore, is not only impossible—it is undesirable. Complete determinacy can only be had through the reckless settling of doubts and disagreements. Planning agents, we have seen, ought to proceed in a more cautious and thoughtful manner. Since human beings are not omniscient and lack the ability to think through the consequences of every one of their options, it would be foolish to decide *up front* how to act under all circumstances. Rational planning typically proceeds in a more incremental fashion, by initially settling the ends and basic strategies to be pursued, and then filling in the details over time as the future becomes clearer and more concrete. If legislators know that they want to exclude passenger cars, motorcycles, mobile homes, tractor trailers, and taxis from the park, they might simply prohibit vehicles without worrying about borderline cases such as riding lawn mowers. Similarly, if they want to eliminate restraints of trade, but are not sure or cannot agree about which practices restrain trade, they might content themselves with an open-ended standard and leave the development and refinement to others.

It is no surprise, therefore, that U.S. constitutional law is highly (though obviously not completely) indeterminate. Because constitutional provisions can only be changed through an onerous and costly amendment process, it would make little sense for the text to be extremely specific and detailed. Were the Constitution (in the words of John Marshall in *McCulloch v. Maryland*) "to partake of the prolixity of a legal code," it would lock the nation into a rigid scheme of governance and deny future generations the ability to adapt to new and changed circumstances. Though constitutional law sometimes appears to be more holes than cheese, "we must never forget that it is a *Constitution* we are expounding."[47]

Legal indeterminacy, therefore, is a feature, not a bug. Perfectly precise rules, even if they could be constructed, would inevitably be arbitrary and likely create havoc. In many instances, it is better to let others fill in the details when they are in a superior position to judge which course of action is best. As Hart emphasized long ago, by repressing the existence of borderline cases, formalists deny judges the prospect of shaping the law in accordance with social aims and consequences. They squander the moral opportunities afforded by the penumbra.[48]

The same might be said of interpretive methodology and judicial reform. While strict forms of textualism and judicial restraint increase predictability, they also bring pathologies in their wake. For it is inevitable that rigidly following the plain meaning of statutes will lead to absurdities, and strictly applying the law come what may will generate morally monstrous results. Providing judges at least *some* discretion to adjust the law in light of its consequences is the only rational and decent thing to do.

I don't mean, of course, to trivialize the anxieties associated with legal uncertainty. To be at the mercy of someone else's discretion can be a terrifying place to be. As the old adage goes, it is often better for the law to be clear than to be right. But formalists forgot that the converse also holds: it is often better for the law to be right than to be clear. Striving for a fully planned life is not a rational pursuit—it is a sign, rather, of mental illness. A reasonable legal system is one that strikes a balance between clarity, predictability, and constraint on the one hand, and correctness, flexibility, and discretion on the other. The way in which these trade-offs are struck in large part defines the character of a legal system. Indeed, as we will see later on, it is also one of the most important social facts determining the content of the law.

9

HARD CASES

Rump Formalism

At the time Hart published his critique of legal formalism in the late fifties and early sixties, this school of thought was on its last legs in the United States. Formalism had been the target of a ferocious onslaught by American jurists, beginning with Holmes in the late nineteenth century and continuing with the legal realists such as Karl Llewellyn, Herman Oliphant, Underhill Moore, and Max Radin in the first half of the next century. On their view, formalism was a characterization of American law that could not survive serious scrutiny.[1]

These critics argued, for example, that the general principles cited by the formalists are so abstract as to be meaningless. Given their minimal content, these norms are incapable of resolving any concrete dispute, a point put best by Holmes when he declared: "General propositions do not decide concrete cases."[2] According to the realists, formalist principles are mere ciphers whose primary function is to permit courts to reach, under the guise of deductive logic, any outcome they think best.

The realists denied not only that legal principles could be used deductively to decide actual cases, but also that they could be derived inductively from past judicial decisions. Just as philosophers of science had noted that there are an infinite number of hypotheses compatible with a finite set of data, the realists argued that any principle could be made to fit any string of past cases. The evidence, in other words, radically underdetermines the choice of legal principle. Nor are the norms of common law reasoning capable of narrowing down the options. Competent lawyers understand that opinions can easily be read in multiple ways: troublesome opinions can be distinguished so as to diminish their legal significance, while favorable opinions can be construed broadly to justify the desired position. Indeed, these strategies are precisely what law students learn in their first year. They are taught to use common law reasoning in order to argue both sides of the case.

Similarly, the realists argued that statutes could be read strictly or loosely, depending on one's objective. Llewellyn, for example, pointed out that the accepted canons of statutory interpretation are contradictory. For any thrust in favor of one reading, there was a parry in favor of another.[3] Thus, one well-accepted canon dictates that "A statute cannot go beyond its text," while another equally well-accepted canon requires that "To effect its purpose a statute may be implemented beyond its text." On this view, textual *and* purposive interpretations are acceptable in American law, and opportunistic lawyers or judges may simply take their pick.

Clearly, the realist critique of formalism is a system-specific objection. According to the realists, American legal practice is incapable of securing the formalist dream of complete determinacy. General principles of the sort formalists tout have too little content and, given the standard norms of common law and statutory construction, more substantial ones cannot be derived in a consistent manner.

Hart's attack on formalism, by contrast, is a comprehensive critique. No legal system can be completely determinate, according to Hart, because complete guidance of conduct is impossible. Even when legal authorities frame their rules using general terms, the open texture of language and thought necessarily leaves certain contingencies unaddressed. This was the upshot of the Limits of the Social argument. Social facts cannot pick out norms that settle every possible question and, as a result, the law will necessarily be moderately indeterminate.

Because Hart's critique of formalism is conceptual, it extends beyond the mere confines of the United States to every possible legal system. There can be no legal system in which the formalist dream of complete determinacy is achievable. Hart's rebuttal of the more extreme versions of legal realism has the same universal scope. The partial determinacy of language and the concepts it expresses ensure that some form of communicated guidance will be effective and, thus, the law in every system will regulate some, although not all, cases.

To be sure, the "Limits of the Social" argument exposes legal positivism to a certain liability. For if it can be shown that the formalists were basically right all along, and that American law is a completely determinate system, then not all law can be determined by social facts alone. The legal theorist would have to appeal to morality in order to explain the comprehensive guidance that the law offers. A demonstration that formalism is true, in other words, would be tantamount to a proof that positivism is false.

In this chapter, we will examine just such an alleged proof. For as astonishing as it may seem, Hart and the legal realists did not actually manage to land the coup de grace against the formalists. While they did permanently discredit certain aspects of the classical program, such as conceptualism, formalism's claims about legal determinacy and the role of the judge nevertheless survived. We will see that shortly after *The Concept of Law* was published, Ronald Dworkin mounted a spirited and sustained campaign to salvage a rump version of formalism as a serious jurisprudential account. As Dworkin argued, judges do not seem to behave as the positivists and realists claimed they must. They never act, in other words, as though they exercise legislative power, but always assume that there is law that settles the case before them. Thus, in none of the cases we examined at the beginning of the last chapter did the judges say: "I am now in the penumbra of a rule and therefore free to legislate as I see fit." Quite the contrary, they acted as though one of the parties had the legal right to prevail, and it was their duty to discover whether the plaintiff or defendant was the bearer of this right. Indeed, hard cases are so terrifying for law students because they are not permitted to respond to their professors in the way the positivist suggests. They cannot say that the question is a trick, that there is no right answer.

According to this new objection, then, positivism is to be faulted not for its total embrace of formalism, but rather for its total *rejection* of it. For an examination of judicial practice indicates, according to Dworkin, that there is a right answer to every legal question and that judges are legally required to apply that answer to cases that come before them. Legal positivism, in other words, is refuted by the reality of judicial decision making. Whether there is indeed a mismatch between the theoretical commitments of legal positivism and empirical observations of legal practice is a question we will take up in the second half of the chapter.

Right Answers in Hard Cases

Rules vs. Principles

In his effort to resuscitate the formalist position on legal determinacy, Dworkin began by introducing a distinction between two different kinds of legal norms: rules and principles.[4] Rules, according to Dworkin, are "all or nothing" standards. When they apply, they are dispositive of the case at hand. The norm requiring three witnesses for a will, therefore, is a rule: if a will is attested by only two witnesses, it is legally invalid. End of story.

By contrast, principles do not dispose of the cases to which they apply. They lend support to certain outcomes—they have what Dworkin called "weight"—but they are not necessarily conclusive. Valid principles, therefore, may and typically do conflict. When they clash, the proper method for resolving the conflict is to select the position that is supported by the principles that have the greatest aggregate weight.

According to Dworkin, legal principles are most conspicuously at play in hard cases. In the notorious case of *Riggs v. Palmer*,[5] for example, Elmer Palmer was worried that his grandfather would change his will and remove him as a beneficiary. In order to preempt this possibility, Palmer poisoned his grandfather. Though Palmer was sent to jail for murder, he nevertheless petitioned the probate court for his share of the estate. Palmer had the plain language of the New York statute of wills on his side: the rules, after all, did not make explicit exceptions for murderous beneficiaries. On the other hand, it seemed highly unlikely that the legislature intended this result. In order to resolve this interpretive difficulty, the majority of the court of appeals did not appeal to another rule, but to a principle instead. They took the principle that no person should profit from his own wrong to provide a strong reason to read into the statute an exception for murderous beneficiaries. Because executing the will as written would enable Palmer to profit from his own wrong, and since the contrary principles that privilege the plain reading of the text were not as compelling, the majority concluded that Palmer was not legally entitled to his share of the estate.

In *Riggs*, the court applied legal principles in order to interpret an unclear rule; in other hard cases, judges use principles to help establish the existence of rules that had not been previously acknowledged. As an example of the latter, Dworkin cited *Henningsen v. Bloomfield Motors*. In this case, Mr. Henningsen bought his wife a car for Mother's Day. Ten days after the purchase, Mrs. Henningsen was driving the car when the steering wheel suddenly spun in her hands, causing the car to collide with a wall and totaling it. When Mr. Henningsen demanded that Bloomfield Motors replace the car, they refused, citing a provision in the sales contract that held the dealer liable only for defective parts, not for any damage caused by those defective parts.[6] During litigation, the lower courts accepted the dealer's argument that Mr. Henningsen had waived liability by signing the contract, and so denied Henningsen's claim. On appeal, the New Jersey Supreme Court could find no explicit rule that would authorize it to ignore such a waiver, but nevertheless held for Henningsen. In support of its decision it cited a number of legal principles, including "Freedom of contract is not such an immutable doctrine as to admit of no qualification in the area in which we are concerned"[7] and "In a society such as ours . . . the manufacturer is under a special obligation in connection with the construction, promotion and sale of his cars."[8] These principles, the court reasoned, were of such great importance that they outweighed contrary principles, such as those supporting the freedom to contract, which militated in favor of enforcing the waiver.

Against Strong Discretion

Having argued that courts rely on legal principles to decide disputes in which the clearly applicable rules have run out, Dworkin sought to use these hard cases as confirmation of the formalist thesis on legal determinacy. For as he pointed out, judges in these cases do not stop looking at the available legal materials when they fail to find a clearly applicable rule. They do not, in other words, act like legislators who must compensate for the inevitable imperfections of legal regulation by figuring out which course of conduct is morally best, all things considered. Rather, they continue to act as *judges:* officials who engage in legal reasoning so as to decide which party has the legal right to win. They assume that there are norms that resolve the dispute in question and they are under a legal obligation to find these norms and apply them to the case at hand. Thus, in *Henningsen,* even though the all-or-nothing rules had run out, the court looked to the various legal principles that were applicable in the case, balanced them against each other, and declared the principles that supported recognizing a duty of care for the automobile manufacturer outweighed those that supported recognizing the validity of the consumer waiver.

In contrast to Hart's contention, Dworkin argued that judges never enjoy legal discretion. Even in cases where the clearly applicable rules have run out, legal principles exist which determine the right answer to the legal question at issue. Positivists, on the other hand, ignore the existence of these norms. They consider cases that are ungoverned by rules, such as *Riggs* and *Henningsen,* to be ungoverned by law. Legal positivism,

, therefore, has an impoverished conception of legal reasoning: it is a model of rules only.[9]

Dworkin was careful to point out that there are several "weak" senses in which judges must exercise discretion even in hard cases.[10] Judges must exercise discretion in the sense that they are required to use their judgment in reasoning from legal principles to legal conclusions. They also sometimes have discretion in the sense that they have the final say in a particular case. Dworkin denied, however, that judges must exercise what he calls "strong" discretion, namely, the idea that they must look beyond the law and apply nonlegal standards to resolve the case at hand.[11] Contrary to Hart's claims, when judges resort to principles in hard cases, they are not extending the law; they are finding it. And if they are finding the law, then the principles that they are applying must be legal norms.

Dissenting from Classical Formalism

In claiming that judges never exercise strong discretion, Dworkin was clearly aligning himself with the formalists' position on the determinacy of the law. Judicial decision making, they both agreed, is completely dominated by legal reasoning. Moreover, both accepted a restrictive conception of the judicial role. From the legal perspective, judges may never change the law but are always obligated to apply it in cases that arise before them.

Yet Dworkin clearly did not accept every doctrine of classical formalism. For example, he rejected conceptualism. On his model, there are not a handful of general principles that can be used to resolve cases via conceptual analysis and deductive logic. Dworkinian legal principles are legion and they compete against each other in difficult cases. Nor do they obey a rulelike, top-down, all-or-nothing logic. Principles have a dimension of weight that must be compared with other principles to determine the correct legal decision. The model for Dworkinian legal reasoning, therefore, is not geometry but morality. Just as moral reasoning is often thought to involve the careful balancing of competing moral principles in order to determine the morally correct course of action, legal reasoning employs the same highly discretionary weighing procedure to resolve difficult cases.

Not only did Dworkin dissent from the classical formalists' logic of legal principles, he also rejected their canonical method for discovering the existence of these norms. Dworkin insisted that legal principles could not be found simply by consulting their social source or, as he called it, their "pedigree." Principles are binding not simply because they have been endorsed by past decisions of authoritative bodies, but because they are morally appropriate. These legal norms, in other words, can be discovered only through moral reasoning.

Dworkin's justification for this claim was empirical: he asserted that judges rely on certain principles to resolve hard cases because of their perceived moral legitimacy. "The origin of [the *Riggs* and *Henningsen* principles] as legal principles," he writes, "lies not in a particular decision of some legislature or court, but in a sense of appropriateness developed in the profession and the public over time. Their continued power depends upon this sense of appropriateness being sustained. If it no longer seemed unfair to allow people to profit by their wrongs, or fair to place special burdens upon oligopolies that manufacture potentially dangerous machines, these principles would no longer play much of a role in new cases, even if they had never been overruled or repealed."[12]

While Dworkin claimed that judges derive legal principles via moral reasoning, he noted that judges also care about pedigrees as well. In his early writings, Dworkin did not specify the relevance of past political decisions for the interpretation of the law, although, as we will see in the next chapter, he was soon to develop an extremely elaborate account of how social and moral facts interact to determine the existence and content of a legal norm.

The New Trouble for Positivism

Having established the formalist thesis on legal determinacy, Dworkin concluded that Hart's theory must be rejected. For as we saw in the last chapter, Hart's positivism is a moderately *anti*-formalist theory of law. On his view, the formalist ambition of complete determinacy is necessarily unachievable. In any legal system, many cases that courts face will not have correct answers, and judges will enjoy substantial discretion to make new law to resolve the dispute at hand. According to Dworkin, such a view simply cannot be squared with the way in which common law judges actually make decisions. Judges never act as though they enjoy strong discretion, but rather assume that the law furnishes norms to resolve the case at hand which they are required to find and apply.

Indeed, Dworkin's critique was directed not solely at Hart's theory, but at all versions of legal positivism. For on Dworkin's reckoning, all positivistic theories are committed to a moderate version of antiformalism.[13] All positivists are moderate antiformalists on his view because they subscribe to an austere metaphysics of law. On this construal, legal positivists believe that all law is necessarily determined by social facts alone. In order for a norm to be legally valid, it must have a social pedigree: it must have been enacted by a legislature, instituted by an administrative agency, issued by a minister, imposed by a court, and so forth. Moreover, its legal validity depends only on this social pedigree. Moral properties may never play a role in the validity of legal norms.

According to Dworkin, this austere metaphysics commits the legal positivist to a rudimentary, and ultimately impoverished, conception of legal reasoning. Most obviously, if the legality of a norm depends only on its social pedigree, never on its moral properties, legal reasoning will necessarily be an amoral activity. Determining the validity of a norm, interpreting its content, and applying it to the facts of the case could not involve any moral reasoning. Legal reasoning would be consumed with a sociological inquiry into the social source of a norm and a logical inquiry into how this norm can be applied to resolve the factual case at hand.

More to the point, the exclusive reliance on social facts precludes the legal positivist from embracing the Determinacy thesis, a core tenet of legal formalism. For according to Hart's Limits of the Social argument, it is impossible for social facts to pick out a complete set of rules for all conceivable cases. Pedigreed norms will frequently run out, leaving many gaps and unresolved inconsistencies. And because positivists deny that nonpedigreed moral norms are law, they cannot fill the legal void. Thus, courts will lack the legal resources to decide many hard cases. When the social facts run out, they will have no choice but to exercise their substantial discretion by looking beyond the law and plugging the gap through a fresh act of legislation.

On the other hand, a natural law metaphysics that allowed moral facts to determine legal content would have no such result. For even when the pedigreed rules run out, nonpedigreed norms would be available to resolve the disputes. A richer metaphysics of law, in other words, would lead to a more robust and denser legal terrain. For once legal reasoners are permitted to look to morality, gaps and inconsistencies can be resolved and the slide to antiformalism halted.

Dworkin's challenge to legal positivism, therefore, presents a clash between two very different conceptions of legal practice. On the positivist account, law is determined by social facts alone, legal reasoning is necessarily amoral, and legal systems are moderately antiformalist. In hard cases, the law will typically run out, there will be no right answer, and judges will enjoy substantial discretion to repair the breach by looking outside the law to morality. On Dworkin's account, by contrast, an examination of legal practice indicates that hard cases are completely regulated by law, there are always right answers, and judges lack strong discretion. As a result, law cannot be determined by social facts alone, and legal reasoning must involve moral reasoning, at least in hard cases.[14]

Inclusive and Exclusive Positivism

Let us recap our story up to this point. According to the objection we canvassed in the last chapter, legal positivism is committed to legal formalism. Legal positivists privilege social facts in the determination of the law and thus deny judges the opportunity to appeal to moral considerations to decide cases. However, judges routinely rely on moral considerations to decide hard cases. Since formalism is false, the objection concluded, legal positivism must be false as well.

First Objection
    (1) IF (Positivism) THEN (Formalism)
    (2) NOT (Formalism)

---

    (3) NOT (Positivism)

In response, Hart denies the first premise of the objection. He argues that legal positivism is not committed to legal formalism; in fact, it is committed to a moderate version of *anti*-formalism. Insofar as legal facts are determined by social facts alone, and social facts are incapable of settling every question about what is to be done, it follows that the law will be moderately indeterminate on positivistic accounts.

The objection we canvassed in this chapter aimed to capitalize on Hart's defense of legal positivism. Dworkin agreed that legal positivism entails a moderate form of antiformalism but claimed that an examination of American legal practice strongly suggests that the law is completely determinate. For judges always assume that the law settles every case and take themselves to be obligated to find and apply the law. Since legal positivism is committed to moderate antiformalism, and moderate antiformalism is false, Dworkin concluded, legal positivism must be false as well.

Second Objection
    (1) IF (Positivism) THEN (Moderate Antiformalism)
    (2) NOT (Moderate Antiformalism)
    _____
    (3) NOT (Positivism)

Given the logic of this second objection, it is easy to imagine two responses that legal positivists might offer. Positivists might either reject Dworkin's characterization of legal positivism as committed to moderate antiformalism (the first premise) or deny his characterization of American legal practice as committed to formalist determinacy (the second premise). Either way, Dworkin's objection would fail.

According to the first reply, positivists would reject the first premise. Positivism is not committed to moderate antiformalism because it is not committed to an austere metaphysics that reserves law determination to social facts alone. Moral norms that lack social pedigrees may still be legal norms, on this view, just so long as these moral norms are ultimately validated by a social rule of recognition. Thus in hard cases, when the pedigreed primary norms run out, the secondary rule of recognition could require judges to take nonpedigreed legal principles into account to resolve the dispute. In this way, positivists could grant to Dworkin his interpretation of American legal practice while retaining their jurisprudential commitment to the primacy of social facts: nonpedigreed principles would help determine the content of the law, and hence resolve hard cases, only because social facts required that they play such a role.

According to the second response, legal positivists would affirm the first premise of the objection. On this view, positivists are moderate antiformalists who deny that hard cases always have right legal answers—when the pedigreed primary norms run out, so does the law. Positivists, however, would reject the second premise and hence deny Dworkin's characterization of American legal practice as formalist in nature. The fact that American judges always assume that there are norms that settle disputes and that they are obligated to find and apply does not, on this reply, imply that these norms are *legal* norms. Rather, it merely indicates that American law requires judges to appeal to extralegal norms when the legal norms run out. At most, judicial behavior suggests that hard cases have morally correct answers, not legally correct ones.

In the remainder of this chapter, we will examine these two responses. As we will see, the proper response to the second challenge depends on the proper role that social facts play in positivistic theory. Those who believe that social facts play a minimal part in the determination of legal content favor the first response, in which positivism is compatible with a characterization of American legal practice as a virtually determinate legal order. Whereas others who regard social facts in a maximal fashion opt for the second response, which characterizes positivism as committed to a moderate version of antiformalism and denies that hard cases usually have right answers.

Inclusive Legal Positivism

Let us begin our discussion of the first response by distinguishing between two different claims a positivist might make about the relationship between social and legal facts. The first claim maintains that legal facts are *ultimately* determined by social facts alone. Call this the "Ultimacy" Thesis.

> *Ultimacy Thesis:* Legal facts are ultimately determined by social facts alone.

The second claim drops the "ultimately" qualifier and maintains that legal facts are determined by social facts alone. Not only do social facts determine the content of the law at the highest level, but they do so at every point in the chain of validity. Under no conditions may the truth of a legal proposition depend on the existence of a moral fact. Call this the "Exclusivity" Thesis.

> *Exclusivity Thesis:* Legal facts are determined by social facts alone.

The distinction between the Ultimacy and Exclusivity theses is often formulated in Hartian terms. According to this translation, the Ultimacy Thesis requires that the rule of recognition be a *social* rule. It does not, however, place any restrictions on the kind of criteria of legal validity that the rule sets out. As far as the Ultimacy Thesis is concerned, moral criteria of legal validity are possible, provided that they are accepted and practiced by officials from the internal point of view. The Exclusivity

Thesis, on the other hand, not only requires that the rule of recognition be a social rule but insists that it set out criteria of legal validity to test legal norms based solely on their social pedigree. In other words, the rule of recognition may never set out a test of legality that conditions a norm's validity on its moral properties. The criteria of legal validity may test a norm based only on whether it was enacted by the legislature via majority vote, was recognized by the actions of courts or administrative agencies, or had some other social source.

As portrayed throughout this book, legal positivism is necessarily committed to the Ultimacy Thesis. One who thinks that moral facts play some role in the ultimate determination of legal content is by definition a natural lawyer. It might be wondered, however, whether one who accepts the Ultimacy Thesis, but rejects the Exclusivity Thesis, can nevertheless be considered a legal positivist in good standing.

Many legal positivists, often called "soft" or "inclusive" positivists, have thought so.[15] Moral tests of legality are acceptable, on their view, just in case these tests themselves have social pedigrees. For as long as the criteria of legality are set out in a rule whose existence is underwritten by a social fact, the law will have an ultimate social foundation.

One attractive feature of inclusive legal positivism is that certain constitutional provisions may thus be taken at face value. For example, the Eighth Amendment to the United States Constitution prohibits "cruel and unusual punishment." Similarly, Article I of the German Constitution states that "human dignity shall be inviolable" and that it is the "duty of all state authority" to respect and protect it. These provisions seem to condition legal validity on moral considerations. Thus, according to this interpretation, provisions that violate human dignity are not legally valid in the German legal system. Inclusive legal positivists can explain how such phenomena are possible: because officials in these systems accept that cruelty and dignity are relevant to legal reasoning, these moral considerations are ultimately backed by social fact and hence can determine the content of the law.

Rejecting the Exclusivity Thesis also provides inclusive positivists with a way of rebutting Dworkin's objection. For once legal positivists allow rules of recognition to validate norms simply by virtue of their moral properties, they no longer need be staunch antiformalists. They may concede that hard cases have right answers even though the pedigreed primary rules have run out. According to the inclusive legal positivist, therefore, the explanation for why common law judges act as though there is always law to find is that they are following a rule of recognition that requires them to apply moral norms in hard cases. Judges would be obligated to apply nonpedigreed norms to interpret preexisting rules (as in *Riggs*) or to establish the existence of previously unacknowledged rules (as in *Henningsen*). Since the rule of recognition itself has the appropriate social pedigree—it is practiced by legal officials—it may validate primary norms that themselves do not have social pedigrees. Judges would be finding the law even as they engage in moral reasoning because they would be using norms that are picked out at the highest level by some social fact.

While inclusive legal positivists are able to reject moderate antiformalism, they cannot agree with Dworkin and the formalists that the law is, or can ever be, *completely* determinate. For according to the Limits of the Social argument, the fact that the rule of recognition is a social rule places constraints on how comprehensive its guidance can be. Thus, in the rule of recognition we have just considered, the concept HARD CASE has an area of open texture and will cause gaps in its guidance. Judges dealing with borderline hard cases will have no choice but to make law, instead of applying it. At best, legal positivism is compatible with virtually determinate legal orders, ones which almost always provide right answers to legal questions.

Exclusive Legal Positivism

Inclusive legal positivists accept the Ultimacy Thesis, but reject the Exclusivity Thesis. "Exclusive" (or "hard") legal positivists accept both theses. On this uncompromising view, a norm counts as law only when it has a social pedigree and is ascertainable without resort to moral reasoning.[16]

It is important to note that exclusive legal positivism does not preclude the existence of laws that contain moral concepts. For example, it is a rule of American contract law that unconscionable contracts are not enforceable. Likewise, it is a rule of American tort law that individuals owe a duty of reasonable care to others. Exclusive positivists do not deny that these laws exist, even though the concepts these norms employ—UNCONSCIONABLE and REASONABLE—are moral concepts. Rather, exclusive positivists claim that these rules are law because they have social pedigrees, for example, they have been passed by a legislature, decided by judicial precedent, or enacted by administrative rulings. They deny, in other words, that moral facts can be responsible for their existence or content.

Because exclusive legal positivists deny the title "law" to any norm lacking a social pedigree, they reject the formalist claim that there is a right answer to every legal question. Indeed, the Limits of the Social argument implies that the law contains many gaps and unresolved inconsistencies, and that judges have no choice but to act as legislators when encountering these legally unregulated cases. Thus, exclusive legal positivists accept Dworkin's claim that legal positivism implies a moderate form of antiformalism.

Moreover, exclusive legal positivists agree with Dworkin's observation that American judges generally assume that there are norms that resolve hard cases and that they are legally obligated to find and apply. But, they contend, Dworkin has misconstrued the evidence: judicial behavior in hard cases does not show that formalism is true and that judges lack strong discretion. For in hard cases, where the pedigreed primary norms run out, American judges are simply *under a legal obligation to apply extra-legal standards*. In other words, the fact that American judges are under an obligation to apply nonpedigreed norms does not imply that they are compelled to apply preexisting law; rather, they are merely under an obligation to reach outside the law and apply the norms of morality instead. Thus, when the court in *Henningsen* applied the principle that automobile manufacturers owe a duty of care with respect to the construction, promotion, and sale of their cars, it was satisfying its legal charge to look beyond the law to morality in order to decide the case.

It might be objected that if American judges are under a legal obligation to apply nonpedigreed norms, then by definition these norms are *legal norms*. What else is the law except those standards that judges are legally required to apply in cases that arise before them?[17] As Joseph Raz has pointed out, however, this assumption is false. The law of a particular legal system does not consist of all those rules that judges are under an obligation to apply. When interpreting a congressional statute, for example, judges are supposed to use the rules of English grammar. Yet the rules of English grammar are not part of U.S. law. Similarly, in cases involving parties from different jurisdictions, judges are often required to apply the law of a foreign jurisdiction. Yet the obligation to apply foreign rules does not transmute them into local rules. The distinction between normative systems is preserved even when one system borrows from another.

Analogously, the exclusive legal positivist claims, the fact that some legal systems impose an obligation on judges to look to morality in order to resolve hard cases does not ipso facto incorporate morality into the law of those systems.[18] Judicial practice in the American legal system, therefore, does not require the legal positivist to give up the idea that the law is ultimately *and* exclusively determined by social facts. For when pedigreed standards run out, American judges are simply under a legal obligation to exercise strong discretion, by looking outside the law to morality in order to resolve the case at hand.[19]

Inclusive vs. Exclusive Positivism

Just as positivists are able to fend off the first objection, it appears that they have excellent responses to the second one as well. To Dworkin's charge that positivism is inadequate because it is committed to a moderate form of antiformalism, the inclusive legal positivist responds by denying the underlying allegation. Hard cases might have right answers, on this view, provided that the secondary rule of recognition requires the application of moral norms when the pedigreed primary norms run out. In this way, the inclusive legal positivist accounts for judicial behavior in hard cases without giving up on the priority of social facts in the determination of law. Moral facts determine the law because social facts ultimately determine that they play such a role.

The exclusive legal positivist, on the other hand, accepts Dworkin's claim that legal positivism is committed to moderate antiformalism. The law is determined by social facts alone, and since social facts cannot settle all questions in advance, the law will contain many gaps and inconsistencies. Nevertheless, the exclusive legal positivist denies that Dworkin has given them any reason to accept formalism. For even when judges are required to look to morality to resolve hard cases, exclusive legal positivists simply say that judges are responding to their obligation to apply extralegal standards when the legal norms run out.

Both the inclusive and exclusive legal positivist, therefore, can respond to Dworkin's challenge. We might wonder, nevertheless, which positivistic response is the better one. Is the inclusive legal positivist right in allowing the law to depend on moral facts as long as it ultimately rests on social facts? Or is the exclusive positivist correct in denying that the law may be determined by moral facts under any circumstances?

Labeling Problems

Before I launch into a discussion of the comparative merits of inclusive vs. exclusive positivism, I should concede an important point about the nature of this debate. In Chapter 1 I said that many nonphilosophers believe legal philosophers to be solely concerned with a "labeling" problem. The labeling problem in jurisprudence involves determining whether to attach the label "law" to some object.

Although I argued that legal philosophers are not primarily interested in such problems, I must confess that the debate between exclusive and inclusive legal positivism is essentially such a dispute. The point of contention, after all, is whether it is proper to call a nonpedigreed norm that judges are legally bound to apply a *legal* norm. Both the exclusive and inclusive legal positivist, in other words, agree that judges are bound to apply moral norms when the pedigree standards have run out. They just disagree about how to describe what they are doing: for the inclusive legal positivist, judges are *applying* legal norms; for the exclusive legal positivist, they are *creating* legal norms.

In this regard, the immediate outcome of this debate does not affect what judges should do; it only concerns how to describe what they are doing. But before readers skip the rest of the chapter (if they have even gotten this far), I would urge them to be patient and soldier on. Not only is the debate between these two camps of legal positivism interesting, even fun, but its resolution will provide tools for solving other jurisprudential problems. In particular, we will see in the next few chapters that the reasons for preferring one set of labels over another are the same considerations that militate in favor of engaging in legal reasoning in one way rather than another. The debate between inclusive and exclusive positivism will ultimately turn out to have not only terminological but practical implications as well.

The Logic of Planning

Let us return to the Planning Theory. Recall that, according to the Planning Theory, laws are plans or planlike norms. Their function is to guide and organize the conduct of members of a community both over time and across persons. Laws guide conduct in the same way that plans do, namely, by cutting off deliberation and directing the subject to act in accordance with the plan. By settling matters in favor of the directed action, laws cut down on deliberation and bargaining costs and compensate for cognitive incapacities and informational asymmetries, thereby enabling community members to achieve goals and realize values that would otherwise be beyond their grasp.

If the law is to guide conduct in the manner of plans, then it follows that its existence and content cannot be determined by facts whose existence the law aims to settle. For if the existence or content of the law were determined in such a manner, then the proper way to ascertain its existence or content would be to deliberate about the merits of different courses of action. But the point of having plans is to obviate this very activity. It would be self-defeating, in other words, to have plans do the thinking for us if the right way to discover their existence or content required us to do the thinking ourselves! Call this the "Simple Logic of Planning" argument (a more general form of the argument will be presented later on).

> *SLOP:* The existence and content of a plan cannot be determined by facts
> whose existence the plan aims to settle.

For example, suppose I want to know whether I have a plan to go to Mexico for winter vacation. If I do have such a plan, then the right way to discover its existence cannot require me to first figure out whether I ought to go to Mexico this winter for vacation. After all, the whole point of having such a plan is to settle that very question. Deliberation on the merits would violate the logic of planning because I would be doing the activity that the plan is supposed to do for me. If I must deliberate in order to discover the plan, then I do not have the plan.

The problem with inclusive legal positivism is that it too violates SLOP. If the point of having law is to settle matters about what morality requires so that members of the community can realize certain goals and values, then legal norms would be useless if the way to discover their existence is to engage in moral reasoning. Legal norms that lack pedigrees are like can openers that work only when the cans are already opened.

Exclusive legal positivism, by contrast, is not "sloppy." Because the existence or content of the law can be determined only by social facts, there is no danger that the process of legal discovery will defeat the very purpose of having law. Social facts are determined through empirical observation, not moral deliberation. As such, they are fitting grounds for law. They enable the planlike nature of legal norms to accomplish their function, namely, to settle deliberation on the merits and thereby guide and organize members of the community so as to solve moral problems and seize moral opportunities.

Notice further that exclusive legal positivism does not violate the logic of planning by recognizing the existence of legal norms that contain moral concepts. Consider the rule that prohibits the enforcement of unconscionable contracts. Although this rule does not settle every moral question that arises with respect to contract enforcement—it does not, for example, tell us when a contract is unconscionable—it is not thereby useless. For the rule does settle a very important issue about contract enforcement, namely, whether unconscionable contracts ought to be enforced. Judges who follow such a rule, in other words, will not engage in unrestricted moral deliberation: they will focus on the issue of unconscionability, ask themselves whether the contract in their case is unconscionable, and refuse to enforce those contracts that they deem to be so. To serve as a plan, we might say, it is not necessary for a law to *eliminate* moral reasoning. Rather, it need only displace the need for some such deliberation. As long as it takes certain issues "off the table" and channels deliberation in a particular direction, the rule will fulfill its function as a plan.

The Planning Theory, therefore, would follow the exclusive legal positivist's lead in responding to the objections we have been discussing in the past two chapters. Thus, in reply to the first objection, which accuses legal positivism of being committed to a formalistic conception of judicial decision making, the Planning Theory would distinguish sharply between judicial decision making and legal reasoning. Whereas legal reasoning is necessarily amoral, judicial decision making need not be. Indeed, when the pedigreed norms run out (which they must, given the Limits of the Social argument), the social planning that the law provides runs out as well. The fact that judges routinely rely on moral considerations in such instances simply indicates that they are engaged in further social planning.

In reply to the second objection, which accuses legal positivism of being committed to moderate antiformalism and hence to an amoral conception of legal reasoning, the Planning Theory pleads guilty. But the Planning Theory is not concerned by Dworkin's observation that, at least in some systems, judges are under a legal obligation to apply norms that lack social pedigrees. Again, it interprets this requirement as a mandate to engage in further social planning. The pedigree-less norms that they eventually apply are then understood as generating new plans/laws, not finding old plans/laws. For if the old plans/laws could be found only through moral reasoning, there would be absolutely no point in having them in the first place.

Planning and Indeterminacy

The responses I have just endorsed may seem to raise the following serious problem. Suppose a judge must decide whether to enforce a contract and, as it happens, the pedigreed norms have run out. Assume that the proper way to resolve such cases in this system is to look to the principles of morality and that those principles require the judge to enforce the contract in question. It would seem to follow that the judge is legally obligated to enforce the contract. But, then, enforcing the contract is the law! Contrary to the Planning Theory, the law must have been determinate all along: the legal obligation to look to morality generates a legal obligation to enforce the contract even in the absence of pedigreed norms requiring such an action.

The Planning Theory, it would seem, cannot have it both ways. On the one hand, it claims that, in the absence of a pedigreed norm, the judge is not legally required to enforce the contract. Yet, it also admits that the law can obligate the judge to look to morality. Because morality recommends the enforcement of the contract, the judge can satisfy this legal obligation only by enforcing the contract. But, then, the judge is legally obligated to enforce the contract. The Planning Theory must be inconsistent: judges cannot be legally obligated to enforce the contract and not legally obligated to enforce the contract at the same time.

The contradiction, however, is merely apparent. The inconsistency is generated only because the objection uses an insufficiently fine-grained conception of legal obligation. According to the Planning Theory, one cannot simply assert or deny that a person is legally obligated to perform some action; strictly speaking, a person can be legally obligated to perform some action *only under some description of that action*. In the above case, a proper description would specify that the judge is legally obligated to enforce the contract under some descriptions, but not under others. Under the act-description "making the morally best decision," the judge is legally required to enforce the contract (and the promisee has a legal right to that decision). But under the act-description "enforcing the contract," the judge is not legally required to enforce the contract (and the promisee does not have a legal right to that decision).

An analogy might help here. Consider someone who flips a switch in order to turn on the light and unwittingly scares away a burglar. Did the person perform an intentional act? As Donald Davidson pointed out, this question is not well formed.[20] Under some descriptions, the act was intentional (namely, "turning on the light"); under other descriptions, it was unintentional (namely, "scaring away the burglar.") Strictly speaking, actions are neither intentional nor unintentional—only actions under descriptions are. The Planning Theory says the same thing about legal obligation. For any action, we cannot ask whether it is legally required or not. We must ask the question only relative to some description of the act. Under some descriptions, the act will be legally required; under others, not. Thus, when we describe the act of enforcing the contract in the above case as an "enforcing of the contract," the judge is not legally obligated to perform this action; but when we describe the very same event as "doing the morally required action," the judge is legally obligated to enforce the contract.

No doubt, some will see in this response a desperate desire to save the Planning Theory at all costs. In order to respond to the challenges we have discussed in the past two chapters, the Planning Theory has to argue that (1) judges can be legally obligated to apply nonlegal rules and (2) their legal obligations to apply these rules arise only under some descriptions, but not under others. Like Ptolemaic astronomy, the Planning Theory must add epicycle upon epicycle to save the doctrine from incoherence.

It is crucial to see, however, that these moves are not ad hoc responses to the objections we have considered, but natural consequences of thinking about the law in terms of social planning. As for the first assumption, we have already seen why the Planning Theory must deny that the legal obligation to apply a nonpedigreed norm converts that moral norm into a legal norm. For according to SLOP, the existence and content of a plan cannot be determined by facts whose existence the plan aims to settle. Since the aim of legal norms is to answer moral questions, moral facts that resolve these questions cannot determine the existence or content of the answers. Hence, the insistence that pedigree-less moral norms cannot count as law.

To see why legal obligations apply not to particular actions themselves, but only to actions under descriptions, we should begin by reminding ourselves that the point of planning is to guide and organize conduct by obviating deliberation on the merits. The more deliberation obviated, the more complete the guidance. For example, the law might forbid "unreasonable restraints of trade." Or it might declare that "pricefixing, bid rigging, and market allocation schemes" are prohibited. Both descriptions might apply to the same sets of acts, but they represent very different plans. The former plan is highly incomplete because it picks out the actions in question under a morally loaded description. The guidance it provides does not obviate the need for deliberation on the moral merits of various business practices. The latter provides more complete guidance, not because it picks out more actions than the former, but because it picks out those actions in a way that settles more issues than the former. It is possible to identify the prohibited acts without deliberating on whether price-fixing is an unreasonable restraint of trade.

To use an optical metaphor, we might say that two plans may be trained on the same actions but have different resolutions. A plan that settles more issues has greater resolving power than one that requires the subject to engage in extensive deliberation on the merits. The plan that prohibits price-fixing, for example, presents a much sharper image of the actions it proscribes than the one that prohibits unreasonable restraints of trade, because the former settles more questions about which actions are impermissible.

Indeed, as we argued in the last several chapters, planning is normally a cumulative process whereby the resolving power of the law increases over time. Planning begins by settling some issues but may present only a blurry image of the actions regulated. New subplans home in on the actions using finer descriptions, thereby obviating further deliberations on the merits. As I argued in Chapter 7, legislation frequently proceeds in this incremental fashion, specifying very broad standards at the outset, and either delegating rule-making authority to agencies or courts to fill these plans out or engaging in further legislation to settle matters left open by the original legislation. The legal point of view becomes more focused over time, until the actions that fall within its purview are so finely described that they can be identified without any deliberation at all.

Legal Obligation Revisited

Let's return now to statements of legal obligation. According to the Planning Theory of law, to say that X is legally obligated to do A (where "legal" is used perspectivally) is to say that from the legal point of view, X is obligated to do A. The legal point of view purports to represent the moral point of view. It states that the norms of the legal system are morally legitimate and binding. Since norms of the legal system are plans, the legal point of view claims that the plans of the system are morally legitimate and binding.

Recall, however, that the legal point of view is not a complete normative theory. While it takes a stand on those issues resolved by the norms of the system, it is silent on those questions left open by the law. Or put in terms of planning, the legal point of view resolves only those questions settled by the plans. Thus, if the plans demand that A be done, but not whether B is an alternative description of A, then from the legal point of view, A is obligatory under the description A, but not under the description B.

Legal obligations apply to actions under certain descriptions, not actions themselves, because perspectival statements of legal obligation are supposed to report the legal point of view. Because plans always guide actions *under certain descriptions,* perspectival statements of legal obligations must be sensitive to the descriptions under which they are identified. If some action, like price-fixing, is prohibited by a plan that sets out a morally loaded description, like "unreasonable restraints of trade," then the law has only settled that the action not be taken under the morally loaded description, not a morally neutral one. To characterize an action as legally obligatory just because it falls under some description set out in some preexisting rule runs the risk of misrepresenting the resolving power of the law. It may end up describing the law as providing far sharper guidance than it has in fact provided.

Once we bear in mind the relativity of legality to act-descriptions, we can also see that inclusive legal positivists were misled by Dworkin's challenge. Dworkin correctly pointed out that judges in hard cases are bound by law. They are not legally free to decide in any way that they wish, but are rather directed to find and apply the legally correct answer. Inclusive legal positivists thought that the only way to respond adequately to this challenge is to show that *the decision itself* is grounded in some social fact. Legal positivism can be saved only if the particular action the judge is bound to perform is given a social foundation. Hence, they postulated that in hard cases the rule of recognition sets out moral criteria of legality, thereby tying the judicial decision to some social fact.

The better response, however, is to point out that judicial decisions can be legally regulated under one description but legally unregulated under another. Dworkin has presented a false choice: in hard cases, judges can be either applying law and enforcing preexisting rights or making law and creating new rights. Since the former is true, Dworkin concludes, the latter cannot be. In this regard, the inclusive legal positivists bought into this false choice. They imagined that if judges are finding the law in hard cases, then they cannot be making it. In truth, however, judges can do both. They can apply the law by acting as morality requires them to do and enforce preexisting rights by deciding for the morally entitled party. Yet they can also make new law and create new rights by recognizing that one of the two parties to the suit should win. Under one description, "deciding for the morally entitled party," the decision is legally mandated; under another, "deciding for the promisee," it is legally unregulated.

The moral of the story is that it is a mistake to think that the realm of actions can be divided into those that are legally obligatory, those that are legally permissible, and those that are neither. Legality does not track actions themselves—it tracks actions under certain descriptions. With respect to one particular action, the law may regulate according to one description of the action but be silent according to another. The law is completely determinate, then, when it regulates every action under every possible description.[21] The law will be indeterminate, in turn, whenever the law does not regulate some action under some possible description. This will occur in a number of situations, including when the action falls within the penumbra of some rule but not the core of a more specific rule, the core of a morally loaded rule but not the core of a more specific morally neutral rule, or the core of two inconsistent rules when there is no rule that resolves such conflicts. Since actions inevitably fall within one of these categories, it follows that the law will never be completely determinate.

10

THEORETICAL DISAGREEMENTS

The Other Bush v. Gore

During the first debate of the 2000 U.S. presidential election between George W. Bush and Al Gore, the moderator asked both candidates about the kind of judges they would nominate if elected. Bush answered that he favored "[p]eople who will strictly interpret the Constitution and not use the bench for writing social policy." Gore, on the other hand, rejected strict interpretation (or, as it is more usually called, strict constructionism), which is the method of interpreting a legal text strictly according to its so-called plain meaning. Instead, he accepted living constitutionalism. "The Constitution," Gore said, "ought to be interpreted as a document that grows with our country and our history."[1]

We now know that, strictly construed, Bush's response is incoherent. For as Hart demonstrated in his critique of formalism, it is impossible for a judge both to strictly construe a legal text and to never make social policy when deciding cases. Because natural language is irreducibly open textured, some cases will inevitably fall within the penumbra of general terms. A strict constructionist judge will have no choice in these situations but to look beyond the text and create new law.

My aim, however, is not to score this particular debate. Rather, I am concerned with whether such debates pose a serious challenge to legal positivism. As we discussed in the last chapter, all legal positivists believe that the law ultimately depends on social facts. Thus, whether the constitution of a legal system ought to be read strictly or as a living document is an issue that is resolvable only by reference to facts about the group in question. However, the debate between Bush and Gore did not seem like a sociological one. Bush, for example, did not argue for strict constructionism by pointing to a convention among officials to read the

Constitution strictly according to its plain meaning. Indeed, it would have been foolish to do so: Bush was aware that strict constructionism is not the norm in federal courts and intended to use his power as president precisely to change judicial practice. Nor did Gore try to gain advantage by pointing out that strict constructionism is a highly controversial methodology. If legal positivism were the correct theory of law, such a retort would have been a slam dunk.

Rather than being a dispute over social facts, the debate between Bush and Gore focused on questions of democracy and trust. For Bush, strict constructionism protects the legislature against the courts. As he warned during his surrebuttal: "[Gore will] put liberal activist justices who will use their bench to subvert the legislature, that's what he'll do." Gore, on the other hand, seemed more concerned with updating the Constitution to keep current with progressive conceptions of morality. The Constitution, he said, must "grow with our country and our history." Insofar as the crux of this debate was ideological, not sociological, a natural law model that grounds the law in moral facts seems to characterize the nature of the dispute far better than a positivistic one.

Debates about proper interpretive method pose an even greater difficulty for legal positivism. As Ronald Dworkin has argued, the mere fact that such disputes take place indicates that law cannot rest on the kind of facts that positivists believe form the foundation of legal systems. For positivists have maintained that the criteria of legal validity are determined by convention and consensus. But debates over interpretive methodology demonstrate that no such convention or consensus exists. In other words, disagreements about interpretive method are impossible on the legal positivist position. Nevertheless, they seem not only possible, but pervasive.

These objections, we can see, are instances of yet another form of the challenge from legal reasoning. According to this version, legal positivists cannot account for a certain type of disagreement that legal reasoners frequently have, namely, disagreement concerning the proper method for interpreting the law. The only plausible explanation for how such disagreements are possible, this version of the objection continues, is that they are political disputes that are resolvable only through moral reasoning. Contrary to legal positivism, the law does not and cannot rest on social facts alone, but is ultimately grounded in considerations of political morality.

In the first half of this chapter, we will discuss Dworkin's presentation of this new objection. In contrast to the other two critiques discussed in the previous chapter, we will see that the third critique of Dworkin's is extremely powerful and not so easily dismissed. In fact, whether positivists have any defense against it is a matter that will occupy us for the rest of the book.

In the second half of the chapter, we will discuss Dworkin's natural law alternative to legal positivism. According to Dworkin, disagreements about interpretive methodology are possible because legal reasoning is a form of moral reasoning. Indeed, as we will see, Dworkinian legal interpretation is an intense exercise in moral and political philosophy. To determine proper interpretive methodology, as well as to apply it in any particular case, the legal reasoner must engage in extremely abstract philosophical reflection and confront questions that have baffled humanity for millennia.

Legal Disagreements

At the beginning of *Law's Empire,* Dworkin claims that the law is a social phenomenon with a special structure. Legal practice is "argumentative," by which he means that it largely consists of participants advancing various claims about what the law demands and defending such claims by offering reasons for them.[2]

Because of the centrality of argument to legal practice, philosophers must study the different modes of argumentation that participants actually use when engaging in legal reasoning. Dworkin maintains, however, that modern jurisprudence fails utterly in this regard. Following the dominant approaches in legal philosophy, he claims, many of the disagreements that legal participants engage in either do not exist or are complete nonsense.

The Grounds of Law

To formulate this charge, Dworkin begins by introducing two related sets of distinctions. He first distinguishes between "propositions of law" and "grounds of law."[3] A proposition of law is a statement about the content of the law in a particular legal system, such as "the law forbids states to deny anyone equal protection within the meaning of the Fourteenth Amendment" and "the law requires Acme Corporation to compensate John Smith for the injury he suffered in its employ last February." Propositions of law may be true or false. The proposition "motorists are not legally permitted to drive in California over 65 miles per hour" is true, whereas "motorists are not legally permitted to drive in California after sunset" is false.

Propositions of law are true by virtue of the "grounds of law." In California, for example, a proposition of law is true (roughly speaking) if a majority of state legislators vote for a bill that contains text to that effect and the governor then signs it. These acts of legislation make propositions of California law true and hence are grounds of law in the California legal system.

Given the distinction between propositions and grounds of law, Dworkin argues that two different types of legal disagreements are possible.[4] The first type involves disagreements about whether the grounds of law have obtained in a particular instance. Parties could clash, for example, over whether Congress passed a certain law by the requisite majorities or whether the president vetoed the bill. Dworkin calls these disputes "empirical disagreements."

The second type of disagreement does not relate to whether the grounds of law have obtained; rather, it involves conflicting claims about what the grounds of law *are*. For example, one party to a dispute might argue that a statute is valid because Congress has the authority to enact a certain kind of legislation and has so acted. The second party might concede that the procedural conditions for enactment have been met but nevertheless claim that Congress lacks the authority to so legislate. These parties are not embroiled in an empirical disagreement, inasmuch as they agree about the historical record. According to Dworkin, they are engaged in a "theoretical" disagreement about the law. They are disagreeing about the identity of the grounds of law, that is, about what must take place in their legal system before a proposition of law can be said to be true.

These Dworkinian distinctions, it should be noted, have analogues in Hart's theory of law. For example, the grounds of law are those facts set out in the rule of recognition. If the California rule of recognition states that all bills passed by a majority of both houses of the state legislature and signed by the governor are valid laws of California, then the facts of bicameral passage and executive signature are the grounds of law in the California legal system. Similarly, theoretical disagreements are simply disputes about the content of the rule of recognition, whereas empirical disagreements are disputes about whether the conditions set out in the rule of recognition have obtained in a particular case.

The Plain Fact View

Having introduced these distinctions, Dworkin sets out his characterization of legal positivism. Legal positivism, according to Dworkin, accepts the "plain fact" view of the law. The plain fact view is constituted by two main theses. First, it maintains that the grounds of law in any community are fixed by consensus among legal officials. If officials agree that facts of type f are grounds of law in their system, then facts of type f are grounds of law in their system. Second, the plain fact view holds that the only types of facts that may be grounds of law are those of plain historical fact. The plain fact view, in other words, does not allow moral facts to be grounds of law.[5]

It should be apparent that the "plain fact view" is just another label for exclusive legal positivism. Inclusive legal positivists, we have seen, do not accept the second tenet of the plain fact view because they believe that the law can be determined by moral facts (provided there is an official convention to apply moral norms in certain cases). Dworkin, therefore, is claiming that all positivists are exclusive legal positivists, which is clearly false. However, as we will see in the next section, this error is harmless and his critique is effective against inclusive legal positivists as well.

With the groundwork laid, Dworkin proceeds to argue that, on the plain fact view, theoretical disagreements are impossible. The reason is simple. According to its first tenet, a fact f is a ground of law only if there is agreement among legal officials that it is a ground of law. Disagreements among legal officials about whether f is a ground of law, therefore, are incoherent: without consensus on whether f is a ground of law, *f is not a ground of law.* On the plain fact view, we might say, theoretical disagreements are self-defeating. Once they occur in a legal community, the questions at issue immediately resolve themselves in favor of the naysayers. Coherent disagreements about the law can only involve conflicting claims about the existence or nonexistence of plain historical facts. They must, in other words, be empirical disagreements.

For example, suppose there is a widespread dispute about whether the speed limit in California is 55 mph. Using Dworkin's terminology, the dispute concerns the truth-value of the proposition of California law "The speed limit is 55 mph." There are two possible explanations for this dispute: (1) Theoretical: One side believes that some fact f makes this proposition of California law true whereas the other side believes that f, though obtaining in this case, is not a ground of California law and hence cannot make this proposition true; (2) Empirical: Both sides agree that f, if it obtained in this case, would make this proposition true, but disagree about whether f has obtained in this case.

On the plain fact view, this dispute cannot be interpreted in the first way, namely, as a dispute over the legal relevance of f. Since the grounds of California law are fixed by consensus on the plain fact view, any pervasive disagreement about whether f is a ground of California law would indicate the *absence* of consensus about f, and hence would eliminate the possibility that f is a ground of California law. This leaves the second explanation as the only sensible one. The disputants must be disagreeing over whether the agreed-upon ground of law has obtained in this particular case—they must be disagreeing about the obtaining of a plain historical fact.

TVA v. Hill

Having argued that theoretical disagreements are impossible on the plain fact view, Dworkin proceeds to argue that these disputes do in fact take place. He makes his case by presenting a number of examples where it is plausible to suppose that legal participants all agree about the historical record but dispute its legal significance. For example, in *Tennessee Valley Authority v. Hill*, several conservation groups sued the Tennessee Valley Authority (TVA) to prevent it from completing a $100 million dam project.[6] They claimed that the dam would threaten the existence of the snail darter—a three-inch fish of no particular scientific, aesthetic, or economic interest—and hence would violate the Endangered Species Act of 1973. The TVA, however, argued that the Endangered Species Act did not apply to a project authorized, funded, and substantially constructed before it was passed and, hence, should not be construed to prohibit the dam's completion.

The Supreme Court sided with the conservationists. Although Chief Justice Burger, writing for the majority, admitted that halting the project would involve an enormous waste of public funds and, from a policy perspective, could not be justified, he noted that the text clearly requires the government to terminate projects posing risks to species designated as "endangered." Furthermore, he could find no indication that Congress intended otherwise. Burger thus concluded that the Court had no choice but to issue the injunction, even at so late a date.

The dissent, led by Justice Powell, argued that courts should not construe texts to lead to absurd results, except where it can be demonstrated that such results were intended by the legislature. Because it would be ludicrous to shut down a nearly completed $100 million construction project simply to save an unimportant, albeit endangered, fish and because Congress did not clearly endorse this result, the Court is obligated to give an interpretation that "accords with some modicum of common sense and the public weal."[7]

Dworkin argues that the disagreement between Burger and Powell is ultimately theoretical in nature.[8] Both sides agreed that the Endangered Species Act of 1973 is valid law, that halting the construction of the dam is terribly wasteful even in the light of the benefits to the snail darter, and that Congress never considered this type of case when drafting or voting on the legislation. Their disagreement concerned the *legal relevance* of these facts. According to Burger, the plain meaning of the text determines the law even when absurdities follow, unless compelling evidence can be found to show that Congress did not intend the absurd result. Powell, on the other hand, argued that plain meaning does not determine the law when absurdities follow unless compelling evidence can be found that Congress did intend the absurd result. Burger and Powell disagreed, in other words, about when the plain meaning of a statute is a ground of law.

Dworkin infers from *TVA v. Hill,* and other cases like it, that theoretical disagreements not only take place but abound. Because the plain fact view cannot account for the possibility of these disputes, Dworkin concludes that it does not capture the argumentative structure of legal practice, and as a result must be rejected.

Comparing Critiques

Dworkin's critique of legal positivism in *Law's Empire* bears many similarities to his earlier one discussed in the last chapter. In both challenges, Dworkin characterizes legal positivism as committed to a form of exclusive legal positivism. Both also claim that positivism cannot explain judicial behavior in hard cases. And, as we will soon see, both maintain that the proper explanation for such behavior is that judges look to morality to resolve the legal matters at hand. Despite these commonalities, however, Dworkin's latter critique is a different and vastly more effective one.

Dworkin's first critique purports to show that in hard cases judges take morally relevant facts to be grounds of law. It does this by examining cases such as *Riggs* and *Henningsen* where judges regard themselves as bound by principles whose legal authority derives from their moral worth. But legal positivism is committed to the Exclusivity Thesis, which precludes moral grounds of law. Hence, the first critique concludes that legal positivism cannot explain judicial behavior in hard cases.

Whereas the first critique seeks to exploit the alleged fact that judges often take the grounds of law to be moral in nature, the second critique tries to capitalize on the alleged fact that judges often disagree with one another about what the grounds of law are. The dispute in *TVA*, for example, was grounded in a dispute about whether to privilege the statutory text even in the face of absurd results. Positivism cannot explain such disagreements, the second critique concludes, because it is committed to the plain fact view, according to which the grounds of law are fixed by agreement.

Thus, though *Riggs, Henningsen,* and *TVA* are hard cases, they are hard for different reasons. *Riggs* and *Henningsen* are hard because, although the courts agreed on the grounds of law, figuring out whether such grounds obtain in a particular case is a demanding question about which reasonable people may disagree. By contrast, *TVA* is hard because to determine the correct outcome of the case, the Court first had to resolve what the grounds of law were, and reasonable people can disagree about that question as well.

As we saw in the previous chapter, hard cases like *Riggs* and *Henningsen* are not hard for the positivist to accommodate. For example, the positivist may take the exclusivist route and claim that, in such cases, judges are legally obligated to apply extralegal norms. Or she can take the inclusive route and simply admit that the grounds of law can be moral in nature, provided that there is a convention among judges to regard those facts as grounds of law. But cases like *TVA* cannot be explained away in either manner. For exclusive and inclusive legal positivists both insist that the grounds of law are determined by convention. How can they account for disagreements about the legal relevance of certain facts whose legal relevance, by hypothesis, presupposes agreement on their legal relevance? How can positivists explain an aspect of legal practice that on their view is necessarily self-defeating?

Incoherence and Insincerity

At this point, legal positivists might consider several different responses to Dworkin's challenge. They might, for example, concede that theoretical disagreements are indeed incoherent and those who engage in them are deeply confused. But this implication, positivists will argue, does not undermine legal positivism. For they will point out that incoherent disagreements are not necessarily *impossible* ones. And while taken in isolation, the fact that positivism depicts legal participants as acting incoherently in some cases counts against this jurisprudential account, it must be remembered that the test of a theory is how well it fits the totality of the data. If Hart's account does a better job than Dworkin's in accounting for the range of legal phenomena *taken as a whole,* we might conclude that legal participants are in error and that theoretical disagreements are indeed impossible.[9]

The methodological point raised in this response is clearly correct: no jurisprudential theory can be expected to validate *every* intuition that lawyers have about the practice in which they engage. Mistakes are always possible. Still, I think that the response underestimates the theoretical importance of the point in question and for that reason fails. The idea that the criteria of legality are determined by consensus is not just one aspect of legal practice among many; on current accounts of legal positivism, it is *the fundamental ground rule of law.* What ultimately makes it the case that some rule is a binding legal rule is that it is validated by some standard accepted by officials of the group. And herein lies the problem for positivists: the prevalence of disagreements about the criteria of legality, and the complete absence of criticism for engaging in these disputes, strongly suggests that legal practitioners do not follow the ground rules that positivists claim they do. To be sure, this evidence is not dispositive. It is possible that lawyers are so confused about the practice in which they are engaged that they are simultaneously committed to mutually incompatible sets of fundamental ground rules; sometimes they act on ground rules that privilege official consensus, other times on ground rules that do not. Yet, such an explanation is uncharitable in the extreme. As a methodological matter, any theory that imputes that much irrationality and ignorance to experts should be severely penalized and deemed presumptively unfit.

Alternatively, the positivist might argue that legal participants who engage in theoretical disagreements are simply acting insincerely and opportunistically. They are aware, in other words, that such disputes are incoherent, but nevertheless engage in them in an effort to bamboozle others into accepting the methodologics that they favor from a political perspective.

It should be granted, of course, that lawyers and politicians are not always honest and often seek to advance their own self-interest or political ideology under the guise of legal reasoning. The debate between Bush and Gore, for example, was not a detached jurisprudential discussion. The political implications of the interpretive dispute were crystal clear: strict constructionists do not find a right to abortion in the Constitution and generally favor overturning *Roe v. Wade;* living constitutionalists, on the other hand, accept such a right and would not support the judicial retrenchment of abortion protections. As Gore bluntly put the point during the debate: "[A] lot of young women in this country take this right for granted and it could be lost. It is on the ballot in this election, make no mistake about it."[10]

The problem with the "bamboozlement" response, however, is that it is hard to understand why anyone would dare try such a strategy. If the fundamental ground rule of law precludes controversial interpretive methodologies, then the mere advancement of one would automatically result in a charge of duplicity. While the response is correct in claiming that many legal practitioners who engage in theoretical disagreements are acting in bad faith, no one, except for the legal positivist, thinks they are acting in bad faith *merely because* they are engaged in theoretical disagreements. Rather, their motivations are called into question because the methodologies they advocate suspiciously produce the political results they favor.

Putting Dworkin's challenge in the language of conceptual analysis we have been using throughout this book, we can say that Dworkin has shown it a truism about legal practice that, absent some authoritative settlement of the matter, theoretical disagreements are legitimate. Debates about whether legal texts ought to be read strictly or loosely; in accordance with original public meanings, evolving social mores, deeply rooted traditions, framer's intentions, expected applications, or moral principles; with deference to past judicial interpretation, administrative agencies, treatise writers, or laws of other nations; or in conjunction with legislative history or similar textual provisions, or in isolation, are absolutely commonplace occurrences in many modern legal systems. Dworkin has pointed out that legal positivism, at least as it is currently conceived, cannot make sense of this truism and hence is incapable of accounting for a central feature of legal practice.

Constructive Interpretation

Having argued that legal positivism cannot account for the coherence of theoretical disagreements, Dworkin proceeds to show how they are indeed possible. In order to provide for such an account, Dworkin looks to another realm where theoretical disagreements are pervasive: literary interpretation.

The Literary Analogy

As Dworkin points out, when critics differ over the interpretation of a literary text, they are not necessarily engaged in an empirical disagreement. Critics often agree about which text is the canonical version of the work, the ideas the author intended to convey, and the nature of the social environment within which the piece was created. Their arguments are often theoretical in nature, in that they are based on general disagreements about the correct way to interpret literature. For example, some believe that the critic's job is to uncover the intentions of authors. Others believe that the author's role in tradition ought to be considered, so that the interpretation of a text must await events that occur after the author is dead. Still other literary theorists emphasize formal considerations, such as literary structure, style, and technique, to the exclusion of social, political, and economic factors. These general disagreements about literary interpretation play prominent roles not only in literary theory, but also, explicitly or implicitly, in the various disputes critics have about particular literary texts.

How do we make sense of these sorts of disagreements? Dworkin surmises that they are ultimately based on disparate views about the aesthetic value of literature.[11] Different aesthetic theories generate different accounts of literary interpretation. For example, Dworkin cites with approval the view of Stanley Cavell, who claims that the prominent role many assign to artistic intention in interpretation is based on the modernist predilection to locate artistic value in creative genius. Likewise, intention will be less important in aesthetic theories that emphasize not creativity and originality, but rather, say, tradition or political emancipation.

Literary interpretation is a species of what Dworkin calls "constructive" interpretation. Constructive interpretation is the process of "imposing purpose on an object or practice in order to make of it the best possible example of the form or genre to which it is taken to belong."[12] When interpreting a novel, for example, the interpreter seeks to impose on the text an aesthetic purpose that will make it the best possible novel it can be. All else being equal, interpretations that engage richer themes, more interesting characters, or more gripping plots will be preferable.

The analysis of literary interpretation as constructive interpretation, therefore, provides the requisite logical room for theoretical literary disagreements. Because literary criticism is always directed toward making the text the best that it can be, people can disagree about the proper interpretation of a text because they disagree about the aesthetic merits of literature. In fact, the pervasiveness of theoretical literary disagreements can be neatly explained by the frequency of disputes about what makes literature valuable.

Dworkin argues that the process of legal interpretation should be viewed similarly, as a form of constructive interpretation. In order to determine what the grounds of law are, the legal interpreter imposes a purpose on legal practice in order to make it the morally best social practice it can be. The grounds of law are just those facts that best further this moral purpose.

Just as in the literary case, treating legal interpretation as constructive interpretation would account for the possibility of theoretical interpretations in law. Disagreements about the grounds of law would be predicated upon disagreements about the moral purpose of law and/or its relation to practice. Thus, unlike the positivist position, this account need not treat theoretical disagreements as incoherent or insincere: insofar as the content of the law is dependent on which principles portray legal practice in its morally best light, genuine *moral* disagreements will induce genuine *legal* disagreements.

The analogy between literary interpretation and interpretations of social practices such as the law is anchored by the fact that, according to Dworkin, "both aim to interpret something created by people as an entity distinct from them."[13] Works of art and social practices are distinct entities in that their creators produce them with the intention that their beliefs about the meaning of the work should depend on the meaning of the work, rather than the other way round. Authors do not, in other words, take themselves to have authority over the meaning of their creations. With respect to novels, for example, Dworkin claims: "An author is capable of detaching what he has written from his earlier intentions and beliefs, of treating it as an object in itself. He is capable of reaching fresh conclusions about his work grounded in aesthetic judgment: that his book is both more coherent and a better analysis of more important themes read in a somewhat different way from what he thought when he was writing it."[14]

Because novels are intended to be distinct creations that are detachable from the author's antecedent design, it is possible that an author will end up changing his mind about the proper interpretation of the work he created, as John Fowles reportedly did when he saw the movie adaptation of *The French Lieutenant's Woman*. Fowles formed a new belief about, not a new intention for, his book. "Any full description of what Fowles 'intended' when he set out to write *The French Lieutenant's Woman* must include the intention to produce something capable of being treated that way, by himself and therefore by others, and so must include the intention to create something independent of his intentions."[15]

Likewise, those who create a social practice aim to produce an entity whose content is determined by the point or purpose of the practice, as possibly distinct from the creators' antecedent design.[16] These intentions are revealed in the very structure of the practice created, specifically, in the distinction between what people think that the practice demands and what it in fact demands.[17] That everyone believes that a practice requires a certain form of behavior is not conclusive—it is always possible that they have misunderstood its justification and that a better interpretation would reveal their mistake.[18]

One clarification is in order before we proceed. When Dworkin claims that creators of texts or social practices aim to create an entity whose content is to be determined by its point, I don't think we should take him to mean that these individuals actually have this idea in mind during acts of creation. Dworkin, for example, explicitly rejects the idea that ascertaining an intention during literary interpretation involves recovering a conscious mental state.[19] The interpreter, rather, aims to capture a sense of what the creators attempted to achieve, even if they do not consciously recognize this themselves. Therefore, we should understand Dworkin's main contention as being a claim about what these creators would have accepted as a realization of their practical ambitions. Although these individuals might not have consciously imagined that they were creating a text or practice whose content should be determined by the purposes that portray it in its best light, they would nevertheless be committed to accepting that description as capturing, at least implicitly, what they were aiming at when they created what they did.

Fit and Justification

Now it is tempting to reject constructive interpretation out of hand, on the grounds that the role of the interpreter should not be to portray a text or a practice in its best light, but rather in its *true* light. After all, if the correct interpretation of *Murder on the Orient Express* is one that makes it the best novel that it can be, what prevents a critic from claiming that the book is really about Hamlet and his indecision over killing his uncle?

This objection, though, is based on a misconception of "best-lights" analysis. As Dworkin points out, to interpret *Murder on the Orient Express* as "Hamlet" would not present the book in its best light, given that there is nothing in the Christie novel to indicate that it is about an indecisive Dane. A novel that on its surface bears no relation to the story or set of themes that it is really about is, in fact, a bad novel.

Thus, an interpretation makes an object the best that it can be when it both "fits" and "justifies" the object better than any rival interpretation. An interpretation "fits" the object to the extent that it approves of the object's existence or its properties. In the case of a social practice, for example, one purpose fits better than another whenever the former recommends behavior that more closely matches observed conduct than the latter. A purpose is "justified" to the extent that it is a purpose worth pursuing.[20]

In her search for the optimal interpretation, the constructive interpreter must balance these twin desiderata. Some interpretations that present a practice in a more valuable light than others might fit it less well. They may present more rules as mistakes that must not be repeated. The interpreter must deal with these trade-offs by compensating for losses of fit with gains in value. Constructive interpretation ends in equilibrium, where increasing value no longer offsets decreasing fit. The resulting interpretation will present the object in its best light, which for Dworkin is its true light.

Interpreting Legal Practice: The First Phase

As we noted earlier, propositions of law are true in a particular legal system only when the grounds of law specific to that system are satisfied. Thus, the Dworkinian interpreter must begin the process of legal interpretation by identifying the grounds of law of the system using the method of constructive interpretation. Only after the grounds of law are determined can the interpreter ascertain which propositions are true.

In this section, we will discuss the first stage of Dworkinian interpretation, namely, the one in which the interpreter imputes a point to the practice that presents it in its best light and then uses this point to ascertain the grounds of law for the particular system. In the next section, we will see how the interpreter tests propositions of law by assessing whether the grounds of law culled from the first stage have obtained in the case at issue.

Conceptions of Law

During the initial stage of legal interpretation, the interpreter attempts to choose the "conception of law" that places legal practice in its best light. A conception of law, according to Dworkin, is an interpretation of a particular legal practice. It purports to identify (1) the purpose of this practice and (2) the set of facts such a purpose commends as the grounds of law. A conception of law presents legal practice in its best light when it best fits and justifies the practice. It fits the practice to the extent that the facts it specifies as the grounds of law are actually recognized by legal officials as the system's grounds of law. It justifies legal practice to the extent that the purpose it assigns to legal practice is morally justifiable.

In *Law's Empire,* Dworkin considers the appeal of three different conceptions of law: conventionalism, pragmatism, and law as integrity. Conventionalism and law as integrity are "nonskeptical" conceptions of law, in that they accept that individuals have legal rights, as opposed to pragmatism, which denies that they do. In what follows, I will briefly present Dworkin's sophisticated discussion of the two nonskeptical conceptions. My aim in doing so is to give the reader a flavor for the sort of arguments Dworkin believes an interpreter should employ when analyzing legal practice. As we will see, the method he uses—constructive interpretation—is intensively abstract and relentlessly philosophical.

Conventionalism

According to Dworkin, both conventionalism and law as integrity attribute the same general purpose to law: to guide and constrain officials by requiring them to exercise coercive force only when sanctioned by the rights and responsibilities that flow from past political decisions. These nonskeptical conceptions differ, however, based on the particular reasons they give as to why past decisions should be respected. On the conventionalist picture, the particular point of demanding deference to the past is to guarantee that the use of coercion will be predictable and hence will not unfairly upset expectations.

Because the specific aim of the law is to give individuals fair warning of coercion, the conventionalist holds that legal officials ought to respect those conventions that explicitly designate which institutions have power to make law and how their utterances are to be construed. Thus, on the conventionalist conception, the grounds of law in systems such as our own are determined by convention: a proposition of law is true just in case the grounds of law conventionally accepted by legal officials have obtained in the particular case.

Predictability, however, is not the only value recognized by the conventionalist. Conventionalists seek to reserve for officials a measure of flexibility so that they can continually develop the law. Accordingly, they believe that the scope of legal conventions should remain limited, so as to leave certain cases legally unregulated. When conventions run out, legal officials can then fine-tune the rules to particular cases. To be sure, the use of coercion in these cases will deprive some of fair warning. Yet the conventionalist believes that the loss of predictability will ultimately be offset by the gain in flexibility.

Before we proceed to set out Dworkin's evaluation of conventionalism, we should pause briefly to note the relationship between conventionalism and legal positivism. At first glance, conventionalism appears to be a positivistic conception of law, for both privilege social facts in the determination of legal content. (Indeed, conventionalism appears to be a form of *exclusive* legal positivism, for the conventions it recognizes pick out legal norms based on their institutional pedigrees.) It is crucial to see, however, that conventionalism is not a positivistic theory at all. For while both theories privilege social facts, only positivism does so at the ultimate level. According to the legal positivist, the grounds of law are *ultimately* determined by social facts. By contrast, conventionalism privileges conventions at the nonultimate level: conventions determine the content of the law only by virtue of the fact that morality requires that they do so. Conventionalists, in other words, are natural lawyers who believe that political morality requires them to act as though they were exclusive legal positivists.

Having presented conventionalism, Dworkin proceeds to argue that it neither fits nor justifies our legal practice. Conventionalism fails to fit legal practice for the now-familiar reason that judges do not give up looking for law when the conventional sources run out. Even when the legal community is divided on how to read a statute or past judicial decisions, judges nevertheless argue about, and seek to discover, the correct interpretation of these texts. Conventions, therefore, do not exhaust the range of facts that legal participants take as grounds of law.

Nor does conventionalism justify legal practice. As we saw, the conventionalist believes that the best way to render the law both predictable and flexible is to demand that officials exercise coercion either when authorized to do so by convention or, if no convention exists, when it is socially beneficial. However, Dworkin argues, it is not obvious that slavishly following conventions is the best way to achieve the optimal mix of predictability and flexibility. For surely there will be cases when conventions should be ignored and legal officials given flexibility to change the law in the manner they see fit. Although this will make the law less predictable, it is plausible to suppose that, at least on some occasions, the attendant flexibility of the law will more than compensate.

Law as Integrity

Having concluded that conventionalism neither fits nor justifies existing legal practice, Dworkin attempts to demonstrate that another conception, law as integrity, does succeed at its interpretive task. Law as integrity agrees with conventionalism that the general point of legal practice is to constrain official conduct through the requirement that coercive force be justified by past political decisions. But in contrast to conventionalism, law as integrity does not hold that fidelity to the past is sanctioned by the predictability gains that such actions would inevitably bring, or by any other instrumental benefit. Rather, the point of this constraint is to require officials to act with *integrity*: if the law has treated one member of the community in a certain way in the past, the law must similarly treat others similarly situated in the present.

Because the constraint of law is not, according to law as integrity, justified by its effect on predictability, the rights and responsibilities that "flow from" past political acts are not those singled out as authoritative by official convention. Rather, they are determined by the demands of integrity. Integrity requires the community to act according to the set of principles and policies that present past political acts in their best light. "[Integrity] requires government to speak with one voice, to act in a principled and coherent manner toward all of its citizens, to extend to everyone the substantive standards of justice or fairness it uses for some.

If government relies on principles of majoritarian democracy to justify its decisions about who may vote, it must respect the same principles in designing voting districts. If it appeals to the principle that people have a right to compensation from those who injure them carelessly as its reason why manufacturers are liable for defective automobiles, it must give full effect to that principle in deciding whether accountants are liable for their mistakes as well."[21] In other words, law as integrity requires communities to act in every area according to one coherent set of principles. Integrity is violated when the rules in one legal domain can be justified only by principles that would not justify, or would be inconsistent with, the rules in another domain. The grounds of law demanded by integrity, therefore, are the set of principles and policies that place all past political decisions in their best light.

According to Dworkin, law as integrity is a better fit than conventionalism for two main reasons. First, law as integrity is able to explain why judges persist in their efforts to construe legal texts even when they disagree about proper interpretive methodology. Since the grounds of law are not determined by convention, but rather by a constructive interpretation of past political decisions, judges are not absolved of their interpretive responsibilities simply because their colleagues are not on the same page. Rather, each is obligated to identify for himself or herself which principles and policies present the practice in its best light and to interpret the law accordingly.

Moreover, law as integrity fits another feature of our legal practice that is inexplicable by other conceptions of law. As Dworkin points out, the American legal system strongly disfavors "checkerboard" laws. It would violate the Equal Protection Clause of the Fourteenth Amendment, for example, if, pursuant to a political compromise, a state prohibited only women who were born on odd days from having an abortion, while permitting those born on even days. Law as integrity nicely explains why such political compromises are legally shunned: checkerboard statutes render the law incoherent in principle. And when the state fails to act on a coherent set of principles, it fails to act with integrity.

Finally, Dworkin argues that law as integrity presents legal practice in a morally justifiable light. When the law is seen as consisting of the rights and responsibilities that flow from the set of principles and policies that both fit and justify past political acts, the community speaks with one voice toward all of its members, and a true fraternal association is formed. Members of this fraternal association see themselves bound not so much by circumstance or the necessities of political compromise as by a common set of principles.[22]

The creation of fraternal association is significant, according to Dworkin, because the obligation to obey the law, and consequently the state's moral permission to use coercion, can only apply in such communities. Dworkin rejects the prevailing theories of political obligation, namely, consent, fair play, and natural duty theories, and claims that obligations arise by virtue of membership in fraternal associations. Because communities that respect the virtue of political integrity are fraternal associations, members are ipso facto under an obligation to respect the common scheme of principle that the group endorses through its political actions.

Interpreting Legal Practice: The Second Phase

Both conventionalism and law as integrity are constructive interpretations of legal practice. Each seeks to present legal practice in its best light, although they disagree about the proper way to do so. Conventionalism maintains that the law is seen in its best light when conventions determine the grounds of law. In order to interpret the law on the conventionalist model, a judge does not engage in further constructive interpretation. During the second phase of legal interpretation, where propositions of law are tested for truth, the judge simply inquires into what the applicable conventions require and acts in accordance with these requirements.

Unlike the conventionalist, a judge that follows law as integrity does not stop engaging in constructive interpretation at the first phase of legal interpretation. Law as integrity claims that the law is seen in its best light when the grounds of law are taken to be the set of principles and policies that both fit and justify the law. Law as integrity is, thus, *doubly* interpretive. To present legal practice in its best light at the first phase of legal interpretation requires the judge to present past legal decisions in their best light at the second phase as well. Hence, according to Dworkin, in order to ascertain the truth of any proposition of American law, the interpreter must engage in another round of constructive interpretation and seek to determine which moral principles fit and justify past political acts.

For example, suppose a judge wishes to resolve a particular legal issue about negligence law and, in the course of his research, comes across a judicial opinion that is apparently on point and binding. According to law as integrity, in order to determine the resolution of the issue compelled by the opinion, the judge must first determine which principles fit the outcome of the case in question. Once he has established a set of principles that fit the case tolerably well, the judge must go on to determine whether these principles are required by more abstract principles that apply to negligence law more generally. The judge will thus be required to review the most promising theories of negligence liability, such as corrective justice, economic efficiency, and civil recourse, and test their fit with the existing case law and statutory materials. It is possible that the principles that adequately fit negligence law more generally do not fit the original opinion, in which case the interpreter might conclude that the original opinion is mistaken and, as a result, should not be followed.

Law as integrity would counsel the judge not to stop at negligence law. For he must always be on guard for the possibility that some theories that are apt for negligence law might not fit as well when other tort cases are considered. Thus, he should expand his inquiry to include tort law more generally. Once this round has been completed, the judge must broaden his reach to other areas of private law, such as property and contract law, as well as to public law such as criminal, administrative, and constitutional law. Finally, the judge should expand the inquiry to encompass the entirety of the law to determine which sets of principles will fit and which will not. Along the way, he will have to confront a range of collateral issues, such as whether civil liability should ever be imposed for reasons of policy instead of principle, and whether fit in negligence law should be affected by lack of fit in other areas of the law.

Once fit has been ascertained, the interpreter must then form judgments about the moral justification of the various sets of principles he has assembled. He must confront questions such as whether a set of principles that ascribes value to wealth per se is better than one that does not, whether a theory of justice that requires injurers to bear the costs of accidents is morally superior to one that shifts costs to victims in a certain range of circumstances, and whether a conception of political morality that treats corrective justice as reducible to distributive justice is better justified than one where the two accounts are kept distinct. Determinations of fit and justification must then be combined to rank the various theories, and finally applied to the particular case.

Interpretation and Meta-Interpretation

In the first half of this chapter, we set out Dworkin's second critique of legal positivism. Rather than criticizing positivists for neglecting cases where judges look to moral facts as grounds of law, Dworkin points out that judges often disagree about what the grounds of law are. Positivists cannot account for these cases, according to Dworkin, because they hold that the grounds of law are determined by social convention. Since controversiality is inconsistent with conventionality, legal positivists must deem theoretical disagreements conceptually incoherent. Yet, Dworkin notes, theoretical disagreement is a pervasive feature of legal practice.

In the effort to explain how theoretical disagreements are possible, Dworkin argues that the grounds of law are determined not by social convention, but by constructive interpretation. In order to discover which facts determine the content of the law, legal interpreters must figure out which facts both fit and justify past political decisions. Constructive interpretation is bound to elicit a significant amount of disagreement, insofar as questions of political morality and social value are apt to be highly controversial, especially in pluralistic societies.

In the next several chapters we will explore Dworkin's challenge to positivism and his proposed alternative. But before we do so, we have a terminological problem that must be solved. Because Dworkin works with a very different conception of law than the Planning Theory, it is necessary to find a more general framework within which to discuss and compare these two jurisprudential accounts.

The terminological problem is this: Dworkin assumes that fundamental disagreements about legal interpretation are disagreements about the "grounds of law." If one party believes that judges ought to take into account some fact f when interpreting a legal text and another party disagrees, according to Dworkin, their dispute concerns whether f is a ground of law. Since Powell, for example, believed the statutory interpretation ought to be affected by considerations of "common sense and the public weal," he believed that moral facts help determine the content of the law.

According to the Planning Theory, however, moral facts *never* determine the content of the law. As we saw in connection with the Simple Logic of Planning argument of the last chapter, the content of plans cannot be determined by facts whose very existence the plans are supposed to settle. Since laws are plans that are supposed to settle moral questions, moral facts cannot be grounds of law. Thus, the moral fact that it would be absurd to halt the TVA dam cannot make the proposition "A federal court is legally required to issue an injunction to halt the TVA dam" true or false. Only social facts may do so.

It follows from the Planning Theory that when judges disagree with one another about the relevance of some moral fact to the interpretation of a legal text, they cannot be disagreeing about the grounds of law. To understand the nature of these disagreements on the Planning Theory, we must recall an important feature of plans discussed in Chapter 5, namely that they are typically defeasible. When I plan to go to the movies tonight, I am not planning to go *come what may*. I realize that there are compelling reasons that might arise that would force me to reconsider my decision, for example, I suddenly get sick, the movie theater increases the price of admission tenfold, my house catches fire, and so on. "Unless compelling reasons arise," therefore, is an implicit codicil that typically attaches to our plans and conditions their applicability.

In everyday life, these clauses are left extremely vague. Our plans do not specify the compelling reasons that would force reconsideration, but we know them when we see them. The law, however, regulates the manner of its own defeasibility: it identifies the kinds of reasons that suspend the law's injunctions. The necessity defense states that criminal prohibitions are suspended when obeying the injunction would do more harm than disobeying it. Doing more harm, therefore, is a compelling reason that defeats a criminal law in those systems that accept such a defense.

Properly understood, the debate between Burger and Powell in *TVA* concerned the suspension clauses that implicitly attach to congressional statutes. In particular, their disagreement was over whether absurd results defeat a congressional directive, permission, or authorization. According to Burger, absurd results never defeat unless Congress intended that they do so. According to Powell, absurd results always defeat unless Congress intended them not to do so. Thus, on Burger's view, the Endangered Species Act required courts to issue injunctions to halt federal projects harming a certified endangered species *unless doing so would be absurd and Congress intended that the injunction not be issued*. On Powell's characterization, the law required courts to issue injunctions *unless doing so would be absurd and Congress did not intend that the injunction be issued*.

On the Planning Theory, therefore, when Powell held that the Endangered Species Act did not bar the completion of the dam because halting its completion would have been morally absurd, he was not finding preexisting law. Rather, he was following (what he took to be) a suspension policy of not applying the Endangered Species Act when it gives absurd and unintended results. When Powell determined that the conditions set out in this implicit policy did obtain in *TVA*—that the morally neutral description "halting a $100 million nearly completed dam to save the snail darter" refers to an event also referred to by the morally loaded description "acting absurdly by issuing an injunction"—he was attempting to increase the guidance provided by the law and hence to create new law in the process.

Because Dworkin's account and the Planning Theory disagree about whether a fact ought to merit the label "ground of law," it is imperative that we switch to a more neutral vocabulary. In the remainder of the book, I will instead speak of "interpretive methodologies." An interpretive methodology is a method for reading legal texts. Textualism, for example, is an interpretive methodology. It claims that legal texts ought to be read in accordance with their plain meaning. Law as integrity is another interpretive methodology. It states that legal texts should be read in accordance with the principles that portray them in their best moral light. Burger's position in *TVA* is an interpretive methodology because it claims that all congressional statutes have implicit suspension clauses that require interpreters to ignore congressional commands, permissions, and authorizations when absurd results obtain and Congress intended that interpreters act this way.

The advantage of talking about "interpretive methodologies" is that it is neutral as to whether their outputs are preexisting law and hence whether the facts that they countenance are grounds of law. For example, suppose that Powell is right about the proper way to read congressional statutes. Dworkin would understand his interpretive methodology as one that outputs preexisting law and that treats moral considerations as grounds of law. The Planning Theory, by contrast, would view the interpretive methodology as one that always creates new law when applied by a court, insofar as it requires judges to determine whether absurdity follows the strict application of a congressional statute, an assessment that is moral in character.

Meta-Interpretation

In what follows, I will not be concerned with these labeling issues. Whether we should understand interpretive methodologies as always outputting preexisting law or, in certain circumstances, new law will be of no moment going forward. Rather, the main focus will be on the intensely practical issue of choosing interpretive methodologies. Suppose someone argues that authoritative texts of their legal system ought to be read according to their plain meaning. Another insists instead that these texts should be read according to the intentions of those who enacted them. How are disputes like this supposed to be resolved?

For our purposes, any theory that takes up this question will be known as a "meta-interpretive" theory. I call it a theory of *meta*-interpretation insofar as it does not set out a specific methodology for interpreting legal texts, but rather a methodology for determining which specific methodology is proper. It provides participants of particular systems, in other words, with the resources they need to figure out whether to endorse textualism, living constitutionalism, originalism, pragmatism, law as integrity, and so on.

The theory that Dworkin uses to derive the grounds of law in a particular legal system, therefore, sets out his theory of meta-interpretation. According to this meta-interpretive theory, an interpretive methodology is proper for a particular legal system just in case it is required by the principles that place that system in its best moral light. As we saw, Dworkin believes that this meta-interpretive procedure will yield "law as integrity" as applied to the American legal system. Hence I will say that, according to Dworkin, "law as integrity" is the proper interpretive methodology for the American legal system.

One final translation is required. Whereas Dworkin refers to any individual who engages in any stage of legal interpretation as an "interpreter," I will be careful to distinguish between "interpreters" and "meta-interpreters." In my sense, a meta-interpreter is someone who evaluates interpretive methodology in the first stage of legal interpretation. An interpreter, on the other hand, is someone who uses a particular interpretive methodology to interpret a legal text in the second stage of legal interpretation. Marking this distinction in roles is important, for as I will argue in the next chapter, Dworkin's meta-interpretive theory neglects considerations of trust, to the extent that it ignores the limitations of both interpreters and meta-interpreters.

With this new terminology in mind, we can redescribe the plain fact view and the argument from theoretical disagreements. The plain fact view, it turns out, is a meta-interpretive theory. It claims that interpretive methodology is determined by the methodology accepted by all legal officials in a particular system. The problem with the plain fact view, as Dworkin points out, is that it rules out the possibility of meta-interpretive disputes. If officials disagree about interpretive methodology, then according to the plain fact view, there exists no proper methodology. However, since meta-interpretive disagreements are not only possible but common, the plain fact view cannot be a correct meta-interpretive theory. This is the argument from theoretical disagreements.

Dworkin's ambition, therefore, was to develop a meta-interpretive theory that created logical room for meta-interpretive disagreements. Constructive interpretation, he believed, made this possible. If interpretive methodology is fixed by the principles that present legal practice in its best light, then disputes could center either on which principles place legal practice in its morally best light or which methodology is required by such principles. Disputes between conventionalists and proponents of law as integrity—both interpretive methodologies—could thus be made intelligible by imagining that meta-interpreters disagree about the proper constructive interpretation of particular legal systems.

11

DWORKIN AND DISTRUST

Philosopher Lawyers

Many pre-law advisors in American colleges tell their advisees to major in philosophy, believing that philosophy courses teach undergraduates the same analytical and argumentative skills that students learn in law school and that lawyers use in everyday legal practice. Whether or not this is actually so—I have my doubts—such counsel is certainly sound on Dworkin's model of law. As we have seen, Dworkinian legal reasoning is, from start to finish, thoroughly philosophical. One cannot hope to be a good Dworkinian lawyer unless one is also a good philosopher in general, and moral philosopher in particular. "Lawyers are always philosophers," Dworkin writes, "because jurisprudence is part of any lawyer's account of what the law is, even when the jurisprudence is undistinguished and mechanical."[1]

In this chapter, I would like to examine this relentlessly moral-philosophical approach to legal reasoning, beginning with its theory of meta-interpretation. Although I believe that Dworkin's account marks an important advance over those that have been offered by legal positivists, it is nevertheless fundamentally misguided. In particular, I will attempt to show that Dworkin's theory recommends a meta-interpretive practice that defeats the very purpose of law. Generalizing from the Simple Logic of Planning argument introduced in Chapter 9, I will argue that the content of laws, insofar as they are plans, must be discoverable in a way that does not require the resolution of questions that laws are meant to resolve. This argument undermines Dworkin's theory of meta-interpretation, for on his account the only way to discover the content of the law is to engage in moral and political philosophy, which is the very sort of inquiry that the law aims to obviate.

I realize, of course, that this argument will probably not impress a Dworkinian. The incompatibility of their account with mine, they would reply, merely indicates that my account is wrong. In order to defuse such a response, I will go on to test one of Dworkin's two main arguments in favor of his theory. Recall that Dworkin argues for the propriety of constructive interpretation by reference to the intentions of legal creators. He contends that those who create social practices, like those who create works of art, do so with the aim that the meaning of their creations should be determined in the light of the principles and purposes that will make their works the best that they can be. If those who create legal systems intend their content to be determined in a manner that can be discovered only using moral and political philosophy, Dworkin might argue, then so much the worse for the Planning Theory.

As I will attempt to show, however, Dworkin cannot justify his theory by reference to the intentions of legal creators, because it is implausible to suppose that these creators are necessarily committed to a "best-lights" analysis. Such a commitment would be present only when those who create legal practice place great trust in the philosophical ability and ethical character of their fellow citizens and impute to them roughly the same values, beliefs, and interests. But those who do not have faith that members of the group can sufficiently approximate and converge on the findings of ideal inquiry would, I will argue, dismiss Dworkinian meta-interpretation as unwise and inappropriate.

Not only is it possible to imagine a legal system based on such lack of trust and common ethical framework, but as I will go on to suggest, the American legal system is a notable case in point. The framers and ratifiers of the American constitutional order would not have had the intentions Dworkin generally ascribes to legal creators, for they did not regard the political community to be trustworthy and unified enough to rationalize such intentions. In other words, if we actually attend to the point of view of legal creators, we will find that accounts of meta-interpretation that urge legal actors to be moral philosophers are untenable.

I should note at this point that even if I succeed in showing Dworkin's account to be flawed, this would not imply that the Planning Theory is correct. Quite the contrary: as I argued in the last chapter, no positivist theory of which I am aware has yet shown that theoretical disagreements are possible. Whether the Planning Theory can account for this aspect of legal practice is a matter that we will take up in the following two chapters.

The General Logic of Planning Argument

The Planning Theory maintains that the fundamental aim of all legal systems is to rectify the moral deficiencies of the circumstances of legality. The complexity and contentiousness of communal life is apt to forestall the promotion of many moral objectives, such as the maintenance of order, prevention of undesirable and wrongful behavior, promotion of distributive justice, protection of rights, and the provision of facilities for private ordering and fair settling of disputes. What rights do individuals have, and which merit public protection? Which distribution of goods is the just distribution? Against which moral metric is behavior to be assessed? These questions are apt to provoke serious doubts and disagreements. Without some mechanism for determining which specific goals and values the legal system ought to pursue, there is a significant risk that the massive amount of coordinated behavior necessary for the law to achieve its moral mission will not take place.

According to the Planning Theory, the primary mission of the law is to resolve these very issues. Legal institutions aim to settle questions about specific political objectives through social planning: the plans created are supposed to distribute rights and responsibilities in such a way that the exercise of the allocated powers and observance of the assigned duties achieves the selected goals and realizes the designated values.

If we suppose that the law's aim is to resolve doubts and disagreements about moral matters, then its content cannot be discovered in the manner that Dworkin suggests. For if in order to determine proper interpretive methodology members of the group were required to engage in moral and political philosophy to discover the proper justification for legal practice, they would effectively unsettle the very matters that the law is meant to settle.

Consider, in this regard, the myriad of moral questions that a Dworkinian meta-interpreter must answer. At the outset of the process, the meta-interpreter must assemble a list of competing conceptions of law, each of which posits a unique moral justification for legal practice and a distinct set of grounds of law required by such a justification. Having conjured up the various possibilities, the meta-interpreter must then apply the criterion of "fit." This will require a survey of all relevant aspects of legal practice in order to determine whether participants in the legal system actually behave as the various principles require. The meta-interpreter, though, cannot simply measure a principle's fit. She must also assess whether, and to what extent, the principle is "justified" from a moral point of view. This will lead her to form judgments on most of the core questions in political philosophy, such as the relation of rights to utility, the priority of justice over other political goals, the value of protecting settled expectations, the requirement of consent, the moral status of group membership, the existence conditions for true community, and the demands of integrity, among others. Once the meta-interpreter has addressed the issues of fit and justification, she must then combine the two metrics into one overall ranking. This will, no doubt, require another foray into political theory, so that she can determine the morally proper weight to assign to each measure. The meta-interpreter must then rank the various principles and choose the option that ranks highest. The interpretive methodology appropriate for the legal system will be the one that is required by the principles that score highest on the combined measures of fit and justification.[2]

The moral philosophizing may not end here, however. If the actor in question happens to be interpreting texts of the American legal system, Dworkin will advise her to engage in another round of abstract moral and political theorizing. For according to law as integrity, the grounds of law are determined by the principles and policies that place all past decisions in their best moral light. Hence, in order to ascertain the truth of any proposition of American law, the interpreter must again (!) seek to determine which moral principles fit and justify past political acts, and then apply those principles to the question at hand.

Seen from the perspective of the Planning Theory, however, this methodology defeats the purpose of law. Having to answer a series of moral questions is precisely the *disease* that the law aims to cure. Dworkinian legal interpretation thus ends up reinfecting the patient after the contagion has been neutralized.

Notice that this objection is a generalization of the Simple Logic of Planning argument introduced at the end of Chapter 9. Recall that SLOP claimed that the existence and content of a plan cannot be determined by any fact whose very obtaining the plan aims to settle. The idea behind SLOP is that it would defeat the purpose of having plans if, in order to figure out whether a plan exists or what its content is, one had to resolve a question that the plan was designed to answer.

Extending this argument to legal interpretation yields the "General Logic of Planning argument."

GLOP: The interpretation of any member of a system of plans cannot be
determined by facts whose existence any member of that system aims to
settle.

The General Logic of Planning argument is more general than the simple version in two respects. First, SLOP concerns the existence and content of plans, whereas GLOP applies to their interpretation. As we saw
at the end of the last chapter, the Planning Theory allows for the possibility that the interpretation of a plan will result in the creation of a new
plan (such as when the proper interpretation is determined by moral
facts). Thus, GLOP precludes the possibility that *any* interpretation—
those that result in new plans as well as those that discover preexisting
plans—can be determined by facts whose existence any law of the system aims to settle. Second, SLOP concerns the existence and content of
a single plan, whereas GLOP applies to the interpretation of a plan that
is an element of some larger system. The idea is that interpreting a plan
should not require the interpreter to answer a question that another
plan is supposed to answer, lest the point of having a system of plans be
undermined.

Dworkin's theory of meta-interpretation, therefore, turns out to violate
GLOP. If laws are designed to settle moral questions, then the interpretation of a law cannot be determined by any moral fact whose existence it,
or any other law of the system, was designed to settle. But constructive
interpretation trains its sights on these very facts and hence undermines
the settlement function of the law.

It is important to see that this violation of the logic of planning is
different, and far more troubling, than the one committed by inclusive
legal positivism. In Chapter 9, we saw that by according nonpedigreed
moral norms the status of law, inclusive legal positivism violates SLOP:
it permits moral considerations to determine the existence and content
of legal norms, despite the fact that legal norms aim to settle the existence of these moral considerations. The problem, in other words, is that
inclusive legal positivism requires the legal interpreter to answer questions that have not yet been answered when the very purpose of legal
norms is to answer such questions in the first place.

The objection offered here against Dworkin's theory is not that it represents as settled moral questions that have not as yet been settled;[3]
rather, it actually *unsettles* those questions that have been *settled*. Insofar
as the Dworkinian meta-interpreter must delve into moral philosophy in

order to answer questions about the justification of state coercion, Dworkinian meta-interpretation renders the previous decisions by legal institutions on these moral questions moot. It puts issues back on the table that had previously been taken off and, in doing so, frustrates the ability of the law to guide, organize, and monitor conduct in complex, contentious, and arbitrary environments.

The Evolution of Distrust

As I mentioned earlier, I doubt that a Dworkinian would be fazed by this objection. GLOP would be perceived as a threat only if Dworkin's theory were already committed to seeing the law as a method of social planning whose aim is to solve the moral deficiencies of the circumstances of legality. That Dworkin does not subscribe to the Planning Theory of Law is apparent not only from the fact that he has proposed an account of interpretation so obviously at odds with it, but also from his description of the abstract aim of law. For example, he writes: "[T]he most abstract and fundamental point of legal practice is to guide and constrain the power of government in the following way. Law insists that force not be used or withheld, *no matter how useful that would be to ends in view, no matter how beneficial or noble these ends,* except as licensed or required by individual rights and responsibilities flowing from past political decisions about when collective force is justified."[4] As this passage indicates, Dworkin does not see the law as the means by which governments pursue their goals. To the contrary, the function of law is to restrain, rather than enable, the goal-seeking behavior of governments.

In order to adjudicate between Dworkin's theory and the Planning Theory, I would like to evaluate Dworkin's arguments in favor of the former. I will focus on Dworkin's claim that those who create legal systems necessarily intend for the content of the law to be determined by the principles and policies that portray the particular legal system in its best light. I argue that they do not so necessarily intend. The main problem is that Dworkin's meta-interpretive theory is overly demanding, by which I mean that it requires meta-interpreters to engage in highly abstract and intricate thought processes in order to determine the correct method for reading legal texts. "Best-lights" analysis is so philosophically demanding that it is appropriate only for legal systems inhabited by extremely trustworthy individuals. For all other regimes, including, as I show, our own, the requirement that participants attempt to work out the moral principles that best fit and justify their practice would likely lead to organizational disaster.

In this section, I will examine the ideology of trust that formed the basis of the American constitutional order. My aim here is twofold. First, I wish to challenge one of Dworkin's basic justifications for his meta-interpretive theory, by showing that the creators of some legal systems would not have the intentions that Dworkin ascribes to them. Second, I hope to develop further the idea introduced in previous chapters that plans are powerful tools for managing trust and distrust. Plans, we said, are able to overcome the complexity, contentiousness, and arbitrariness associated with massively shared activities and large-scale social interactions more generally, by enabling planners to compensate for the lack of trust and to capitalize on its presence. Thus, I will suggest that legal systems are not simply distributions of authority and responsibility, but of trust and distrust as well. The birth story of the American republic not only reveals the original distribution of faith and suspicion, but also exemplifies in a very dramatic fashion the ways in which attitudes of trust and distrust can and do affect the institutional design of legal systems. Although the basic plot may be familiar to many, this fascinating tale bears repeating in some detail, to shed light on the complex role that considerations of trust play in the life of legal systems and its implications for proper meta-interpretive practice.

Before I begin the historical discussion of the American constitutional founding, one important caveat is in order here. Obviously, I am not a professional historian, and the narrative I will present is not meant to be original, authoritative, or comprehensive. In the sections that follow, I rely almost entirely on the classic account of the American founding presented by historians such as Bernard Bailyn and Gordon Wood. No doubt, some will disagree with their interpretation of the facts, in which case they may not accept the conclusion I offer. But even if the story I tell is wrong in the broad strokes or fine details, I think the exercise is nonetheless important, in that it shows the relevance of constitutional history to assessing philosophical claims.[5]

Radical Whiggism

In order to appreciate the attitudes of trust and distrust held by the creators of the American constitutional system, it is important to begin with the intellectual history of the revolutionary period. As historians such as Bailyn, Wood, and J. A. Pocock have argued, the Whig tradition in England, and particularly its more radical strains, exercised a decisive influence on the American political thinkers of the revolutionary genera-tion.[6] The radical Whigs, such as James Harrington, Algernon Sidney, John Trenchard, Thomas Gordon, and Viscount Bolingbroke, empha-sized the tendency of political power to corrupt, and accordingly viewed politics as an eternal struggle between rulers and the ruled.[7] In the words of Trenchard and Gordon, authors of the highly influential *Cato's Letters:* "Whatever is good for the people, is bad for their Governors; and what is good for the Governors, is pernicious to the people."[8]

For the radical Whig, rulers cannot be trusted with power. Power is intoxicating and addictive; the more acquired, the greater the need. As Bailyn describes the Whiggish sentiment toward authority and its sometimes excitable forms of expression: "Most commonly the discus-sion of power centered on its essential characteristic of aggressiveness: its endlessly propulsive tendency to expand itself beyond legitimate boundaries. . . . All sorts of metaphors, similes and analogies were used to express this view of power. The image most commonly used was that of the act of trespassing. Power, it was said over and over again, has 'an encroaching nature'; '. . . if at first it meets with no control [it] creeps by degrees and quick subdues the whole.' Sometimes the image is of the hu-man hand, 'the hand of power,' reaching out to clutch and to seize: power is 'grasping' and 'tenacious' in its nature; 'what it seizes it will retain.' Sometimes power 'is like an ocean, not easily admitting limits to be fixed in it.' . . . Sometimes it is motion, desire and appetite all at once, being 'restless, aspiring and insatiable.' Sometimes it is like 'jaws . . . always opened to devour.' "[9]

Political power, by itself, is not evil; it can be used legitimately, in order to secure liberty and to promote the common good. For the Whig, what turns power into a malignant force is the corruptible nature of man, and his propensity for vanity and self-aggrandizement. For the radical Whig, the most effective check on the relentless ambition of rulers is the con-stant vigilance of the people acting through the political process.[10] And, in the event that such actions do not curb tyranny, the people reserve the right to rebel and overthrow the government.

While radical Whiggism was relegated to the fringes of oppositional politics in England, it achieved orthodox status in the colonies.[11] Ameri-cans had a better opportunity than the English to see the central premise of radical Whig thought play itself out: a government not accountable to its subjects will neglect their common interests. Americans were ruled by a distant power that resisted all efforts at political reform and constantly sought to increase its influence through patronage and bribery. The colonists' exclusion from the corridors of power was social and geographical, as well as political.[12] As in all colonial settings, social standing was determined largely by one's proximity to the imperial power, and London society was an ocean away.[13] Far removed from the centers of power, and excluded from the social circles of their rulers, the colonists were free to imagine the worst about every political move emanating from London, and paranoia, even full-fledged conspiracy theories, abounded.[14]

Radical Whiggism, with its jaundiced view of authority, resonated with the revolutionary generation and confirmed the sense of oppression and insult that Americans had personally felt toward the Crown and Parliament. Yet, for all their distrust of power, the colonists did not apply their suspicions to themselves as they prepared for Revolution. Like the radical Whigs before them, the Americans subscribed to the classical doctrine of republicanism, which maintained that people could be trusted to exercise power responsibly. They assumed that Americans were a homogeneous people who shared a community of interests, and believed "the People" could work together for the common good.[15] It was generally accepted, a New York pamphleteer wrote, "that the bulk of the people both mean, and think, right."[16] Even Tory writers admitted this much: "That the great body of the people can have any interest separate from their country, or (when fairly understood) pursue any other, is not to be imagined."[17]

These claims were premised on an "organic" conception of society, where the interests of all members were common, and the good of the whole inured to the good of its parts.[18] This corporate ideal was not unique to American thinkers, but was rather a staple of republican thought and a conception of the good society invoked since antiquity.[19] Subscribers to this organic conception took a dim view of division in the body politic, which they regarded as a sign of disease, fomented by selfish individuals who refused to subordinate their private ends to the public good. Once the conflict with their corrupt rulers was behind them, American thinkers of the revolutionary generation firmly believed that dissent and faction could be kept to a minimum, and that most citizens would discharge their civic responsibilities virtuously and in unison.[20]

So great was their faith in themselves during the heady days of Revolution that Americans stretched republicanism to utopian dimensions.

Americans knew that republics were especially fragile forms of government, that they demanded an extraordinary degree of public virtue from their citizens, and that few peoples had proven themselves worthy of a republic. Nonetheless, the Americans were convinced that they had the requisite character and skill. American society was young and innocent, and its people industrious, resourceful, and prudent. The colonies had yet to be tainted by the decadence of Europe. Nor did the colonies possess a monarchy or an aristocracy; hence, they were not required to share power with these corrupting influences.[21] The divisions that from time to time emerged in colonial politics, as well as the rising colonial displays of luxurious living and aristocratic pretense, were blamed on the machinations of the Crown. Indeed, such deviations from virtue were taken by many to be compelling reasons for revolution. It was necessary to break free from the Old World, patriots argued, before its vice permanently infected American life.[22] As Thomas Paine wrote in *Common Sense*, admonishing those "whose office it is to watch the morals of a nation," "If ye wish to preserve your native country uncontaminated by European corruption, ye must in secret wish a separation."[23]

The First Wave: Demoting the Executive

In the years following the Declaration of Independence, Americans got a chance to try out the theories of government they inherited from English oppositional thought. Their experiment in self-government catalyzed a rapid evolution of American political theory in the years between 1776 and the ratification of the Constitution in 1789. Traditional Whig theory, with its faith in the legislature as an antidote to executive overreaching, gave way to a radical Whig preference for direct popular involvement in government, which was in turn eclipsed by the federalist perspective, immortalized in the Constitution, with its emphasis on separation of powers.[24] This remarkable transformation can be tracked by reference to the state constitutions drafted between 1776 and 1789.[25]

It is unsurprising, given the Whiggish distrust of the Crown, that the early state constitutions radically restructured the office of the executive. In order to protect themselves from tyranny, Americans did not merely opt for the traditional British approach to political reform: they were not simply content to extend their charter of rights or to add further barriers to the encroachment by the executive. They sought, rather,

to divest the executive of most of his power to rule society—to eliminate, in the words of Thomas Jefferson, "the kingly office."[26]

Although in the new state constitutions the people's representatives
elected the executive, often by joint ballot in the two houses of the legislature, Americans nevertheless still regarded executive power as a danger
that needed to be contained.[27] Whiggism taught that power corrupts;
based on the English experience, this lesson was chiefly associated with
the executive rather than the legislative branch. To make matters worse,
the people could be too trusting and deferential to a powerful figure; it
was not uncommon for men to end up "worship[ping] a creature of
their own creation."[28] To the American reformers, elected magistrates
posed as much threat to liberty as hereditary ones.

In the new state governments, the executive was stripped of virtually
every power and prerogative traditionally enjoyed by the Crown.[29] The
executive no longer had the authority to assemble or dismiss the legislature, declare war, make peace, lay lengthy embargoes, erect courts, grant
charters to corporations, or coin money. The executive also lost the
power to appoint members of his own administration, to elevate judges
to the bench, or to dismiss judges, even for cause. In addition, the executive
was denied any say in legislation: his signature was no longer required
for a law to be valid, nor was he granted a qualified veto.[30] The intention was to relegate the governor to a mere "magistrate,"[31] as he was
called in the Virginia Constitution, whose sole function was simply to
execute the laws passed by the legislature.

Of the few powers retained, the executive generally was required to
share them with the councils of state. The council members were not advisors chosen by the chief executive, as were the members of the privy council of the Crown, but rather controllers and overseers of the governor
chosen by the legislature, or even made up of legislators.[32] In Pennsylvania, the executive was totally eliminated and replaced with an executive
committee of twelve, all elected by popular suffrage. For the Pennsylvania
Whigs, apparently, even an administrator seemed "too monarchical."[33]

The American reformers also believed that frequent rotation out of
office and prohibitions on reelections were necessary to curb the executive's tyrannical potential.[34] In 1776–1777, the executive's term was
fixed at a mere year in all but four states.[35] In seven of the new constitutions, the executive was subject to a term limit, ranging from one to three
one-year terms.[36] As if these controls were not enough, most state constitutions reserved to the legislature the right to impeach the executive.[37]

In the new revolutionary governments, the legislature was, by far, the dominant governmental actor, reflecting the traditional Whig disposition against a strong executive. The new state legislatures possessed many powers denied the House of Commons, as they assumed most of the (formerly royal) powers and prerogatives stripped from the executive. Legislatures also exercised many judicial functions, such as hearing private petitions, granting divorces, trying cases in equity, and extending equity jurisdiction to common law courts on an ad hoc basis.[38] They were also granted the right to appoint and dismiss members of the executive and judicial branches.

Although the American reformers took the separation of powers to be essential for the protection of liberty,[39] it is clear from the above description that their understanding of the principle differed significantly from our own, as well as from the one that they were to adopt only a short time later. As Gordon Wood has shown, the early understanding of separation of powers was radically asymmetric: the primary focus was to insulate the legislature and the judiciary from executive influence, but not vice versa.[40] Because Americans had experienced a long history of magisterial control of the legislative and judicial processes, they were determined not to permit this manipulation to continue. The executive had to be isolated from the other branches so that it could no longer use its power to corrupt. The legislature, on the other hand, was trusted to act in accordance with the common good.[41] By allowing it to dominate the other branches, they were ensuring that the people's interests would always remain paramount.[42]

The Second Wave: Reining in the Legislature

The revolutionary period began with an abundance of pride and trust in the new state legislatures, which seemed the antithesis of the English tyranny the Americans had rejected. From the outset, the state legislatures were structured to be responsive to the people in unprecedented ways. The states adopted short and regular terms for their assemblies, with the House of Representatives elected annually in every state except South Carolina.[43] States also expanded the suffrage to make the legislatures more representative of the people, and enlarged the legislatures, in some cases two- or threefold, to make them less susceptible to threats or blandishments from the executive.[44] Bribery and other forms of voter influence by candidates were prohibited; certain states, such as New York, experimented with secret ballots. In contrast to the gutting of the executive branch, though, these checks on legislative supremacy were minor. The enormous power given the legislatures, and the relatively few checks on their power, reflected the American confidence in the capacity of the electorate to select the best candidates for office and to monitor the legislators' activity through the electoral process.

It did not take long, however, for this trust to break down. Reports of legislative abuses started circulating almost immediately, proving that free and open elections had failed to select for the "natural aristocracy" of leadership, to the surprise and disappointment of the revolutionary generation.[45] Some abuses were imagined, but in other cases politicians pushed through legislation that benefited their constituencies at the expense of the general welfare. Such self-dealing was taken as evidence that state legislators could not be trusted to exercise power in the best interests of the people. With the growing distrust of the legislative branch, Americans developed new institutions, and new understandings of existing ones, in order to yoke legislatures to the wishes of the people.[46] Wood lists three devices that were increasingly being used to check the state legislatures: constitutions, conventions, and instructions.

Perhaps the most significant and enduring development was the emerging conception of the constitution as fundamental law, constraining the operations of government and unalterable by the usual legislative means.[47] While in the late 1770s and early 1780s many state legislatures routinely revised their constitutions, treating them as ordinary legislation, this practice became particularly disfavored as the 1780s wore on. If constitutions could be changed so easily, many began to reason, the safeguards adopted would be rendered useless. Only a constitutional convention, where the people were truly represented, could alter the framework that empowered the government to operate.

This reconceptualization of the constitution was intimately connected with a reinterpretation of the citizens' convention. Historically, conventions were considered inferior to duly constituted legislatures and thought to lack the authority to make law; American radicals reversed this hierarchy. Radicals argued that conventions had a mandate superior to that of legislatures, because they were the means by which the sovereign People acted directly.[48] By the late 1770s conventions and congresses were routinely called in order to create or revise legislation, and by the 1780s, they were considered indispensable to any constitutional change.[49] The people acted "out of doors" not only to regulate the economy by combating monopolization, profiteering, and monetary depreciation, but to realize any political goals about which they had complaints. The more radical committees encouraged widespread acts of disobedience to the legislature, which led to rioting in all major cities. As Wood describes the rise of conventions in postrevolutionary America, "No legislative assembly, however representative, seemed capable of satisfying the demands and grievances of large numbers of Americans."[50]

In addition to convening such extralegislative bodies to assert their will and check the power of legislatures, several states began asserting the people's right to instruct their representatives on how to vote on particular issues. The Massachusetts Constitution of 1780, for instance, proclaimed the people's right to "give instructions to their representatives."[51] The proliferation of instructions signaled both a breakdown of trust between the representatives and their constituents, as well as the erosion of the organic conception of society Americans originally assumed.[52] Politics was becoming increasingly, and intensely, parochial: each locality, and perhaps different segments within it, represented potentially competing sets of interests that acted to ensure that its interests were protected and advanced in government. Representatives were no longer entrusted to deliberate on the nature of the common good and the best means to pursue it, but rather to act purely as mouthpieces of the factions that had elected them.

The Third Wave: Losing Faith in the People

The radical Whigs believed giving the people a more direct role in government, through the use of instructions and conventions, frequent elections, and broad suffrage, would act as a corrective to the legislative abuses that surfaced soon after independence was declared. As Thomas Jefferson reflected late in life, "the sickly, weakly, timid man, fears the people, and is a Tory by nature. The healthy, strong and bold, cherishes them, is formed a Whig by nature."[53]

But by the latter half of the 1780s, it was clear to most leading lights of the Revolution that the American experiment in republican politics had gone awry. In part, they were alarmed by the proliferation of conventions and popular mobs that threatened to undermine the rule of law.[54] The people were perverting their liberty, much as the king had misused his power. But beyond the specter of anarchy and licentiousness, America's political thinkers feared that the people had become tyrants, using law as the instrument of their domination. James Madison famously cataloged the popular complaints about the republican crisis in his *Vices of the Political System of the United States,* a memorandum prepared for the Constitutional Convention in 1787. Among the many defects that characterized the laws created by the majoritarian state legislatures, their multiplicity, mutability, and injustice loomed large.

Madison bemoaned the state legislatures' prodigious output of new and intemperate laws. "The short period of independency has filled as many pages as the century which preceded it. Every year, almost every session, adds a new volume."[55] Not only did statutory volume grow at an alarming pace, but statutory volatility did as well. "We daily see laws repealed or superceded, before any trial can have been made of their merits: and even before a knowledge of them can have reached the remoter districts within which they were to operate."[56]

Most alarming, though, was the injustice of the statutes being passed. Madison was primarily referring to the stay laws that prevented the collection of valid debts, the tender laws that required creditors to accept depreciated paper money in satisfaction of their claims, and the confiscation of alien property that violated the Treaty of Paris and other international agreements. Such actions were so disturbing because they called into question the fundamental premises of republicanism.[57] As Madison noted: "If the multiplicity and mutability of laws prove a want of wisdom, their injustice betrays a defect still more alarming: more alarming not merely because it is a greater evil in itself, but because it brings more into question the fundamental principle of republican Government, that the majority who rule in such Governments, are the safest Guardians both of public Good and of private rights."[58]

Madison was expressing the deepest fears of the Americans Whigs that the tyranny of the state legislatures ultimately had to be laid at the door of the people. With annual elections, proportional representation, and constituency instructions, legislatures were as popularly representative as could be imagined; hence, the legislation being produced was a direct translation of the will of the people. It was precisely in response to the demands of the majority that legislatures enacted the stay and tender laws to protect debtors from creditors. The upper houses could not act to prevent such injustice because the senators were popularly elected and were either unwilling or unable to resist their constituents. Nor, given the executive's ineffectual role, could he provide a bulwark against the encroachment of the legislature.

The radical Whig experiment of involving the people directly in government had exposed the fallacy underlying all of Whig thought: the Americans were not a homogeneous people who privileged their common interests, but a diverse and diffuse bunch, riven by factions and motivated by private interests. The trust reposed in the people was now thought to have been misplaced. As Washington wrote to Jay, "We have, probably, had too good an opinion of human nature in forming our confederation."[59] What was needed was a reformation of republican government, one where the power was ultimately derived from the people, but without requiring that the people be virtuous.[60] Indeed, the structure of the federal government that the framers eventually created sought to harness the people's vice and turn it into a virtue.[61]

Economizing on Virtue

The delegates to the Constitutional Convention of 1787 were convinced that the domestic crisis could be averted only by the creation of a strong national government. It was imperative that this new federal government be granted the authority to collect tax revenues from the states, to raise an army, to prevent state violations of international treaties, to regulate interstate commerce, and to prohibit the abrogation of contractual obligations by state legislatures. The problem, of course, was to ensure that such a powerful entity, one that could enforce its will against the states, would remain in the ultimate control of the people and would not be used as an instrument of tyranny.[62]

According to the federalists' diagnosis, the root cause of the domestic crisis was the problem of faction.[63] The people were seemingly unable to resist temptation and submerge their selfish desires in favor of the common good, and were particularly vulnerable to demagogues, who were able to pander to the parochial interests of their constituents. "The people choose a man, because he will vote for a new town, or a new county, or in favour of a memorial; because he is noisy in blaming those who are in office, has confidence enough to suppose that he could do better, and impudence enough to tell the people so, or because he possesses in a supereminent degree, the all-prevailing popular talent of coaxing and flattering."[64] The federalists believed, however, that the inability of the people to choose responsible leaders would be less of a liability in a national setting.[65] Enlarging the electorate would not only expand the pool of talent, but also raise barriers for the less distinguished to achieve political visibility. Only those with national reputations for integrity and wisdom, and who did not make bald appeals to purely local interests, could hope to win a national election. As John Jay explained in Federalist No. 3, "[A]lthough town or country, or other contracted influence, may place men in State assemblies, or senates, or courts of justice, or executive departments, yet more general and extensive reputation for talents and other qualifications will be necessary to recommend men to offices under the national government."[66]

This "extended republic" argument stood the conventional reasoning about republics on its ear. It had been assumed, following Montesquieu, that republics were limited to small areas: only in small communities would individuals possess common interests and feel the appropriate fraternal sentiments that motivate virtuous behavior.[67] The American experience, though, taught that small communities were unsuitable homes for republican government. In small communities, the power of factions is too great and the pool of talented leaders too small. Only by enlarging the electorate can factions be neutralized and the risk of demagoguery decreased.

The federalists had not lost total faith in the people, though. They were confident that popular elections would produce the correct results—that the people would choose the best leaders—if temptation could be significantly diminished. The enlargement of the electorate would, paradoxically, present the people with a constrained set of choices, thereby reducing the risk that private advantage would trump public virtue.

In addition to the safeguards that extending the republic would provide, the federalists sought to minimize the tyrannical potential of the federal government by avoiding great concentrations of power and diffusing authority throughout various legal institutions. The most salient division of power was federalism itself. The federal government, although supreme, was not legally omnicompetent; it was granted only a limited set of powers, which were enumerated in a written document. The remainder was reserved exclusively to the states. Should the federal government seek to overstep its bounds, the federalists predicted, the states would rise up in protest and resist such encroachments. "But ambitious encroachments of the Federal Government, on the authority of the State governments, would not excite the opposition of a single State or of a few States only. They would be signals of general alarm. Every Government would espouse the common cause. A correspondence would be opened. Plans of resistance would be concerted. One spirit would animate and conduct the whole."[68]

The framers separated powers horizontally as well as vertically. Since the crisis of the postrevolutionary period resulted from the fact that the legislature was "drawing all power into its impetuous vortex,"[69] the Constitution walled off the branches of government and assigned distinct governmental functions to the Congress, the president, and the federal courts. The separation of powers, thus, finally achieved symmetry: not only was the executive forbidden from exercising legislative or judicial powers, but the legislature was similarly prohibited from exercising executive or judicial powers. Ironically, the framers sought to contain the ambition of their leaders precisely by harnessing it. It was precisely because men lust after power that the coordinative branches would resist encroachments by each other. The "parchment barriers" of the Constitution would be respected only because, in the famous words of Madison, "ambition must be made to counteract ambition."[70]

The framers divided power not only by allocating different powers to different institutions, but also by requiring various institutions to share the same basic powers. In doing so, the framers hoped to economize on the small degree of virtue present in the system.[71] Bicameralism, for example, was justified in part as a means of preventing legislative tyranny. "The danger will be evidently greater where the whole legislative trust is lodged in the hands of one body of men, than where the concurrence of separate and dissimilar bodies is required in every public act."[72] Likewise, for the executive veto: "[A] negative in the Ex: it is not only necessary for its own safety, but for the safety of the minority in Danger of oppression from an unjust and interested majority."[73]

Dworkin and the Whigs

The Early Republic

Let us now return to Dworkin's argument for his meta-interpretative theory. Is Dworkin correct in maintaining that legal creators are necessarily committed to creating a practice whose content must be understood in its morally best light? It was in order to test this claim that I detailed the American history of trust and distrust between the revolutionary period and the founding. As we saw, the revolutionary generation accepted a theory of government, radical Whiggism, that was profoundly wary of power. Although these Americans believed that authorities were capable of using the law for the common good, they were equally convinced that, without constraints, authorities would succumb to the siren song of power and abuse their positions. They would inevitably transmogrify into tyrants and deprive the people of their liberty in order to feed their insatiable appetite for domination.

The power eventually entrusted to the federal government under the Constitution did not evidence a renewed faith in mankind. Rather, the decision to create a system of dual sovereignty with federal supremacy resulted from an emerging sense of distrust in the people as the guardians of liberty. The framers' distrust of officials was met by their distrust of the electorate, necessitating the transfer of power from the states and their legislatures to the federal government. To the extent that those of the federalist persuasion had faith in the people to choose correctly, they had this confidence only in certain limited contexts, where temptation was significantly reduced and the set of options heavily constrained.

We also saw that the core principles of American constitutionalism— separation of powers and checks and balances—reflect this pervasive sense of mistrust. Authority is distributed across multiple institutions, ensuring that dangerous concentrations of power are kept to a minimum. Indeed, the institutional arrangements mandated by the Constitution, such as distinct branches of government, federalism, bicameralism, and the executive veto, actually seek to leverage this distrust in order to prevent power from growing beyond its proper sphere. The federalists counted on different institutions to be jealous of their prerogatives—for ambition to counteract ambition—and to be zealous in the enforcement of the boundary lines of power.

Clearly, this worldview is at odds with the assumptions that animate the "best-lights" theory. The degree of analysis and judgment that Dworkin's account demands would have undoubtedly struck these Whigs as unreasonable. Not only would they have thought the average person unlikely to possess the competence necessary to engage in a philosophical investigation into the moral vindication of the regime with its attendant judgments of fit and justification. They would also have been skeptical about whether such a discretionary procedure would be faithfully executed. If the electorate could not be trusted to resist the temptation to seek private advantage when selecting and monitoring leaders, it is hard to believe that the electorate would be resolute when determining its legal obligations.

When the American Whigs trusted individuals with power, they did so primarily in contexts where some institutional constraint or check was in place. But in nonjudicial settings, no such constraint exists for Dworkinian meta-interpretation. There are no filter mechanisms that limit options to those least likely to tempt. There is no requirement of deliberation with others; no one that holds a veto over one's interpretation requiring one to reconsider. The constitutional structures that seek to control the allure of private advantage are entirely absent from Dworkinian meta-interpretation.

Dworkin does, of course, mention one constraint on interpretation, which is that of fit. The principles that portray the practice in its morally best light must fit the existing practice sufficiently well. However, as we have seen, arriving at a judgment of fit is very challenging. It not only requires that meta-interpreters know how the entire system works, but also demands that they entertain various theories of politics in order to establish which ones give results that most closely match the practice. Furthermore, determining the relation of fit to justification is a philosophical assessment, which is difficult to make and even more difficult to police. In this context, the difference between an honest mistake and an abuse of discretion would be very hard to detect.

In judicial settings, of course, institutional checks are present. Judges must explain their rulings to the public and are usually subject to some review, whether by a higher court, legislature, or future constitutional convention. Courts are, therefore, constrained in their behavior: they cannot simply offer any interpretation they wish, but only those that will preserve their professional reputations and survive on appeal. However, because Dworkinian meta-interpretation is so abstract and uses techniques unfamiliar to most nonphilosophers, the normal institutional checks are bound to be ineffective. It is doubtful that many people are conversant enough in philosophical method to be able to distinguish between a good philosophical argument made sincerely and a bad philosophical argument offered strategically. Guards can protect borders only when they are clear about where those borders lie.

Nor does Dworkinian meta-interpretation fit comfortably with the framers' conception of the body politic. As we have seen, the framers rejected the organic conception of society inherited from early republican thought. Rather than seeing the people as a unified group sharing a sense of the common good, they understood the citizenry to be riven by factions and motivated by parochial interests. Dworkinian meta-interpretation, however, is a process that demands a shared background of values, beliefs, and interests. For only in a community unified in its conception of political morality will Dworkinian meta-interpreters converge on the same interpretive methodologies.

Dworkin's main argument for his meta-interpretive theory, thus, appears to rest on a false premise. For it is not true that those who create legal systems always intend to create a practice whose interpretive methodology should be determined by the set of moral principles that portray the law in its best light. In the case of our system, at least, it is unlikely that the framers and ratifiers of the American Constitution would have had such intentions, insofar as they did not regard the political community as trustworthy and unified enough to rationalize so difficult, creative, and value-laden a procedure.

Note that nothing I have said undermines Dworkin's claim that those who create legal practice necessarily intend "to create an entity distinct from themselves." Dworkin is right to point out that the intent to create something implies the intent to create an autonomous entity with a life of its own. Creators, therefore, necessarily delegate a certain degree of interpretive freedom to their audience. However, a grant of limited freedom does not imply the total privilege associated with constructive interpretation. Dworkin seems to have overlooked the enormous middle ground between taking the meaning of an object to be determined by its creator and allowing the audience to engage in "best-lights" analysis.

The Present System

It is, of course, possible that Dworkin would concede all of this. He might acknowledge that, given their radically Whiggish worldview, the founders of the American legal system would not have intended to create a practice whose content is to be determined by a "best-lights" analysis. Nevertheless, he might claim that the designers of the current system did have such intentions. Of course, this concession would undermine the generality of his meta-interpretive theory, because the theory would not be applicable to every legal system, or even to secular, industrialized, capitalist, pluralistic, constitutionally democratic ones. Still, he might be satisfied if "best-lights" analysis could be used to determine interpretive methodology for the present American system.

Nevertheless, I am not sure whether even this more limited claim is sustainable. Insofar as the American constitutional system remains committed to the principles of separation of powers and checks and balances, and continues to affirm the arrangements of federalism, bicameralism, and executive veto, Dworkinian interpretation seems to be at odds with the attitudes that underlie our current system. Our legal system, as well as the political culture in general, remains notably Whiggish in character: despite over 200 years of revision, its basic institutional arrangements reflect an abiding suspicion of power. Likewise, the current order continues to reject the organic conception of society. The American system is a liberal democracy predicated on the fact of pluralism. It assumes that moral principles are constantly and vigorously contested in the public sphere and thus protects the rights of individuals to speak their minds, organize with others who share their views, and participate in the political process so as to change the law.

To be sure, there have been many important changes to the American legal system since the founding. The extension of the franchise to racial minorities and women, the change from indirect to direct elections in senatorial elections, and the rise of statutory law over common law all signal a growing trust in the populace. Analogously, there has been increased trust in the federal government and its officials to wield power in a responsible manner, as evidenced by the additional grants of power to Congress in the Reconstruction amendments to protect individual rights, as well as the rise of the administrative state during the New Deal.

These changes, though important, should not be exaggerated. Like the transfer of power to the federal government at the founding, the additional authority granted to federal officials was motivated in large part by a sense of distrust of individuals and state governments. Congress was given the power to enforce individual rights because, as events such as the *Dred Scott* case, the Civil War, and the passage of the Black Codes demonstrated, state governments and the federal judiciary were no longer trusted to protect liberty. Likewise, the rise of the administrative state reflected a sense that nongovernmental entities could not be trusted to respect workers' rights, provide a social safety net for the down and out, or protect the environment. In other words, the fact that certain members of a group are given additional rights and responsibilities does not necessarily show that there has been an overall increase in the amount of trust accorded to all members. As is often the case, some actors are entrusted with greater powers because the designers of the system have lost faith in others and have transferred authority from one subgroup to another.

As I have argued, the distrust pervading the American legal system, past and present, gives the lie to Dworkin's claim that creators of legal systems necessarily intend that interpretive methodology be determined by a "best-lights" analysis. The same basic point, I believe, suffices to impugn the interpretive methodology that Dworkin argues best fits and justifies current American practice, namely, law as integrity. Even assuming for the sake of argument that Dworkin's meta-interpretive theory is correct, law as integrity would not be the best methodology for the legal system currently in force in the United States, for it fails decisively at the level of "fit." Because so many of the core rules of American constitutional law rest on principles of abiding distrust toward individuals with power, the importance of checking discretion, and the fact of pluralism, any conception of law that requires for its implementation a great deal of philosophical competence, moral rectitude, and political homogeneity will clash irredeemably with such a legal structure. It is noteworthy in this respect that the only provision of American constitutional law that Dworkin mentions to bolster his claim that law as integrity fits the American system is the Equal Protection Clause of the Fourteenth Amendment.[74] Had he taken into account other constitutional principles, such as separation of powers and checks and balances, and the institutions of federalism, bicameralism, executive veto, written constitutionalism, bill of rights, judicial review, Electoral College, fixed periodic elections, jury system, civilian control of the military, and so on, he might have endorsed a different interpretive methodology.

Taking Trust and Diversity Seriously

We might say that Dworkin's argument in favor of his theory of legal interpretation founders because it does not take trust seriously. As we have seen, his theory of meta-interpretation is enormously demanding, requiring great intellectual ability and ethical character to apply successfully. Unless the designers of a legal system manifest extreme trust in the competence and character of members of their community, mandating philosophical analysis for meta-interpretive reasoning is bound to be regarded as a dangerous feature of legal practice.

Nor does Dworkin's theory of meta-interpretation take moral diversity seriously either. From the perspective of institutional design, best-lights analysis makes sense only in a community that roughly shares the same interests, beliefs, and values. In pluralistic societies, however, where diversity and competition are the norm, Dworkinian meta-interpreters would rarely converge on common methodologies and hence would be at odds about the proper way to interpret their law.

Just as Dworkin's meta-interpretive theory makes no concessions to the limitations and differences of *meta-interpreters,* it is similarly insensitive to the varying levels of competence, character, and diversity of *interpreters* as well. On Dworkin's theory, interpretive methodology is determined by the principles that best fit and justify legal practice, with the notable exception, it would appear, of those principles that relate to the intellectual abilities, moral character, and ethical differences of those who must interpret the law.

The examination of the ideological origins of the American constitutional order not only shows that the intentions of legal creators are sometimes at odds with the demands of best-lights analysis. I believe it also provides additional evidence for the claim that the Planning Theory is a plausible description of legal practice. Insofar as questions of trust and difference are crucial to any endeavor that depends on the actions of others to accomplish its objectives, the fact that legal designers are intensely concerned with the competence, character, and diversity of actors when allocating rights and responsibilities seems to lend credence to the view that they treat the law as a planning activity. What this means for a theory of meta-interpretation is the subject of the next two chapters.

12

THE ECONOMY OF TRUST

In Chapter 1, I argued that fundamental questions about legal interpretation—what I am now calling issues of meta-interpretation—can be answered only by first determining the nature of law. If we want to know how to interpret the Eighth Amendment, the New York Statute of Wills, or any other legal text, we must know which facts ultimately determine the content of law, for only by using these can we adjudicate disputes between rival interpretive methodologies. Correct theories about the nature of law provide us with this information: they tell us what necessarily follows from the fact that something is law. To know how to interpret the law, then, we must answer the Implication Question.

In this chapter, I use our answer to the Identity Question to develop a theory of meta-interpretation. As I try to show, the Planning Theory entails that the attitudes of trust and distrust presupposed by the law are central to the choice of interpretive methodology. Roughly speaking, the Planning Theory demands that the more trustworthy a person is judged to be, the more interpretive discretion he or she is accorded; conversely, the less trusted one is in other parts of legal life, the less discretion one is allowed. Attitudes of trust are central to the meta-interpretation of law, I argue, because they are central to the meta-interpretation of *plans*—and laws are plans, or planlike norms.

Indeed, seasoned legal participants such as judges, litigators, and legal academics—whom I will refer to collectively as "lawyers"—have at least implicitly recognized the law as a practice of social planning and have demonstrated this precisely through their greater sensitivity to issues of trust. They routinely justify their choice between free and constrained interpretation by adverting to the degree to which certain people can be trusted to act competently and in good faith. However, this lawyerly attention to trust is strikingly missing from philosophical discussions of interpretation. Legal philosophers have simply not recognized the importance of competence and character for assessing interpretive methodology. Dworkin's theory of meta-interpretation, of course, is a dramatic example of this neglect.

To acknowledge that lawyers understand the importance of trust is not, of course, to say that lawyers have nothing to learn from philosophical discussions about the nature of law. Quite the contrary: although I believe that lawyers tacitly accept the idea that legal activity is, at bottom, a practice of social planning and are accordingly more alert to the ways in which issues of trust affect meta-interpretation, this insight remains untheorized, and its implications for meta-interpretive practice misunderstood. Thus, in the second half of this chapter I argue that lawyers fail to fully appreciate the role of trust in answering meta-interpretive questions because they fail to recognize the importance of the conceptual concerns they are often so quick to dismiss. In other words, while philosophers have examined questions of legal interpretation within an *institutional* vacuum, lawyers have typically engaged such issues within a *philosophical* vacuum—with similarly detrimental results.

Plans and Trust

As I intend to show, the Planning Theory entails that attitudes of trust and distrust presupposed by the law are central to the determination of interpretive methodology. Trust matters in the interpretation of law because trust matters in the interpretation of plans. Let us begin, therefore, by reflecting on simple plans that are adopted outside of a legal context.

Plan's End

Suppose a financial advisor develops an investment plan for one of her clients. Having figured out the best course of action, the advisor drafts a document setting out the plan and presents it to the client. If the advisor does her job well, of course, doubts about the proper interpretation of the document will rarely arise. The requirements of the plan will be obvious. Nevertheless, we can ask the meta-interpretive question about this plan: which methodology is the proper one to use when interpreting the document? For example, should the client follow the text literally or, alternatively, construe its meaning so that it always leads him to make the correct financial choice?

It is tempting to answer as follows: since the point of planning is to achieve certain ends, texts that set out plans should always be interpreted solely in the light of those ends. Otherwise, the interpreter would be acting counterproductively and irrationally. Thus, if following the literal text of the financial advisor's plan would lead the client to do something financially detrimental, then he must not interpret it to require this action.

The flaw in this response is not hard to spot. Allowing someone to interpret an investment plan solely in accordance with the end of making money would defeat the point of having a plan. The client has sought out financial advice precisely because he does not *know* which means are best suited to his financial goals. The plan is supposed to help compensate for his ignorance. If the client must interpret the plan so that it best achieves the desired financial result, then the plan will be doing no work.

This point may be made more vivid by filling out the story. Suppose the client is completely clueless about financial matters and seeks out the advisor for extensive help. Consequently, the advisor prepares an extremely comprehensive investment plan. The document specifies in great detail every stock that the client should buy, the dates on which he should purchase them, and the target prices at which to sell. It leaves virtually nothing to the client's discretion. The document does not say: "Sell IBM when the price stabilizes;" rather, it says: "Sell IBM at 90."

The detailed nature of the document reveals the plan's modus operandi. The plan aims to enable the client to achieve his financial goals precisely by denying him all but the smallest degree of freedom to pursue these goals directly. It allocates decision-making authority between the plan and the client in such a way that the *plan*—not the client—settles most questions about which means are best suited to the end of making money. This distribution of authority is itself based on an underlying distribution of trust. Because the advisor does not trust the client, she judges that the best allocation accords the lion's share of decision-making authority to the plan, while reserving a tiny remainder for the client.

Interpreting the investment plan exclusively in terms of its financial purpose, therefore, would frustrate its point. The plan allocates decision-making authority so as to compensate for the client's lack of competence.

An uncompromising purposive approach to interpretation, however, defeats this compensatory function by redistributing decision-making authority. It allocates a degree of power to the client that would be appropriate only in a more trusting environment.

Managing Trust and Distrust

As we have seen, the investment plan attempts to compensate for the client's lack of competence in financial matters. It does so by claiming the bulk of the decision-making authority for itself. The plan's comprehensive nature, as well as its use of concepts that require little judgment to apply, leave virtually no room for the client to deliberate about the best means to achieve his end.

Plans do not merely allow planners to compensate for their lack of trust in others; they also enable them to *capitalize* on such trust where it exists. Suppose the advisor prepares an investment plan for a client in whom she places significantly more trust. As a result, she drafts a far less detailed document. For example, the text recommends that the client purchase various kinds of stocks (blue-chip, biotech, start-up telecom, oil, and so forth) and gives examples of each category. But it does not take any firm stands. It merely instructs the client to invest in each kind of company based on the best information that the client has available to him. Furthermore, unlike its more comprehensive cousin, this plan establishes target ranges for each stock listed, rather than an exact price at which to sell. Because the advisor places greater trust in this second client, she drafts a plan that accords him greater discretion. Such a plan will enable the client to take greater advantage of information that might arise in the future. A more detailed plan would constrain him too much: it would deny him the discretion he needs to best promote his financial goals.

Plans, we have seen, are sophisticated devices for managing trust and distrust: they allow people to capitalize on the faith they have in others or compensate for its absence. In our first investment scenario, we saw two ways in which plans cope with distrust: through detailed provisions and through the use of nonevaluative concepts that require little discretion to apply. In our Cooking Club story in Chapter 5 we saw another way, namely, by denying important roles to those who lack the competence or character to perform the requisite tasks.

In our second investment scenario, we saw how the use of more general directions and evaluative concepts enables a financial planner to make the most of the trust she holds in the client. Shared plans also enable planners to capitalize on their trust in others, either by shifting important functions to those who can be relied upon to handle such matters, or by empowering these individuals with planning power via authorizations.

In most instances, of course, particular plans aim both to compensate for the lack of trust *and* to capitalize on its presence. A plan may be used to help cope with a degree of distrust, but the distrust may not run so deep that the plan need be very detailed. A shared plan may allocate important tasks to those trusted to handle them, while denying them to those who cannot be so trusted. An authorization may empower an individual in a certain domain, but accompanying instructions may limit the exercise of that power, and additional directives may require the power holder to exercise it in certain ways.

Respecting the Economy of Trust

As we have seen, plans are sophisticated tools for managing trust and distrust. Plans can play this management role because they can have any content, can come in different varieties and sizes, and can be combined to form complex networks. Some plans direct, while others authorize; some are dense, others are spare; some use evaluative concepts, others do not; some withhold power, while others confer it; and some are free-standing, while others are embedded within a large set of plans regulating their use.

Let us call the distribution of trust upon which a plan is predicated the plan's "economy of trust." The first investment plan has an economy of trust that is stingy to the client but generous to the advisor; the second plan's economy of trust, by contrast, is more egalitarian, in that it bestows much greater faith on the client. Our previous discussion suggested that plans can play their role in trust management only if the interpretive methodology respects their economy of trust. In other words, the interpretive methodology must not allocate decision-making power in a manner inconsistent with the attitudes of trust presupposed by the plan.

Although we will refine this formulation as we proceed, we can say generally that the more generous a plan's economy of trust, the more discretion the applier should have to depart from the literal meaning of the text in the name of the plan's purpose; conversely, a more distrustful set of attitudes should lead to a more restrictive methodology, demanding greater adherence to the text or to the planner's specific intentions or expectations. Thus, it would not be consonant with the first investment plan's economy of trust to accord the client a great deal of freedom to depart from the plan's literal language. The plan, after all, presupposes a lack of faith in the client's competence—this is why it exists and takes its specific form. To allow the client to depart from the detailed text whenever he thought that following it would lead to a financial loss would undo the very point of having such a plan.

Conversely, a radically textualist approach to the second investment plan would be inconsistent with its economy of trust. Departures from literal interpretation, at least under some circumstances, would accord with the trust attitudes that motivated the formulation and adoption of the plan. Suppose the client stumbles on inside information suggesting that some biotech company whose stock he owns will be bought out by a big pharmaceutical house. To interpret the plan so that he must sell the biotech company simply because the price of its stock falls within the target range set by the plan, even though he has good reason to anticipate a future increase in that price, would not be consistent with the judgments of competence that motivated the formulation and adoption of the plan.

Law and Trust

We can now see why attitudes of trust are normally important for the meta-interpretation of plans. Insofar as the aim of a plan is to capitalize on trust and compensate for distrust, the proper way to interpret the plan must not frustrate this function. It must not, in other words, permit interpreters to exercise competences and other character traits that the plan denies they have and for whose absence it seeks to compensate; nor may it refuse them the use of capacities that the plan assumes they possess and on whose possession it wishes to capitalize. The only way to respect a plan's trust management function is to defer to its economy of trust, namely, the attitudes of trust and distrust that motivated its creation.

Let us now consider meta-interpretation in law. I claim that the choice of methodology to interpret legal texts should be determined in a similar manner, namely, by deferring to economies of trust. A distrustful system requires a constraining methodology, such as textualism, whereas a more trusting system demands one according greater interpretive discretion. This relationship holds, I will now show, because one of the main roles the law plays is to manage trust and distrust, and the only way to respect this function is through fidelity to these attitudes.

Law and the Management of Trust

Recall that in the circumstances of legality, moral problems are numerous and serious, and their solutions complex, contentious, and arbitrary. As we saw in Chapter 6, members of a community in the circumstances of legality would face grave difficulties solving these moral problems by themselves. The complexity of the problems would severely tax their competence. Many would simply not know what to do; some might not know what to do but, tragically, think that they do; and some who might know what to do would need to expend significant time and energy figuring it out and convincing others to act likewise. Complexity would also provide those who lack good character with a pretext to evade their responsibilities. Even if they knew how to behave appropriately, they could still credibly feign ignorance or assert that they were required to do very little. The contentiousness of these problems would ensure that convergence on solutions would be difficult, costly, and sometimes impossible. And the arbitrariness of the solutions would thwart the ability of the community to capitalize on any faith they might have in one another in order to do what they morally ought to do.

Even if members of the community should miraculously agree on a set of solutions, difficulties would nevertheless arise when the opportunity for implementing these solutions arrived. Since people are usually bad judges when they have an interest at stake, disputes about how to apply these agreed-upon principles to concrete cases can be expensive, difficult to resolve, and liable to create further dissension. Even when everyone agreed about what ought to be done in particular situations, there would still be the danger that those who lack good character would renege on their responsibilities. This concern would be compounded by the mere *perception* that some lack the appropriate character to act fairly and responsibly. Without a method for assuring trustworthy actors that their participation and forbearance won't be exploited, this distrust could be corrosive and thwart the possibility of cooperation.

As we can see, the problems of the circumstances of legality are largely (although not exclusively) problems of trust: either members of the community cannot be trusted to do what they ought to do, can be trusted but need help realizing their potential, or do not trust each other enough to engage in the social cooperation necessary to solve the serious and numerous problems that can arise. According to the Planning Theory, the fundamental aim of the law is to rectify these deficiencies; moreover, the law pursues this aim by managing trust: it compensates for and capitalizes on the trust and distrust that its officials hold toward members of the community, as well as the trust and distrust that members of the community feel toward one another.

The law manages trust through social planning. Legislators are supposed to identify those who are trustworthy and assign them tasks that take advantage of their trustworthiness; conversely, they are to identify those who are less reliable, plan out their behavior in greater detail, and deny them the ability to abuse or exploit their power. Judges, in turn, are supposed to resolve disputes over these rights and responsibilities fairly and efficiently. Finally, law enforcement personnel may be required to impose sanctions on those who break the rules. In such ways, those who do not know how to solve existing moral problems, or falsely think they do, will be given the appropriate guidance; those who would have discovered the solutions only in a costly manner will now be able to do so cheaply; those who lack good character and wish to evade responsibilities will be subjected to standards by which their behavior can be monitored; those who disagree about the proper resolution to moral problems, or who are faced with a choice among arbitrary solutions, will be given a common blueprint off of which act; those who might engage in self-deception will have their disputes adjudicated before a neutral arbiter; those who are tempted to free ride will have incentives to cooperate; and those worried that others will free ride will be given assurances to the contrary.

To be sure, the law must solve moral problems without creating new ones in the process. Thus, power must not be granted to those who cannot be trusted to use it properly. The task of institutional design, therefore, is to capitalize on trust while simultaneously compensating for distrust: to allocate enough power so that problems may be solved, but not so much that this power can be abused and exploited. This tension was the focus of the story we told in the last chapter. The framers sought to economize on virtue by selecting those with enough talent and integrity to act in the public spirit, while checking their natural proclivity toward self-aggrandizement through diffusions of power and bureaucratic competition.

It should be noted that not every legal problem is an issue of trust. Political conflict does not always arise because of a lack of competence or character. Questions about how to allocate resources, or how to choose between conflicting but equally valid visions of the good life, can be disputed between similarly trustworthy parties. Social planning overcomes these potentially dangerous disputes by settling the matter: it determines which of these alternative courses of action are to be followed. However, it must not be forgotten that even when the law must resolve disputes, questions of trust are still relevant. For legal authorities must still determine whether the parties need detailed guidance on how to implement the winning vision, or whether the losing party needs to be monitored so that it does not evade the terms of the settlement.

Undoing the Law

Once we recognize that the law seeks to rectify the moral deficiencies of the circumstances of legality principally by compensating for lack of trust and capitalizing on its existence, we see that the interpretation of the plans created by the law must be consistent with the legal system's economy of trust. A simple example will help make this point. Suppose that the designers of a particular legal system strongly distrust the competence and character of community members. This outlook is enshrined in the system's institutional design: authority is widely dispersed throughout the system, executive and judicial officers are forbidden from legislating, lengthy waiting times are set up before legislation can be passed, there are severe sanctions for abuse of discretion, statutes are set out in detailed codes with few open-ended standards, and so on.

Now imagine that this distrustful system is combined with an interpretive methodology according officials a great deal of discretion. This methodology does not require them to hew too closely to the plain meaning of legal texts, but rather allows them to deviate from the plain meaning when they think that the texts have been poorly drafted or will produce unreasonable results. When reading statutes, officials in this system tend to interpret grants of power broadly and constraints narrowly, ignore legislative texts that give a result with which they mildly disagree, refuse to defer to the interpretation of regulations by the appropriate administrative agencies, and so forth. All of this is permitted according to the system's interpretive methodology.

The obvious problem with applying this methodology to a legal system informed by distrust of its participants, however, is that such an interpretive methodology grants officials too much freedom from the point of view of the system designers. By according officials a large degree of interpretive discretion, it provides them with opportunities to expand their powers, reduce restrictions, and further increase their discretion beyond the level contemplated by the designers. The methodology frustrates the compensatory aim of the rules: it denies incompetent actors some of the guidance they need to solve moral problems; it denies members of the community some of the means to monitor the unscrupulous and hold them accountable; it denies the self-deceived some of the protection they need to keep themselves honest; and it denies those who worry about free riding some of the assurances they require to induce cooperation. The resulting distribution of power and authority, in other words, is incompatible with the distrustful views of the regime. The interpretive methodology requires that officials exercise capacities that the institutional design denies they possess and whose absence it seeks to offset.

Likewise, a system that takes a more optimistic attitude toward human nature and cognition would be ill-served by a highly restrictive interpretive methodology. While such a methodology protects the law from exploitation by the unscrupulous, it also prevents members of the community from capitalizing on the faith invested in them by the rules. By curtailing the officials' interpretive discretion, it precludes them from pursuing the objectives they were entrusted to serve.

To be sure, the argument just presented is incomplete, in that it does not tell us how to ascertain a system's economy of trust, or how interpretive methodology ought to track it. The limited point being made here is that systemic attitudes of trust (conceived in some plausible way) must play an important role in meta-interpretation if legal systems are to manage issues of trust. If the proper interpretive methodology for a particular legal system fails to harmonize with its economy of trust, the system will be unable to compensate for lack of trustworthiness and to capitalize on its existence. Indeed, as I will now argue, not only must trust matter in meta-interpretation if the law is to plan effectively, but lawyers are normally aware of this.

Lawyers and Trust

Even a cursory glance at what lawyers say about legal interpretation reveals that issues of trust lie at the very heart of their concerns. Consider, for example, the following statements:

And if [legislators] are dispersed, so that their minds cannot be known, then those who may approach nearest to their minds shall construe the words, and these are the sages of the law whose talents are exercised in the study of such matters.—Plowden[1]

Relieve the judges from the rigour of text law, and permit them, with praetorian discretion, to wander into it's [sic] equity, and the whole legal system becomes incertain.—Thomas Jefferson[2]

Constitutions are not designed for metaphysical or logical subtleties, for niceties of expression, for critical propriety, for elaborate shades of meaning, or for the exercise of philosophical acuteness or judicial research. They are instruments of a practical nature, founded on the common business of human life, adapted to common wants, designed for common use, and fitted for common understandings. The people make them, the people adopt them, the people must be supposed to read them, with the help of common-sense, and cannot be presumed to admit in them any recondite meaning or any extraordinary gloss.—Joseph Story[3]

Obviously there is danger that the courts' conclusion as to legislative purpose will be unconsciously influenced by the judges' own views or by factors not considered by the enacting body. A lively appreciation of the danger is the best assurance of escape from its threat but hardly justifies an acceptance of a literal interpretation dogma which withholds from the courts available information for reaching a correct conclusion.—Stanley Reed[4]

[The court] should assume, unless the contrary unmistakably appears, that the legislature was made up of reasonable persons pursuing reasonable purposes reasonably.—Henry Hart and Albert Sacks[5]

The number of judges living at one time who can, with plausible claim to accuracy, "think [themselves] . . . into the minds of the enacting legislators and imagine how they would have wanted the statute applied to the case at bar," may be counted on one hand.—Frank Easterbrook[6]

[T]he United States Code is not the work of a single omniscient intellect.–Richard Posner[7]

A society that adopts a bill of rights is skeptical that "evolving standards of decency" always "mark progress," and that societies always "mature," as opposed to rot. Neither the text of such a document nor the intent of its framers (whichever you choose) can possibly lead to the conclusion that its only effect is to take the power of changing rights away from the legislature and give it to the courts.—Antonin Scalia[8]

Enlightenment statesmen were very unlikely to think that their own views represented the last word in moral progress. If they really were worried that future generations would protect rights less vigorously than they themselves did, they would have made plain that they intended to create a dated provision.—Ronald Dworkin[9]

As these quotes demonstrate, issues of trust play a prominent role in debates about legal interpretation. Some of the writers cited above argue that since judges can be trusted with discretion—either because they are "sages of the law" (Plowden) or because "a lively appreciation of the dangers" of discretion is enough to protect them from wayward action (Reed)—they should engage in purposive interpretation. Others argue that any type of discretion is dangerous since judges cannot be so trusted—either because their judgment is "praetorian" (Jefferson) or because imagining what legislators would have done is so difficult that those with such ability "may be counted on one hand" (Easterbrook). Some believe that judges must have interpretive flexibility because legislators are not "omniscient" (Posner), while others believe that judges should defer to legislative purpose insofar as legislators are "reasonable persons pursuing reasonable purposes reasonably" (Hart and Sacks). Some claim that the framers were concerned with moral "rot" and would have wanted judges to stick closely to the text of constitutional provisions (Scalia), while others respond that the framers believed in "moral progress" and would have trusted future generations to interpret the Constitution in accordance with moral values (Dworkin).

Even when questions of trust are not directly broached in discussions of legal interpretation, they often lie just below the surface. For example, when Coke writes, "The wisdom of the judges and sages of the law has always suppressed new and subtle inventions in derogation of the common law," he is not so subtly implying that legislators cannot be trusted with the power to override rules made by more learned judges.[10]

That lawyers take trust seriously in meta-interpretation further confirms the claim that attitudes of trust bear directly on the question of proper interpretive methodology. In fact, this supporting evidence is not unrelated to the earlier argument about the implications of the Planning Theory. Insofar as lawyers are legal participants par excellence, they are apt to have deep appreciation for the planning nature of law. And awareness of the law as a planning activity inexorably leads one to grasp that trust is central to meta-interpretation.

Determining the Economy of Trust

As we have seen, many seasoned legal practitioners believe that judgments of competence and character ought to play a central role in determining interpretive methodology. Generally speaking, it is thought that the more trustworthy interpreters are judged to be, the more interpretive discretion they should be given. Lawyers are not, however, always of the same mind about *whose* judgments should be authoritative. In this section, I would like to compare two well-known meta-interpretive arguments and show how each assesses the trustworthiness of interpreters from a different point of view.

Two Points of View

In *A Matter of Interpretation*, Antonin Scalia argues that constitutional provisions ought to be interpreted in accordance with the original meaning of the text, rather than with an "evolving sense of decency." A judge living today should not, for example, interpret the Eighth Amendment according to the meaning that she assigns to the term "cruel" if that meaning diverges from the late eighteenth-century understanding, for such evolutionary methodologies flout the fundamental function of constitutions. "It certainly cannot be said that a constitution naturally suggests changeability; to the contrary, its whole purpose is to prevent change—to embed certain rights in such a manner that future generations cannot readily take them away. A society that adopts a bill of rights is skeptical that 'evolving standards of decency' always 'mark progress,' and that societies always 'mature,' as opposed to rot."[11]

On Scalia's view, the purpose of a constitution is to prevent untrustworthy future generations from rescinding rights that the present generation feels should be protected. But, he argues, granting judges the power to interpret the constitutional text in accordance with changing conceptions of morality would, in effect, permit future generations to change the constitution and thereby defeat its raison d'etre.

Now consider Richard Posner's defense of what he calls "pragmatic adjudication." Posner claims that it is proper to accord courts the discretion to decide cases in accordance with their judgments of the general welfare because judges are generally trustworthy. Insofar as they are routinely chosen from the intellectual elite of American society, judges will normally have the competence to wield such power responsibly. He writes:

Judges of the higher American courts are generally picked from the upper tail of the population distribution in terms of age, education, intelligence, disinterest, and sobriety. They are not tops in all these departments but they are well above average, at least in the federal courts because of the elaborate pre-appointment screening of candidates for federal judgeships. Judges are schooled in a profession that sets a high value on listening to both sides of an issue before making up one's mind, on sifting truth from falsehood, and on exercising a detached judgment. Their decisions are anchored in the facts of concrete disputes between real people. Members of the legal profession have played a central role in the political history of the United States, and the profession's institutions and usages reflect the fundamental political values that have emerged from that history. Appellate judges in nonroutine cases are expected to express as best they can the reasons for their decision in signed, public documents (the published decisions of these courts); this practice creates accountability and fosters a certain reflectiveness and self-discipline. None of these things guarantees wisdom, especially since the reasons given for a decision are not always the real reasons behind it. But at their best, American appellate courts are councils of wise elders and it is not completely insane to entrust them with responsibility for deciding cases in a way that will produce the best results in the circumstances rather than just deciding cases in accordance with rules created by other organs of government or in accordance with their own previous decisions, although that is what they will be doing most of the time."[12]

Both Scalia's and Posner's arguments are meta-interpretive in nature. Each argues for (or against) a specific methodology as the proper way to read legal texts in the American legal system. Moreover, each grounds his meta-interpretive argument on an assessment of the trustworthiness of legal actors. Scalia thinks that judges ought to be denied the discretion to appeal to current views of morality based on skepticism about the moral character of future generations; Posner believes judges should be accorded such discretion based on confidence in their expertise.

A closer look, however, reveals an important difference in the structure of their arguments. While both look to judgments of trustworthiness in selecting an interpretive methodology, only Posner appeals to his own judgments. Posner seeks to accord judges discretion in interpretation because *Posner* deems them to be sufficiently trustworthy. By contrast, Scalia aims to curtail judicial discretion based not on his personal skepticism, but rather on the fact that the *designers* of the American legal system were insufficiently confident in the trustworthiness of future generations.

Accordingly, we can distinguish between two different meta-interpretive procedures. Let us call Posner's argument an instance of the "God's-eye" method. The God's-eye method pegs proper interpretive methodology to *actual* competence and character. A meta-interpreter seeking to determine which methodology she ought to use would, on this account, be directed to evaluate her own trustworthiness. If she thought highly of herself, she should accord herself great discretion in interpretation; conversely, if she were less confident, she should constrain herself to a greater degree.

Scalia's argument, on the other hand, is an instance of what I will call the "Planners" method. According to this approach, a meta-interpreter should not assess her own trustworthiness, but rather defer to the views of the system's planners regarding her competence and character. Her task is to extract the planners' attitudes of trust as they are embodied by the plans of the legal system, and then to use these attitudes to determine how much discretion to accord herself. Planners' confidence in competence and character should yield significant levels of interpretive discretion; doubt and suspicion ought to issue in low levels of discretion. Insofar as the Planners method requires meta-interpreters to defer to *imputed,* rather than actual, competence and character, its recommendations may diverge from the God's-eye approach whenever the legal system is founded on false beliefs about the abilities and dispositions of actors.

To make the contrast between the God's-eye and Planners methods more concrete, consider an argument advanced by Daryl Levinson regarding the psychological foundations of American constitutionalism. As Levinson points out, federalism and separation of powers presuppose that government officials are "empire builders."[13] But, he argues, this assumption is mistaken. Unlike dictators, democratic representatives do not personally benefit from increases in the power of the institutions of which they are members. Moreover, in a minimally functioning democracy, officials who act in an imperialist or avaricious manner will be punished by their constituents. Levinson concludes that "the kind of agency-driven empire-building feared by the Framers should be a much less significant concern than contemporary constitutional law credits."[14]

Let us assume that Levinson is correct. Should any of this affect meta-interpretation? This depends on whether one embraces the God's-eye or Planners perspective. Levinson's finding might lead a supporter of the God's-eye view to accord government officials greater discretion in interpretation. After all, officials are not in fact empire builders, and hence the dangers of unfettered discretion are not nearly as great as the framers believed. On the Planners view, however, nothing has changed. The fact that the framers were wrong about empire building is immaterial—what matters is that they thought they were right.

It should be pointed out that the Planners method is not the same as "originalism."[15] Originalism is usually understood to be a specific interpretive methodology: it dictates that legal texts be interpreted in accordance with the intent of those who enacted them. The Planners method, by contrast, describes an approach to meta-interpretation, that is, a way to select interpretive methodologies: it requires that proper interpretive methodology be a function of the attitudes of trust of those who designed various aspects of the legal system in question. Now, where the planners assume a high level of distrust toward group members, it may indeed follow from such trust attitudes that an interpreter should cabin discretion when construing certain textual provisions, and that the best way to cabin discretion is through privileging original intent. In such a case, the Planners approach would justify the use of original intent methodology. But it is also possible that attending to the trust attitudes of legal planners might actually demand the rejection of original intent methodology.[16]

Playing God

Lawyers rarely offer meta-interpretive arguments. In most instances, they simply use a particular interpretive methodology without stating that they are using it or attempting to justify their choice. Of course, as we have seen, lawyers are sometimes self-conscious about their interpretive behavior and proffer arguments supporting their pick. Posner and Scalia are notable examples. But even when volunteering such justifications, jurists are almost never explicit about their underlying meta-interpretive theory. They simply make meta-interpretive arguments, hoping that the criteria to which they appeal are accepted by their interlocutor as the proper determinants of interpretive methodology.

Recently, however, legal academics have become more reflective regarding meta-interpretive practice. Although no one has developed anything close to a theory, several theorists have nevertheless sought to identify explicitly some meta-interpretive criteria. Such musings have, naturally, led them to appreciate the importance of trust in determining interpretive methodology. Interestingly, though, when these theorists have considered the precise role that trust ought to play in meta-interpretation, by and large they have opted for the God's-eye approach.[17]

Unfortunately, while these theorists openly advocate the God's-eye method, they fail to provide any basis for their preference.[18] In fact, for all their emphasis on the importance of institutional competence, they never explain why such considerations are crucial in the selection of interpretive methodologies. They treat the relevance of competence as self-evident, a claim so obvious as not to need explanation.

No doubt, the God's-eye view has its intuitive appeal. After all, who would be in favor of heeding ideas one believes to be false? Nevertheless, I think that this approach to legal meta-interpretation is inconsistent with the logic of planning and, as such, frustrates the ability of the law to achieve its fundamental aim.

This point can best be made by returning to the example of the distrustful legal system encountered earlier in the chapter. In that system, the planners hold a very distrustful view of the competence and character of officials and, as a result, they aim to develop a certain legal framework for coping with such problems: they attempt to diffuse authority through the system, forbid executive and judicial officers from legislating, set up lengthy waiting times before legislation can be passed, enforce sanctions for abuse of discretion, and so on. Accordingly, they draft a constitution that sets out these rights and duties in very clear, detailed, and precise language.

Let us imagine, by contrast, that legal officials operating in such a system think of themselves as eminently trustful. As a result, they believe that the contemplated constraints are unnecessary and, in fact, impede their valuable work. In keeping with the God's-eye view, they use their charitable views about their own trustworthiness and assume large degrees of discretion in interpretation: they read grants of power broadly, interpret constraints narrowly, ignore statutes when these texts give a result with which they mildly disagree, refuse to defer to the interpretation of regulations by the appropriate administrative agencies, and so forth.

The obvious difficulty with this mode of proceeding, however, is that the very aim of the designers in creating the constitution is frustrated. The designers wanted to compensate for their distrust of officials by severely constraining their discretion; yet by following the God's-eye view, the officials are able (wittingly or unwittingly) to defeat this aim. Those deemed to be incompetent are encouraged by this meta-interpretive approach to judge themselves competent; those regarded as unscrupulous are given the latitude to evade their responsibilities; those feared to be self-deceiving are freed to deceive themselves; and those who worried about free riding are left without assurances.

Troubles arise here because the officials share a view about themselves that differs dramatically from those shared by the system's designers. Matters will likely be worse when no such consensus among officials exists. In these cases, which are bound to be the norm, coordination will be hard to secure and disagreements will be costly to resolve, precisely the sort of difficulties that institutional design is supposed to alleviate. Last, even if implementers are finally able to settle their doubts and disagreements, valuable resources will have been spent in the exercise, resources that could have been used to advance the goals of the system.

Put slightly differently, the core problem with the God's-eye view is that it violates the General Logic of Planning principle. It does so because it requires officials to determine the existence of those facts that their law aimed to resolve. The constitutional plan, in other words, is supposed to settle the question "Who should be trusted to do what?" Yet this is the very question that the God's-eye approach directs meta-interpreters to answer. It demands that meta-interpreters determine their own trustworthiness, and hence unsettles what has been settled.

By violating GLOP, the God's-eye approach recreates, at least partially, the deficiencies of the circumstances of legality. The law aims to cure these deficiencies, in large part, by managing trust: its plans should compensate for distrust and capitalize on trust. However, by requiring those who are regulated by the plans to determine how trustworthy they themselves are, the God's-eye approach reopens Pandora's Box. Those who are untrustworthy can use their untrustworthiness to arrive at different solutions than the ones determined by the law; the trustworthy can fail to exercise their competence and character and hence not utilize those strengths that the law seeks to exploit; those who disagree about trustworthiness will end up disagreeing about what ought to be done and hence act at cross-purposes; and those who fear free riding will lose some of the required assurances.

It is important to emphasize that this objection is not an empirical one. The claim is not that legal officials who follow the God's-eye approach are less likely to solve moral problems than those who defer to the system planners. The point, rather, is conceptual: given that the law aims to solve moral problems through social planning, it cannot do what it is supposed to do when the logic of planning is violated. To be sure, approaches like the God's-eye one will, on some occasions, manage to solve moral problems. But it is crucial to see that when this is so, the success is a legal accident. The problems have not been solved in the way that the law is supposed to solve them: they have not been solved by plan-based reasoning.

Notice that the Planners method of meta-interpretation does not violate GLOP. Because it preaches fidelity to the designers' conception of trust, it does not require the meta-interpreters to answer the question "Who should be trusted to do what?" It takes their answer as correct for the purposes of determining interpretive methodology, and hence does not frustrate the trust management function of the law.

Legitimacy

Thus far, I have described the infirmities of the God's-eye point of view in purely instrumental terms: if the law is to fulfill its aim, then the logic of planning demands that questions of competence and character not be decided by the meta-interpreter. As we will now see, the God's-eye approach suffers from another, related problem: it violates the rights of those who have moral authority to rule.

On the Planning Theory, to rule is to engage in social planning; thus, to have the moral right to rule is to have the moral right to engage in social planning. Anything, therefore, that prevents legitimate rulers from engaging in social planning effectively deprives them of their moral right to rule. Since the argument of the previous section showed that the God's-eye view frustrates the aim of social planning, it follows that the God's eye approach violates the moral rights of legitimate authorities.

Suppose, for example, that the distrustful legal system we just discussed has a good democratic pedigree. Its constitution was ratified by an overwhelming majority of adults in the political community after a full and fair debate. Because the God's-eye view does not require deference to the trust attitudes of those who ratified the constitution, it does not permit the democratic majorities the right to rule themselves. For if the side that distrusts human nature wins the debate, those taking a more hopeful attitude toward human nature in meta-interpretation sabotage the democratic process. They undo what the majority had the right to do.

This problem with the God's-eye approach, of course, does not arise because of some quirky feature of democratic theory. The same difficulties will crop up for any nonanarchist theory of political legitimacy. For any such theory will suppose that some persons have the moral right to plan for the community. Because these planners are the legitimate ones, the theory must deny all others the right to interfere with their social planning. Such a theory, therefore, must require that all others not take the God's-eye point of view. Otherwise, not only will the law not be able to do what it is supposed to do, but the legitimate authorities (whoever they may be) will not be able to do what they have the *right* to do.

Authority and Opportunistic Systems

Having argued that the God's-eye approach to meta-interpretation violates the logic of planning while the Planners method does not, should we infer that the Planners method is the correct approach to meta-interpretation? I think not. I would like to suggest that the correct approach to meta-interpretation depends on the legal system. In many instances, the Planners approach is appropriate, but not in every case.

To know whose attitudes of trust and distrust to privilege, it is important to know *why* the current participants of the legal system accept, or at least purport to accept, the system as designed by its planners. Is the participants' acceptance predicated on their belief that the plans were designed by those having superior authority or judgment? Or, rather, do they believe that these plans are well suited to solve those moral problems that the law should solve, even if the reasons why they think the plans are good are different from the reasons for which they were created?

Let's distinguish between two ideal types of legal systems. In an "authority" system, the reason why the bulk of legal officials accept, or purport to accept, the rules of the system is that these rules were created by those having superior moral authority or judgment. The authoritative provenance of these rules, in other words, is deemed to be of paramount moral importance. In an "opportunistic" system, by contrast, the origins of most of these rules are deemed morally irrelevant. Officials in these regimes accept them because they recognize, or purport to recognize, that these rules are morally good and hence further the fundamental aim of law.

The Planners method is appropriate for authority systems. Because officials attribute moral legitimacy or expertise to the authorities of the system, and since authorities are social planners, it follows that they attribute moral legitimacy or expertise to their activity of social planning. Any view that attributes moral legitimacy or expertise to their activity is committed to imputing moral legitimacy or expertise to their aim of trust management. Attributing moral legitimacy or expertise to the trust management aim of a set of planners would commit one to interpreting the plans created in a way that does not frustrate their aim. Since the Planners method respects the trust management aim of a set of planners, attributing moral legitimacy or expertise to a set of planners commits one to using the Planners method of meta-interpretation. The economy of trust in such a system, therefore, would be constituted by the attitudes of trust and distrust shared by the system's planners.

Officials in opportunistic systems, on the other hand, do not accord any special moral status to the planners of their system. They accept, or purport to accept, the rules because they judge them to be morally good, not because they have a morally legitimate or expert source. Put in terms of the Planning Theory, they think that the plans of the system just so happen to manage trust and distrust correctly; they do not care whether the planners who created them aimed to accomplish this task. In such a case, the economy of trust would be the attitudes of trust shared by the bulk of the current participants of the system, rather than the attitudes of the planners who originally created them. Call this the Participants method of meta-interpretation.

It is an empirical question, of course, whether a specific legal system more closely resembles an authority system or an opportunistic system. For example, do legal participants in the United States accept, or purport to accept, the U.S. Constitution because it was framed by the Founding Fathers and ratified in 1789? Or do they accept it, or purport to accept it, because they think that the scheme of governance that it sets out is a good one regardless of its origin? If the first description is more accurate, then the framer's Whiggish attitudes about human nature are relevant to the question of meta-interpretation; if the second better describes social reality, then the Constitution would truly be a living document, insofar as the attitudes of trust that determine interpretive methodology would be those held by the bulk of the current participants in the American legal practice.

For what it's worth, I believe that the United States legal system strongly resembles an authority system. The reverence in which the "Founding Fathers" are held, the privileging of democracy to the exclusion of all other modes of political legitimization, the political impossibility of criticizing the Constitution, and the veneration with which the text is treated all bespeak a belief that the authority of the Constitution stems from its special provenance. As Hendrik Hertzberg has aptly observed:

[I]n the public square the Constitution is beyond criticism. The American civic religion affords it Biblical or Koranic status, even to the point of seeing it as divinely inspired. It's the flag in prose. It's something to be venerated. It's something to be preserved, protected, and defended, as the President swears by God to do. In the proper place (a marble temple in Washington), at the proper times (the first Monday in October, *et seq.*), and by the proper people (nine men and women in priestly robes), it is to be interpreted, like the entrails of a goat.[19]

Because legal participants in the United States accord the Constitution an authoritative source, those who interpret it must be sensitive to the attitudes of trust held by those who designed it. But as we will see in the next chapter, this privileging of the attitudes of constitutional designers does not entail that originalism is the proper methodology for constitutional interpretation; nor does it mean that only the framers' attitudes matter. The entrails of a legal system are messy and evolving, and their interpretation no simple matter.

13

THE INTERPRETATION OF PLANS

Textualism vs. Purposivism

Meta-interpretive debates cover a wide range of topics, including whether to rely on parliamentary intent and legislative history, defer to administrative agencies, follow judicial precedent in constitutional and statutory interpretation, recognize evolving social mores, accept the authority of treatise writers, and so on. But the principal disagreement over interpretive methodology has always been between those who favor stricter forms of interpretation versus those who prefer looser ones. Advocates of textualism insist that the plain meaning of legal texts be followed. For them, the letter of the law controls. By contrast, those who favor some form of purposivism maintain that it is proper in some instances for interpreters to bypass the literal reading of an authoritative text. When the text recommends a course of action that is contrary to the purpose for which it was enacted, purposivists believe it a dereliction of duty to follow the letter of the law.

Nonlawyers are often perplexed by this debate. Some think it obvious that legal texts ought to be construed strictly. If the law says "No vehicles are permitted in the park," then no vehicles are permitted in the park—end of story. A judge who, in order to best serve the spirit of the law, interprets the statute to permit an ambulance to go through the park is not *really* interpreting the statute—she is changing it.

Others take the opposite tack. They cannot see the point of sticking to the letter of the law when doing so would be counterproductive. The function of the law, to them, is to make our lives better off. What justification could there possibly be, on this view, for not letting an ambulance go through a park if that is the quickest route to the hospital? From this perspective, textualism appears to confirm the layman's worst suspicions about lawyers and the law.

353

Unfortunately, both of these views are misinformed. As to the first, the debate between textualism and purposivism is not *whether* judges should follow the law; the dispute concerns, rather, *how* to follow the law. The textualist believes that judges follow the law only when they heed it to the letter. The purposivist, on the other hand, denies that the literal interpretation of the text is the law. Judges follows the law only when they interpret legal texts purposively, not literally.

Consider, for example, Plowden's famous description of purposivism:

> [I]t is not the words of the law, but the internal sense of it that makes the law, and our law (like all others) consists of two parts, viz. of body and soul, the letter of the law is the body of the law, and the sense and reason of the law is the soul of the law. . . . And the law may be resembled to a nut, which has a shell and a kernel within, the letter of the law represents the shell, and the sense of it the kernel, and as you will be no better for the nut if you make use only of the shell, so you will receive no benefit by the law, if you rely only upon the letter, and as the fruit and profit of the nut lies in the kernel, and not in the shell, so the fruit and profit of the law consists in the sense more than in the letter. And it often happens that when you know the letter, you know not the sense, for sometimes the sense is more confined and contracted than the letter, and sometimes it is more large and extensive.[1]

Plowden, thus, denies that the text of the law is the law. It is simply the shell, which must be discarded in favor of the purposive core that ultimately determines proper legal interpretation.

As for the contrary reaction that the only rational interpretive methodology is a purposivist one, it should now be clear why a meta-interpreter might be tempted toward stricter forms of construction. As we saw in the last chapter, the Planning Theory suggests that attitudes of trust are central to the choice of interpretive methodology. If those regulated by the law are greatly distrusted, then they should not be accorded the discretion necessary to bring the interpretation of a text in line with its purpose. Constraining an untrustworthy interpreter to follow the text strictly might actually achieve a better result than allowing the interpreter to pursue the targeted goals or values directly.

By the same token, if the legal system places greater trust in certain members of the legal community, it might be appropriate for interpreters to look past the literal wording of a legal text in order to act in accordance with its purpose. The point of planning, after all, is to further some goal or realize some value. It would thus be self-defeating for a faithful agent to interpret a law in a way that impeded the aim the law is meant to serve.

The debate between textualists and purposivists, therefore, cannot be resolved a priori. In order to know whether interpreters should have discretion to depart from the text when doing so furthers the purpose of the text in question, one must look to the system in which the text is situated and determine its economy of trust. Indeed, in many instances, it is possible to interpret this meta-interpretive debate precisely as a dispute about the economy of trust of particular legal systems. The textualist maintains that the economy of trust of a given legal system does not support the level of trust necessary for purposive interpretation. The purposivist, on the other hand, sees the judgments of competence and character underlying the plans of the system as sufficiently approving to sanction departures from the text in appropriate circumstances.

In this chapter, I develop a theory of meta-interpretation in some detail, using the Planning Theory as my guide. My aim in doing so is not simply to set out a method that lawyers can use to improve their meta-interpretive arguments. I also try to demonstrate that many of the meta-interpretive arguments that lawyers have actually made conform, albeit in an inchoate and unreflective manner, to the process of meta-interpretation that the Planning Theory recommends.

The Planning Theory of Meta-interpretation

Before I begin this discussion, however, I would like to formally introduce the cast of characters who will play important roles in the account I will develop. Although we have already encountered these individuals, it will be helpful to explain in detail who they are and how they are related.

Who's Who in Meta-interpretation

The four most important groups that play a role in meta-interpretation are the officials, actors, planners, and, of course, meta-interpreters. By "officials" I refer to those who occupy offices in a particular legal system. They include judges, senators, administrative officials, ambassadors, police officers, county clerks, city comptrollers, bailiffs, and so on. By "actors" I mean those persons who are delegated legal rights and responsibilities so that they may contribute in some way to the political goals of the system. Actors include not only officials, but ordinary citizens as well. They exclude, however, infants and the severely mentally challenged insofar as the law does not rely on them to further its objectives.

By "planners" (or as I will sometimes say "designers") I refer to those actors who have created, modified, or extinguished the institutions of a particular legal system, or affected the relationships between institutions. In the American system, for example, legal planners ordinarily include legislatures, courts, administrative agencies, and executive officials, but also constitutional conventions and the electorate itself.

Because legal systems always contain mechanisms for revision, the planners change as the structure of the system changes. The designers of the present American system include not only the framers and ratifiers of the Constitution of 1787, but the numerous agents who have changed the complexion of the system over the past two hundred years. The framers and ratifiers of the Fourteenth Amendment are as much the designers of the current regime as the framers and ratifiers of the original Constitution. Insofar as the meta-interpreter focuses on the current system, the relevant set of planners for meta-interpretation is the current one, namely, those whose planning has not yet been modified or extinguished by subsequent planners.

Last, by "meta-interpreters" I mean those persons who attempt to discover which interpretive methodology is appropriate for an actor in a given legal system to use. Planners, nonplanning actors, and even nonactors can be meta-interpreters. For example, a federal judge who attempts to ascertain what method she should use to interpret the United States Constitution is a meta-interpreter who also happens to be a planner; an American law professor who writes an article critiquing such a judge is a nonplanner (but actor) meta-interpreter; and a French law professor critiquing his American colleague is a nonactor metainterpreter.

Meta-interpretation can be either "self-regarding" or "other-regarding." A self-regarding meta-interpreter attempts to determine which interpretive methodology is appropriate for her to use, for example, a Supreme Court justice arguing that a certain method of statutory interpretation is appropriate for her to follow. An other-regarding meta-interpreter seeks to select a methodology for other actors to apply, for example, a citizen who considers how judges should read statutes. For the sake of simplicity, however, I will assume in what follows that meta-interpreters are always legal actors, and that meta-interpretation is always self-regarding.

Thus, I ignore cases where the meta-interpreter is a nonactor, or where an actor attempts to determine how some other actor should read legal texts. Nothing of consequence hinges on this simplifying restriction.

The Economy of Trust

In the last chapter, I argued that proper meta-interpretation is always faithful to the attitudes of trust and distrust presupposed by the rules of the system. The meta-interpreter extracts these attitudes and uses them to determine how much discretion to accord interpreters. A proper meta-interpretive theory, in other words, should always respect a system's economy of trust. An interpretive methodology that requires a high degree of discretion for its implementation is appropriate only for a system whose economy of trust is rather generous. Conversely, a highly restrictive technique befits a system whose economy is significantly more miserly.

In contrast to Dworkin's model, this theory does not demand that interpretive methodologies be justified from the moral point of view. The meta-interpreter need not know why citizens should obey the law, the relation of justice to fairness, or the proper demands of community. He may have no opinions about how trustworthy members of his community really are. On this account, interpretive methodology is pegged not to the truth of any abstract philosophical or social-scientific theory, but rather to the law's presuppositions concerning the trustworthiness of legal actors.

Because this account is significantly more modest than Dworkin's account, it will be compatible with a much larger set of trust attitudes. One need not have an especially rosy picture of human nature to believe that individuals can effectively defer to the attitudes of others. Moreover, unlike the God's-eye method, this account necessarily respects the law's trust management function. Because its prime directive is to defer to the trust attitudes presupposed by the rules, the planner's method will never license interpretive methodologies that are inconsistent with the system's distribution of trust and distrust.

As I argued at the end of the last chapter, the proper way to determine a system's economy of trust is to determine the reasons why legal officials accept, or purport to accept, the rules of the system. In an authority system, where the bulk of the officials credit the system's designers with superior authority or judgment, the attitudes of these designers will determine the system's economy of trust. In an opportunistic system, by contrast, the attitudes of current officials will determine its economy of trust. For simplicity's sake, we will concentrate on authority systems. To adjust for opportunistic systems, it will usually suffice to replace "official" for "planner" in the discussion that follows. How meta-interpretation should proceed in customary legal systems will be addressed at the end of this chapter.

The Importance of Role

Thus far, I have proposed the following meta-interpretive principle: interpreters should be given as much discretion in interpretation as they are otherwise accorded in their system's economy of trust. Notice that this principle has the following implication: because economies of trust are rarely egalitarian—certain groups will be trusted more than other groups with respect to certain domains—it would be surprising if one methodology were appropriate for every subgroup in the system. It is entirely likely that a highly discretionary methodology will be fitting for certain officials, a highly constraining one will suit others, and some third method will be appropriate for the citizenry. Strictly speaking, therefore, there is no such thing as the correct interpretation of a legal text. Legal interpretation is always *actor-relative:* a text is interpreted correctly only in relation to an actor and her particular place within the system's economy of trust. Consequently, the meta-interpreter must always be careful to keep her position in the system in full view, and to tailor her interpretive method so as to harmonize with the degree of trust accorded to her.

While the meta-interpretive principle I introduced has certain virtues— for example, it takes the trust attitudes of all planners seriously—it is nonetheless too crude. As formulated, the principle selects methodologies based on the amount of interpretive discretion they confer, not the type. But since different methodologies may grant interpreters similar degrees of discretion, simply deferring to the system's trust economy may not yield a unique interpretive methodology. For example, as I show later on, certain types of textualism confer roughly the same degree of discretion on interpreters as some purposive ones. The principle I proposed cannot inform the choice between such methodologies.

A more powerful principle is therefore needed. Recall that, according to the Planning Theory, legal systems are enterprises for solving moral problems. Legal planners assign roles to actors with the understanding that their contributions will advance the fundamental aim of the law. I suggest proper interpretive methodology is determined not only by the level of trust accorded actors, but by their roles as well. An interpretive methodology is proper for an interpreter in a given legal system just in case it best furthers the objectives actors are entrusted with advancing, on the supposition that the actors have the competence and character imputed to them by the designers of their system.

On the Planning Theory, the meta-interpreter must complete three tasks. First, she must ascertain the basic properties of various interpretive methodologies. She must attempt to discover, for example, whether certain methodologies require a great deal of expertise to implement or comparatively little, and whether they are easy to abuse or hard to manipulate. Second, the meta-interpreter must attempt to extract certain information from the institutional structure of the legal system in question: the planners' attitudes regarding the competence and character of certain actors, as well as the objectives that they are entrusted to promote. Finally, the meta-interpreter should apply the information culled from the first two tasks in order to determine the proper interpretive methodology. She must ascertain which interpretive methodologies best further the extracted objectives in light of the extracted attitudes of trust.

Corresponding to these three tasks are three basic stages of meta-interpretation, which I will call "specification," "extraction," and "evaluation." In each stage, the meta-interpreter attempts to answer the following questions:

1. *Specification*—What competence and character are needed to implement different sorts of interpretive procedures?
2. *Extraction*—(a) What competence and character that the planners believed actors possess led them to entrust actors with the task that they did? (b) Which systemic objectives did the planners intend various actors to further and realize?
3. *Evaluation*—Which procedure best furthers and realizes the systemic objectives that the actors were intended to further and realize, assuming that they have the extracted competence and character?

Specification

Meta-interpretation can only proceed on the supposition that there are nontrivial differences between at least some interpretive methodologies.

The Planning Theory locates these distinguishing characteristics, in large part, in the diverse intellectual and moral demands that methodologies place on interpreters. Different interpretive procedures require for their implementation different types of competence and character, or require the same capacities but to a lesser or greater extent.[2]

In attempting to isolate the prerequisites of any methodology, the meta-interpreter must draw on his judgments about the knowledge, skill, talent, temperament, and personality demanded by certain intellectual operations. Questions that meta-interpreters must ask themselves include: what type and level of expertise are needed to successfully implement a given procedure, how difficult is it for others to detect mistakes or abuse, and which methodologies create the appearances of improprieties even where none exist. In answering these questions, the meta-interpreter must always keep the institutional context in view. An interpretive methodology that would require a great deal of probity to implement successfully in one context might, in another context, require very little. Thus, the meta-interpreter might predict that even an untrustworthy person would scrupulously follow a highly discretionary methodology in the presence of mechanisms that seek to check and control abuses of discretion.[3]

Meta-interpretive battles are often fought and won at the specification stage. Insofar as it is easier to justify a less demanding methodology, advocates of particular hermeneutical styles tend to minimize, while critics emphasize, the degree of competence and character needed for successful implementation. Purposivists, for example, have consistently played down the risk of manipulation and self-deception associated with the search for legislative intent. Justice Reed went so far as to claim that the "lively appreciation of the danger" that interpretation "will be unconsciously influenced by the judges' own views"[4] would significantly reduce such a threat. In other cases they have recognized the dangers posed by liberal construction and have advocated the use of additional evidence of intent, most notably legislative history, in order to constrain judicial discretion. Requiring courts to justify their interpretations by reference to the hard facts of legislative history, they argued, would prevent judges from dressing up their own policy views in the garb of legislative intent. "Strong judges are always with us," James Landis, an early proponent of legislative history, admitted. "But the effort should be to restrain their tendencies, not to give them free rein. . . ."[5]

Modern textualists, by contrast, have mocked these judgments as psychologically and politically naive. According to Easterbrook, "The number of judges living at one time who can, with plausible claim to accuracy, 'think [themselves] . . . into the minds of the enacting legislators and imagine how they would have wanted the statute applied to the bar,' may be counted on one hand."[6] The use of legislative history as a constraining device has also been subject to scathing criticism. Textualists believe that, rather than constraining judges, legislative history merely gives judges another avenue by which to confirm their own subjective political preferences. As Justice Scalia has expressed this view: "[T]he manipulability of legislative history has not *replaced* the manipulabilities of these other techniques; it has *augmented* them."[7]

Extraction

Extraction as Explanation

Once the intellectual and ethical prerequisites of various interpretive methodologies have been ascertained, the meta-interpreter must assess whether, from the system's point of view, interpreters and other actors have the competence and character needed to implement these methodologies effectively. According to the Planning Theory, the systemic view of trust is determined by the attitudes of trust held by the current legal planners. Consequently, the meta-interpreter must seek to unearth the attitudes about appropriate trust embedded within the system's institutional arrangements.

Extraction, on this model, is essentially an explanatory process. The meta-interpreter attempts to show that a system's particular institutional structure is due, in part, to the fact that those who designed it had certain views about the trustworthiness of the actors in question and therefore entrusted actors with certain rights and responsibilities. The views extracted through this practice are those that best explain the construction and adoption of the *texts* that guide the practice, for it is these actions that create the rules. The Planning Theory thus contrasts markedly with Dworkinian meta-interpretation, in that it makes no attempt to justify morally the principles derived from the legal texts. It is enough to show that they explain the shape that the practice currently takes.

The term "extraction" itself is meant to highlight a crucial fact about the relevance of designers' attitudes: their views on the trustworthiness of actors are legally significant only insofar as they played a causal role in the actual design and adoption of the authoritative texts. Not every judgment about appropriate trust that the planners of a system harbor, therefore, is relevant to meta-interpretation. The mere fact that the designers are trusting souls is immaterial—if these judgments do not embed themselves within the institutional structure of the system through the formulation and adoption of the authoritative texts, they are, legally speaking, irrelevant.

Before we proceed, several qualifications are in order. Recall that legal activity is the activity of social planning, and that the results of social planning are normally publicly accessible. It follows, then, that if the content of the law is to be determined ultimately by designers' judgments, these judgments must themselves be publicly accessible. Purely private thoughts, therefore, cannot count as meta-interpretive determinants.

Judgments of trust can be made publicly accessible in many ways. The most obvious manner is through explicit expression. The designer might have made a statement that the measure will be, is, or was supported for thus-and-so reason. Expression can also be implicit, as when a designer votes for a measure containing a statement about the justifications for the regulation. Or the designer's judgments of competence and character might be revealed simply by voting for a certain measure, much as one's desire for a beer is revealed in the act of ordering a beer at a bar. Thus, drafting or voting for a bill that is extremely comprehensive and detailed, containing directives with few moral concepts and whose violation is met with severe sanctions, would bespeak a distrustful attitude on the part of legislators. Similarly, the act of framing and ratifying a centralized constitution with broad grants of power to actors who will engage in top-down social planning indicates a trusting attitude on the part of constitutional designers toward those authorized to act.

It should also be noted that during extraction the meta-interpreter always seeks to uncover *common* attitudes of trust. Insofar as legal design is often the product of shared agency, it is unlikely that each participating designer will hold precisely the same attitudes about the trustworthiness of actors. It seems reasonable to assume, for example, that the framers did not all come to their Radical Whiggism for the same reasons. Some distrusted human nature due to personal experience,[8] others because of their Calvinist background,[9] and still others because it was the orthodoxy of the day.[10] What matters in meta-interpretation, however, is that they all held attitudes of distrust, although for different reasons, and that these attitudes were causally responsible for their official actions.[11]

The meta-interpreter must be alert to the possibility, however, that the designers of a legal system shared no common vision of trust, or that the vision that they shared is so general that it rules out only the most bizarre interpretive methodologies. In such cases, a meta-interpretive theory has little to say so far as questions of trust are concerned. Fortunately, trust is not the only meta-interpretive determinant and, as we will see later on, a meta-interpretive theory might still issue in a unique recommendation even though issues of trust do not play a role.

Absolute vs. Relative Judgments

During extraction, it is crucial for the meta-interpreter to differentiate between several types of judgments about actor trustworthiness. The most important distinction is between absolute and relative judgments. An "absolute" judgment of trustworthiness concerns an individual's level of confidence in the competence or character of another. A "relative" judgment of trustworthiness, on the other hand, concerns the level of confidence in the competence or character of another *as compared to* some third person. Negative absolute judgments about someone's abilities are thus compatible with positive relative judgments about those abilities when assessed against another, less capable individual. I have very little confidence in my ability to hit a home run against a major league pitcher. But I have much greater confidence in my ability to hit a home run against a major league pitcher when compared to my three-year-old daughter's chances of doing the same.

When the designers of a system allocate authority to an individual based on positive absolute judgments of that person's trustworthiness, I will say that the system places a "high absolute trust" in that individual. Allocations that are premised on negative absolute judgments place "low absolute trust" in that individual. Similarly, when designers of a system allocate significantly more (less) authority to one individual than another, we will say that the system places a high (low) relative trust in that individual as compared to the other.

When examining a legal system, the meta-interpreter should be careful not to infer that the system places high absolute trust in certain individuals from the simple fact that they are the recipients of broad grants of power. The grant might simply indicate a significantly higher degree of confidence in the grantee relative to other actors in the system. That the federal government was given great powers in the Constitution, for example, did not indicate that the founders held especially positive absolute judgments of human nature. Rather, it manifested precisely the opposite: because the electorate was distrusted, it was thought that authority should be transferred from the main locus of their power, that is, the state governments, and distributed to a different set of institutions. To some extent, the federal government was accorded a higher relative trust than the states, in part because it was thought that the national government would be manned by a higher caliber of politician. However, the marginal confidence in elites was not immense, as evidenced by the numerous limitations and safeguards placed on federal power by the framers. The moral here is that high relative trust is compatible with low absolute trust and vice versa.

General vs. Particular Judgments

The meta-interpreter must also distinguish between general and particular judgments about trustworthiness. General judgments about trustworthiness relate to the basic psychological nature of individuals: their intelligence, drives, character, and so forth. Particular judgments, by contrast, concern particular actions in particular settings. Positive general judgments are compatible with negative particular judgments. Someone might believe that judges are in general very smart and honorable, but that they are not particularly good economists. Likewise, someone can trust another with respect to one action in one setting, but distrust him with respect to some other action in the same or in another setting. The head of the FDA might be trusted to oversee the testing of pharmaceuticals, but not to allocate the electromagnetic spectrum for communication purposes.

The meta-interpreter must be on guard for the possibility that a change in setting will challenge the relevance to meta-interpretation of particular judgments of trustworthiness. For example, in the late eighteenth and most of the nineteenth century, American courts generally followed the English "no recourse" rule and eschewed legislative history when construing statutes.[12] Because detailed records of legislative procedures were not kept, and because judges were no longer involved in the legislative process, it was thought that they could not be relied upon to use the existing legislative materials. However, when legislatures began keeping extensive records and printing technology improved their accessibility, judges were no longer distrusted in this regard.[13] A late nineteenth-century meta-interpreter could have justifiably concluded that, given the high absolute trust placed in the intelligence and training of judges and the increased availability of dependable records, the particular distrust of courts with regard to legislative history should no longer be credited in meta-interpretation.[14]

Scope of Extraction

In order to preserve the modesty of proper meta-interpretation, the Planning Theory does not demand that each meta-interpreter engage in a massive unearthing of the entire institutional structure. Before extraction can begin in earnest, the meta-interpreter must first figure out which parts of a system's trust economy should be targeted for extraction. Unlike Dworkin's account, which requires *every* meta-interpreter to survey the *entire* legal system and determine the *complete* set of moral principles that best fit and justify the system before interpretive methodology can be ascertained, the Planning Theory requires each meta-interpreter to assess initially whether to limit himself to his institutional neighborhood or go substantially beyond his location in the system's trust economy. The scope of extraction is determined by the particular judgments of trust that underlie the meta-interpreter's role: roughly speaking, the greater the trust, the greater the scope of extraction. Thus, it is plausible to claim that police officers should not consider delicate issues of constitutional structure when determining how to interpret the laws they are applying. A police officer usually confronts only a small part of the overall regime and it would not be expected that he fully understand the basic principles animating the system and how such principles interact with his particular role in the practice. For him, issues of trust that touch his particular station, despite their peripheral status, would have greater relevance than core issues with which he has little contact. Federal judges, by contrast, play a central role in the management of the system. They are required to understand how the overall system works and how the various rules relate to one another. For them, the meta-interpretive perspective stretches across the entire institutional landscape.

By using the term "extraction," I do not mean to suggest that the meta-interpreter must derive the designers' views solely by examining the texts that set out the structure of the legal system. In many instances, their views will be obvious. The bailiff knows that the designers of the system trust the judge more than him; he need not (and should not) consult the Constitution or the Federalist Papers for confirmation. But in other situations, more detailed historical investigation will be warranted. As I argued in connection with Dworkin's theory, historical evidence confirms what a rational reconstruction of the American system would suggest, namely, that the designers of the early American republic were concerned about the trustworthiness of officials and citizens and fashioned the core constitutional principles so as to reflect these attitudes. In extracting the planners' attitudes about trust, transcripts of public debates, and cultural works that shed light on the zeitgeist usually provide invaluable assistance in reconstructing a system's economy of trust.

Synthesis

There is one sense, though, in which the term "extraction" is apt to mislead. Because legal systems are built and rebuilt over time, usually by the hands of many individuals, it would be extremely surprising to find a coherent set of views about trust underlying the totality of the legal texts. As a general matter, the task of the meta-interpreter is not merely to *recover* these disparate attitudes of trust but also to *synthesize* them into one rational vision. Thus, a system's economy of trust is constructed during meta-interpretation, not simply found. I would therefore like to conclude this section by saying a few words about the principles that should govern this synthesis—although, given space constraints, my discussion will be considerably limited and speculative.

As in ordinary conflict-of-law situations, source is the most important determinant for the ordering of trust judgments. In systems where constitutional law takes precedence over statutory law, judgments of trust that underwrite constitutional provisions trump disparate judgments that underlie statutory texts. In systems such as the American one, then, judges usually need go no further than an examination of the Constitution, for any judgments extracted from these fundamental provisions will take precedence over all others.

Difficulties arise, however, when disparate judgments emerge from sources of the same rank. Consider, for example, the conflict that arises between the Fourteenth Amendment and the preceding amendments to the U.S. Constitution. The first amendments were originally predicated on certain positive relative judgments of trustworthiness of the states vis-à-vis the federal government. The basic idea animating the constitutional structure was that state legislatures are more competent than Congress to promote the general welfare of their citizens, given their better access to information and more responsive political base, and are less likely than Congress to infringe basic liberties, given their relative lack of power. As a result, the states were permitted to retain their police power and were exempted from the Bill of Rights. Congress, on the other hand, was empowered to act only in those situations in which collective national action was deemed superior to individual state action, and prohibited from legislating in a way that violated certain basic rights.

The Fourteenth Amendment was based on a different, and conflicting, set of relative judgments. Insofar as traditional attitudes toward the trustworthiness of the state legislatures and their ability to protect basic liberties could no longer be maintained after the Civil War, the Fourteenth Amendment not only imposed substantive limitations on state legislation through the Equal Protection Clause, but also empowered Congress to protect equality and other constitutional rights through federal legislation. The Fourteenth Amendment thus assumes attitudes of trust that are contradicted by the attitudes of trust that underlay the first twelve amendments. How should such conflicts be resolved?

My suggestion is that we approach the synthesis of conflicting trust judgments in roughly the same manner that philosophers of science treat the revision of inconsistent theories.[15] For example, when a scientist faces highly credible evidence that contradicts an accepted theory, she will be forced to adjust her theory in light of the recalcitrant data. The generally accepted method in the philosophical literature for synthesizing these conflicting elements is called "minimal" revision: the scientist ought to give up as little of the theory as possible in order to achieve consistency. Thus, the scientist should attempt to retain the central premises of the theory—the "hard core" in Lakatos's helpful terminology[16]—but jettison more peripheral elements in order to reestablish consistency. It may not, of course, be possible to keep the hard core intact, in which case certain central elements will have to be revised away. But in most situations, such revolutionary change will not be necessary, and adjustment of more marginal elements will ensure a consistent synthesis.

Analogously, we can treat the trust attitudes underlying a system's institutional arrangements as a "theory of trust." This theory sets forth various hypotheses concerning the general competence and character of individuals and how particular settings affect their trustworthiness. When a revision of a legal system injects conflicting trust judgments into this "theory," the meta-interpreter should then engage in minimal revision: she should synthesize judgments of trust by holding the most recent judgments fixed and revising the earlier judgments as little as possible so as to render them consistent. Hence, in the above example, the attitudes associated with the Fourteenth Amendment would be held constant, while the judgments associated with the first twelve amendments would be minimally revised so as to ensure consistency. A plausible revision, therefore, would be that the state legislatures are deemed more trustworthy than Congress to provide for the general welfare of their citizens, but not to protect their basic liberties.[17]

On this reading, the ratification of the Fourteenth Amendment brought about a major "redistribution" in the American economy of trust. Trust was redistributed from the states to Congress, such that the federal government, not the states, was now entrusted with the responsibility for protecting the people's basic rights. One might also plausibly argue that the Fourteenth Amendment brought about a fundamental realignment in the trust relations involving Congress and the federal courts. Whereas Congress had previously been seen as the chief threat to liberty, and the courts as the principal bulwark against congressional malfeasance, the new regime accorded equal trust to Congress and the courts to protect basic constitutional liberties. As Doug Laycock has argued, "Congress did not entrust the fruits of the Civil War to the unchecked discretion of the Court that decided Dred Scott v. Sanford. . . . The amendments vested independent responsibility for enforcing the new rights in both Congress and the courts."[18] The meta-interpretive upshot of this synthesis would be that, in addition to the Court, Congress has the independent authority to interpret the scope of constitutional liberties through their Section 5 enforcement power. According the Court exclusive authority to interpret the Constitution for the other branches of government would thus be inconsistent with the post–Civil War economy of trust.[19]

Objectives

After extracting the trust attitudes of legal designers, meta-interpreters are charged with extracting the objectives that various actors are entrusted with serving. This extraction is accomplished in much the same way as before: the meta-interpreter seeks the best explanation for why legal texts assign certain individuals certain tasks.[20] Again, it is not necessary for the meta-interpreter to show that these objectives are morally worthwhile from the God's-eye point of view—as long as the designers of the system have parceled out rights and responsibilities so that individuals will achieve certain ends, those ends are the only ones relevant in determining interpretive methodology.

When the meta-interpreter is a legal official, extraction will focus on her role. She will, in other words, set out to determine what part she has been meant to play in the shared activity of social planning. Sometimes the role of the officials is quite clear. The bailiff is supposed to keep order in the courtroom. Other times, the objectives that an official is meant to serve can be quite controversial. What, for example, is the role of the judge in a democratic society? Is it to implement the will of the people, protect minority rights, promote social justice, collaborate with the legislature, police the legislature to ensure it does not tamper with political representation, enforce interest group bargains, adjudicate disputes, or some combination thereof? Different people answer these questions differently—which, as we will see, has important implications for meta-interpretive debates.

Just as modesty demands that judgments of trust determine the scope for extracting the economy of trust, it likewise demands that they be employed to delimit the boundaries for extracting the objectives that legal actors are required to serve. How deep and wide a meta-interpreter should look when extracting objectives depends on the degree of trust otherwise accorded the interpreter by the system. The prison guard need not understand the ultimate goals that he serves by doing his job, whether it is to punish the wicked, deter crime, implement the democratic will, or enrich those who build prisons. He is trusted to perform only certain limited tasks and therefore should concentrate solely on the relatively specific goals associated with his role, such as to foil escapes and protect prisoners from each other. On the other hand, those accorded greater trust, such as judges, high-ranking executive officials, and legislators, should plumb the constitutional texts and extract the more general and distal goals associated with their powerful positions within the system.

Judgments of trust will have the greatest impact on the scope of extraction for ordinary citizens. For it would clearly exceed the competence of nonprofessionals to consider all of the goals and values that the legal texts regulating their conduct aim to serve and realize. In some cases, of course, the aim of the law is obvious. The rules regulating motor vehicle use are clearly designed to improve safety (although that is not all that they are designed to achieve). In other areas of regulation—taxes, securities regulation, sales law, product liability—the objectives are much less transparent, and frequently complicated. Comprehensive extraction of the system's total set of plans by laypersons would, thus, be inconsistent with most economies of trust.

Evaluation

Because the Planning Theory treats legal systems as planning systems that are designed to achieve certain political and moral ends, it ranks interpretive methodologies according to their capacities to advance those ends. In assessing their potential, though, the Planning Theory adds a crucial proviso: it insists that the evaluation of methodologies be conducted against the background of trust extracted from the current institutional arrangements. An interpretive methodology is appropriate for an interpreter just in case it best furthers the goals that legal actors are entrusted with advancing *on the supposition that* the interpreter and certain other actors have the extracted competence and character.

To evaluate interpretive methodologies, the meta-interpreter engages in a thought experiment: for any given methodology, she imagines what the world would be like if the interpreter claimed to be following the methodology when interpreting legal texts *and* possessed the competence and character that the designers attribute to him as well as to others. Worlds where, say, interpreters claimed to be using highly discretionary procedures, but were very untrustworthy, would be ones in which these procedures were usually flouted. Other worlds, where trustworthy interpreters claimed to be using constraining procedures, would be ones where these procedures were routinely and faithfully implemented.

While engaging in this thought experiment, the meta-interpreter grades interpretive methodologies according to their performance in the imagined circumstances. Methodology M ranks above methodology N just in case the goals that legal actors are entrusted with advancing are better served in the imagined circumstances when M is claimed to be followed than when N is claimed to be followed. The interpretive methodology that is ranked highest when all methodologies are considered is the correct one for the particular legal system. In the case of ties, the procedures that rank highest are all deemed correct and, to the extent that they give different results, the law is indeterminate at these conflicting points.

Relations between Trust and Discretion

The method of evaluation I have just described is completely general: it can be used to evaluate any methodology in any authority system and for any actor within that system. In this section, I would like to explore some of the relations that hold between appropriate methodology and certain subsets of authority systems and legal actors. This will, hopefully, illuminate important connections that obtain between a system's economy of trust and the proper allocation of interpretive discretion.

In general, systems of *low absolute* trust are incompatible with *highly discretionary* interpretive procedures. This relation obtains for the following reason: worlds in which untrustworthy individuals claim to be using highly discretionary interpretive methodologies are ones in which these procedures will not be followed and, hence, will not serve a useful function. This is most clearly true for systems whose goals include the protection of liberty and autonomy. Worlds in which corruptible individuals use manipulable procedures are ones in which they will interpret the law to their own liking. The ends of liberty and autonomy will not be met because the law will be incapable of protecting citizens against abuse by officials.

While regimes of low absolute trust rule out highly discretionary procedures, it should not be assumed that these systems require highly *constraining* interpretive methods. High relative trust, despite low absolute trust, might actually support a significantly discretionary methodology. To show this, I would like to consider John Manning's attempt to demonstrate that textualism was the most appropriate interpretive methodology for the early American constitutional structure. As I will argue, his argument for constraint in interpretation does not succeed, as he focuses on absolute trust at the expense of relative trust.

Manning begins his meta-interpretive argument by pointing out that the American system was constructed on the basis of a sharp separation between legislative and judicial power. The aim in separating powers, according to Manning, was both to increase predictability and decrease official discretion. History had shown the founders that when powers are commingled, legislators could not be trusted to enact clear rules, given their incentive to reserve discretion for the future; nor could they be relied upon to follow those rules that they did enact, given their interest in revising any rule yielding an undesirable consequence. It would make little sense, Manning concludes, to distrust judges with the power to make law while at the same time trusting them with the discretion to interpret the law in accordance with their conception of equity and reason.[21]

Although Manning has produced a meta-interpretive argument of the right form—he explicitly links appropriate interpretive method to systemic trust and roles—his conclusion may be doubted for his failure to consider all of the relevant premises. As I have argued, the meta-interpreter must consider judgments of *relative,* as well as *absolute,* trustworthiness in assessing a system's economy of trust. While it is true that the American constitutional order is built on a distrustful view of human nature, it does not follow that everyone is distrusted to the same extent. As the history of the framing of the Constitution shows, the movement toward judicial independence in the late 1780s was precipitated by a sharp increase in the trust awarded judges relative to legislators, inasmuch as judges were seen as having better technical legal skills and as not facing the same pressures from constituents to act in derogation of common law rights. This increase in the relative trust of judges not only resulted in the creation of an independent judiciary but also fueled the greater acceptance of purposive interpretation. Courts were now thought capable of correcting the errors of legislatures, both by narrowing poorly drafted and highly unjust legislation and by extending statutory language to cover unanticipated situations in a small range of cases.[22] The New Jersey Supreme Court description of its approach to statutory interpretation was typical: "We do not consider ourselves bound by the strictly grammatical construction of the words of the act. The intention of the legislature should be our guide; or, rather, in a case of this nature, we should not hesitate to adopt a construction which the words will clearly warrant, free from the inconveniences which must flow from other interpretation."[23]

Manning's meta-interpretive mistake thus lies in his concern with absolute trust and disregard of relative trust. While highly discretionary modes of interpretation, such as Dworkinian ones, are ruled out by low absolute trust, it does not follow that highly constraining methods, such as textualist ones, remain the only viable options. Even if all officials are distrusted, law creators may be more distrusted in certain ways than law-appliers, and thus it will be appropriate to accord the latter significant discretion in interpretation.

Just as high relative trust will normally sanction a significantly discretionary interpretative methodology, low relative trust normally suggests a highly constraining one. The deference that is normally shown administrative agencies in statutory interpretation is justified, at least in part, by the greater experience and expertise of administrative agencies as compared to courts with respect to the underlying issues at stake.[24] Provided that courts find an agency interpretation reasonable and based on the relevant considerations, they will inquire no further into its appropriateness and acquiesce. Likewise, juries are required to defer to the interpretation of the law given by trial courts, given the comparative expertise of the court over the lay juror.[25]

Discretion, Text, and Purpose

In the previous section, I argued that actors who enjoy high relative trust should normally be accorded significant discretion in interpretation. It is important, however, not to conclude from this that high relative trust compels *purposive* interpretation. While purposive interpretation is significantly discretionary, not all significantly discretionary methods of interpretation are purposive. One might plausibly argue, for example, that even if judges are thought to be better lawyers than legislators and more likely to act in the public interest, they should still not look to purpose when interpreting legislative texts. To see why this might be so, I would like to consider the argument made by Frank Easterbrook, who, drawing on the results of public choice theory, has argued for a discretionary, but textualist, interpretive methodology.

According to the familiar public choice story, legislation is a good that is subject to the laws of supply and demand. Legislators will supply legislation to those who are most willing to pay for it, where payment generally takes the form of monetary contributions to reelection campaigns. Given collective action problems, however, the public usually will not demand legislation that is broadly redistributive in nature. The larger the group, the less each individual benefits from such redistribution, and hence the less interest each individual has in paying for such a benefit. Only small interest groups are capable of mobilizing forces to overcome such free riding problems, thus ensuring that they, and not the public at large, will capture the economic rents that come from legislation.

Public choice theory predicts not only that legislators will succumb to the siren song of special interests, but also that legal systems will be designed so as to shield courts from similar pressures. Legislation is valuable to interest groups only if courts enforce it. If courts were subject to political influence by interest groups, however, they would enforce legislation only when supportive interest groups were ascendant; as soon as these groups lost power, the benefits of legislative redistribution would vanish. An independent judiciary is essential to interest group politics, on this picture, because independence ensures the durability and hence value of legislation. Courts must be "above politics," in other words, if politics is to flourish. Indeed, some public choice theorists, such as William Landes and Richard Posner, argue that the best explanation for why the framers drafted Article III, which rendered the judiciary independent through the granting of life tenure and protection against salary reduction, was to provide for predictable long-term enforcement of interest-group bargains, thereby maximizing the value of legislative enactments for these constituencies.[26]

Although the constitutional structure, on the public choice explanation, is designed to establish the durability of private-interest legislation, it is also meant to reduce the rent seeking that will inevitably take place. According to Easterbrook, for example, the constitutional requirements of bicameralism, presentment, and publication exist in order to constrain Congress by cutting down on the amount of legislation and by driving "bargains into the open where they may be scrutinized."[27]

Notice that on this public choice "extraction," the American economy of trust is quite distrustful of legislators. But the distrust here is directed to their *character*, not their competence: they are taken to be self-interested maximizers, not servants of the public interest. By contrast, the system places a significant degree of confidence in courts, for it entrusts them with the enforcement of interest group bargains. In keeping with this picture of judges, these accounts are often called "faithful" or "honest" agent theories of adjudication.

Easterbrook has argued for textualism on the basis of this public choice construal.[28] Purposive interpretation is a nonstarter, he claims, for such methodologies assume the existence of legislative purpose. Although legislators often present legislation as motivated by public-spirited considerations—concerns that could in principle be extrapolated to unanticipated cases—public choice theory predicts that statutes are much more likely to be the result of self-interest bargaining. Gaps in statutes are usually intentional; if the parties had reached an agreement on such cases, they would have included the terms of the bargain in the statute.[29] As Easterbrook explains, "Interest-group legislation requires adherence to the terms of the compromise. The court cannot 'improve' on a pact that has no content other than the exact bargain among the competing interests, because the pact has no purpose."[30]

Notice that Easterbrook's version of textualism, as opposed to Scalia's, accords judges wide discretion in construing statutes. This discretion rests primarily in the courts' responsibility to distinguish between statutes that were enacted pursuant to interest group bargaining and those that were truly public spirited. Judges are supposed to take a "beady-eyed" approach, scrutinizing statutes for the telltale signs of rent seeking. Legislation that is relatively detailed, erects barriers to entry, subsidizes one group by another, or prohibits private contracting in response to the new statutory entitlements indicates interest group activity. Easterbrook even advocates that courts make extensive inquiries into legislative history, a practice that is anathema to a Scalian textualist. He recommends that judges ask: "Who lobbied for the legislation? What deals were struck in the cloakrooms? Who demanded what and who gave up what?"[31]

Easterbrook opines that the behavior of judges will be "influenced, if not determined"[32] by their understanding of the sources and functions of legislation. "A judge who believes with New Dealers that markets are flawed and that 'experts' employed by the government can correct these 'imperfections' will take a path very different from that of a judge who believes that most legislation grows out of a struggle among interest groups to appropriate the benefits produced by other people."[33] The former will treat statutes as normally being premised on purposes that can be extended to unanticipated cases and will interpret them in such light; the latter will assume the worst and will usually stick to the written terms of the legislative contract.

It is hard to know whether Easterbrook means this to be a descriptive or a normative claim. If meant as a descriptive hypothesis, one might wonder how Easterbrook knows why judges actually adopt the interpretive methodologies that they do. Understood as a normative claim, though, it seems that Easterbrook is on surer footing. As I have argued, considerations of appropriate trust and purpose are the sorts of reasons that are proper to use when justifying meta-interpretive choice. If the aim of legislation is to cure market failures, and regulators are deemed to be experts in such matters, then one might conclude that purposive interpretation is proper. On the other hand, if the role of legislators is to capture economic rents and distribute them to those who most demand it, then textualist interpretation may be more appropriate.

Yet, it is important to note that Easterbrook's meta-interpretive claim is incomplete to the extent that he focuses exclusively on the function and capacities of legislators and ignores those of judges. If regulators indeed are experts in a certain field and judges are not, then perhaps the latter should not second-guess the texts that the former produce. Expert regulators, after all, are less apt to draft language that yields unreasonable results or that fails to anticipate many possibilities. The greater competence of regulators might then suggest textualism, not purposivism.

Conversely, even if legislators are not experts, but generally act as agents of interest groups, the pull toward textualism might still be resisted. For example, as Jonathan Macey has persuasively argued, the fact that legislators will tend to conceal their rent-seeking behavior behind a public-interest façade is the best reason for judges to take them at their word.[34] By interpreting legislation in accordance with the public-spirited purpose on the face of the legislation, courts will frustrate this political subterfuge, thereby forcing legislators to be more honest about their true motivations. The deficiency of legislative character would thus suggest purposivism, not textualism.

Cynical vs. Aspirational Textualism

As I have argued, the textualisms of Scalia and Easterbrook are both based on a cynical reading of the American economy of trust. Strict construction is appropriate, they claim, because certain officials are deemed to be deeply disingenuous. These textualists, however, part company in their assessment of the objects of distrust. For Scalia, the villain is the *willful judge;*[35] for Easterbrook it is the *rent-seeking* legislator. Accordingly, Scalia's textualism seeks to cabin judicial discretion; Easterbrook, on the other hand, seeks to increase it.

Not all forms of textualism are quite so cynical. The textualism of Akhil Amar, for example, is aspirational in nature. Amar argues that the function of the United States Constitution is to facilitate public discourse among free and equal citizens. The document is supposed to serve as a democratic "focal point," giving individuals a common language and framework within which to debate pressing political issues. Only an interpretive methodology that places an emphasis on the text, as opposed to technical legal doctrine, can fulfill this democratic mission. "Emphasis on the Constitution's writtenness—its general textuality and its specific textual provisions—has certain democratic virtues. The Constitution is a compact document that most Americans can read. With modest effort, even layfolk can become familiar with its words and basic layout. . . . The text of the document itself constitutes a democratic focal point—an open meeting hall, a common language—that can structure the conversation of ordinary Americans as they ponder the most fundamental and sometimes divisive issues in our republic of equal citizens."[36]

Amar, like Scalia and Easterbrook, bases his methodology on a certain lack of confidence in members of the community. But these doubts concern the citizenry, not officials, and are related to their competence, not their character. According to Amar, textualism is required because this method does not presuppose professional legal training—it is not "inherently exclusionary." The assumption here is that citizens will sincerely participate in public deliberation provided that the meaning of the Constitution is rendered sufficiently transparent to them.

These attitudes of trust can be seen to be presupposed by the text of the Constitution. As Amar points out, "[o]ur Constitution is written in remarkably compact prose. The full text, including amendments, runs less than 8000 words—a half-hour's read for the earnest citizen."[37] The fact that the Constitution is a "compact and concrete document,"[38] not a prolix legal code, would seem to imply that its framers deemed such a text appropriate to its readership, namely, "We the People."

Competition

As we have seen, attitudes of trust are extremely important in meta-interpretive debates. Meta-interpreters routinely inspect a system's economy of trust in order to determine appropriate interpretive methodology. If the relationship between planners and meta-interpreter is a trusting one, then increased discretion is inferred; the more skeptical it is, the greater constraint is deduced.

Trust attitudes are not, however, the only considerations that must be taken into account. The competitive relationship between social planners is itself a crucial meta-interpretive determinant. This is so because legal plans do not merely manage trust; they manage *conflict* as well. Plans, as we have noted before, are extremely useful tools for settling political disputes. When plans play a conflict-management function, I would now like to argue, the more competitive the planning relationship is, the more constraining the interpretive methodology; conversely, the more collaborative the exercise of social planning, the more interpretive discretion is warranted.

To see this, suppose a city council passes a ban on bringing dogs into restaurants. The regulation is motivated by numerous complaints of restaurateurs who think that the practice of bringing animals into food establishments is unsanitary and unappetizing. Since the members of the council agree with the restaurateurs on the merits, they unanimously approve a bill that states: "No dogs are permitted in restaurants."

Imagine that someone tries to bring his dog into a school cafeteria located in the city. The principal demands that the person leave with the dog, whereupon the dog owner sues the principal for violation of his civil rights. The question arises before the judge as to whether a school cafeteria is a "restaurant" within the meaning of the city regulation. Imagine further that the legal system in question is not a particularly distrustful one, so that there is no trust-based reason for denying judges interpretive discretion. A credible argument might then be made that the judge ought to interpret the regulation purposively. Since the ban was motivated by a belief that bringing dogs into eating establishments is both unsanitary and unappetizing, the purpose of the regulation would best be served by applying it to cover school cafeterias as well.

Now, change the example slightly. Suppose that opinion on the city council is split between those who believe that it is unsanitary and unappetizing to bring dogs into any establishment that sells food, including restaurants, supermarkets, and delis, and dog lovers who think that "Canine-Americans" have rights as well. Imagine further that a compromise is worked out where dogs are banned only from restaurants. In this revised scenario, the application of the prohibition to cafeterias would seem to be problematic. The aim of the regulation was not to improve the sanitary and appetizing conditions of all establishments that sell food. After all, the regulation that sought to serve that end was defeated. The ban, rather, was a compromise between two opposing forces. To apply the ban to school cafeterias would stretch the rule past the negotiated middle ground and hence unsettle the bargain.

Generalizing, we can say that the more competitive the process of social planning, the greater the pull of textualism. There are at least two reasons for this correlation. First, when planners are divided over goals and values, the settlements reached will likely be based on a very thin consensus on objectives. Indeed, the bargain may be grounded in no more than a common need to reach a deal. Without a thick set of purposes with which to work, purposive interpretation becomes unworkable. Second, in the absence of a wide and deep consensus on objectives, social planning cannot take a top-down approach. Lacking the resources to forge agreement on broad social policies, it must content itself with resolving local disputes.

To extend these local settlements in a more global fashion would therefore undo them. To move up the planning tree would permit one side greater power than it could have secured during social bargaining and hence would defeat the conflict-management function of the law.

In the previous section we saw these kinds of arguments deployed by Easterbrook. Easterbrook distinguished between rent-seeking and public-interest legislation and claimed that textualism is appropriate for the former given the competitive nature of the decision making. Jeremy Waldron has offered an argument in support of textualism for the latter cases as well.[39] Even when officials are eminently trustworthy and act for the "right" reasons, Waldron argues, the competitive nature of their deliberations compels a privileging of statutory texts in interpretation.

Waldron premises his arguments on a sophisticated reading of modern democratic legal systems. According to Waldron, democratic decision-making is best characterized as the quest for settlement in the face of pervasive disagreement. Despite widespread conflict concerning questions of justice, rights, and values, political actors must nevertheless decide how to act together. The institutions of democracy are designed to enable the representatives of these opposing positions to deliberate with one another and to forge a local consensus on matters of moral importance.

As Waldron points out, modern legislatures are large, multimembered chambers. They aim to represent a large array of political viewpoints and enable legislators to speak for diverse constituencies on important matters of public policy. And because political deliberation is not an intimate discussion among a small group of like-minded individuals, debates within these chambers are governed by formal rules of parliamentary procedure. These policies structure public deliberation, allowing large-scale discussions to take place. They determine how debates are initiated and concluded, who has the right to speak, who may interrupt, who sets the agenda and how to set it, when and how voting takes place, and so on.

In particular, Waldron emphasizes the role that "textuality" plays in parliamentary debate. In order to engage in a legislative discussion, a motion must be reduced to writing and introduced. A change to the resolution under discussion must be accompanied by a written amendment to the motion and offered up to the chamber for approval. Waldron argues that the textual nature of legislative motions is crucial for organizing large-scale conversations involving diverse viewpoints. Vague proposals may be appropriate for debate among small groups of like-minded individuals who understand each other. In the absence of shared understanding about political beliefs and values, however, making one's ideas explicit is crucial. "If any one says, in the rather cozy way that people have who share tacit understandings, 'Come on, you know what I mean,' the answer is likely to be: 'No, I don't know what you mean. You had better spell it out to me.' "[40]

Finally, majority decision making is necessary for any settlement of conflict in the midst of deep disagreement. For a consensus on normative issues is practically unattainable in deliberative environments where many different points of view are represented. As Waldron points out, majority voting is able to settle disputed matters of principle because it is a "content-independent" procedure. The winning proposition is one that is identified by counting heads, not by considering the very merits that formed the basis of the dispute.

Waldron argues that the structure of legislatures and political deliberation realizes a distinctive value of mutual respect. In modern democracies, opposition and conflict are not shoved under the rug. Disputes are aired before votes are cast. Moreover, majoritarian decision procedures do not discredit the losing parties. When a side does not prevail, members can at least take comfort in knowing that their views were accorded equal weight in the political calculus, and that their defeat was not a wholesale repudiation of their arguments and values. They might have lost a political battle, but they will live to fight another day. They can hope to muster better, more persuasive arguments for their position and sway enough to secure victory in the next dispute.

Waldron believes that these considerations strongly militate in favor of textualism. In an environment riven by deep divisions over principles of justice, fairness, and value, it is unlikely that consensus will form on purposes of individual items of legislation. Nontextual modes of interpretation require inputs that modern democracies simply do not and cannot produce. More importantly, to privilege the beliefs, values, intentions, hopes, and expectations of legislators is to ignore the importance that the text plays in settling conflict between opposing viewpoints. The textuality of legislation is necessary to ensure that all participants are on the same page. To depart from the common script is to disrespect the multiplicity of opinion and the techniques that democracies use to respond to that diversity.

Waldron's support for textualism is especially interesting from the perspective of the Planning Theory because he roots his meta-interpretive argument in considerations of institutional design. The respect for diversity supports textualist interpretation, in other words, not because it is an important value seen from the God's-eye point of view. Rather, as Waldron shows, textualism is presupposed by the very structure of legislatures and democratic deliberation, namely, in the size of their assemblies, the rules of parliamentary procedure, the textuality of resolutions, and majoritarian decision making.

We might recast Waldron's argument as follows: the rules of democratic institutions aim to settle the question of how we should settle our disputes. They demand that we do so in a respectful manner, by requiring that all views have a hearing, by not assuming that everyone "knows" the question under consideration, and by according everyone an equal say in resolving the dispute. And because the value of respect gives shape to democratic decision making, it must be respected when interpreting the rules made in a democratic fashion. For if we did not respect the textuality of law when interpreting it, the respect generated by the process of legislation itself would be lost or significantly diminished.[41]

The Possibility of Theoretical Disagreements

Let us return to Dworkin's challenge regarding theoretical disagreements. Is it really true that no positivistic theory can account for meta-interpretive disputes?

Before addressing this issue, notice that the meta-interpretive theory developed in this chapter shares many similarities with Dworkin's account of meta-interpretation. The Planning Theory concedes that the plain fact view, or any other account that privileges interpretive conventions as the sole source of proper methodology, ought to be rejected. Because theoretical disagreements abound in the law, interpretive methodology may be fixed in ways other than specific social agreement about which methodologies are proper.[42] The Planning Theory also agrees with Dworkin that when theoretical disagreements abound, ascertaining proper interpretive methodology involves attributing aims and objectives to the law. One cannot understand disagreements over interpretive methodology unless one sees them, at least in part, as disputes about the point of engaging in a particular practice of law. Finally, the Planning Theory maintains, with Dworkin, that in such cases proper interpretive methodology for a particular legal system is primarily a function of which methodology would best further the objectives that the system aims to achieve.

Here, however, the agreement ends. Although ascertaining interpretive methodology involves attributing purpose to legal practice, the Planning Theory, of course, does not treat this attributive process in a Dworkinian manner, namely, as an exercise in moral and political philosophy. The Planning Theory, rather, seeks *social facts*. That some set of goals and values represents the purposes of a certain legal system is a fact about certain social groups that is ascertainable by empirical, rather than moral, reasoning. Proper interpretive methodology is established by determining which methodology best harmonizes with the objectives set by the planners of the system in light of their judgments of competence and character.

A virtue of this type of proposal is that, insofar as interpretive methodology need not be determined by a specific convention about proper methodology, it is able to account for the possibility of theoretical disagreements. Participants in a practice can disagree over proper interpretive methodology because they disagree about whether their practice is best described as an authority or an opportunistic system, and hence to whose judgments they ought to defer. Even if they agree about the general nature of the practice, they can differ about any of the three steps of meta-interpretation. They might disagree about the demands imposed by particular methodologies, the ideological purposes of the system, its distribution of trust and distrust, or which methodology best harmonizes with such purposes and judgments of competence and character. In fact, this chapter has been filled with these sorts of disagreements.

Note further that this theory is positivistic. Because it takes a regime's animating ideology as its touchstone, this account may end up recommending an interpretive methodology based on a morally questionable set of beliefs and values. The legal system in question, for example, may exist in order to promote racial inequality or religious intolerance; it may embody ridiculous views about human nature and the limits of cognition. Nevertheless, the positivist interpreter takes this ideology as given, and seeks to determine which interpretive methodology best harmonizes with it.

As just mentioned, this account of legal interpretation is positivistic in the most important sense, namely, it roots interpretive methodology in social facts. That a legal system has a certain ideology is a fact about the behavior and attitudes of social groups. The account privileges social facts not out of fanatical desire to save positivism at all cost, but, as mentioned earlier, because the alternative is inconsistent with the logic of planning. Imputing to legal systems judgments of trustworthiness and political objectives that are morally justified undercuts the basic division of labor between those whose role it is to settle such matters and those whose role it is to implement such settlements.

It is possible, then, for the positivist to maintain that the grounds of law are determined by social facts *and* to account for theoretical disagreements about those very grounds, Dworkin's contention notwithstanding. The commitment to the social foundations of law, I have tried to show, can be satisfied in the absence of a specific convention about proper interpretive methodology just in case a consensus exists about the factors that ultimately determine interpretive methodology. In authority systems, the law will be grounded in social facts whenever there is a consensus among the bulk of the current officials concerning which texts are legally authoritative, as well as a consensus among those who created and adopted these texts about the competence and character of legal actors and the objectives they ought to pursue. The fact that interpretive methodology is determined by these factors not only renders theoretical disagreements possible but explains why such disagreements are so prevalent. For it is highly likely that meta-interpreters will disagree with one another about the content of the planners' shared understandings and which methodologies are best supported by them.

To be sure, it is a consequence of this approach that, in the absence of the relevant shared understandings, disagreements about proper interpretive methodology will be irresolvable. And even if shared understandings do exist, they may be quite thin and thus will provide neither side much leverage in interpretive debates. I do not think, however, that these implications undermine the solution I am offering to Dworkin's challenge. First, while thin shared understandings may not determine a unique methodology, they might nevertheless rule out certain interpretive stances. There may be no right answer to these disputes, but there are usually *wrong* ones. For example, I have argued that Dworkin's theory of law as integrity is inconsistent with the American economy of trust. I think similar claims could be made about Richard Posner's theory of legal pragmatism.

Second, as we saw in the previous section, extremely thin shared agreements may support particular interpretive methodologies. As Waldron argued, textualism seems appropriate for parties who face deep and pervasive disagreements on principles. For when there is no further purpose to the settlement of a dispute other than settling the dispute, the text will be the only thing they share and the only thing they have to go on when deciding on what to do.

Third, and more importantly, a theory of law should account for the *intelligibility* of theoretical disagreements, not necessarily provide a resolution to them. An adequate theory, in other words, ought to show that it makes sense for participants to disagree with each other about the grounds of law. Whether a unique solution to these disputes actually exists is an entirely different, and contingent, matter, and a jurisprudential theory should not, indeed must not, demand one just because participants think that there is one.

The Death Penalty Revisited

In Chapter 1, we noted that the constitutionality of capital punishment is hotly contested in the United States. This legal debate centers on the proper way to interpret the Eighth Amendment's "cruel and unusual" clause. Some believe the provision ought to be read in accordance with the intentions of those who framed it. Since the framers plainly did not regard the death penalty as cruel and unusual, they conclude it is constitutionally permissible. Others believe that the provision ought to be read literally: since "cruel" means cruel, and the death penalty is cruel and unusual, the death penalty is unconstitutional—the framers' intentions notwithstanding.

The Planning Theory helps explain why the interpretation of this clause is legally controversial. Suppose one thinks that the United States has an authority system. Imagine further that one believes that the framers and subsequent constitutional planners had a very distrustful opinion of human beings in general, and judges in particular. These Whiggish planners were skeptical of future generations and of people in positions of power, and designed a system to cabin their discretion. One might conclude from this economy of trust that judges ought to use interpretive methodologies that do not presuppose the very competence and character that the system's economy of trust presupposes they lack. Requiring judges to hew to the original intent of constitutional designers, the thought goes, will minimize the potential for judicial mischief. It will prevent judges from imposing their potentially faulty views on others, as well as restrict their ability to exploit textual vagueness for their own political ends.

Others might claim that the framers did not hold particularly distrustful views of human beings or judges. They might point out that the American system is a democracy that bestows sovereignty on "We the

People." Democratic systems place a significant degree of absolute trust in citizens insofar as they grant them ultimate political power. Moreover, the U.S. system is a constitutional democracy that grants life tenure and the power of judicial review to federal courts, an allocation of authority that bespeaks a fairly high degree of trust in judges as compared to the legislature. Finally, they might point out that the clause in question is fairly thin and vague. It is not a detailed and comprehensive list of prohibited punishments, nor does it prohibit those punishments that "we deem to be cruel and unusual." This high degree of trust placed in the courts relative to legislatures might suggest to them that courts should be permitted a fair degree of discretion when enforcing constitutional rights. When a legislature's conception of just punishment both is cruel and falls outside the range of accepted opinion, courts should be able to strike down such legislative actions.

These antioriginalists might also challenge the originalist's contention that the U.S. regime is an authority system. The text of the Constitution, they might point out, has been relatively stable for over two hundred years. Why would those who currently participate in the practice allow themselves to be governed by the "dead hand of the past"? It is more plausible, they might say, that current participants accept the constitutional system because they regard it as independently justifiable. If so, then the conception of cruelty held by those several centuries ago would hold little relevance to current legal decisions. Just as no one thinks that flogging is constitutional, despite the fact that the framers considered it neither cruel nor unusual, antioriginalists might rely on a shared understanding of the moral weight and content of the Eighth Amendment to argue that the death penalty is unconstitutional.

There is much more to say, of course, about the debate between originalist and antioriginalist methods of constitutional interpretation. My intention here has not been to exhaust every argument that either side might muster for their position, but rather to demonstrate that the Planning Theory has the resources to explain why the interpretation of this clause would be legally controversial. In a legal system as complex and old as the U.S. regime, there really is something for everyone. And the fact that decent meta-interpretive arguments can be made by both sides ensures that political controversies will also be expressed, as they so often are in the United States, in legal terms.[43]

Customary Legal Systems

Thus far, I have discussed how meta-interpretation should proceed in authority and opportunistic systems, regimes in which plans predominate. Not all laws are plans, however: customary rules, we have seen, are merely planlike. These planlike norms must be analyzed differently than plans, given that they can, and often do, arise unintentionally and hence are not created in order to manage trust. It might be thought, therefore, that legal systems whose rules are not purely the result of design, but often arise through customary means, might not have economies of trust. How, then, should interpretive methodology be determined in what I will call "customary" legal systems, namely, regimes in which customs predominate over self-conscious acts of social planning?

In answering this question, let us begin by reminding ourselves that although the fundamental aim of the law is to solve those problems that cannot be solved as efficiently by custom, tradition, persuasion, consensus, and promise, the law still ought to rely on such nonlegal means when doing so is more efficient than social planning. Thus, when custom furnishes better solutions than planning, or does so at a lower cost, legal systems should prefer to incorporate customary solutions over legislative ones. Accordingly, we can distinguish at least two reasons why custom is said to be superior to planning as a method for solving moral problems.

First, as Friedrich Hayek emphasized in his critique of planned economies, customary rules are often superior because they arise "from below," in a bottom-up fashion. As such, they are capable of evolving over time and adapting themselves to changed circumstances. Second, as Edmund Burke argued, customary practices are likely to be good practices because they have stood the test of time. The likelihood that generations have been wrong all along, and that some individual or group has finally discovered "the truth," should be severely discounted, both in theory and in practice.

Based on these justifications, we can define two ideal types of customary legal systems. In a Hayekian system, the bulk of officials believe that the outputs of customary processes ought to be followed because bottom-up decision making can solve moral problems better than top-down social planning. In a Burkean system, the bulk of officials believe that customs should be continued insofar as their persistence is strong evidence of their moral worth.

Once we focus on the accepted reasons for following legal customs, we can start to see how customary systems can have economies of trust. Hayekian and Burkean systems are distrustful systems, in that both take a jaundiced eye toward social planning. On their view, human beings are just not very good at self-consciously ordering the affairs of others. These suspicious economies of trust, therefore, would be inconsistent with interpretive methodologies, such as Dworkin's law as integrity, that are highly discretionary. To allow judges to interpret the law in accordance with extremely abstract and novel philosophical theories would presuppose the very competencies that Hayekian and Burkean systems disown.

While both of these systems are skeptical, their economies of trust are not identical. Hayekian systems look askance at top-down, centralized forms of social planning, while Burkean systems reject any form of revolutionary regulation. Because the objects of their distrust differ, each system favors different interpretive methodologies. For example, Hayekian systems reject methodologies that treat legal texts as exemplifying general principles and interpret their provisions so as to further the principles exemplified. Given its preference for bottom-up, case-specific forms of reasoning, the Hayekian economy of trust is inconsistent with purposive methodologies that broaden texts so as to further promote high-level legal principles. Burkean systems, on the other hand, favor methodologies that permit interpreters to depart from textual provisions so as to promote and realize principles that are supported either by the strongly rooted traditions of the culture or by other parts of the legal system.

14

THE VALUE OF LEGALITY

If you ever want to see a great philosopher in the flesh, go to London and take the Tube to Euston Square; upon leaving the station, take a left and walk down Gower Street to University College; enter the main building and ask a guard for directions to the South Cloister; proceed to the South Cloister and find a large wooden cabinet. In this cabinet, behind a plane of glass, you will find the great philosopher. He sits at his writing desk every day facing passersby. You are free to ask him any question you'd like. He is unlikely to respond, however, so don't take offense. He is, after all, dead and has been so for nearly two hundred years.

The philosopher in the box is none other than Jeremy Bentham, the father of modern legal positivism. In his will, Bentham bequeathed his body to his friend Dr. Southwood Smith, instructing Smith to dissect the cadaver before medical students and the general public; following the dissection and lecture on human anatomy, Bentham directed that his head be mummified, bones reassembled, and skeleton dressed in his clothes and perched on his usual chair at his usual writing desk with his usual walking stick "Dapple" at his side. He did not explain his reasons for this kooky plan, but they are not difficult to divine. Bentham was a paragon of the Enlightenment, passionately committed to scientific inquiry and firmly convinced of its potential for improving the human condition. Detesting the resurrectionists who opposed human dissection, he believed that people should give over their dead bodies to science. By displaying his preserved skeleton in public, he sought to demystify the body, and death itself, thereby helping to lift the shroud of superstition that religion had thrown over such natural phenomena.

Bentham took the same irreverent and unromantic attitude toward legal systems. He sought to demystify the law, exposing its irrational beliefs and rituals to the bright light of reason. As H. L. A. Hart has explained, Bentham's advocacy of legal positivism was a central element of this debunking strategy.

> Bentham contemplated and elaborately documented the abuses of the English law of his day, the fantastic prolixity and obscurity of its statutes, the complexity and expense of its court procedure, the artificiality and irrationality of its modes of proof. He was horrified by these things, but even more horrified by the ease with which English lawyers swallowed and propagated the enervating superstition that these abuses were natural and inevitable, so that only a visionary would dream of their radical reform. He believed that only those who had been blinded to the truth that laws were human artefacts could acquiesce in these absurdities and injustices as things to be ascribed to nature; and one way of opening men's eyes was to preach to them the simple but important doctrine that laws were but expressions of the human will. Law is something that men add to the world, not find within it.[1]

For Bentham, legal positivism is a liberating doctrine because it exposes the contingency and mutability of the law. Since the law is created by human activity, it could always have been created otherwise. Once this fact is appreciated, there will be no excuse for accepting the status quo. Since law is fixable, where it is broken, it ought to be fixed.

But for every legal positivist who regards his theory of law as therapeutic and progressive, there is a natural lawyer who sees it as desiccated and distorting. According to these critics, legal positivism is like Bentham's bequest, a well-intentioned idea taken to absurd extremes. In its zeal to demystify, even shock, it trivializes and transmogrifies. Natural lawyers regard legal positivism as a sort of philosophical taxidermy: it hollows out and drains the law of its moral guts and lifeblood, then wheels out and displays the stuffed mount as though it were the real thing.

In this concluding chapter, I examine two influential critiques of legal positivism posed by the theory of natural law. Each faults legal positivism for its austerity and neutrality; on their view, questions about what law *is* simply cannot be divorced from questions about what law *ought* to be. Addressing these concerns is important not only in order to defend the Planning Theory—which is also a demystifying theory of law—but also because it allows us to recapitulate certain aspects of the jurisprudential outlook developed in this book, and deepen others in the process.

Central and Peripheral Cases

Let us return one last time to our five-year-old child. Suppose she asks you to explain what a "theory" is. You respond by giving her a list of examples. You say that those who believe the Earth is flat have a theory of geography; those who think that the moon is made out of green cheese have a theory of astronomy; those who believe that the stork delivers babies have a theory of reproduction; and those who think that some numbers are luckier than others have a theory of probability.

Obviously, there is something wrong with your explanation. The problem is not its accuracy: after all, you have given her a list of genuine theories. Rather, the hitch is that by failing to provide any examples of *good* theories, you have omitted a crucial element of the definition; the theories you did mention, though genuine, are *faulty*. To explain the nature of a theory, in other words, one must make clear that a theory is supposed to be true. When a theory is true, it is successful; when it is false, it is defective. If you don't understand that a theory necessarily aims at the truth—an objective that it may or may not achieve—then you simply don't understand what a theory is.

As John Finnis has argued, legal positivists make the same basic mistake when providing an explanation of the nature of law. Whether trying to debunk the law's pretensions to authority, or constructing a general theory of law, legal positivists have spent an excessive amount of time focusing on morally inadequate systems and tailoring their theories to fit these regimes. Their obsession with the Nazis and the Problem of Evil, however, has blinded them to a basic jurisprudential truth: a wicked regime is a botched legal system, much as "the Earth is flat" is a failed scientific theory.

According to Finnis, one truly understands the nature of law only when one understands its moral point or purpose.[2] Legal regimes that satisfy this objective are the "central" or "focal" examples of what law is. Wicked regimes, on the other hand, fail to satisfy the objective that law is supposed to serve. They are, to use Finnis's terminology, "peripheral," "watered-down," or "borderline" instances of law; they are law only in a "sense," "manner of speaking," "qualified sense," or "extended sense."[3] Because legal positivists focus their energies almost exclusively on these watered-down versions, they neglect to see them as watered-down, as not *really* law.

There is much to be said in favor of Finnis's criticism of traditional legal positivism. Finnis is correct in pointing out that legal positivists have failed to appreciate the distinction between just and unjust legal systems. Positivists, of course, see that there is a difference between these kinds of regimes, but they think the difference is moral, not jurisprudential. They believe, in other words, that a theory about the nature of law cannot distinguish the unjust from the just system. Each is a genuine legal system, and there is nothing more to be said.[4]

In this respect, positivists are mistaken. As I argued in Chapter 7, it is part of the nature of law that law must conform to morality. Law has a moral aim; when it fails to satisfy this aim, the law fails by its own terms. Thus, when legal systems solve moral problems, we do not regard these events as happy accidents. In contrast to criminal organizations, whose moral benefits are purely adventitious, legal systems are supposed to produce such benefits. When they do, they fulfill their fundamental aim.

While Finnis is right to claim that there is a jurisprudential difference between just and unjust regimes, I believe that he mischaracterizes the distinction. He says that only just regimes can be ideal or central cases of law, whereas unjust regimes are, at best, peripheral, watered-down or borderline instances of law. But a regime is not peripheral, watered down, or borderline merely because it is unjust. An unjust regime that satisfies the identity conditions of legality set out in Chapter 7 is a genuine legal system that simply does not do what it is supposed to do. It differs from, say, the current Afghan government, which *is* a borderline legal system because of the weak hold it has on much of the territory over which it claims authority.

To use a well-worn analogy, unjust regimes are like broken clocks. Broken clocks are not diluted, peripheral, borderline clocks. They differ from merely decorative clocks, which do lie on the borderline of clockhood. Broken clocks are real, but defective, clocks. They do not do what objects of their type are supposed to do.

Finnis, it seems, has conflated two senses in which regimes that are just and satisfy the identity conditions of legality are central or ideal types of law. They are ideal in the sense of being pure, unadulterated, core instances of legal systems. To use Platonic terminology, they fully partake of the Form of Legality; in more modern language, they completely instantiate all of the essential properties of law. But these systems are also ideal in another sense: they are excellent and exemplary instances of law. They both fully possess the essence of law *and* do what things with that essence are supposed to do.

Because Finnis does not distinguish between these two senses of "ideal," he slides from the failure of an unjust system to be ideal in the second sense to a failure to be ideal in the first sense. From the fact that a regime does not do what it is supposed to do, he concludes that it is an impure, diluted, watered-down, borderline instance of law. This clearly does not follow. A defective instance of a kind is not ipso facto an attenuated version of its kind—it is not, again to use Platonic language, a mere shadow of the exemplary instances. Indeed, it is only because unjust legal regimes instantiate the property of legality that it makes sense to regard them as *unjust* (as opposed to merely being undesirable or evil).

A proper theory of law must not be so hard-boiled that it denies the jurisprudential significance of injustice; yet it must not be so starry-eyed that it exaggerates this significance. The Planning Theory tries to walk this line by affirming that it is part of the nature of law to have a moral aim, while at the same time denying that the failure to attain this end undermines the law's identity as law. Unjust systems have all the properties that make legal systems the things that they are, but they do not do what things of this sort are supposed to do. While they may be pure and unadulterated, they are nonetheless poor and defective.

The Rule of Plans

Perhaps the most famous assault on legal positivism was unleashed by Lon Fuller in his book *The Morality of Law*. He faulted legal positivists for ignoring the connection between the nature of law and the Rule of Law. By insisting that the existence of law is independent of moral facts, positivists fail to see that a regime would not be law if it consistently flouted the moral principles that constitute the Rule of Law.

To establish this claim, Fuller employed what might be called the Deconstructivist Strategy, namely, he tried to show the various steps one can take to *destroy* a legal system.[5] He began by imagining a regime headed by a well-meaning but hopelessly inept king named Rex. Rex believes that the regime he has inherited is antiquated and irrational, and wishes to engage in radical reform. Accordingly, he repeals all the laws of the old system and starts anew.

Because Rex finds it difficult to generalize, he decides against replacing the old set of rules with a new code of law. Rather, he resolves to solve each particular controversy as he sees fit. Unfortunately, Rex's plan causes great confusion. Because the citizenry cannot detect any pattern to Rex's decisions, they cannot predict how he will decide in any particular case. As a result, they clamor for Rex to develop a set of general rules by which their conduct will be judged.

Rex acquiesces and does his best to construct a comprehensive legal code containing numerous rules. However, he declines to make this code public. Needless to say, the citizenry are outraged by Rex's secrecy. Stunned by the fury his actions have caused, Rex acquiesces yet again and decides to promulgate a set of rules. The catch is that the rules to be applied will be determined after controversies have occurred. At the end of each year, Rex will publish a list of rules to be used when resolving the cases of the previous year. These rules will not be binding on controversies that arise in the future. The citizenry explain that rules are useful to them only when known *in advance.*

In order to accommodate their reasonable concerns, Rex decides to draft a public code of rules to be applied to future controversies. Once it is published, the citizenry study the new code, only to discover that its provisions are extremely obscure. Responding to public criticism for greater clarity and guidance, Rex revises this code with outside help. Unfortunately, the code's new provisions, while crystal clear, are massively contradictory. Another revision produces internal consistency but imposes requirements that are physically impossible to satisfy. Yet another change in the code produces a consistent, prospective, satisfiable set of rules. Regrettably, the drafting of this code takes so long that its regulations are seriously out of step with changes in social and economic conditions. In an effort to modernize the code, Rex amends its provisions daily.

Needless to say, these constant fluctuations make the task of planning everyday life extremely difficult for the citizens of the realm. Rex heeds their complaints and commits himself to keeping the code stable. While he keeps his promise and rarely amends the code, it turns out that the rules Rex does apply when deciding cases bear no relation to the code's provisions. As the citizens plot to remove Rex from his throne, the king dies, old before his time and deeply disillusioned with his people.

According to Fuller, Rex successfully destroyed the old legal system but failed to replace it with a new one. Each attempt fell short because it flouted a necessary requirement for the existence of law. A legal system cannot exist, according to Fuller, if it (1) lacks rules; (2) does not make its rules public; (3) drafts its rules obscurely; (4) engages in retroactive legislation; (5) enacts contradictory rules; (6) enacts rules that are impossible to satisfy; (7) constantly changes its rules; or (8) does not apply the rules it adopts.[6] Each of these failures constitutes the flouting of a general moral principle; as a group, these principles constitute the ideal known as the "Rule of Law." These principles require that legal standards be general, promulgated, clear, prospective, consistent, satisfiable, stable, and applied. While it is impossible, indeed undesirable, that each principle be fully satisfied by any legal system (imagine the deficiency of a legal system whose rules are so stable that they never change), the wholesale flouting of any particular principle results in the failure to create or maintain an existing legal system.

Fuller notoriously claimed that these principles constitute an "inner" or "internal morality" of law.[7] It is a *morality* on his view because its observance necessarily generates certain moral goods: any system that obeys the Rule of Law will provide its citizenry with a fair opportunity to obey the law. The morality is *internal,* rather than external, in that its value does not depend on the substantive political objectives that the rules aim to serve. According to Fuller, even wicked legal systems that obey such principles give their citizenry a reasonable prospect to comply, and thus to avoid being punished for disobedience.

From the fact that regimes that violate the Rule of Law are not legal systems, Fuller concluded that law and morality are necessarily connected. Rex's regime failed to attain legal status, on Fuller's view, because it failed to observe the moral principles whose satisfaction is necessary for law to exist. Contrary to legal positivism, therefore, the existence of the law does depend on moral facts.

Much ink has been spilled over the question of whether the principles Fuller identifies are best characterized as moral, and hence, whether he has discovered an important link between law and morality.[8] Although my sympathies lie with those who reject Fuller's characterization, I want to sidestep this thorny question. Instead, I would like to provide an alternative explanation for why Rex's regime is not a legal system. Its failure to attain the status of law, I maintain, has nothing to do with its inability to generate certain moral goods. Rather, it stems from the fact that regimes that flout these principles are simply not engaged in the basic activity of law: they are not engaged in social planning.

It is easy to see that Fuller's eight requirements are derivable from the Planning Thesis. The first two requirements—that laws must be general and public—follow immediately from the claim of the Planning Thesis that legal planning is social in nature. As I argued in Chapter 7, legal planning is social in the sense that it regulates the bulk of communal activity via general, publicly accessible policies. The next five requirements—that law must be clear, consistent, prospective, satisfiable, and stable—follow from the fact that planning is characterized by a set of associated dispositions. As I argued at the beginning of Chapter 5, planners are disposed to fill in their plans over time, to render plans that are consistent with one another and with their beliefs and to resist reconsidering their plans absent compelling reasons to do so. Finally, that legal officials must apply those rules that have been enacted follows from the fact that planning is a composite activity, involving not only plan adoption, but also plan application. If judges did not apply those rules created by the legislators, they would not be applying the plans adopted by the legislators, and hence would not be engaged in the same planning activity as other officials.

Rex did not destroy his legal system, therefore, because he was an unjust social planner, although his actions did cause significant injustice. Nor did he fall short because he was an inefficient social planner, though the means he chose fit poorly with the ends he sought to achieve. Rex was unsuccessful in his legal endeavors because *he was not a social planner at all.* He simply lacked the dispositions that human beings, as planning agents, normally possess. (Indeed, if the members of the Cooking Club acted as Rex did, there would be no club either.) The positivist, therefore, can agree with Fuller that observance of his eight principles is necessary for the existence of a legal system and yet deny that the existence of law depends on moral facts.

What Is the Value of Legality?

Once we appreciate that Fuller's eight principles state necessary conditions for the existence of social planning, their value becomes apparent. Let us begin by distinguishing the autonomous benefits of the Rule of Law from the instrumental ones. The autonomous benefits are those that arise from the mere observance of the principles, irrespective of the ends that the rules of the system in question aim to achieve. The instrumental benefits, on the other hand, are those generated exclusively from the fact that they enable individuals to achieve worthy ends.

Fuller's discussion highlights two important autonomous benefits of the Rule of Law. First, it enables members of the community to predict official activity and hence to plan their lives effectively. Second, the Rule of Law constrains official behavior and hence protects citizens from arbitrary and discriminatory actions by officials. These benefits arise because, as we have emphasized numerous times in this book, plans are capable of promoting predictability and accountability. Instead of guessing how officials will evaluate one's conduct, or worrying that they will lie about their evaluation, one can simply go about one's business, relying on the existence of a plan or policy.

Unfortunately, Fuller neglected to mention a third autonomous benefit that attends social planning, namely, the enormous cognitive energy saved by not having to think about the best way to regulate our lives and to convince others about the rectitude of our judgments. Even when the rules are misguided or corrupt, we are at least spared from having to deliberate and debate about what should be done.

It is a curious feature of much of the writing on this subject that it restricts itself to extolling the Rule of Law's autonomous benefits. One gets the sense that this political ideal is cherished simply because it allows us to stay out of court. These defensive accounts, however, neglect the Rule of Law's instrumental benefits. The Rule of Law is valuable not only because it allows *us* to plan our lives, but because it enables *the law* to plan our lives. The law is morally valuable, I have argued, because we face numerous and serious moral problems whose solutions are complex, contentious, and arbitrary. The only conceivable way for us to address these moral concerns is through social planning. Morally and prudentially speaking, we desperately need norms to guide, coordinate, and monitor our actions. If a regime did not normally produce standards that were general, promulgated, clear, prospective, consistent, satisfiable, and stable, and then did not apply them to cases that arose, it would not provide the guidance, coordination, and monitoring we need to solve the problems we ought to solve.

Consider, for example, the principle that Fuller describes as the essence of the Rule of Law, namely, the eighth requirement that officials apply the rules enacted. Imagine that officials were not required to apply the enacted rules, but were free to evaluate conduct in light of their best judgment. Clearly, such behavior is antithetical to a system of social planning. Plans are supposed to settle in advance what is to be done; if officials are not required to apply those norms they deem mistaken, then the norms cannot bring about the results that plans are designed to achieve.

The Rule of Law, we can say, is the Rule of Social Planning: its value derives entirely from the benefits that social planning generates and is best served when legal structures maximize these benefits. It should come as no surprise, therefore, that the Rule of Law is a perennial source of political contestation. When theorists disagree about the optimal form of social planning, they will disagree about the Rule of Law. Those, for example, who place great faith in social planning will regard centralized, comprehensive, codified, top-down, and directive-intensive statutory law as embodying the ideals of legality. They will look askance at the common law, perhaps agreeing with Bentham when he described it as "Dog law." "When your dog does anything you want to break him of, you wait till he does it, and then beat him for it. This is the way you make laws for your dog: and this is the way the judges make law for you and me. They won't tell a man beforehand what it is he *should not do* . . . they lie by till he has done something which they say he should not *have done,* and then they hang him for it."[9] By contrast, those who have great faith in spontaneous ordering and distrust social planning will likely take a kinder attitude toward the decentralized, bottom-up, authorization-intensive, and conservative approach of the common law. Thus, on Hayek's reckoning: "The freedom of the British which in the eighteenth century the rest of Europe came so much to admire was thus not, as the British themselves were among the first to believe and as Montesquieu later taught the world, originally a product of the separation of powers between legislature and executive, but rather a result of the fact that the law that governed the decisions of the courts was the common law, a law existing independently of anyone's will and at the same time binding upon and developed by the independent courts. . . ."[10]

It would be a mistake, I think, to interpret this dispute as a disagreement over the content of the Rule of Law.[11] The disputants agree that it is the ideal of rational social planning—they simply disagree over *how to engage in* rational social planning. For another example, consider the debate over judicial review and parliamentary supremacy. For many, review by an independent judiciary is the sine qua non of the Rule of Law.[12] A system whose courts do not have the power to check legislative and executive action, or are subject to political control, is one in which the law does not reign supreme. Others believe that judicial review by politically unaccountable courts is the antithesis of the Rule of Law, the very definition of the "rule of men."[13] This debate is nothing but a dispute over optimal institutional design. Both sides agree that accountability is necessary to safeguard against official misconduct; they simply disagree over which accountability mechanism is most efficient: interbranch competition or elections. Because the answers to such questions are not at all obvious, we should not expect debates about the Rule of Law to disappear any time soon.

Thinking Inside the Box

Though questions about optimal social planning are intensely controversial, legal systems simply cannot avoid them, for their task is precisely to engage in optimal social planning. Legal systems have no choice but to decide how to balance the needs for guidance, predictability, and constraint on the one hand against the benefits of flexibility, spontaneity, and discretion on the other. Legal systems, therefore, not only must heed the Rule of Law but also must have views about how the Rule of Law itself is best heeded.

One way of summarizing the argument of the last few chapters is to say that the Rule of Law is served only when those who engage in legal interpretation are faithful to the vision of the Rule of Law that the legal system presupposes and embodies. For it would undermine the role of law as a system of social planning if interpreters relied on their own ideas about how to balance freedom versus constraint when construing the authoritative texts. They must neither attempt to exercise competencies and other character traits that the system denies they have and for whose absence it seeks to compensate, nor deny themselves the use of capacities that the law assumes they possess and whose possession it wishes to utilize. They must not overstep their bounds and take on unassigned roles or attempt to further different objectives than they have been entrusted to serve. And they must not interpret in a collaborative mode when the envisioned political relationships are competitive, or act competitively when the relationships are collaborative.

The Rule of Law flourishes, therefore, only when legal interpreters possess a great deal of self-discipline. They must, in other words, resist the impulse to take legal interpretation as an invitation to philosophize about the great moral and political questions of their time. Instead, they must suspend their moral judgment and show fidelity to the legal point of view. To be able to think *inside* the box, we might say, is the ultimate passive virtue of the legal interpreter. For the logic of planning is respected only when the process of legal interpretation does not unsettle those questions that the law aims to settle.

To be sure, the fact that the law aims to settle questions about what is to be done does not imply that there will be agreement about what the law is. Indeed, I have claimed as a virtue of the Planning Theory its ability to account for the possibility, indeed the prevalence, of theoretical disagreements, thus answering Ronald Dworkin's critique of legal positivism. Deferring to the legal point of view is not a simple and uncontroversial exercise; figuring out which conceptions of political morality and human nature are presupposed by the law, and which methodology best furthers the law's objectives in light of these conceptions, is undoubtedly a difficult and contentious task. Some legal systems may be so complex that excellent meta-interpretive arguments can be made for rival interpretive methodologies. Indeed, there may be no rational resolution to certain theoretical disagreements, and hence no ultimate truth about which interpretive methodology is uniquely appropriate to a particular legal system.

Just as there are no assurances that the law will always succeed in settling questions about what is to be done, there is no guarantee that being faithful to the law's point of view will solve the problems that ought to be solved. For if those who created the law were incompetent or depraved, deferring to their judgments will be useless or worse. But when legal authorities have done their job, when they have crafted a set of plans that are capable of solving moral problems, then fidelity to their judgments about competence, character, goals, and values is essential to allowing members of the community to accomplish what they could not do otherwise and allowing the authorities to enjoy the powers they have a right to exercise. By contrast, natural law theories and the God's-eye view threaten to snatch defeat from the jaws of victory by counseling legal interpreters to unsettle that which has been settled.

Although it is not a particularly inspiring or romantic description, the law is, in the end, an instrument. And like all instruments, it can be used for good or bad purposes. When the law is used for bad purposes, it is imperative not to paper over this fact by denying the identity of the instrument doing the damage. And when the law is used for good purposes, it is important not to become complacent and assume that it is guaranteed to succeed. As with all instruments, there are correct and incorrect ways to use the law; if we use it incorrectly, it will not do what it is supposed to do and authorities will not do what they are entitled to do.

Unfortunately, this instrument does not already come complete with a user manual. And, of course, such a manual cannot be legislated: one would need instructions for how to use the instructions. Hope is not lost, however, for we are rational, reflective creatures capable of engaging in philosophical thought. We can consider the kind of instrument that the law is and attempt to derive the correct operating procedures from our understanding of its nature. With enough luck, we might actually figure out how it works.

NOTES

ACKNOWLEDGMENTS

INDEX

NOTES

Abbreviations

AL Joseph Raz, *The Authority of Law: Essays on Law and Morality* (Oxford: Oxford University Press, 1979)

CL H. L. A. Hart, *The Concept of Law,* ed. Joseph Raz and Penelope Bullock, 2d ed. (Oxford: Oxford University Press, 1994)

EJP H. L. A. Hart, *Essays in Jurisprudence and Philosophy* (Oxford: Oxford University Press, 1983)

LE Ronald Dworkin, *Law's Empire* (Cambridge, MA: Harvard University Press, 1986)

PJD John Austin, *The Province of Jurisprudence Determined,* ed. Wilfred E. Rumble (Cambridge: Cambridge University Press, 1995)

PRN Joseph Raz, *Practical Reason and Norms,* 2d ed. (Oxford: Oxford University Press, 1999)

1. What Is Law (and Why Should We Care)?

1. By contrast, law departments in Continental universities are often called departments of jurisprudence.

2. Admittedly, the line between analytical jurisprudence and the interpretive branch of normative jurisprudence is not always very clear. Is it possible, for example, to understand the concept of a tort, and how it differs from, say, a crime, without understanding why we hold people liable for the torts that they commit? It would seem that, in these cases at least, one couldn't do analytical jurisprudence without engaging in normative jurisprudence as well.

403

3. Unfortunately, the term "legality" has its own ambiguities. Sometimes, it refers to the property of being legal or lawful. Thus, we might ask about the legality of making a U-turn in the middle of the street. Other times, "legality" refers to a value or set of values, in particular, those values associated with the Rule of Law. The principles of legality, for example, require that laws be clear, prospective, promulgated, etc. On the value of legality, see Chapter 14.

4. See Joseph Raz, "The Problem about the Nature of Law," in *Ethics in the Public Domain* 196–198 (Oxford: Oxford University Press, 1994).

5. Jeremy Bentham, *Of Laws in General,* ed. H. L. A. Hart, 9 (London: Athlone Press, 1970).

6. It is also sometimes said that legal philosophers are never interested in the meaning of the word *law.* Just as chemists care about the chemical composition of water, not the semantic properties of the word "water," legal philosophers care about the nature of a certain social practice and its products, not the word used to refer to the practice. But this position is also too strong. There seems to be no reason why legal philosophers should not opine on the meaning of "law," as well as the metaphysics of law. For an excellent analysis of the word "law," see Jules Coleman and Ori Simchen, "'Law,'" 9 *Legal Theory* (2003). While I see no reason why investigating the semantic question should not be considered to be part of the proper province of jurisprudence, we will have very little to say about it in this book. Our main concern will be with investigating the nature of law, not the word "law."

7. The distinction between the identity of an entity and its necessary implications dates back to Aristotle. See, e.g., Aristotle, *Topics* I.5, 102a18–25. See also, Gareth B. Matthews, "Aristotelian Essentialism," 50 *Philosophy and Phenomenological Research* (Autumn 1990): Supplement, 251–262. For a modern elaboration, see Kit Fine, "Essence and Modality," 8 *Philosophical Perspectives* (1994).

8. Nor have legal philosophers been careful to distinguish between the Identity and Implication questions. Consider, for example, the notorious "Separability Thesis," which is usually formulated as the claim that "there is no necessary connection between law and morality" (see, e.g., Jules L. Coleman, *Markets, Morals and the Law* 4 [Cambridge: Cambridge University Press, 1988]). Tradition tells us that legal positivists accept the Separability Thesis whereas natural lawyers deny it. Recently, a number of philosophers have questioned whether the Separability Thesis is an issue between these two schools of thought. See, e.g., Joseph Raz, "Authority, Law and Morality," in *Ethics in the Public Domain* 226–227 (1994); Jules Coleman, "Beyond the Separability Thesis: Moral Semantics and the Methodology of Jurisprudence," 27 *Oxford Journal of Legal Studies* (2007); Leslie Green, "Positivism and the Inseparability of Morals," 83 *New York University Law Review* (2009). For example, Raz argues that no legal positivist can plausibly deny that there is a necessary connection between law and morality.

As he points out, it is plausible to suppose that the social order that law necessarily brings about is morally desirable. It follows that all legal systems have some morally desirable aspects to them, even if on balance the harm created outweighs that good, and hence law and morality are necessarily connected. But I think that the Separability Thesis is best seen as a claim about the identity of law, not its necessary implications. The positivists, in other words, concede that law and morality may share some necessary properties in common. They maintain, nonetheless, that law and morality are not *essentially* connected, that the properties that make law what it is are nonmoral in nature. The natural lawyers, on the other hand, insist that a social institution is a legal institution because it possesses some desirable moral properties. They believe that morality is part of the identity of law. Understood in this manner, then, the Separability Thesis is a point of contention between legal positivists and natural lawyers.

9. The terminology "conceptual analysis" is slightly confusing insofar as it might suggest that the object of analysis is a concept, rather than entities that fall under the concept. As I will be using the term, however, it denotes a process that uses a concept to analyze the nature of the entities that fall under it. As Raz notes, even though Hart called his book *The Concept of Law,* his theory is best understood as the analysis of the nature of law, rather than the concept. See Joseph Raz, "Can There Be a Theory of Law?" in *The Blackwell Guide to the Philosophy of Law and Legal Theory,* ed. Martin Golding and William Edmundson, 324–325 (Malden, MA: Blackwell Publishing, 2004).

10. For a dissenting view in legal philosophy, see Brian Leiter, "The Naturalistic Turn in Legal Philosophy," in Brian Leiter, ed., "New Directions in Analytic Jurisprudence," *American Philosophical Association Newsletter on Philosophy and Law* (Spring 2001): 142–146.

11. Another way of distinguishing true statements from truistic ones is by examining our interpretation of their respective denials. If we are content to impute strange beliefs to the speaker, then the speaker is merely denying a true statement; but if we are totally baffled by the denial and as a result infer that the speaker has changed the subject on us, then the speaker is denying a truism. On the role of truisms (or what Frank Jackson calls "subject-determining platitudes") in conceptual analysis, see Frank Jackson, *From Metaphysics to Ethics: The Role of Conceptual Analysis,* chap. 2 (Oxford: Oxford University Press, 1996). See also Michael Smith, *The Moral Problem,* chap 2 (Oxford: Blackwell, 1994).

12. To answer an Implication Question about X, it is often necessary to answer Identity questions about entities other than X. Thus, to figure out the relation between law and morality, it is necessary to have some understanding of the identity of morality.

13. For similar intuitions, see H. L. A. Hart, *The Concept of Law,* 2d ed., 207, ed. Joseph Raz and Penelope Bullock (Oxford: Oxford University Press,

1994) (hereafter CL); and Joseph Raz, *Practical Reason and Norms,* 2d ed., 164 (Oxford: Oxford University Press, 1999) (hereafter PRN).

14. Cf. Ronald Dworkin, *Justice in Robes,* chap. 6 (Cambridge, MA: Harvard University Press, 2006).

15. Answers to an Implication Question need not be truistic either. For even if there were complete agreement on the identity of an entity, some might not know, or be able to see, that some truth necessarily follows from various truths about the identity of that entity, especially when the derivation is subtle or complicated. Disagreements might also arise when the derivation of a necessary truth about the entity in question depends on truths about other entities and these latter truths are controversial as well.

16. In some instances, conceptual analysis can be completed only by consulting a scientific theory. For example, the analysis of the concept WATER tells us that something is water just in case it has the same internal structure as the stuff that is in the lakes, rivers, and oceans that we see around us. But the concept alone does not specify what the internal structure of water is (the ancient Greeks grasped the concept WATER even though they didn't know that water is H_2O). In order to know the internal structure of water, one must look to the a posteriori theory that tells us about the inner structure of material bodies, namely, chemistry. To give a more complete answer to the question "What is water?" therefore, one must look to a scientific theory that tells us about the constitution of water.

Traditionally, legal philosophers have not treated the concept LAW like the concept WATER, namely, they have not supposed that discovering the nature of law requires deference to another outside a posteriori theory. Even though Hart claimed that *The Concept of Law* was "an exercise in descriptive sociology" (CL vi), his analysis bears little resemblance to standard procedure in the social sciences—he didn't perform or examine any detailed case studies, engage in statistical analysis, etc.—nor did he consult findings in that field. He seemed to have assumed that the nature of law could be determined exclusively by conceptual analysis.

A few philosophers, however, have rejected Hart's approach and suggested instead that the concept LAW does require that we consult some other theory in order to determine the proper application of the concept. One popular position is that the concept LAW makes implicit reference to the best social scientific theory. The law, on this view, is what social science tells us law is, or would tell us if it were correct. This approach is plausible, at least at first glance, because the law is a social institution and social science is in the business of analyzing the nature of other social institutions. See David Lyons, *Ethics and the Rule of Law* 57–59 (Cambridge: Cambridge University Press, 1984); Brian Leiter, *Naturalizing Jurisprudence: Essays on American Legal Realism and Naturalism in Legal Philosophy* 183–192 (Oxford: Oxford University Press, 2007). My own view is that Hart was right with respect to the concept of law. Social science cannot tell us what the law is because it studies *human* society. Its deliverances have no relevance for the legal philosopher because it is a truism that nonhumans could have law. Science fiction, for example, is replete with stories involving alien civilizations with some form of legal system. These examples show that it is part of our concept of law that groups can have legal systems provided that they are more or less rational agents and have the ability to follow rules. Social scientific theories are limited in this respect, being able to study only human groups, and hence cannot provide an account about all possible instances of law.

17. "Is Justified True Belief Knowledge?" 23 *Analysis* (1963): 121–123. Gettier attributes the view of knowledge he critiques to Plato at *Meno* 98; Roderick Chisholm at *Perceiving: A Philosophical Study* 16 (Ithaca, NY: Cornell University Press, 1957); and A. J. Ayer at *The Problem of Knowledge* 34 (London: Macmillan, 1956). Bertrand Russell made the same point in 1912. See Bertrand Russell, *The Problems of Philosophy* 132 (Oxford: Oxford University Press, 1994).

18. CL vi.

19. Ibid.

20. Of course, the fact that one set of components are sufficient to create a legal system does not entail that they are necessary. In practice, induction from one case of law to all cases is rendered plausible through the subtle use of caricature: the hypothetical legal system is constructed so that certain abstract features of law are made especially prominent, even slightly exaggerated, thus drawing our attention to those properties whose ordinariness might cause them to be overlooked. The expectation is that we will recognize that the features present in the hypothetical legal system are in fact present in every legal system. For a use of this device, see the introduction to Chapter 6.

21. Richard Posner, *Law and Legal Theory in the UK and USA* 3 (New York: Oxford University Press, 1997).

22. See, e.g., Glanville L. Williams, "Language and the Law" (pt. 4), 61 *The Law Quarterly Review* 389 (1945). ("[E]very question of the form 'What is . . . ?', or 'What is the nature of . . . ?', or 'What is a . . . ?', or 'What is the nature of a . . . ?' (followed in each case by the name of a class, quality or relation) is a request for the definition of a word.")

23. According to tradition, the classical exponents of this position were Aquinas and Blackstone. See Thomas Aquinas, *Summa Theologica*, IaIIae.95.2, in Aquinas, *Political Writings*, ed. R. W. Dyson, 130 (Cambridge: Cambridge University Press, 2002); William Blackstone, *Commentaries on the Laws of England*, Introduction, section 2. This interpretation of Aquinas and Blackstone has been contested by John Finnis, see John Finnis, *Natural Law and Natural Rights* 364–365 (Oxford: Oxford University Press, 1980) and John Finnis, "Blackstone's Theoretical Intentions," 12 *Natural Law Forum* (1967), though accepted by Mark Murphy, see Mark Murphy, "Natural Law Jurisprudence," 9 *Legal Theory*

(2003). The idea that the extreme injustice of a rule precludes its status as law has also been associated with Gustav Radbruch (often called the "Radbruch formula"). See Gustav Radbruch, "Statutory Lawlessness and Supra-Statutory Law," (1946), trans. Stanley Paulson in 26 *Oxford Journal of Legal Studies* (2006). The Radbruch formula has been endorsed by the German Constitutional Court in upholding the murder conviction of a former East German border guard. See 95 BVerfGE 96 (1996). It has also been accepted by a number of contemporary theorists. See, e.g., Robert Alexy, *The Argument from Injustice: A Reply to Legal Positivism,* trans. Stanley Paulson and Bonnie Litschewski Paulson (New York: Oxford University Press, 2002); Neil MacCormick, *Institutions of Law* 277–279 (Oxford: Oxford University Press, 2006); Philip Soper, *The Ethics of Deference* 96–99 (Cambridge: Cambridge University Press, 2002); Michael Moore, *Educating Oneself in Public* 303–304 (Oxford: Oxford University Press, 2000); Deryck Beyleveld and Roger Brownsword, *Law as a Moral Judgment* 13–18 (London: Sweet & Maxwell, 1986); and Mark Greenberg, "The Standard Picture and Its Discontents," 1 *Oxford Studies in the Philosophy of Law* (Oxford: Oxford University Press, 2010). Ronald Dworkin claims that wicked regimes are legal systems only in the "pre-interpretive" sense. See Ronald Dworkin, *Law's Empire* 101–108 (Cambridge, MA: Harvard University Press, 1986) (hereafter LE).

24. "The Study of Jurisprudence," 5 *Law Magazine and Review,* 4th Service 382 (1880). For similar comments expressing the jaundiced attitudes of practicing lawyers to jurisprudence in the Victorian era, see Neil Duxbury, "English Jurisprudence Between Austin and Hart," 91 *Virginia Law Review* 71–77 (1995).

25. My presentation in this section was greatly influenced by Mark Greenberg, "How Facts Make Law," 10 *Legal Theory* (2004).

26. See generally Bruce Ackerman and Neal Katyal, "Our Unconventional Founding," 62 *University of Chicago Law Review* (1995).

27. See, e.g., Joseph Raz, *The Authority of Law: Essays on Law and Morality* 37 (Oxford: Oxford University Press, 1979) (hereafter AL); Jules Coleman, *The Practice of Principle* 75 (Oxford: Oxford University Press, 2001); Gerald J. Postema, "Coordination and Convention at the Foundation of Law," 11 *Journal of Legal Studies* (1982).

28. See, e.g., Ronald Dworkin, "'Natural Law' Revisited," 34 *University of Florida Law Review* (1981); Beyleveld and Brownsword, *Law as a Moral Judgment* 11; Nicos Stavropoulos, "Interpretivist Theories of Law," available at http://plato.stanford.edu/entries/law-interpretivist; Greenberg, "How Facts Make Law" (Greenberg uses the label "anti-postivism" as opposed to "natural law theory"). No doubt, this description of the natural law position is contentious. Some theorists characterize natural law theories as merely holding that immoral or unreasonable laws are *defective as laws.* See, e.g., Murphy, "Natural

Law Jurisprudence," 254, who calls this the "weak" reading of the natural law thesis. My reason for rejecting this characterization is threefold. First, as Murphy himself recognizes, the weak reading of the natural law thesis is consistent with the central tenet of legal positivism. A positivist can coherently maintain that the law is ultimately grounded in social facts alone but that immoral laws are defective as law. Indeed, I will propose such a theory later on. My characterization of natural law theory in the text is meant to capture the traditional understanding that natural law theory is a *rival* to legal positivism. Second, the weak reading of the natural law thesis cannot explain why so many natural lawyers have claimed that unjust rules are not laws. On my characterization, natural lawyers accept this view because they hold that legal facts are ultimately determined by social and moral facts and, in the case of unjust rules, the right sort of moral facts are missing. Third, the weak reading of the natural law view, while not uninteresting, is not so interesting that the dispute over it should constitute the major debate in analytical jurisprudence. As I intend to show in this book, the debate over whether the law ultimately rests on moral facts is capable of playing such a role.

29. U.S. Constitution, amend. VIII.

30. See, e.g., Cass Sunstein and Adrian Vermeule, "Interpretation and Institutions," 101 *Michigan Law Review* (2003).

2. Crazy Little Thing Called "Law"

1. Thomas Hobbes, *Leviathan,* ed. Richard Tuck, 2d ed., chap. 13, p. 89 (Cambridge: Cambridge University Press, 1996).

2. See, e.g., *The Cambridge Encyclopedia of Hunters and Gatherers,* ed. Richard Lee and Richard Daly, 1–4 (Cambridge: Cambridge University Press, 1999).

3. The anthropological literature suggests that intergroup violence between hunter-gatherers was quite extensive. See Azar Gat, *War and Human Civilization* (Oxford: Oxford University Press, 2006).

4. Hobbes, Leviathan, p. 89.

5. U.S. Constitution, art. I, §8.

6. U.S. Constitution, art. VII.

7. "Norm" is also used by European lawyers to refer to what Anglo-American lawyers call a "rule."

8. Another reason for its use is that rules are often contrasted with principles (a rule being an all-or-nothing standard, whereas principles lend support to various options without being conclusive) and sometimes with standards (rules being objects that can be applied without evaluation, whereas standards must be applied using evaluation). On these distinctions, see Chapter 9. Since rules, principles, and standards are all normative entities—they purport to tell you what to do or what is valuable, desirable, acceptable, and so on—they are all norms.

9. How a norm acquires its aim to guide and evaluate depends on the kind of norm it is. Moral and logical norms acquire their aim from their intrinsic validity. Personal plans, on the other hand, derive their function from the intentions with which they are created.

10. Charles S. Peirce, *Selected Writings* 100 (New York: Courier Dover Publications, 1966).

11. In this connection, see John Austin's famous response to the natural lawyer in *The Province of Jurisprudence Determined*,158, ed. Wilfred E. Rumble (Cambridge: Cambridge University Press, 1995) (hereafter PJD) ("Suppose an act innocuous, or positively beneficial, be prohibited by the sovereign under the penalty of death; if I commit this act, I shall be tried and condemned, and if I object to the sentence, that it is contrary to the law of God, who has commanded that human lawgivers shall not prohibit acts which have no evil consequences, the Court of Justice will demonstrate the inconclusiveness of my reasoning by hanging me up, in pursuance of the law of which I have impugned the validity.")

12. See David Hume, A *Treatise of Human Nature,* book III, part I, end of section I.

3. Austin's Sanction Theory

1. Letter from Mrs. Austin to M. Guizot (Dec. 31, 1860), in 2 *Three Generations of Englishwomen: Memoirs and Correspondence of Mrs. John Taylor, Mrs. Sarah Austin, and Lady Duff Gordon,* ed. Janet Ross, 102 (London: Murray, 1888).

2. James Fitzjames Stephen, "English Jurisprudence," 114 *Edinburgh Review* 484 (1861).

3. The following discussion of Austin's sanction theory is based on the account given in his *The Province of Jurisprudence Determined.*

4. Technically, Austin regarded the corporate body of the King, the peers, and the electors of the House of Commons as the sovereign. See PJD 192–196.

5. PJD 209–210. See also Hart's description of Austin's view at CL 74.

6. For Hart's discussion of Austin's command theory of law, see CL 18–25. See also 82–85.

7. Hart actually requires that there be a general belief in the *likelihood* that the sanctions will be applied. I have dropped the likelihood requirement in the text, for as Hart himself notes, Austin only required that the rules impose the "smallest chance of incurring the smallest evil," PJD 23. See CL 282.

8. Since ought-claims are normative, such an inference would be an instance of DINO reasoning.

9. CL 27.

10. The distinction between positive and negative aspects of freedom is adapted from, though not identical to, Isaiah Berlin's famous two concepts of

liberty. See Isaiah Berlin, "Two Concepts of Liberty" in *Liberty,* ed. Henry Hardy (Oxford: Oxford University Press, 2002).

11. Necessarily, the law is supposed to provide its subjects with moral reasons to comply with its demands. The imposition of a legal duty is supposed to make it the case that one morally ought to heed that duty. Because not everyone responds to moral reasons, the law usually attempts to provide self-interested reasons for complying with its directives in the form of sanctions. The law need not impose sanctions as a matter of necessity, but normally finds it prudent to add threats of punishments as an additional inducement to obey the law.

12. CL 33–35.

13. On the distinction between threats and offers, see Robert Nozick, "Coercion," in *Socratic Puzzles* (Cambridge, MA: Harvard University Press, 1999).

14. See, e.g., Hart's comments in CL 40.

15. In order for X to command Y to perform some action A, it is not enough for X to intend that Y do A. On most accounts, X must (1) intend that Y do A *and* (2) intend that Y do A because of the first intention.

16. Hans Kelsen, *General Theory of Law and State* 34 (Cambridge, MA: Harvard University Press, 1945).

17. I am assuming here that X commands Y to do A only if X intends that Y do A. Because unintentional intending is impossible, so is unintentional commanding.

18. Kelsen, *General Theory of Law and State* 36. See also CL 42–44.

19. In response, it might be argued that the *Senate,* not individual senators, creates legislation and hence commands senators to pay their taxes. The objection in the text, in other words, confuses corporate bodies with their members. Once we recognize this distinction, we can see how Austin explains the reflexivity of law: corporate legislative bodies are agents separate from their individual members and hence can command their members to act in a certain way. However, as Hart argued in a slightly different context, this solution is unavailable to Austin, for the existence of corporate legislative bodies depends on the existence of power-conferring rules. See CL 76.

20. Kelsen, *General Theory of Law and State* 34–35. See also CL 44–49.

21. CL 47–48.

22. Ibid., 52–54.

23. Ibid., 61–63.

24. Austin, following Hobbes, tried to explain the persistence of law by relying on the notion of a tacit order: if Rex II does not overrule Rex I's commands, then Rex II should be understood to have tacitly ordered that they be followed. Yet, as Hart pointed out, this response leads to absurdity. For if courts apply rules from a previous regime merely with the expectation that the sovereign will

eventually acquiesce, it would be difficult to explain why courts restrict themselves to applying these rules, as opposed to rules that have been repealed but that they find more appealing and that the sovereign might accept after the fact. Surely, the best explanation for why courts apply unrepealed rules of a previous regime is that *they think it is already law,* not that they hope it will turn into law some time down the road. See ibid., 63–65.

25. Ibid., 71–73.

26. Ibid., 55–57.

27. Wilfrid Sellars, "Truth and 'Correspondence'" 59 *Journal of Philosophy* 44 (1962).

4. Hart and the Rule of Recognition

1. CL 100–110.

2. CL 91. For Hart's theory of social rules, see 54–57 and 86–88. For an excellent description of Hart's theory, see generally Raz, PRN 49–58.

3. CL 92.

4. CL 92.

5. CL 92–93.

6. CL 93–94.

7. CL 94.

8. CL 95.

9. CL 97.

10. See, e.g., U.S. Constitution, art. V and art. VI, §2.

11. CL 106.

12. CL 110.

13. On Hart's account of the internal point of view, see Scott J. Shapiro, "What Is the Internal Point of View?" 75 *Fordham Law Review* (2007).

14. CL 115–116.

15. CL 107–108.

16. CL 107.

17. For a similar interpretation, see Raz, AL 92.

18. U.S. Constitution, art. I, §8.

19. The Supremacy Clause of Article VI, §2 does impose such a duty on state judges.

20. U.S. Constitution, art. VI, §3.

21. CL 57–61.

22. CL 106.

23. Ibid.

24. See, e.g., U.S. Constitution, art. V.

25. CL 95, 103.

26. CL 108–110.

27. This phrase is from the title of Chapter 5 of *The Concept of Law.*

28. CL 113–117.

29. Hart's reduction of social rules to social practices is seen most clearly in his claim that statements asserting the existence of a rule of recognition are simply "external" statements, namely, descriptive statements about the existence of a practice. See CL 110. For an even clearer expression of this reduction, see Hart's description of the Practice Theory in the Postscript, CL 255.

30. Joseph Raz has argued that this watered-down conception of the internal point of view renders acceptance by alienated officials unintelligible, for self-interest is a reason of the wrong kind for accepting the rule of recognition. A nonlegal example might help to make the point. My self-interest justifies my judgment that I ought to do my homework, but it cannot justify my judgment that you ought to do your homework—only your self-interest can do that. My self-interest only gives me a reason to act *as though* I believe that you ought to do your homework. Any such avowal would be insincere. Now consider the case of law. The rule of recognition, as we said, imposes a duty on judges to apply the primary rules. Accepting the rule of recognition, therefore, commits a judge to accepting the primary rules. But the primary rules specify how others are to act. Hence, to accept the rule of recognition commits a judge to accepting that others ought to act as the primary rules suppose. If so, then a judge's self-interest is the wrong kind of reason to accept the rule of recognition, for it cannot justify accepting norms requiring others to act in certain ways. Acceptance of the rule of recognition, therefore, is akin to accepting that others ought to do their homework; only non-self-interested reasons can justify a good-faith acceptance of such norms. For Raz's discussion, see "Hart on Moral Rights and Legal Duties," 4 *Oxford Journal of Legal Studies* 129–131 (1984).

31. In the discussion that follows, I have benefited enormously from Allan Gibbard's reinterpretation of G. E. Moore's naturalistic fallacy. See Allan Gibbard, *Thinking How to Live* 21–37 (Cambridge, MA: Harvard University Press, 2003). Gibbard distinguishes between properties and concepts, not facts and judgments, though I rely on the latter distinction because I think it is closer to how Hart would have expressed his account. I should add that though I rely on Gibbard's work, I am not suggesting that he endorses, or would endorse, my interpretation of Hart's theory of law.

32. Strictly speaking, when on Hart's account one describes a rule as imposing an obligation, one expresses several different attitudes, namely, the belief that the rule (1) is normally supported by serious social pressure, (2) is generally thought important, and (3) is generally believed to require sacrifice. Furthermore, to say "You are obligated to do A" is to express these beliefs, as well as the acceptance of a social rule and the judgment that A falls under that rule.

33. For a similar "expressivist" interpretation of Hart's account of internal legal statements, see Kevin Toh, "Hart's Expressivism and His Benthamite Project," 11 *Legal Theory* 75 (2005).

34. CL 210–211.

35. See, e.g., Hart, *Essays on Bentham* 159–160 (Oxford: Oxford University Press, 1982).

36. Gilbert Ryle, *The Concept of Mind* (Chicago: University of Chicago Press, 2002).

37. The criticism of Hart in this paragraph is originally due to Geoffrey Warnock. See G. J. Warnock, *The Object of Morality* (London: Methuen & Co. Ltd., 1971), 61–65.

38. See, e.g., Gerald J. Postema, "Coordination and Convention at the Foundation of Law," 11 *Journal of Legal Studies* (1982); Jules Coleman, "Negative and Positive Positivism" in *Markets, Morals and the Law* (Cambridge: Cambridge University Press, 1988).

39. More specifically, a coordination problem exists just in case two conditions are met. First, the interests of the players must predominately coincide. Second, there must exist at least two proper coordination equilibria. A combination of choices S is a proper coordination equilibrium just in case everyone strictly prefers that everyone choose S over a situation where everyone but one chooses S. To require that a coordination problem contain two coordination equilibria, therefore, is tantamount to requiring the existence of two combinations of choices S and S' such that (1) everyone strictly prefers that all play their part in S, just in case almost all play their part in S and (2) everyone strictly prefers that all play their part in S', just in case almost all play their part in S'.

40. The Coordination Argument need not hold that the selection of an authority structure be a pure coordination problem. It allows the players' preferences to conflict. Some players might prefer that one authority structure be selected over another, while others have the opposite preference. What matters is that everyone prefer universal agreement on a structure given that almost everyone else has chosen to follow that structure. Coordination games of partial conflict are often known as "The Battle of the Sexes" in the game theory literature.

41. See David Lewis, *Convention: A Philosophical Study* (Cambridge, MA: Harvard University Press, 1969).

42. See Lewis, *Convention* 70 and, generally, Andrei Marmor, *Social Conventions: From Language to Law* (Princeton: Princeton University Press, 2009). Postema refers to this property as "ambiguity" at Postema, "Coordination" 174.

43. A number of readers have offered the following response on behalf of Hart: my objection assumes that the bad man cannot accept the rule of recognition because he does not accept the law as a guide to his conduct. But the bad man can accept the rule of recognition because the acceptance of the rule of recognition is just the acceptance of a standard that distinguishes legally right from legally wrong conduct. It is akin to a rule of grammar: just as one can accept a rule of grammar and yet not be committed to following it, one can accept the rule of recognition without deciding to be law-abiding. This response is highly problematic, however. For it is not clear what it would mean to accept

the rule of recognition *as a rule* in such a weak sense. If the bad man does not believe that the rule of recognition correctly distinguishes courses of conduct that he has reason to follow from those he does not, what does it mean to say that it correctly distinguishes legally right from legally wrong conduct? To treat the rule of recognition as a rule, one must think that conduct that violates it is *defective* in some way. But the bad man does not believe that legally wrong conduct is defective. To the contrary, he thinks the rule of recognition is defective! The analogy to rules of grammar, therefore, is inapt: the bad man thinks that an ungrammatical sentence is a defective sentence, but he does not think that violation of the law is a defective act.

44. In later writing, Hart claimed that Joseph Raz's distinction between "committed" and "detached" statements allows him to explain how the bad man can describe the law in normative terms and engage in legal reasoning. See, e.g, Hart, *Bentham* 153–161. On Raz's distinction, see Raz, PRN 171–177; AL 153–157; Joseph Raz, *The Concept of a Legal System: An Introduction to the Theory of Legal System,* 2d ed., 234–238 (Oxford: Oxford University Press, 1980). According to Raz, someone who issues a committed statement expresses acceptance of a rule. The vegetarian who exhorts himself, saying, "I must not eat this hamburger," is making a committed statement. A detached statement, on the other hand, does not express a personal acceptance of a rule. Rather, it expresses some other point of view from which a particular rule is accepted as legitimate. Thus, when a meat eater says to his vegetarian friend, "You must not eat that—it's a hamburger!" he is expressing his friend's point of view, not his own. According to Raz, committed and detached statements express the same normative proposition but have different truth conditions. Committed statements have normative truth conditions, whereas detached statements have exclusively descriptive truth conditions. If vegetarianism is not morally required, then the statement "You must not eat that!" is false under the committed interpretation, but it is true under the detached interpretation because my friend is indeed a vegetarian and, from his point of view, it is wrong to eat meat. Hart seized on Raz's theory of normative statements and argued that the bad man can describe the law in normative terms and engage in legal reasoning because legal statements can be detached. Thus, when the bad man ascribes legal validity to a rule, he is not expressing his acceptance of the rule of recognition, but rather the point of view of those who accept the rule of recognition. This detached statement is true just in case there is judicial acceptance of a rule of recognition that validates the rule in question, regardless of whether the utterer accepts that rule of recognition himself.

Unfortunately, Raz's distinction between committed and detached statements is a mysterious one. First, the distinction presupposes an unorthodox semantic theory. According to Raz, both committed and detached statements express the same proposition but have different truth conditions. The usual semantic assumption is that propositions are individuated according to their truth conditions.

Second, the idea that a statement can be both detached *and* normative seems incoherent. In what sense can a statement express a normative proposition—a proposition about what ought to be done—and yet have descriptive truth conditions? Unless this can be explained, relying on the notion of a detached statement to solve the problem of the bad man merely substitutes one mystery for another.

45. Raz makes the same point (and I probably got it from him). See Raz, "Incorporation by Law," 10 *Legal Theory* 6 (2004).

46. Raz, "Hart on Moral Rights," 130–131.

47. Notice that the natural lawyer does not face similar problems. For on the natural law view, those who deny, like the bad man, that certain demands are morally legitimate must also deny that these demands are law. They cannot figure out and redescribe the content of the law, for there is no law to figure out and redescribe.

5. How to Do Things with Plans

1. It should be noted that in *The Concept of Law* Hart accepted the reduction of moral rules to social rules, though he repudiated this position in the Postscript. See Hart, CL 256.

2. Michael E. Bratman, *Intention, Plans and Practical Reason* 28–30 (Stanford, CA: Center for the Study of Language and Information, 1999).

3. Bratman, *Intention* 32–35.

4. Bratman, *Intention* 30–32. It should be noted that the pragmatic justification for the requirements of rationality set out in the text, as well as the content of the requirements themselves, are the subject of philosophical controversy. For alternative accounts, see John Broome, "Normative Requirements," *Ratio* 12 (1999); R. Jay Wallace, "Normativity, Commitment, and Instrumental Reason," 3 *Philosophers' Imprint* (2001); and Kieran Setiya, "Cognitivism about Instrumental Reason," 117 *Ethics* (2007). For Bratman's rejoinder, see his "Intention, Belief, Practical, Theoretical" in *Spheres of Reason*, ed. Simon Robertson (Oxford University Press, 2009) and "Intention, Belief and Instrumental Rationality," in *Reasons for Action*, ed. David Sobel and Steven Wall (Cambridge: Cambridge University Press, 2009).

5. Similarly, it follows that when a planner recognizes that her plan applies, she should not deliberate about the merits of the case at hand. The plan is supposed to settle the matter of whether she should act in a certain way and, thus, to deliberate before execution undermines the fundamental purpose of the plan. The planner rationally executes the plan because she adopted it and it applies, and for no other reason.

6. See, e.g., David Hume, *A Treatise of Human Nature,* book III, part II, section II.

7. See, e.g., Ludwig von Mises, "Economic Calculation in the Socialist Commonwealth," in *Collectivist Economic Planning*, ed. Friedrich A. Hayek (London: G. Routledge, 1935); Friedrich A. Hayek, *Individualism and Economic Order*, chaps. 7–9 (Chicago: University of Chicago Press, 1948).

8. See, e.g., Joseph Raz, *The Morality of Freedom* 118–119 (New York: Oxford University Press, 1988); Jules L. Coleman, *Risks and Wrongs* 62–64 (Oxford: Oxford University Press, 2002).

9. The phrase "joint activity" might be thought ambiguous as between a mere collection of actions and an integrated whole that has actions as its parts. My cooking dinner and your tying your shoes is a joint activity in the first sense because it is a collection of two individual actions, but not in the second sense because these actions bear no relation to one another. I am using "joint activity" in the second sense. Thus, our joint activity of cooking together is an integrated whole because we don't merely want to, say, make a salad and cook fish, but to make a meal that has making salad and cooking fish as its parts. Notice further that joint activities understood as integrated wholes need not be created by shared activities. I might have cooked fish by myself and you might have made a salad by yourself and, having realized our luck, we might combine forces to have a meal together. We will have engaged in the joint activity of cooking dinner though not as a shared activity. The possibility of joint activities that are not shared activities is essential for the noncircularity of defining shared activities in terms of joint activities. On this last point see, Michael Bratman, *Faces of Intention* 96–97 (Cambridge: Cambridge University Press, 1999).

10. A plan may be designed for a group not only when it has been formulated before the conduct takes place, but also when it has been endorsed after the pattern of behavior has arisen. Consider a group of people who have been acting in a certain fashion and come to realize that they should continue acting in this way because the sum total of their individual actions adds up to a valuable joint activity. For the purposes of shared agency, the recognition and endorsement of this pattern of behavior by members of the group count as designing their shared plan and enable the group to act together.

11. How would we know that Dudley and Stephens did not intend to paint the house? Suppose that halfway through his painting the fresh coat, Stephens announces that he quits. Dudley replies that it doesn't matter to him—after all, he will get his money regardless. If we assume that Dudley is rational, sincere, and hasn't changed his mind since he accepted the job, we can infer from this exchange that Dudley never formed an intention that they paint the house. This is so because to intend that they paint the house entails a rational commitment on the part of Dudley to the joint activity of their painting the house. This commitment, if present in a rational participant, must express itself in some form of action designed to result in their painting of the house. Dudley might pick up the brush and paint the house himself, or notify me of Stephens's departure, or

try to convince Stephens that he shouldn't leave. The fact that Dudley does nothing indicates that he is not so committed. He has the singular intention to do as I say and, hence, to scrape the paint off the house, but not the plural intention that *they* paint the house. Yet, despite the fact that Dudley is not so committed to the joint activity, it will be true that they share a plan if Stephens changes his mind and returns to the job.

12. Because Dudley and Stephens do not intend to act together, they are not subject to the same rationality constraints as Henry and I are. Dudley must fill in all his subplans related to scraping, ensure that they are consistent with all his other subplans, and not reconsider prior decisions absent a good reason. Dudley must also make sure that he does not totally interfere with Stephens's painting. But beyond that, Dudley need not worry about Stephens's subplans. Suppose Stephens does not know how to paint. Dudley is under no rational requirement to help Stephens paint the house; after all, Dudley gets paid regardless of whether Stephens paints. Of course, since I know that Dudley is not rationally required to help Stephens, I should give Stephens very detailed instructions on how to paint the house. Unlike them, it is rationally incumbent on *me* to ensure that the housepainters know what they are doing.

13. According to Michael Bratman, two individuals act together only when there is a *shared intention* in favor of the joint activity, which in turn obtains only when each of the participants is committed to the success of the joint activity. See *Faces of Intention,* chaps. 5–8. The requirement of a shared intention is too strong, I believe, because it eliminates the possibility of shared agency involving alienated participants. Dudley and Stephens are both alienated from the project of painting my house and yet they can still paint the house together, and do so intentionally, even though neither of them intends that they paint the house together. The requirement that the participants share a plan, instead of an intention, is designed to accommodate cases of alienation, for sharing a plan does not require a commitment to the joint activity. On the importance of accounting for alienation by theories of shared agency, see Christopher Kutz, *Complicity: Ethics and Law for a Collective Age,* 96–103 (Cambridge: Cambridge University Press, 2000).

Of course, some might not share my intuitions about the alienated housepainter case. They might deny that Dudley and Stephens paint the house together; as Margaret Gilbert once said to me, they only manage to paint the house "between them." To adjudicate between these conflicting intuitions, we could appeal to some theoretical considerations about shared agency. For example, Bratman has argued that shared agency is action that is explainable by a complex of mental states that plays three characteristic roles: it must (1) coordinate the actions of each participant toward the realization of the goal in question, (2) coordinate the planning of each participant so that each can achieve the intended goal, and (3) specify a background for bargaining in the case of conflict. See, e.g., *Faces of*

Intention, chap. 6. I claim that the acceptance of a shared plan by Dudley and Stephens is a complex of mental states that plays these three roles—it enables them to coordinate their actions, coordinate their planning, and resolve their conflicts. First, because the shared plan allocates tasks between Dudley and Stephens, their actions will be coordinated toward the goal of painting the house. Second, their planning will be coordinated because each will be committed to different parts of the plan and hence will fill out different subplans. Moreover, their commitment not to interfere with one another will ensure that Dudley will not interfere with those that Stephens adopts and vice versa. Third, if their planning clashes, they can appeal to the shared plan and, if need be, to me to resolve the conflict. Thus, if one accepts Bratman's functionalist theory of shared agency, it seems as though alienated participants such as Dudley and Stephens ought to be able to paint the house together.

14. The analogy here is to individual agency: just as individual action is individual behavior explainable by an individual plan, shared action is group behavior explainable by a shared plan.

15. Many of these customs are coordination conventions, but not all. For example, we do not regard our three-course-dinner custom as an arbitrary solution to a coordination problem (none of us would want to participate in cooking activities that are more or less elaborate) and, as a result, this custom is not a coordination convention.

16. Only customary norms that purport to settle what is to be done are planlike. For example, it is a customary norm in the United States for families to gather together on Thanksgiving, but this norm does not settle the question as to what is to be done on Thanksgiving. The Thanksgiving customary norm, therefore, is not a planlike norm.

6. The Making of a Legal System

1. For a fascinating discussion of these colossal failures of social planning, see James C. Scott, *Seeing Like a State: How Certain Schemes to Improve the Human Condition Have Failed* (New Haven, CT: Yale University Press, 1999).

2. Friedrich A. Hayek, *The Road to Serfdom,* 2d ed., 37 (London: Routledge, 2001).

3. Ibid., 36–37.

4. The reason that the stipulation is prefaced with "For the purposes of island land use policies" is that the plan does not require the group to consider the family in question to be the owner for, say, tithing purposes. As is the case in many jurisdictions, someone can be deemed the owner (to have title) for the purpose of determining who bears the risk of loss, but not for owing property or sales tax.

5. Moreover, since we designed our system of private property and market exchange to increase the amount of food available for the group to eat, our policies are *subplans* of the overall shared plan to boost the agricultural output of the island. They organize the behavior of the group so that the goal of the shared plan can be achieved. It turns out, then, that market activity—an activity that has traditionally been thought to be the paradigm of individualism—on our island is a shared activity. As long as we seek to maximize our own wealth subject to the cost internalizations mandated by our shared plan, we will collectively maximize food production.

6. Robert Ellickson, *Order Without Law: How Neighbors Settle Disputes* (Cambridge, MA: Harvard University Press, 1991) is the *locus classicus* for how communities are often able to order their affairs without resorting to law. The discussion in the text is much indebted to Ellickson's discussion.

7. On the importance that offices play in routinizing authority, see Max Weber, *Economy and Society,* ed. Guenther Roth and Claus Wittich, chaps. 11 and 14 (Berkeley: University of California Press, 1978).

8. The Cooks Island system is sanctionless in the sense that it both does not possess law enforcement personnel and does not privatize law enforcement by requiring ordinary citizens to mete out sanctions on offenders.

9. Grant Lamond helpfully distinguishes between the claim that all legal systems must prescribe sanctions for the breach of certain rules and the claim that all legal systems must authorize the use of physical force under some situations. See Grant Lamond, "Coercion and the Nature of Law," 7 *Legal Theory* 39 (2001). The argument in the text is addressed to the former but can easily be tailored to the latter, namely, that just as the Cooks Island legal system does not prescribe sanctions, it does not authorize physical force in any situation and does not do either because it assumes that such provisions are simply unnecessary.

10. For a similar response, see Raz's discussion of a society of angels and their need for law in PRN 159–160.

11. The term "circumstances of legality" is a reference, of course, to David Hume's famous doctrine of the "circumstances of justice." Hume argued that justice is a virtue only in situations of moderate conflict. He identified the circumstances of justice as ones of (1) modest scarcity, (2) limited altruism, (3) rough equality, and (4) moderate social interdependence. See, e.g., David Hume, *An Enquiry Concerning the Principles of Morals,* part I, section 3 (1751). Other philosophers have added further conditions. Rawls, for example, claims that justice is appropriate also where people have divergent conceptions of the good life. John Rawls, *A Theory of Justice,* 126–130 (Cambridge, MA: Harvard University Press, 1971). See also Hart, CL 193–200. The Planning Theory does not take the circumstances of justice to be sufficient for rendering law valuable. For the circumstances of justice can obtain for a certain community, but the problems of justice posed may be resolvable through nonlegal forms of social ordering. Jeremy Waldron speaks of the "circumstances of politics," which he identifies as

obtaining whenever a group of people must act together over time but persistently disagree about the principles of justice that should regulate their joint activities. See, e.g., Jeremy Waldron, *The Dignity of Legislation* 153–154 (Cambridge: Cambridge University Press, 1999). On the Planning Theory, the circumstances of legality include the circumstances of politics but are not exhausted by them.

12. See generally, Simon Roberts, *Order and Dispute* 82–84 (New York: St. Martin's Press, 1979). Some simple hunter-gatherer groups may inhabit the circumstances of legality. For example, in *The Law of Primitive Man,* Hoebel lamented the fact that Eskimo communities lacked a system of legal authority. On his view, the absence of formal legal rules regulating family life led to uncertainty about appropriate forms of sexual contact. This uncertainty generated feuding between men competing for women and contributed to a high homicide rate. "In a society in which manpower is desperately needed, in which occupational hazards destroy more men than the society can well afford, there is additional tragic waste in the killings which the inchoate system permits—indeed, encourages." E. Adamson Hoebel, *The Law of Primitive Man* 99 (Cambridge, MA: Harvard University Press, 1954).

13. Bratman, *Faces of Intention: Selected Essays on Intention and Agency* 5 (Cambridge: Cambridge University Press, 1999).

14. James Madison, "The Federalist No. 51," in *The Federalist,* ed. Terence Ball, 252 (Cambridge: Cambridge University Press, 2003).

15. See, e.g., Thomas Hobbes, *Leviathan,* chaps. 13–15 (1668).

16. See, e.g., John Locke, *Second Treatise of Government,* chaps. 2–3, 8–9 (1690).

17. See, e.g., David Hume, *A Treatise of Human Nature,* book III part II, section VII (1739).

18. Hans Kelsen, *General Theory of Law and State* 21 (Cambridge, MA: Harvard University Press, 1945) ("The law is an organization of force").

19. To be sure, the group that shares a plan might know and agree on the moral facts and hence would not have to deliberate or bargain about how to act. But this does not show that the plan is capable of resolving doubts and disagreement in such an instance; rather, since there are no doubts and disagreements to resolve, there is no way for the plan to fulfill its function in this case.

20. Notice that while the authorization to plan for others merely depends on the mental states of legal officials, the ability to plan depends on the mental states of ordinary citizens as well. Legal authorities can motivate obedience in the normal course only if members of the community are sufficiently virtuous, submissive, or cowardly. Trying to plan for a "stiff-necked people" may simply not be possible and, when this is so, legal authority will not be possible either.

21. I borrow "the inner rationality of law" from Michael Bratman, who in turn adapted Lon Fuller's famous phrase "the inner morality of law." See Bratman,

"Reflections on Law, Normativity and Plans," an unpublished paper presented at a conference at the University of Antwerp, The Normative Dimensions of Law, June 2009.

22. The analogy is from Andrei Marmor, *Social Conventions: From Language to Law,* chap. 1 (Princeton: Princeton University Press, 2009).

23. On the "legal point of view," I am heavily indebted to the work of Joseph Raz. See Raz, PRN 171–177. Raz's use of the legal point of view, however, is tied to his account of detached normative statements, which I reject. For my skepticism, see note 44 of Chapter 4. I explain how my use of this concept differs from Kelsen's in note 26 of this chapter.

24. Since a legal system exists only when it is generally efficacious, i.e., when most members of the community normally obey the law, X will have legal authority over Y in S only when S is generally efficacious. The legal point of view, therefore, ascribes moral legitimacy only to those who are authorized by a master plan of a generally efficacious system.

25. As mentioned in the previous note, X will have legal authority over Y in S only when S is generally efficacious. Hence, it will not be sufficient for a master plan to authorize someone to plan in order for that person to have legal authority. The master plan must be the plan of a generally efficacious planning system.

26. Kelsen sought to answer Hume's Challenge by claiming that legal reasoning is suppositional in nature. To derive a legal judgment from a descriptive judgment, the legal reasoner must presuppose another normative judgment that imputes normative significance to certain social facts. This presupposed normative judgment is that the basic norm of the system is valid. The bad man can engage in legal reasoning because presupposition is easy—anyone, even the bad man, can presuppose the basic norm and hence derive legal judgments. As is well known, however, Kelsen's solution is flawed because presupposition turns out to be too easy. Why can't someone presuppose a basic norm that confers supreme and unlimited authority on, say, me and then interpret my actions as being legally authoritative? Kelsen insisted that the fundamental norms of a legal system be practiced, but this demand is completely ad hoc. The Planning Theory, by contrast, faces no similar difficulty. On the Planning Theory, the legal point of view is the perspective according to which the authorizing norms of the legal system are morally legitimate. But since the authorizing norms form a shared plan, and shared plans must be practiced in order to exist, the legal point of view will attribute moral legitimacy only to those authorized by practiced norms.

7. What Law Is

1. Plato, *The Republic,* Book II, trans. Benjamin Jowett.

2. Or at least this is the way that the federal courts have regarded Section 1. According to Herbert Hovencamp, courts treat the Sherman Act "as 'enabling'

legislation—an invitation to the federal courts to learn how businesses and markets work and formulate a set of rules that will make them work in socially efficient ways." Herbert Hovencamp, *Economics and Federal Antitrust Law* 52 (St. Paul: West Publishing, 1985). See also Frank Easterbrook, "Vertical Arrangements and the Rule of Reason," 53 *Antitrust Law Journal* 135, 136 (1984) ("The Sherman Act of 1890 told the courts to make up a law on the subject of restraint of trade"). Others have imputed to Section 1 more determinate content. See, e.g., Robert Bork, *The Antitrust Paradox: A Policy at War with Itself* 20 (New York: Free Press, 1978).

3. Standard Oil Co. of New Jersey v. United States, 221 U.S. 11 (1911).

4. See United States v. Trenton Potteries Co., 273 U.S. 392 (1927); Continental T. V., Inc. v. G.T.E. Sylvania Inc., 433 U.S. 36 (1977).

5. The key cases were Donoghue v. Stevenson, [1932] A. C. 562 (H. L.) in the United Kingdom and MacPherson v. Buick Motor Co., 217 N.Y. 382 (1916) in the United States.

6. See generally David Strauss, "Common Law Constitutionalism," 63 *University of Chicago Law Review* 891–897 (1996).

7. On distinguishing, see Raz, AL 183–189.

8. See Dan Kahan, "The Secret Ambition of Deterrence," 113 *Harvard Law Review* 429–430 (1999).

9. To say that legal planning regulates most communal activity via general and publicly accessible standards is not to claim that most laws are general and publicly accessible. Most laws in a legal system might be private bills addressed to individuals or secret, but as long as the bulk of the activity regulated is governed by open policies, then the regulation counts as social planning.

10. U.S.S.R. Constitution preamble; Iran Constitution preamble; Sweden Constitution, arts. I and II.

11. Although the account of shared agency I sketched requires that there be one shared plan, it is possible to relax this requirement without changing the essentials of the approach. Thus, we could say that a law is a member of a legal system if it was created in accordance with, and its application is regulated by, a *set of plans* that the relevant official group shares. We can further stipulate that a group shares a set of plans if and only if (1) each plan of the set was designed, at least in part, for that group so that they may engage in a joint activity; (2) the members of the group accept the parts of the plans that apply to them; and (3) the members of the group commit to not interfering with the parts that apply to others. On the planning theory, therefore, the content of a legal system does not depend on the unitary nature of its shared plan. Rather, it ultimately depends on the fact that someone conceived of officials *as a group* and developed a set of instructions for them so that they may govern a community. Whether we treat the instructions addressed to this group as forming one plan or many is, in the end, immaterial.

12. Indeed, it is a noteworthy feature of offices that they can exist even while empty, e.g., papal interregna, where the papacy remains while the College of Cardinals elects the new pontiff.

13. The primary method by which legal systems should resolve moral problems depends on the nature of political morality. On one view, political morality is largely determinate, namely, it provides answers to most political questions. Given this conception of political morality, the law should solve moral problems primarily by revealing these answers to those who need them and secondarily by selecting arbitrary solutions to coordination problems. Others regard political morality as largely indeterminate: it provides very little by way of specific guidance about what the law should be. Political morality, in other words, does not tell us what kind of property, contract, criminal, constitutional, and tax laws we must have. On this conception, the law resolves moral problems primarily through a process that Aquinas called "determinatio," namely, the determination and filling out of the details that are left indeterminate by morality. The law is needed not so much to reveal the answers to moral questions, but rather to *create* them. On this conception of political morality and the role that law plays within it, see Arthur Ripstein, *Force and Freedom: Kant's Political and Legal Philosophy* (Cambridge, MA: Harvard University Press, 2009).

14. H. L. A. Hart claimed that the law has a purpose, which is the guidance of conduct, but clearly did not think that this function was unique to law. See CL 249.

15. For a clear expression of this skepticism, see Leslie Green, "Law as a Means," in *The Hart-Fuller Debate in the Twenty-First Century,* ed. Peter Cane (Oxford: Hart Publishing, 2010).

16. See, e.g., Curtis Milhaupt and Mark West, "The Dark Side of Private Ordering: An Institutional and Empirical Analysis of Organized Crime," 67 *University of Chicago Law Review* (2000).

17. Morally good laws, we might say, are like true beliefs: laws should be moral just as beliefs should be true. Morally beneficial crimes, however, are akin to psychologically comforting beliefs. Beliefs need not make us feel good, although when they do, and they are true, we should count ourselves lucky.

18. See, e.g., Raz, AL 155n13 (Oxford: Oxford University Press, 1979). For Hart's criticism of this position, see Hart, *Essays on Bentham* 155–161 (Oxford: Oxford University Press, 1982).

19. Augustine, *City of God against the Pagans,* ed. R. W. Dyson, 147 (Cambridge: Cambridge University Press, 1998).

20. It follows from the Moral Aim Thesis that if a criminal organization presents itself as dedicated to solving serious moral problems (think of Robin Hood and his Merry Men), it too might be eligible to be a legal system. The fact that others consider it to be mere organized crime does not change the reality of the situation.

21. See, e.g., Raz, PRN 151–152.

22. Raz argues that the law's claim to supreme authority can be discharged simply by it claiming the right to *permit* other normative institutions to operate within its jurisdiction. See ibid. 152. He might then respond to the objection in the text by noting that states claim supreme authority over the federal government by claiming the right to permit the feds to regulate their affairs. Of course, this is a funny way to claim supreme legal authority. For the states permit the feds to regulate in a very strong sense, namely, by accepting federal supremacy. It would follow then that states claim supreme authority over the feds by *denying* themselves supreme authority over the feds. For our purposes, the problem with allowing the claim to supreme authority to be discharged in this manner is that it fails to distinguish Florida from the condo board. For the condo board claims the right to permit the law to operate in its jurisdiction. It does this by stating in its by-laws that Florida law controls. By claiming the right to enact such a by-law, the condo board is claiming the right to permit Florida to operate in its jurisdiction and hence, according to Raz, satisfying the board's claim to supreme authority.

23. See PRN 150–151.

24. Max Weber uses this criterion to define the state, not the law. See Max Weber, "Politics as a Vocation," *From Max Weber: Essays in Sociology,* trans. and ed. H. H. Gerth and C. Wright Mills, 77 (New York: Oxford University Press, 1946).

25. On the medieval Icelandic legal system, see William I. Miller, *Bloodtaking and Peacemaking: Feud, Law and Society in Saga Iceland* (Chicago: University of Chicago Press, 1990).

26. 42 U.S.C. §1973c. It is interesting that parenting is more self-certifying than state legal activity because parents never face preclearance requirements. If I want to enforce the rules of the house, I never have to call the police or file suit against my child in family court; I can simply punish my child.

27. See, e.g., PRN 150.

28. Certain philosophers have argued that not all laws are norms. For example, Raz has claimed that laws that specify the territorial limits of a legal system are not norms because they do not, by themselves, prescribe any action. See Raz, *The Concept of a Legal System: An Introduction to the Theory of Legal System,* 2d ed., chap. 7 (Oxford: Oxford University Press, 1980). If not all laws are norms but all plans are norms, then it would follow that not all laws are plans. I think, however, that Raz's claim is mistaken, for laws that define the territorial limits of a jurisdiction do concern action. They direct individuals to apply certain rules only in certain contexts. Their form is: "With respect to laws of type L, apply them only within the following territorial limits: . . ." Thus, laws defining the reach of a jurisdiction's criminal law direct individuals to apply its criminal law only when actions are performed within those limits. Laws that specify

the territorial limits with respect to taxation require individuals to apply the rules of taxation only to property and activities within those limits as well.

29. City of San Mateo, Ord. 1984–5, §42, 1984.

30. Hammurabi's Code.

31. New York Vehicle and Traffic Law, art. 31, §1192-a.

32. Japanese Constitution, art. 39.

33. Permissions are often formulated using "unless" clauses. Thus the EU regulation: "No oil tanker carrying heavy grades of oil shall be allowed to fly the flag of a Member State unless such tanker is a double-hull tanker" is a conditional permission, for it permits an oil tanker to fly the flag of a Member State only on the condition that it is double hulled. Regulation (EC) No. 457/2007.

34. New Zealand Grown Fruit and Vegetable Regulations 1975, part 4, reg. 21.

35. Pub. L. 108–176, title VII, Sec. 702, Dec. 12, 2003, 117 Stat. 2576, f(1).

36. See Tony Honore, *Making Laws Bind 87 (Oxford: Oxford University Press, 1987)*.

37. U.S. Constitution, art. II, §3.

38. On the use of factors in the law, see Cass Sunstein, *Legal Reasoning and Political Conflict* 28–30, 143–147 (New York: Oxford University Press, 1996).

39. Since the legal point of view is the one according to which laws have the moral effects they are supposed to have, it is always possible to recharacterize the content of the law in a morally approving way from the legal point of view.

8. Legal Reasoning and Judicial Decision Making

1. Smith v. United States, 508 U.S. 223 (1993).

2. Muscarello v. United States, 524 U.S. 125 (1998).

3. Nix v. Hedden, 149 U.S. 304 (1893).

4. In re House Bill no. 1291, 178 Mass. 605 (1901).

5. United States v. Locke, 471 U.S. 84 (1985).

6. Palsgraf v. Long Island Railroad Co., 162 N.E. 99 (N.Y. 1928).

7. Chorlton v. Lings (1868), L.R. 4 C.P. 374.

8. McBoyle v. United States, 283 U.S. 25 (1931).

9. Church of the Holy Trinity v. United States, 143 U.S. 457 (1892).

10. Adams v. Lindsell, 1 B & Ald 681 (1818).

11. Bush v. Gore, 531 U.S. 98 (2000).

12. See, e.g., Brian Tamanaha, "The Bogus Tale of the Legal Formalists," St. John's Legal Studies Research Paper No. 08–0130 (2008).

13. Among American formalists, the standard list includes Christopher Columbus Langdell, Joseph Beale, J. B. Ames, and Samuel Williston.

14. The discussion that follows is much indebted to Thomas Grey, "Langdell's Orthodoxy," 45 *University of Pittsburgh Law Review* 6–11 (1983). See also

Grant Gilmore, *The Ages of American Law* (New Haven, CT: Yale University Press, 1977); Anthony T. Kronman, *The Lost Lawyer: Failing Ideals of the Legal Profession,* chap. 4 (Cambridge, MA: Harvard University Press, 1993).

15. The discussion in this section is based on Grey, "Langdell's Orthodoxy" 12.

16. For examples of authors claiming this connection between formalism and positivism, see Roscoe Pound, *Law and Morals* 46–50 (Littleton, CO: Rothman, 1987) (positivists claim law is a complete logical system and adjudication a mechanical, deductive process); Morris R. Cohen, "Positivism and the Limits of Idealism in the Law," 27 *Columbia Law Review* 238 (1927)(attributing to positivists the assumption that a legal system is complete and closed); Felix Cohen, "The Ethical Basis of Legal Criticism," 41 *Yale Law Journal* 215 (1931) (positivism's commitment to logical consistency and certainty); W. Friedmann, *Legal Theory,* 3d ed., 289 (London: Stevens, 1967) (positivists see law as a complete and self-contained system and legal reasoning as strictly logical); Julius Stone, *The Province and Function of Law: Law as Logic, Justice, and Social Control: A Study in Jurisprudence,* 2d ed., 138–140 (New York: William S. Hein, 1973) (on the positivist commitment to the logical consistency of law).

17. Oliver Wendell Holmes, *The Common Law* (Boston: Little, Brown, & Co., 1909).

18. Pound, *Law and Morals,* 59.

19. See John P. Dawson, *Oracles of the Law* 410–411 (Ann Arbor: University of Michigan Law School, 1968) and John Merryman, *The Civil Law Tradition: An Introduction to the Legal Systems of Western Europe and Latin America* 83 (Stanford, CA: Stanford University Press, 1969). But see Mitchel Lasser, *Judicial Deliberations: A Comparative Analysis of Judicial Transparency and Legitimacy,* chaps. 2 and 6 (Oxford: Oxford University Press, 2004).

20. H. L. A. Hart, *Essays in Jurisprudence and Philosophy* 62–66 (Oxford: Oxford University Press, 1983) (hereafter EJP).

21. For a broader definition of "legal reasoning," see Joseph Raz, *Ethics in the Public Domain,* 327 (Oxford: Oxford University Press, 1994).

22. Hart, CL 126–128.

23. See, generally, Gerald J. Postema, *Bentham and the Common Law Tradition* (Oxford: Oxford University Press, 1989).

24. CL 126.

25. EJP 63–64.

26. CL 126.

27. EJP 65–66.

28. While Hart believed that judges also legislated, he clearly distinguished between the roles of the legislator and the judge in the development of the law. In contrast to legislators, not only are judges required to supply reasons for

their decisions, but also the reasons that they are permitted to rely on are generally regulated by their legal system. See, e.g., EJP 106–107.

29. EJP 103.

30. See, e.g., the quotes cited by Hart on page 1 of *The Concept of Law*: Karl N. Llewellyn, *The Bramble Bush: On Our Law and Its Study*, 2d ed., 12 (New York: Oceana Publications, 1951) ("What officials do about disputes is . . . the law itself"); Oliver Wendell Holmes, "The Path of the Law," in *Collected Legal Papers*, ed. Harold Joseph Laski, 173 (New York, 1920) ("The prophecies of what the courts will do . . . are what I mean by the law"); John Chipman Gray, *The Nature and Sources of the Law*, 2d ed., 125 (New York, 1921) (". . . statutes, are to be dealt with as sources of Law, and not as part of the Law itself"). In the foreword to the second edition of *The Bramble Bush*, Llewellyn acknowledges that the words quoted above "fail to give a proper account" of the nature of a legal institution, pp. 8–10. For Hart's discussion, see CL 126 and 136.

31. For the association of positivism with textualism, see, e.g., Lon L. Fuller, "Positivism and Fidelity to Law," 71 *Harvard Law Review* 661–669 (1958); Anthony D'Amato, *Introduction to Law and Legal Thinking* 63–67 (Boston: Hotei Publishing, 1996) (positivist judges are confined to semantic interpretation of statutes). Often the association is merely implied or presumed. See, e.g., William N. Eskridge, "Interpretation of Statutes," in *A Companion to Philosophy of Law and Legal Theory*, ed. Dennis Patterson, 204 (Malden, MA: Blackwell Publishing, 1999) ("The new textualism is inspired by a particularly dogmatic positivism"); Richard Posner, *Overcoming Law* 155 (Cambridge, MA: Harvard University Press, 1995) (describing "casuistry, strict construction, disavowal of personal responsibility" as "tricks of the legal positivist"); Ofer Raban "Real and Imagined Threats to the Rule of Law: On Brian Tamanaha's 'Law as a Means to an End'," 15 *Virginia Journal of Social Policy and Law* 492 (2008) ("Some positivists seek to distance themselves from Hart's explicit textualism, though they remain committed to principles whose practical implications boil down to textualism"); Patrick Brennan, "Against Sovereignty: A Cautionary Note on the Normative Power of the Actual," 82 *Notre Dame Law Review* 211 (2006) (". . . textualism, a version of legal positivism . . ."); Thomas Mertens, "Nazism, Legal Positivism, and Radbruch's Thesis on Statutory Injustice," 14 *Law and Critique* 282 (2003) (". . . it seems not unreasonable to define 'positivism' as the conviction that one has to obey the law, simply because it is posited, and that examining statutes by reference to unwritten legal principles is not allowed. Some call this 'statutory positivism'").

32. EJP 63–64 (explaining that cases fall into the penumbra when the *words* of the rule to be applied are ambiguous).

33. Fuller, "Fidelity to Law," 663–665.

34. Ibid., 666.

35. Lawyers typically distinguish between "subjective" and "objective" purposes. Subjective purposes are the goals and values that actual lawmakers have sought to further and realize when creating the law in question. Objective purposes, by contrast, are those goals and values that reasonable lawmakers would have sought to further and realize when creating the law in question. Clearly, forms of purposive interpretation that seek to construe legal texts in light of subjective purposes are acceptable from a positivistic perspective, for the existence of subjective purposes is a matter of social fact. By contrast, it might be thought that a positivist would be unable to endorse objective purposive interpretation. An inquiry into objective purposes, after all, is an exercise in moral reasoning. Whether legal positivists can actually accept objective purposive interpretation as a legitimate interpretive methodology is a question we will address in the next chapter.

36. EJP 106.

37. While positivism is not committed to textualism as an interpretive methodology, it is nonetheless true that many positivists seem to accept some such version of this view. As Mark Greenberg has pointed out, legal positivists often assume that the content of the law is simply the aggregation of the ordinary linguistic or mental contents associated with authoritative texts or utterances (where linguistic content includes not only the semantic content of texts but also contents that are communicated by utterances). See his "The Standard Picture and Its Discontents," 1 *Oxford Studies in the Philosophy of Law* (Oxford: Oxford University Press, 2010).

38. For examples of this understanding of positivism, see, e.g., Robert Cover, *Justice Accused: Antislavery and the Judicial Process,* 4th ed., 27–30 (New Haven, CT: Yale University Press, 1984) (arguing that judges committed to positivism must be "will-less" and deferential to written law, however flagrantly immoral); Ingo Muller, *Hitler's Justice: The Courts of the Third Reich,* trans. Deborah Lucas Schneider, 219 (Cambridge, MA: Harvard University Press, 1991) (claiming positivism demands "judges be strictly bound to the law"); Frank Michelman, "Law's Republic," 97 *Yale Law Journal* 1497 (1988) (a positivist court must not "'impose' its members' 'own choice of values' on the people . . ."); John Goldberg, "Unloved: Tort in the Modern Legal Academy," 55 *Vanderbilt Law Review* 1516 (2002) (describing the theory of legal positivism as "one that conceives of the judicial role as confined to following rules made by others"). Some authors make a weaker claim, namely, that positivism *encourages* judges to strictly apply the law: e.g., Richard Posner, *The Problems of Jurisprudence* 139–142 (Cambridge, MA: Harvard University Press, 1990) (arguing that positivism promotes self-abnegating judges who unduly defer to the political branches); Maura Strassberg, "Taking Ethics Seriously: Beyond Positivist Jurisprudence in Legal Ethics," 80 *Iowa Law Review* 914 (1995) ("Positivism, therefore, will tend to discourage decision-makers from considering whether the

case before them is penumbral and will make them loath to admit that any particular case is appropriately penumbral"); J. C. Oleson, "The Antigone Dilemma: When the Paths of Law and Morality Diverge," 29 *Cardozo Law Review* 700 (2007) ("While Austin, Bentham, and Hart all believed that positivists
would defy a law if a certain threshold of iniquity were reached, this trio
may have underestimated the insidious relationship between authority and
obedience").

39. See, e.g., EJP 71–72.

40. 347 U.S. 483 (1954).

41. 381 U.S. 479 (1965).

42. Morton Horwitz, *The Transformation of American Law, 1870–1960* 251
(New York: Oxford University Press, 1992) (claiming legal positivism was "dramatically called into question" by *Brown*); William N. Eskridge, "Metaprocedure," 98 *Yale Law Journal* 966 (1989) (describing the *Brown* decision as inde-
fensible for a legal positivist because segregation was sanctioned by the states
and no contrary "neutral principle" could be found in existing law); Steven D.
Smith, "Why Should Judges Obey the Law?" 77 *Georgetown Law Journal* 125
(1988) (deeming Justice Stewart's *Griswold* dissent positivist because he found
the sodomy law constitutional in spite of his personal moral objection to it).
Other theorists claim, more strongly, that a judicial decision is antipositivist
whenever it uses moral reasoning to decide even an open question of law, not
just when it changes settled law for moral reasons. See, e.g., Richard Primus, "A
Brooding Omnipresence: Totalitarianism in Postwar Constitutional Thought,"
106 *Yale Law Journal* 447–450 (1996) (deeming *Brown* and *Griswold* "antipositivist" decisions because they used moral reasoning to resolve constitutional
ambiguities). It can be difficult to determine whether an author is making the
weaker or stronger claim. For examples of case outcomes attributed generally
to a positivist refrain from moral judgment, see Michelman, "Law's Republic,"
1497 (Bowers v. Hardwick, 478 U.S. 186 (1986)); Sanford Levinson, "Constitutional Rhetoric and the Ninth Amendment," 64 *Chicago-Kent Law Review*
150–151 (1988) (*The Antelope,* 23 U.S. 10 Wheat. 66 (1825), validating property rights in the international slave trade); Eskridge, "Metaprocedure" 971
(Lassiter v. Department of Social Services, 452 U.S. 18 (1981), holding that a
convicted prisoner was not entitled to government-provided counsel for a child
custody suit); Claire Finkelstein, "Positivism and the Notion of an Offense," 88
California Law Review 337 (2000) (United States v. Dotterweich, 320 U.S. 277
(1943), holding a company president criminally liable for a drug shipment of
which he was ignorant).

43. Cover, *Justice Accused* 227–238.

44. Gustav Radbruch, *Rechtsphilosophie,* trans. Kurt Wilk, in *The Legal
Philosophies of Lask, Radbruch, and Dabin* 43–224 (Cambridge, MA: Harvard
University Press, 1950).

45. On this point, see Liam Murphy, "The Political Concept of Law," in *Hart's Postscript,* ed. Jules L. Coleman (Oxford: Oxford University Press, 2001).

46. Hart goes so far as to analogize a court's role in penumbral cases to that of an administrative agency that is delegated legal powers to develop rules from vague standards. See, e.g., CL 132.

47. McCulloch v. Maryland, 17 U.S. 316 (1819).

48. CL 129–130.

9. Hard Cases

1. For an excellent discussion of the American legal realists to which I am much indebted, see Brian Leiter, "American Legal Realism," in *The Blackwell Guide to Philosophy of Law and Legal Theory,* ed. William Edmundson and Martin Golding (Oxford: Blackwell, 2005).

2. Lochner v. United States, 198 U.S. 45, 76 (1905).

3. Karl N. Llewellyn, "Remarks on the Theory of Appellate Decision and the Rules or Canons About How Statutes Are to Be Construed," 3 *Vanderbilt Law Review* 401 (1950).

4. Ronald Dworkin, "Model of Rules I," in *Taking Rights Seriously* 24–28 (Cambridge, MA: Harvard University Press, 1977).

5. Riggs v. Palmer, 115 N.Y. 506 (1889).

6. 32 N.J. 358, 161 A.2d 69 (1960), discussed in Dworkin, "Model of Rules I" 23–24.

7. 32 N.J. at 388, 161 A.2d at 86.

8. 32 N.J. at 387, 161 A.2d at 85.

9. Dworkin, "Model of Rules I" 28.

10. Ibid., 31–34.

11. Ibid., 32–34. In later writing, Dworkin accepts the possibility that some cases may lack right answers, namely, in situations where two or more sets of principles equally fit and justify past political acts, though he considered their occurrence in Anglo-American systems to be "extremely rare" if they exist at all. See Ronald Dworkin, "Is There Really No Right Answer in Hard Cases?" in *A Matter of Principle* 142–144 (Cambridge, MA: Harvard University Press, 1985).

12. Ibid., 40.

13. Ibid., 17.

14. In the early critiques of Hart's theory, it was unclear whether Dworkin meant to challenge the positivistic picture only as applied to legal principles, while conceding that it was right about legal rules, or whether he intended to attack positivism's treatment of all legal norms by arguing that social facts *never* determine legal validity. In later writings it became evident that he saw the problem posed by legal principles as threatening the entire social foundation of positivism. For as we will see in great detail in the next chapter, rules enacted by

competent institutions are binding only because nonpedigreed principles require that these institutions be heeded. When the legislature passes speed-limit legislation, for example, these all-or-nothing rules are valid because the principles of political morality and sound institutional design collectively confer moral legitimacy on the legislature to regulate driving in this manner. According to Dworkin, then, legal positivists are not only unable to explain judicial behavior in hard cases; they are incapable of explaining how legal reasoning ever functions.

15. For this type of response, see Philip Soper, "Legal Theory and the Obligation of a Judge: The Hart-Dworkin Dispute," 75 *Michigan Law Review* (1977); David Lyons, "Principles, Positivism and Legal Theory," 87 *Yale Law Journal* (1977); Jules Coleman, "Negative and Positive Positivism," in his *Markets, Morals and the Law* (Cambridge: Cambridge University Press, 1988); Wilfred Waluchow, *Inclusive Legal Positivism* (Oxford: Oxford University Press, 1994). For a good discussion, see also Kenneth Himma, "Inclusive Legal Positivism," in *The Oxford Handbook of Jurisprudence and Philosophy of Law,* ed. Jules L. Coleman and Scott Shapiro (Oxford: Oxford University Press, 2002).

16. Joseph Raz, exclusive legal positivism's leading advocate, refers to his view as the commitment to the Sources Thesis. The Sources Thesis was first set out in "Legal Positivism and the Sources of Law" in Raz, AL, and received its most vigorous defense in his "Authority, Law and Morality," reprinted in Raz, *Ethics in the Public Domain* (Oxford: Oxford University Press, 1994). Raz further develops his position in his *The Concept of a Legal System,* 2d ed., 212–216 (Oxford: Oxford University Press, 1980); "The Problem about the Nature of Law," "The Inner Logic of the Law," and "On the Autonomy of Legal Reasoning," all appearing in *Ethics in the Public Domain;* and "Postema on Law's Autonomy and Public Practical Reasons: A Critical Comment," 4 *Legal Theory* (1998). I have subscribed to this view in print: see, e.g., Scott Shapiro, "On Hart's Way Out," 4 *Legal Theory* (1998). Other proponents of exclusive positivism include Andrei Marmor, *Positive Law and Objective Values,* chap. 3 (Oxford: Oxford University Press, 2001) and Brian Leiter, "Legal Realism, Hard Positivism, and the Limits of Conceptual Analysis," in *Naturalizing Jurisprudence: Essays on American Legal Realism and Naturalism in Legal Philosophy* (Oxford: Oxford University Press, 2007).

17. See Raz, "Postscript to 'Legal Principles and the Limits of Law'," in *Ronald Dworkin and Contemporary Jurisprudence,* ed. Marshall Cohen, 84–85 (Totowa, NJ: Rowman & Allanheld, 1983).

18. AL 46.

19. See, e.g., Raz, "Legal Principles and the Limits of Law," 81 *Yale Law Journal* 847–848 (1972).

20. See Donald Davidson, "Agency," in his *Essays on Actions and Events,* 2d ed. (Oxford: Oxford University Press, 2001).

21. If the law regulates an action under some description d, it regulates that action under every description that is either synonymous with d or is analytically entailed by d. Thus, the act of my driving my car into the park under the description "Scott drives his car into the park" is regulated by the legal rule that no vehicles are permitted in the park, because the law regulates my act under the description "Scott drives his vehicle into the park" and it is an analytical truth that cars are vehicles.

10. Theoretical Disagreements

1. See transcript of the first presidential debate between Al Gore and George W. Bush, October 3, 2000, available at http://www.debates.org/index .php?page=october-3-2000-transcript.

2. Dworkin, LE 13.

3. LE 4.

4. LE 4–6.

5. LE 7.

6. Tennessee Valley Authority v. Hill, 437 U.S. 153 (1978).

7. Ibid., 196.

8. LE 23.

9. See, e.g., Brian Leiter, "Explaining Theoretical Disagreement," 76 *University of Chicago Law Review* 1215 (2009). For another response to Dworkin's challenge, see Matthew Kramer, *In Defense of Legal Positivism,* chap. 6 (Oxford: Oxford University Press, 1999).

10. See transcript of the first presidential debate between Al Gore and George W. Bush, October 3, 2000, available at http://www.debates.org/index. php?page-october-3-2000-transcript.

11. LE 59–60.

12. LE 52.

13. LE 50.

14. Ronald Dworkin, "How Law Is Like Literature," in *A Matter of Principle* 157 (Cambridge, MA: Harvard University Press, 1985).

15. Ibid.

16. To be precise, Dworkin does not explicitly say that those who create social practices intend that their content should be determined by their point or purpose. What he does say is that they aim to create something as a distinct entity. It is clear, however, that on Dworkin's view, those who intend to create distinct entities ipso facto intend to create objects that must be understood in accordance with their point. For example, with respect to authorial intention he writes: "An author is capable of detaching what he has written from his earlier intentions and beliefs, of treating it as an object in itself. He is capable of reaching fresh conclusions about his work grounded in aesthetic judgments: that his

book is both more coherent and a better analysis of more important themes read in a somewhat different way from what he thought when he was writing it." See ibid.

17. LE 63.

18. The interpretation of a social practice, therefore, is not reducible to what Dworkin calls "conversational" interpretation (LE 64–65). In conversation, speakers aim to communicate their thoughts. In the production of art or social practice, participants aim to create a distinct entity to be judged in accordance with standards appropriate to the type of thing it is. Hence, creative interpretation is not a matter of uncovering the intentions of its creators. It is constructive in nature, namely, it involves imposing a justification on the practice so as to see it as a valuable activity.

19. See, e.g., LE 57. Thus, Dworkin approves of Cavell's contention that Fellini might have "intended" to allude to the Philomel myth when directing *La Strada*, even if Fellini had never heard of that myth when making his film. Fellini can be said to have intended the reference if he would have seen his "ambitions better realized by embracing that intention."

20. The notion of justification used here is always sensitive to the type of object under study. For example, when interpreting a work of art, purposes are to be evaluated from an aesthetic point of view; social practice, by contrast, must be evaluated from a moral point of view.

21. LE 165.

22. LE 211.

11. Dworkin and Distrust

1. Dworkin, LE 380.

2. LE 66.

3. Dworkin's theory does commit this mistake though. Because an interpretation of the law is correct according to Dworkin if it is implied by the principles that best fit and justify past political acts, it is possible for an interpretation to be correct even though no rules of the system have selected these principles as the morally appropriate ones. The Dworkinian interpreter, therefore, must settle questions that may not yet have been settled, when it is the aim of the law to perform this very function.

4. LE 93 (emphasis added).

5. It might be wondered why history matters here: couldn't Dworkin's claim about the intentions of legal creators be disproved solely through a philosophical thought experiment? One could simply *imagine* a legal system created by people who have very little faith in the philosophical abilities and ethical dispositions of their fellow community members. The shortcoming of this approach, however, is that it presupposes a picture of meta-interpretation that Dworkin need not, and

in fact does not, share. For it assumes that meta-interpretive theories, if true, must be true of every *possible* legal system, such that the failure of Dworkin's theory to apply to one legal system—regardless of whether such a system has ever, or would ever, exist—falsifies the theory. Although Dworkin initially treats creative interpretation as a universal method for the interpretation of all social practices, later on in his discussion he seems to restrict its domain to only certain types of legal systems. "Interpretive theories are by their nature addressed to a particular legal culture, generally the culture to which their authors belong. . . . The more abstract conceptions of law that philosophers build are not. . . . But there is no reason to expect even a very abstract conception to fit foreign legal systems developed in and reflecting political ideologies of sharply different character." LE 102–103. It appears from this passage that Dworkin does not envision his theory of meta-interpretation as the sort of traditional "conceptual" account that philosophers usually construct, and thus that he does not mean it to apply to every possible legal system. Its scope is limited to legal systems that are like our own—ones that share the same basic moral and political foundations. It can be no objection, therefore, simply to find a legal system, possible or actual, in which Dworkinian meta-interpretation would be inappropriate. What must be ascertained is whether that system is sufficiently similar to our own such that it would fall within the domain of Dworkin's theory, and so serve as a bona fide counterexample—hence the relevance of American history to our inquiry.

6. See Bernard Bailyn, *The Ideological Origins of the American Revolution* (Cambridge, MA: Harvard University Press, 1992); Gordon Wood, *The Creation of the American Republic, 1776–1787* (Chapel Hill : University of North Carolina Press, 1998); and J. G. A. Pocock, *The Machiavellian Moment: Florentine Political Thought and the Atlantic Republican Tradition,* 2d ed. (Princeton: Princeton University Press, 2003). Pocock characterized the central tenets of Whig thought and the Whig influence in late colonial America in the following terms: "The Whig canon and the neo-Harringtonians, Milton, Harrington and Sidney, Trenchard, Gordon, and Bolingbroke, together with the Greek, Roman, and Renaissance masters of the tradition as far as Montesquieu, formed the authoritative literature of this [colonial intellectual] culture; and its values and concepts were those with which we have grown familiar—a civic and patriot ideal in which the personality was founded in property, perfected in citizenship but perpetually threatened by corruption; government figuring paradoxically as the principal source of corruption. . . . Not all Americans were schooled in this tradition, but there was (it would almost appear) no alternative tradition in which to be schooled." Pocock 507.

7. The views of traditional English Whigs were largely defined by the events of 1688: the Whigs opposed absolute monarchy and the tyrannical tendencies of James II, and favored parliamentary supremacy of the sort that followed the accession of William of Orange to the English throne. See Pocock, *The Machiavellian*

Moment, 422, 488. Through the eighteenth century, the Whigs were characterized chiefly by a preference for stable, mixed government. The radical Whigs, a fixture of Britain's opposition politics from the late seventeenth through mid-eighteenth centuries, had less faith in the capacity of leaders to resist the corrupting effects of political power, and argued for greater popular involvement in government as a corrective. See Wood, *Creation,* 14–16.

8. Wood, *Creation* 18.

9. Bailyn, *Ideological Origins* 56–57.

10. Wood, *Creation* 25.

11. According to Donald Lutz, the American colonists began relying on Whig political theory to argue for self-government already by 1730. Donald S. Lutz, *Popular Consent and Popular Control: Whig Political Theory in the Early State Constitutions* 221 (Baton Rouge: Louisiana State University Press, 1980).

12. Wood, *Creation* 16.

13. See Wood, "Whig Resentment," in *Creation* 75–82.

14. On the role of conspiracy theories in the American colonies, see Bailyn, *Ideological Origins,* chap. 4, especially "A Note on Conspiracy." For a more sympathetic take on colonial attitudes, see Robert H. Webking, *American Revolution and the Politics of Liberty* 5–11 (Baton Rouge: Louisiana University Press, 1988).

15. Lutz, *Popular Consent* 11.

16. Wood, *Creation* 56.

17. Tory William Smith in ibid.

18. On the organic conception of society, see ibid., 57–65.

19. Ibid., 59.

20. Indeed, the colonial experience with limited self-government had been quite encouraging for the Americans. The colonial assemblies were free from the "rotten boroughs" that distorted parliamentary democracy in Britain, and representatives were attentive to the wishes of their localities. The assemblies largely had a free hand in local matters, as English authorities rarely had a reason to get involved. With its virtuous governments of supreme legislatures, colonial America was, in Paul Rahe's words, "in many respects a radical Whig paradise." Paul A. Rahe, *Republics Ancient and Modern: Inventions of Prudence: Constituting the American Regime,* vol. 3, 547 (Chapel Hill: University of North Carolina Press, 1994).

21. Bailyn, *Ideological Origins* 138–140; Wood, *Creation* 97–107.

22. See, for instance, Thomas Jefferson's *Notes on the State of Virginia* for its praise of the virtues of agrarian America. Lutz, *Popular Consent* 10.

23. Thomas Paine, *Common Sense,* 3d ed., Appendix (1776). See Wood's discussion of "American Corruption" in Wood, *Creation* 107–114.

24. See Lutz, *Popular Consent* 41–44.

25. Eighteen different state constitutions were adopted between 1776 and 1789, with another ten constitutions adopted by 1800. Ibid., 43–44. As Lutz

notes, the constitutions provide a better barometer of the state of political thought than the innumerable pamphlets, sermons, letters, and other political writings of the period, whose influence and representative value are hard to assess. Ibid., 42.

26. Jefferson's Third Draft of a Virginia Constitution in Wood, *Creation* 136.

27. Wood, *Creation* 134–135. Pennsylvania, New York, and Vermont, the former corporate colonies, were exceptions in which the executive was chosen by the electorate directly. See 139.

28. John Sullivan to Meshech Weare, Dec. 11, 1775, Force, ed., *American Archives,* 4th Service, IV, 243 in Wood, *Creation* 135.

29. See Wood, *Creation* 136–137, 143–150. In fact, the demotion of the executive was the only feature that significantly distinguished the first state constitutions from the colonial charters they replaced. Lutz, *Popular Consent* 44.

30. South Carolina was an exception: there, the governor had an absolute veto on legislation.

31. Virginia Constitution of 1776.

32. Wood, *Creation* 138–139; Lutz, *Popular Consent,* 93.

33. "An Essay of a Frame of Government for Pennsylvania" 4 (Philadelphia, 1776) in Wood, *Creation* 137–138.

34. See Wood, *Creation* 139–143.

35. Namely, Pennsylvania, Delaware, New York, and South Carolina. Ibid., 139–140.

36. Ibid., 140.

37. Ibid., 141.

38. Ibid., 154–155.

39. Several states explicitly wrote this principle into their constitutions.

40. Wood, *Creation* 157–159.

41. This traditional Whig trust in the legislature, again, rested on assumptions that the people at root share common interests, and that legislators are chosen not to represent particular interests, but for their superior ability to work for the good of the whole. See Lutz, *Popular Consent* 11–13, 50–51, 111–112; Pocock, *The Machiavellian Moment* 519.

42. In spite of the enormous confidence that the radical Whigs placed in the People, their faith was not absolute. Even at the height of revolutionary fervor, virtually every Whig believed that the people alone were not capable, even through their representatives, of ruling society. To aid the people, individuals of talent and integrity must have a place in government. The upper houses of the legislatures would represent the repositories of honor and wisdom. They would act to correct the well meaning but sometimes careless measures enacted by the lower house —they would supply, in Hamilton's metaphor, "ballast" to the ship of state. Even though the Senate was to counterbalance the House of Representatives, providing a degree of wisdom that the people lacked, every state possessing a bicameral legislature, except Maryland, provided for direct elections

of senators. So vital was their faith in the common person, and their desire to avoid acknowledging and supporting the existence of an American aristocracy, that anything other than popular elections seemed inconceivable. See Wood, *Creation* 209–214.

43. Ibid., 166; Gordon S. Wood, *The Radicalism of the American Revolution* 250 (New York: A. A. Knopf, 1992).

44. Wood, *Creation* 167.

45. Pocock, *The Machiavellian Moment* 516–517. In Pocock's words, this differentiation of the people had been "presupposed by every republican theorist from Aristotle to Montesquieu."

46. This conception of the duty of legislators vis-à-vis their constituents is succinctly expressed in the so-called Essex Result, a critique of Massachusetts' proposed 1778 constitution written by Theophilus Parsons: "Representatives should have the same views, and interest with the people at large. They should think, feel, and act like them, and in fine, should be an exact miniature of their constituents. They should be (if we may use the expression) the whole body politic, with all its property, rights, and privileges, reduced to a smaller scale, every part being diminished in just proportion." Quoted in Lutz, *Popular Consent* 111. This radical Whig perspective is a far cry from the traditional Whig view, popular just a few years before, that representatives' chief qualification for office is not a slavish devotion to the wishes of voters but a discerning, and disinterested, perception of what best serves the public good.

47. Wood, *Creation* 328–343.

48. In the words of Gordon Wood: "What was once considered to be a legally deficient body because of the absence of the magistrates or rulers was now for the same reason seen to be 'the most important body that ever convened on the affairs of this State,' an extraordinary representation of the people actually superior in authority to the ordinary legislature." Ibid., 338.

49. Ibid., 342.

50. Ibid., 328.

51. Lutz, *Popular Consent* 115.

52. Wood, *Creation* 194–195.

53. Letter from Jefferson to Lafayette, Nov. 4, 1823, quoted in Wood, *Radicalism* 97.

54. Wood, *Creation* 393–425.

55. James Madison, *The Writings of James Madison: 1769–1783*, vol. 2, ed. Gaillard Hunt, 365 (New York: G. P. Putnam's Sons, 1901).

56. James Madison in *Classics of American Political and Constitutional Thought: Origins through the Civil War*, vol. 1, ed. Scott J. Hammond et al., 372 (Indianapolis: Hackett Publishing, 2007).

57. Madison was not the only one concerned by the actions of state legislatures. The Pennsylvania Council of Censors reported in 1784 on a number of

legislative acts that violated the state's constitution or bill of rights. The legislature had, inter alia, set aside jury verdicts, remitted fines, disallowed causes of action created by the judiciary, given property belonging to one person to someone else, and released persons held as debtors. Lutz, *Popular Consent* 121.

58. Hammond, ed., *Classics of American Political and Constitutional Thought*, 372.

59. Letter from Washington to Jay, August 15, 1786, in *Papers of Jay*, ed. Johnston, III, 208 in Wood, *Creation* 472. The founders came to this revelation at different points. Wood relates the story of how James Madison was disabused of his Whig illusions in 1777 after running a high-minded campaign for Virginia's House of Delegates, refusing to solicit voters or engage in any other conduct "inconsistent with the purity of moral and of republican principles," and ultimately losing to a former tavern keeper. Wood, *Creation* 122.

60. For a discussion of the Founders' resignation that republican virtue of the classical sort was out of reach and impractical, see Rahe, *Republics Ancient and Modern* 742–744.

61. See Lutz, *Popular Consent*, 11, on the federalist "inversion" of the Whig view of virtue.

62. Madison himself saw the point of this objection: "It may be asked how private rights will be more secure under the Guardianship of the General Government than under the State Governments, since they are both founded in the republican principle which refers the ultimate decision to the will of the majority." Wood, *Creation* 506.

63. For the classic statement of this position, see Madison's Federalist No. 10. Larry Kramer has questioned whether the faction theory, as expressed in Madison's "Notes on Ancient and Modern Confederacies" and Federalist No. 10, captures the discontent more widely felt toward the Articles of Confederation. Kramer suggests that most framers were concerned only with the *interstate* dysfunction of the Confederation—the pursuit by each state of its own parochial interests in the absence of a strong national government—and failed to perceive the *intrastate* dynamics producing the bad legislative outcomes: the capture of state legislatures by powerful factions within the states. See Larry D. Kramer, "Madison's Audience," 112 *Harvard Law Review* (1999). It is beyond the scope of this chapter to take a position on whether Kramer is correct, or whether Madison's faction theory was in fact widely shared among the framers. In both accounts, however, deep distrust of others constituted the main motivation behind the Constitution of 1787. See also Akhil Amar, *America's Constitution: A Biography*, chaps. 1 and 2 (New York: Random House, 2005).

64. Wood, *Creation* 501.

65. Ibid., 499–518.

66. Ibid. 512–513.

67. Ibid. 356–357. See Montesquieu, *The Spirit of the Laws*, VIII.16, 132–133 (London: P. Dodesley, 1794).

68. Federalist No. 46 (Madison).

69. Federalist No. 48.

70. Federalist No. 51.

71. On the economy of virtue, see Bruce Ackerman, *We the People: Foundations* 198–199 (Cambridge, MA: Harvard University Press, 1991).

72. Federalist No. 63.

73. James Madison, quoted in *The Records of the Federal Convention of 1787*, vol. 1, ed. Max Farrand, 108 (New Haven, CT: Yale University Press, 1911).

74. LE 176–186. Dworkin mentions federalism, but only to show how this principle is not inconsistent with law as integrity.

12. The Economy of Trust

1. William D. Popkin, *Statutes in Court: The History and Theory of Statutory Interpretation* 12 (Durham, NC: Duke University Press, 1999).

2. *The Papers of Thomas Jefferson*, vol. 9, ed. Julian P. Boyd, 71 (Princeton: Princeton University Press, 1954). See also Letter of Thomas Jefferson to Edmund Pendleton, Aug. 26, 1776 ("Let mercy be the character of the lawgiver, but let the judge be a mere machine. The mercies of the law will be dispensed equally & impartially to every description of men; those of the judge, or of the executive power, will be the eccentric impulses of whimsical, capricious designing man.").

3. Joseph Story, *Commentaries on the Constitution of the United States*, ed. Thomas Cooley, §451 (4th ed. 1873).

4. United States v. Am. Trucking Ass'n, 310 U.S. 534, 544 (1940).

5. Henry M. Hart and Albert M. Sacks, *The Legal Process: Basic Problems in the Making and Application of Law*, ed. William N. Eskridge and Philip P. Frickey, 1378 (Westbury, NY: Foundation Press, 1994).

6. Frank Easterbrook, "Statutes' Domains," 50 *University of Chicago Law Review* 550–551 (1983).

7. In re Wagner, 808 F. 2d 542, 546 (7th Cir. 1986).

8. Antonin Scalia, *A Matter of Interpretation: Federal Courts and the Law*, ed. Amy Gutmann, 40–41 (Princeton: Princeton University Press, 1997).

9. Ibid., 124.

10. Popkin, *Statutes in Court*, 97.

11. Scalia, *A Matter of Interpretation*, 40–41.

12. Richard Posner, "Pragmatic Adjudication," 18 *Cardozo Law Review* 11–12 (1996).

13. Daryl Levinson, "Empire-Building Government in Constitutional Law," 118 *Harvard Law Review* 917 (2005).

14. Ibid., 922–923.

15. Scalia, for example, is not an originalist, but he subscribes to the Planners approach to meta-interpretation.

16. This might be the case when planners are particularly trusting of actors and the best way to serve legislative purpose is by overriding the original understanding of legislators.

17. Adrian Vermeule, *Judging Under Uncertainty: An Institutional Theory of Legal Interpretation* (Cambridge, MA: Harvard University Press, 2006); Cass Sunstein, "Must Formalism Be Defended Empirically?" 66 *University of Chicago Law Review* (1999); Richard Posner, "Reply: The Institutional Dimension of Statutory and Constitutional Interpretation," 101 *Michigan Law Review* 952 (2003); Elizabeth Garrett, "Legal Scholarship in the Age of Legislation," 34 *Tulsa Law Journal* (1999); and William Eskridge, "Norms, Empiricism and Canons in Statutory Interpretation," 66 *University of Chicago Law Review* (1999). Whether Hart and Sacks subscribed to what I have called the God's-eye view is a matter of scholarly controversy. On a plain reading it certainly seems as if they did. Hart and Sacks, for example, famously claimed that legislators ought to be presumed to be "reasonable persons pursuing reasonable purposes reasonably." Hart and Sacks, *The Legal Process*, 1378. For a summary of the literature on this controversy, see Jonathan Macey, "Promoting Public-Regarding Legislation Through Statutory Interpretation: An Interest Group Model," 86 *Columbia Law Review* (1986).

18. In part, these theorists are responding to meta-interpretive arguments that appear to invoke empirical premises but offer no empirical proof. For example, when purposivists argue that relying on legislative history will allow judges to discern what the legislature really meant to do, then surely, these theorists argue, purposivists have the burden of showing that judges are in fact competent to accomplish such a task. In a certain sense, of course, the God's-eye theorists are correct. If purposivists put forward an empirical argument in support of the use of legislative history, but provide no empirical warrant, then they are rationally bound to supply the missing premises. But, it should be noted, even if purposivists do supply the empirical foundation for their argument, this would not prove the appropriateness of purposivism. To show that purposivism is the proper interpretive methodology, purposivists must show why meta-interpretive arguments should be made from the God's-eye perspective.

19. Hendrik Hertzberg, "Framed Up," *The New Yorker,* July 29, 2002.

13. The Interpretation of Plans

1. Eyston v. Studd, 75 Eng. Rep. 688, 695 (K.B. 1574).

2. It is important to bear in mind that the degree of discretion that an interpretive methodology confers on interpreters is not constant across all legal texts, but is rather a function of the kind of text being interpreted. A textualist

methodology, for example, significantly limits discretion in the case of detailed rules, but confers substantial discretion in the case of standards.

3. For example, it is one of the main justifications for judicial deference to administrative interpretation of statutes—so-called *Chevron* deference—that administrative agencies are politically accountable in ways that courts are not and hence can be more readily relied upon to act in hermeneutically responsible ways. See Chevron v. National Resources Defense Council, 467 U.S. 837, 865–866.

4. United States v. Am. Trucking Ass'n, 310 U.S. 534, 544 (1940).

5. James Landis, "A Note on 'Statutory Interpretation,'" 43 *Harvard Law Review* 891 (1930).

6. Frank Easterbrook, "Statutes' Domains," 50 *University of Chicago Law Review* 550–551 (1983).

7. Antonin Scalia, *A Matter of Interpretation: Federal Courts and the Law,* ed. Amy Gutmann, 36 (Princeton: Princeton University Press, 1997). Antitextualists have countered that no interpretive methodology can constrain very willful judges, insofar as every method presupposes a certain degree of honesty and integrity from its users. Textualists cannot discredit nontextualist methods by pointing to the possibility that certain judges might abuse a certain method, for the same possibility is true of textualist methods. See, e.g., Richard Posner, "Statutory Interpretation—in the Classroom and in the Courtroom," 50 *University of Chicago Law Review* 817 (1983).

8. See, e.g., note 59 to Chapter 11.

9. See Marci Hamilton, "The Paradox of Calvinist Distrust and Hope at the Constitutional Convention," in *Christian Perspectives on Legal Thought,* ed. Angela Carmella, Robert F. Cochran Jr., and Michael W. McConnell (New Haven, CT: Yale University Press, 2001).

10. See, e.g., note 6 to Chapter 11.

11. The process of extraction described in the text bears an obvious resemblance to the Rawlsian search for an "overlapping consensus." See, e.g., John Rawls, *Political Liberalism,* 2d ed. (New York: Columbia University Press, 2005). However, the overlapping consensus here relates to attitudes of trust, rather than principles of justice. The above description of legal design also resembles Sunstein's conception of law as a series of "incompletely theorized agreements." See, e.g., Cass Sunstein, "Incompletely Theorized Agreements," 108 *Harvard Law Review* (1995) and Cass Sunstein, *Legal Reasoning and Political Conflict,* chap. 2 (New York: Oxford University Press, 1996).

12. The English rule of "no recourse" to legislative history was first announced in Millar v. Taylor [1769] 3 WLR 1032. For the adherence to the "no recourse" rule by American courts, see Hans Baade, "'Original Intent' in Historical Perspective: Some Critical Glosses," 69 *Texas Law Review* (1991).

13. Legislatures began recording verbal transcripts of legislative debates around the middle of the eighteenth century. Government printing of the Con-

gressional Record started in 1873. Popkin claims that the increased reliability and availability of these records led to the eventual acceptance of legislative history in statutory interpretation. See Popkin, *Statutes in Court,* 122.

14. How a meta-interpreter ought to handle changes in settings might itself depend on the designer's attitudes toward the meta-interpreter. If the system places high absolute trust in the meta-interpreter, then she should have greater leeway to invalidate a particular judgment based on an outdated setting. Similarly, low absolute trust might counsel against such moves.

15. See, e.g., W. V. O. Quine, "Two Dogmas of Empiricism," *The Philosophical Review* 60 (1951); Donald Davidson, "On the Very Idea of a Conceptual Scheme," in his *Inquiries into Truth and Interpretation,* 2nd ed. (Oxford: Oxford University Press, 2001); Isaac Levi, *The Enterprise of Knowledge: An Essay on Knowledge, Credal Possibility, and Chance* (Cambridge, MA: Massachusetts Institute of Technology Press, 1983); Peter Gardenfors, *Knowledge in Flux: Modeling the Dynamics of Epistemic States* (Cambridge, MA: Massachusetts Institute of Technology Press, 1990).

16. Imre Lakatos, *Methodology of Scientific Research Programmes,* ed. John Worrall and Gregory Currie (Cambridge: Cambridge University Press, 1980).

17. Matters are obviously more complicated than this example would suggest. Clearly, the expansion of federal power following the New Deal would suggest a more positive and complex attitude toward Congress with respect to the promotion of the general welfare. The example is intentionally simplistic in order to show how the synthesis of extracted views about trust might proceed.

18. Douglas Laycock, "Conceptual Gulfs in City of Boerne v. Flores," 39 *William and Mary Law Review* 765 (1998). Laycock claims that the original understanding of the Fourteenth Amendment supports this view. See 766.

19. The Supreme Court, by a 5–4 vote, rejected this synthesis in City of Boerne v. Flores, 521 U.S. 507 (1997).

20. The same qualification mentioned earlier in the section is in order here: designers might claim to assign particular tasks to actors in order to bring about certain goals, even though they privately believe that those tasks will actually bring about different goals. As with the extraction of trust judgments, the Planning Theory requires the meta-interpreter to heed the purported, not actual, objectives.

21. John Manning, "Textualism and the Equity of the Statute," 101 *Columbia Law Review* 70 (2001).

22. As William Eskridge has shown, state courts in the 1780s and 1790s, and federal courts in the 1790s and early 1800s, generally rejected a strict textualist approach and were willing to look beyond the words and heed the "equity" of the statute. See William Eskridge, "All About Words: Early Understandings of the 'Judicial Power' in Statutory Interpretation, 1776–1806," 101 *Columbia*

Law Review (2001). Eskridge cites Porter v. Dunn, 1 S.C.L. (1 Bay) 53 (1787) as the only case he could find that pursued a "follow-the-words-notwithstanding-the-consequences" approach to interpretation. See 1014.

23. Woodbridge v. Amboy, 1 N.J.L. 246, 247 (Sup. Ct. 1794).

24. See, e.g., Skidmore v. Swift & Co., 323 U.S. 134, 139 ("[T]he Administrator's policies are made in pursuance of official duty, based upon more specialized experience and broader investigations and information than is likely to come to a judge in a particular case") and Chevron U.S.A., Inc. v. Natural Resources Defense Council, Inc., 467 U.S. 837, 865 (1984) ("Judges are not experts in the field").

25. It is noteworthy that in certain colonies, such as Massachusetts, where distrust of judges ran especially high, jurors were given the power to find the law, not just facts. See William Nelson, *Americanization of the Common Law: The Impact of Legal Change on Massachusetts Society, 1760–1830,* 28–30 (Cambridge, MA: Harvard University Press, 1975).

26. See William Landes and Richard Posner, "The Independent Judiciary in an Interest-Group Perspective," 18 *Journal of Law and Economics* (1975).

27. Frank Easterbrook, "Text, History and Structure in Statutory Interpretation," 17 *Harvard Journal of Law and Public Policy* 63–64 (1994).

28. See, e.g., Easterbrook, "Foreword: The Court and the Economic System," 98 *Harvard Law Review* 14–18 (1984) and "Statutes' Domains," 50 *University of Chicago Law Review* (1983).

29. Although Easterbrook appears here to be making a classic God's-eye argument—i.e., since legislators cannot in fact be trusted to act in the public interest, judges should not engage in purposive interpretation—matters are not so clear. For while he believes that public choice theory gives a reasonably good description of legislative behavior, he also thinks the American legal system is more or less based on such a model of human motivation. See, e.g., Easterbrook, "The State of Madison's Vision of the State: A Public Choice Perspective," 107 *Harvard Law Review* (1994). For Easterbrook, therefore, the designer and God's-eye approach essentially coincide. It is noteworthy that Easterbrook often explicitly resorts to constitutional design in his meta-interpretive arguments. For example, he argues against the practice of using legislative history in statutory interpretation by reference to the constitutional requirements of bicameralism, presentment, and publication. As we saw in the text, Easterbrook believes that these devices, which are "an important part of the design," serve to constrain Congress by reducing the amount of rent seeking and by driving bargains out into the open so that they may be scrutinized. "Enacting a vaporous statute and winking, or putting some stuff in the reports, avoids these constraints—which judges can resist by insisting that words in laws be taken seriously." Easterbrook, "Text, History and Structure," 64. In the interest of interpreting him charitably, I have taken Easterbrook to be making a meta-

interpretive argument of the correct form and have thus read him to be following the designer approach.

30. Easterbrook, "Foreword: The Court and the Economic System," 51.

31. Ibid., 17.

32. Ibid.

33. Ibid.

34. Jonathan Macey, "Promoting Public-Regarding Legislation through Statutory Interpretation: An Interest Group Model," 86 *Columbia Law Review* (1986).

35. Although Scalia believes that the American system is skeptical of all individuals (see, e.g., his argument about the Bill of Rights and future generations in *A Matter of Interpretation: Federal Courts and the Law,* ed. Amy Gutmann, 43 (Princeton: Princeton University Press, 1997)), his argument for textualism depends on a skepticism about judges in particular.

36. Akhil Amar, "Intratextualism," 112 *Harvard Law Review* 796 (1999). See also, Akhil Amar, "Foreword: The Document and the Doctrine," 114 *Harvard Law Review* 45 (2000).

37. Amar, "Foreword," 45.

38. Ibid., 46.

39. Jeremy Waldron, *Law and Disagreement,* chap. 4 (Oxford: Oxford University Press, 1999).

40. Ibid., 74.

41. Waldron does not explicitly say that democratic institutions were originally designed to realize the value of respect, or that we follow them now in order to show respect. But it is hard to see how to understand his argument otherwise, for respect can be taken only if it is first given. If respect were not the reason why we have these procedures, then they could not confer respect. And if they could not confer respect, then respecting statutory texts would be far less important than Waldron believes it should be.

42. It should be noted that sometimes courts settle theoretical disagreements. See, e.g., Edwards v. Canada (Attorney General) [1930] A.C. 124, where the Privy Council rejected originalism as an appropriate method of constitutional interpretation.

43. In the last chapter, I insisted that meta-interpreters in authority systems should be faithful to planners' judgments of competence and character, rather their own. In this chapter, I made the same demand of the choice of objectives. In extraction, the meta-interpreter rejects the God's-eye point of view, deferring to the judgments of the social planners to determine questions of trust, goals, and values. Whereas the second step in meta-interpretation takes the planner's perspective, the first and third steps—specification and evaluation—are conducted from the God's-eye point of view. That is, when ascertaining the properties of various interpretive methodologies and evaluating these methodologies

in terms of their ability to further objectives in light of extracted competence and character, the meta-interpreter is supposed to draw upon his personal judgment, not that of the planners.

One might worry that by embracing the God's-eye point of view during specification and evaluation, the Planning Theory violates the Simple Logic of Planning principle. For in order to determine proper interpretive methodology, it seems that the meta-interpreter must settle certain questions that interpretive methodology aims to settle. Presumably, if an interpretive methodology is a plan or set of plans for resolving interpretive disputes, it must settle issues regarding its own efficiency. Yet, according to the Planning Theory, the meta-interpreter will be required to settle these questions, and hence settle precisely what interpretive methodologies are designed to settle.

The proper response to this concern is to recognize that in systems where meta-interpretive disputes are prevalent, proper interpretive methodologies are not plans, or even as planlike as customary norms. Meta-interpretive disputes arise precisely because no one has settled on how legal texts are to be interpreted. Since interpretive methodologies are not plans or planlike norms, SLOP does not apply. Of course, interpretive methodologies are not completely unplanlike either. The important questions of competence, character, goals, and values have been settled by others and are taken as authoritative in the meta-interpretive process. Thus, unlike Dworkin's account, the Planning Theory's meta-intepretive procedure does not unsettle what the law aims to settle because it does not require the meta-interpreter to answer questions about trust and objectives from the God's-eye point of view before he can figure out how to interpret the law.

14. The Value of Legality

1. H. L. A. Hart, *Essays on Bentham* 26 (Oxford: Oxford University Press, 1982).

2. John Finnis, *Natural Law and Natural Rights,* chap. 1 (Oxford: Oxford University Press, 1980). See especially pp. 16–17.

3. Ibid., 11.

4. I am unsure whether Joseph Raz now believes that the law has a constitutive moral aim. In "About Morality and the Nature of Law," reprinted in Joseph Raz, *Between Authority and Interpretation: On the Theory of Law and Practical Reason,* 177–178 (Oxford: Oxford University Press, 2009), he writes that "the . . . claim, that law by its nature has a moral task, seems both true and interesting. . . . [This claim] sets a critical perspective for judging [the law]. Just as we do not fully understand what chairs are without knowing that they are meant to sit on, and judged (*inter alia*) by how well they serve that function so, the claim is, we do not fully understand what law is unless we understand that

it has a certain task, and is to be judged (*inter alia*) by how well it performs it." Yet, in "Postema on Law's Autonomy and Public Practical Reasons: A Critical Comment," also reprinted in *Between Authority and Interpretation,* 374, Raz writes: "Justice, I believe, is not the law's ultimate aspiration, for there is no one moral virtue that all law by its nature aspires to, other than to be good: that is to be as it should be. This means that it should be just, and generous, and compassionate and many other things. It is important to remember that the law has no specific function (though it, or parts of it, have many such functions). Being good is but a formal function: everything should be good, ie should be as it ought to be."

5. Lon L. Fuller, *The Morality of Law* 33–38 (New Haven, CT: Yale University Press, rev. ed. 1964).

6. Ibid., 39.

7. Ibid., 42–43. See also Lon L. Fuller, "Positivism and Fidelity to Law: A Reply to Professor Hart," 71 *Harvard Law Review* 645–646 (1957).

8. See, e.g., the review by Hart in EJP; Ronald Dworkin, "Elusive Morality of Law," 10 *Villanova Law Review* (1965); and Lon L. Fuller, "A Reply to Critics" in *The Morality of Law* . For later interventions, see Joseph Raz, "The Rule of Law and Its Virtue" in AL 224; Matthew Kramer, *In Defense of Legal Positivism: Law without Trimmings* (Oxford: Oxford University Press, 2003); and Nigel Simmonds, *Law as a Moral Idea* (New York: Oxford University Press, 2007).

9. Jeremy Bentham, *The Works of Jeremy Bentham,* vol. V, ed. J. Bowring, 235, quoted in Gerald J. Postema, *Bentham and the Common Law Tradition* 277 (Oxford: Oxford University Press, 1986).

10. See Friedrich August Hayek, *Law, Legislation and Liberty: Rules and Order,* vol. 1, 85 (Chicago: University of Chicago Press, 1978). For Hayek's views about the predictability of judge-made law, see 116.

11. For contrary views, see Jeremy Waldron, "Is the Rule of Law an Essentially Contested Concept (in Florida)?" 21 *Law and Philosophy* (2002) and Ronald Dworkin, *Justice in Robes* 5 (Cambridge, MA: Harvard University Press, 2006).

12. See, e.g., Raz, "The Rule of Law and Its Virtue," in AL.

13. See, e.g., the Bentham quote in Postema, *Bentham,* 363–364.

ACKNOWLEDGMENTS

Writing this book has been a brutal experience, not only for me but also, and perhaps especially, for those around me. As my friends, family members, and colleagues can attest, I like to talk about my work a little too much and, for the last ten years, I have been working on this book. Many a dinner party has been ruined as a result.

The fact that I have co-opted so many people in this project makes the process of acknowledgment very difficult. In all honesty, I have received so much help over the years that I cannot possibly remember it all. And even if I could accurately recall these kindnesses in order to document them, virtually every sentence of this book would have to be footnoted. As inadequate as it is, I would like to acknowledge some of my greatest debts of gratitude here.

This book began while I was teaching at the Benjamin N. Cardozo School of Law. I am grateful to my friends there who provided help and encouragement at the early stages of the project, especially David Golove, Kyron Huigens, Arthur Jacobson, Melanie Leslie, Ed Stein, Stewart Sterk, and Martin Stone.

The bulk of this book was written while I was a faculty member at the University of Michigan Law School. I am sure that I spoke to everyone on the law faculty about my work in one form or another and would like to thank them for their questions and comments that have helped me clarify and refine my ideas. Daniel Halberstam, Don Herzog, Jim Hines, Bill Miller, Rebecca Scott, and Richard Primus were especially patient and helpful. The medal of valor, however, goes to Scott Hershovitz, who bore the brunt of my obsessions during his first year of teaching. Not only did he respond with good humor and gentle mockery, but his incisive challenges helped me deepen the account presented here in a number of important respects.

I was also fortunate during that time to have been a member of the University of Michigan philosophy department, that rare place on earth where brilliance and decency go hand in hand. I would especially like to thank Elizabeth Anderson,

449

Stephen Darwall, Allan Gibbard, and Peter Railton, all of whom tutored me on recent developments in metaethics and value theory. Chapters 2, 3, and 4 were heavily influenced by these discussions. Special thanks are due to Victor Caston, who talked me down from the ledge many times during the most difficult parts of the writing. His philosophical acuity, generosity, and friendship sustained me.

This book was finished at Yale Law School. Like so many Yale faculty members, I have profited greatly from numerous discussions with Bruce Ackerman over the years. Jim Whitman has been a perennial source of help, support, and friendship; every conversation with him is a treat. Claire Priest read through Chapter 11 and helped tone down my often overheated rhetoric. While no one will confuse me for a real historian, my hope is that, thanks to Claire, that chapter will no longer provoke outright laughter. My conversations with Jack Balkin, Bob Ellickson, Bill Eskridge, Heather Gerken, Bob Gordon, Oona Hathaway, Christine Jolls, Dan Kahan, Harold Koh, Tony Kronman, John Langbein, Daniel Markovits, Nick Parillo, Robert Post, Susan Rose-Ackerman, Jed Rubenfeld, Reva Siegel, and Alan Schwartz have also been extremely helpful.

One of the blessings of teaching at Yale is the superb research assistance. Gabe Mendlow went through the entire manuscript, pointing out numerous howlers, infelicities, and unclarities. He saved me from myself on many occasions. I assigned Erin Miller the unenviable task of reading everything that had been written about legal positivism by a non-philosopher. She rose to the challenge with amazing competence and gusto, helping me to organize the various characterizations into neat categories and to discern a pattern in the blizzard of invectives that often threaten to bury positivism. Chapter 8 simply would not have been possible without her assistance, but Erin also provided invaluable advice on other chapters as well. Justin Schwab provided excellent and diligent copy editing. Jud Matthew did a superb job on Chapter 11, helping me shape, support, and fill out the historical account of the American founding. John Paredes cheerfully and expertly helped with the tedious tasks of proofreading and indexing and, with Alex Sarch, cite checking many of the scholarly references.

During their semester as visiting scholars at Yale, Diego Papayannis and Lorena Ramirez were kind enough to go through the entire manuscript with me at weekly lunches. Their comments were invaluable to me as I made final revisions to the manuscript.

The ideas in this book were tested out in numerous forms over the years, and I would like to thank the many audiences for their indulgence and assistance. In particular, I benefited from the comments of Matt Adler, Larry Alexander, Robert Alexy, Anne Alstott, Horacio Arlo-Costa, Yochai Benkler, Mitch Berman, Carlos Bernal, Brian Bix, Hernan Bouvier, Curtis Bridgeman, Mihailis Diamantis, Tony Dillof, David Dolinko, Ronald Dworkin, Chris Essert, Richard Fallon, Luca Ferrero, Claire Finkelstein, John Gardner, Margaret Gilbert, Antony Hatzistavrou, Peter Hilal, Ken Himma, Adam Hosein, Doug Husak, Shelly Kagan, Rob Kar, Web Keane, Niko Kolodny, Lewis Kornhauser, Matt Kramer, Jody Kraus, Chris Kutz, Andrei Marmor, Ned McClennen, Martha Minow, Michael Moore, Chris Morris, Trevor Morrison, Stephen Morse, Liam Murphy, John Oberdiek, Dennis Patterson, Philip Pettit, Adela Pinch, Gerry Postema, David Plunkett, Christina Redondo, Abe Roth, Veronica Rodriguez-Blanco, Jim Ryan, Adam Samaha, Rodrigo Sanchez Brigido, Fred Schauer, Emily Sherwin, Seana Shiffrin, Ori Simchen, Matt Smith, Larry Solum, Marc Spindelman, Nicos Stavropoulos, David Strauss, Cass Sunstein, Kevin Toh, Bas van Frassen, David Velleman, Jeremy Waldron, Jay Wallace, Fritz Warfield, Ralph Wedgwood, Sheldon Wein, Ernie Weinrib, Carl Wellman, Jonathan Wolff, Gideon Yaffe, and Ben Zipursky.

The penultimate version of this manuscript was the subject of a conference convened by Damiano Canale and Giovanni Tuzet at Bocconi University. I would like to thank them, as well as Giovanni Battista-Ratti, Bruno Celano, Pierluigi Chiassoni, Jordi Ferrer, Diego Papayannis, Giorgio Pino, Francesca Poggi, and Aldo Schiavello for the benefit of their thoughts on my manuscript.

My editor, Michael Aronson; his editorial assistant, Heather Hughes; and the production editor, Meredith Phillips have been wonderful to work with and I am grateful to them for making the publication process so enjoyable.

Les Green, Brian Leiter, and Stephen Perry have been incisive critics of my work over the years. While I am sure I have not answered all of their objections, my attempts to do so have improved my ideas immeasurably.

Mark Greenberg woke me up from my dogmatic, positivistic slumber and helped me see the power of the natural law view. This book is largely a response to our many conversations over the years.

As a reader for Harvard University Press, Arthur Ripstein provided me with an extensive markup of the penultimate version of this manuscript. He not only pointed out dozens of confusions and imprecisions, he suggested ways to fix these problems. In some cases, Arthur actually wrote the copy for me! Never have I been the recipient of such penetrating and thoughtful comments on a manuscript. Arthur is a model for how members of the profession ought to treat one another.

Sidney Morgenbesser made me want to be a philosopher, and Isaac Levi, through tremendous acts of kindness, skill, and effort, helped me to become one. I am forever in their debt.

It has been my good fortune to have been Joseph Raz's student, and it will always remain a source of great pride. Since I met him twenty years ago when I was in law school, Joseph has been a patient tutor, a penetrating critic, and a good friend. There is no one from whom I have learned more about legal philosophy.

My debt to Jules Coleman is immense. Like so many of his former students, I have been the beneficiary of Jules' tireless mentorship; his advice, help, and support have made an enormous difference. More than anything, I would like to thank him for making legal philosophy so much fun. Over the years, we have spent countless hours talking about jurisprudence and our respective takes on the subject. His influence runs through this entire book.

Most of the ideas in this book were developed in 2003–2004 at the Center for the Advanced Study in the Behavioral Sciences, during which time Michael Bratman and I were engaged in a joint project on shared agency. I would like to thank the Andrew Mellon Foundation for making my residency there possible. I would especially like to thank Michael for all the help he gave me during that year and for his continuing support of this project. My joke about Michael is that talking to him is like talking to a much, much smarter version of yourself. Rather than trying to knock you down, Michael always tries to make your arguments the very best they can be. And, incredibly, this is true even when your argument directly challenges *his* work. Anyone who has ever spoken to Michael knows that I am not exaggerating. I still marvel at the luck that allowed me to work with him so closely.

This book was conceived roughly (though not exactly) at the same time as my daughter, Liza, and so I have been living with it almost as long as I have been living with her. She is now ten and my son, Henry (otherwise known as "Drin"), is seven. I will admit that there have been days when I resented the amount of time it has taken to raise them and the extent to which it delayed the completion of this book: the sleepless nights, ear infections, teacher development days, winter breaks, AWOL nannies, dentist appointments, midday assemblies, and so on. But when I compare results, my choice was obviously the right one because my children have turned out so much better than this book. They are simply wonderful and I am so amazed that they are mine.

I am blessed that my parents are alive and well and that I am able to thank them publicly for their love and generosity. I am pretty sure they did not send me to college and law school to become a legal philosopher. Who would do such a thing? But they have supported me every step of the way, which is pretty much the greatest gift parents can give their children. I would also like to thank my sister, Melissa, for her love and friendship and for beating up Steven Paris for me when I was in first grade.

My greatest debt is to my wife, Alison Mackeen. Alison is a very exacting editor. She has extremely high standards for clarity and rigor and I have struggled mightily to live up to them. Fortunately, when I have fallen short she has been there to make up the difference. She edited many parts of this book and improved them dramatically. She also taught me the most valuable lesson in academic writing, which is never to let the reader do any work. If readers find parts of this book not terribly difficult to read, they have Alison to thank.

The last ten years have been both exhilarating and exhausting. We moved so many times, lost so much sleep, got pulled in so many different directions. I could not have made it without her. Nor would I have wanted to try.

Portions of Chapters 4 and 7 first appeared in "Law, Plans and Practical Reason," *Legal Theory*, 8 (387), 2002.

Portions of Chapters 9 and 10 first appeared in *The Hart-Dworkjn Debate: A Short Guide for the Perplexed*, ed. Arthur Ripstein (Cambridge: Cambridge University Press, 2007).

Portions of Chapter 9 first appeared in "Was Inclusive Legal Positivism Founded on a Mistake?" *Ratio Juris*, 22 (326) Oxford: Blackwell Publishing, 2009.

INDEX

Ability to plan: and the possibility of law, 156; and legal authority, 179, 181, 421n20; distinguished from being authorized to plan, 179–180

Absolute judgments of trustworthiness, relative judgments vs., 363–364, 371–373, 376

Actors, 355–356; meta-interpretative role of, 358–359; trustworthiness of, 363–365, 371–372

Adjectival statements (legal authority), 184–186

Alienation: of legal officials, 15, 97, 108–110, 175, 204, 207, 216, 413n13; and coordination conventions, 108–109; and massively shared agency, 144–146, 150; and plans, 144–146, 150; and possibility of shared agency, 418–419n30

Amar, Akhil, on textualism, 376–377

American legal system: constructive interpretation of, 299–300, 310; trust in, 312–330, 345, 366–368, 371–377, 384–385; evolution of distrust in, 312–324, 328–329; radical Whiggism, 313–322; office of the executive, 316–318; legislative power, 318–320; people's role in government, 320–322; and early republic, 324–327; present system, 327–329; as authority system, 351–352; planners of, 356

Amorality of adjudication, 242–248, 276

Analytical jurisprudence, 2, 3; relevance of, 3–4; aversion to, 22–25; practical implications of, 25, 28–32, 399–400. *See also* "What is law?"

Anecdotal Strategy, 21–22

Antioriginalism, 385

Antitrust law, 196–197

Applying a plan, 126–127, 147

Arbitrariness: and coordination conventions, 109–110; of shared activities, 134, 143; positivity of plans, 201; and moral problems, 337

Articles of Confederation, criticisms of, 173

Augustine, 217

Austin, J. L., 20

Austin, John: Hart's lone gunman reconstruction, 21, 54–56; overview, 52–54; obligation, 53; rules as commands, 53; sanction, 53; sovereignty and habits of obedience, 53–54, 73–74; simplicity of theory, 54; Identity and Implication Questions, 56–57; rejection of Egg Principle, 57; Possibility Puzzle solution, 57–59, 77–78; legal concepts as descriptive concepts, 57–58; solution to Hume's Challenge, 58, 77–78; relationship between ought and obligation, 58–59; ignores existence of power-conferring